CLAPTON

CLAPTON

THE AUTHORIZED BIOGRAPHY

Ray Coleman

PAN BOOKS

First published 1994 by Sidgwick & Jackson

This edition published 1995 by Pan Books
an imprint of Macmillan General Books
25 Eccleston Place London SW10 9NF
and Basingstoke

Associated companies throughout the world

ISBN 0 330 33895 1

1 3 5 7 9 8 6 4 2

A CIP catalogue record for this book is available from
the British Library

Typeset by CentraCet Limited, Cambridge
Printed and bound in Great Britain by
Cox & Wyman Ltd., Reading, Berkshire.

SUITAR MAN (CLAPTON)

HE DRINKS LIKES A FISH
AND HE SMOKES LIKE A TRAIN
HE LOOKS LIKE A RAT, AND HE SMELLS LIKE
A DRAIN
HE KNOWS THAT HE'S CRAZY, HE KNOWS
HE'S INSANE
BUT HE DONT FEAR NOTHING EXCEPT
THE SOUND OF HIS NAME ~
   HE'S THE MAN, HE'S THE GUITAR MAN
YOU'D BETTER WATCH OUT WHEN HE
 MAKES HIS STAND
   HE'S THE MAN, HE'S THE GUITAR MAN, HE
CAN HOLD YOUR HEART, IN THE PALM OF
HIS HAND ~
SOMETIMES YOU MIGHT THINK HE'S GONNA
DROP IN HIS TRACKS
BUT DONT BE FOOLED, BY THE WAY THAT HE
ACTS
HE'S JUST PUTTING ON THE AGONY, PUTTING
ON THE STYLE
YOU CAN COUNT YOURSELF LUCKY IF
YOU SEE HIM SMILE
   (CHORUS)

Eric's handwritten poem of self-analysis.

CONTENTS

ACKNOWLEDGEMENTS   ix
INTRODUCTION   xi

1   THE TRAGEDY IN NEW YORK   1

2   THE SALVATION OF MUSIC   14

3   THE BLUES OF CHILDHOOD   29

4   THE 'GOD' OF CREAM   67

5   THE DRUG OF 'LAYLA'   135

6   THE ADDICT   217

7   THE CURED MUSICIAN   274

8   THE MARITAL STORM   307

9   THE ELDER STATESMAN   335

10   THE FRUITS OF STARDOM   359

ERIC CLAPTON ON RECORD   382
GUEST SESSIONS   397
INDEX   443

ACKNOWLEDGEMENTS

THE AUTHOR and publishers wish to thank the publisher Bruno Cassirer of Oxford for permission to reproduce extracts from the book *The Story of Layla and Majnun* by Nizami.

A letter from John and Yoko Lennon to Eric Clapton in 1971 is reproduced in this biography by kind permission of Yoko Ono and the Estate of John Lennon.

Appreciation is expressed to Timothy White, editor-in-chief of *Billboard* magazine, for use of parts of his interview with Eric which was published in that publication's special issue in December 1993 to mark Clapton's thirtieth year in music. And also to Tom Wheeler, editor of the American magazine *Guitar Player*, plus interviewer Dan Forte, for permission to use material from Eric's conversation with that magazine in 1985.

Permission to reproduce lyrics from songs as follows is gratefully acknowledged: 'Layla' © 1970; 'Give Me Strength' © 1974 and 'Wonderful Tonight' © 1977, all published by Throat Music Ltd. Words reproduced by permission of Chappell Music Ltd, London, and Chappell and Co. Inc., New York.

INTRODUCTION

E RIC CLAPTON'S name generates a wide range of emotional responses. There is awe and admiration for the artistry and style which he has marshalled to climb to the pinnacle of his craft. There is deep sympathy for what he has endured as a father whose young son died in tragic circumstances.

He is a complex man whose music, contrasted by the often raging ferocity or blues of his guitar work and the plaintive masculinity of his voice, speaks eloquently for his soul. He is not a stereotypical preening rock star but a supremely gifted guitarist and songwriter who has achieved the goal he set himself more than thirty years ago: to achieve great success entirely on his own terms.

Melodramatic though it may appear, he owes his own physical survival to music. When he plunged into heroin addiction, it was his love of the guitar and his biological need to get back to playing that were largely responsible for his return from the abyss. When he then became an alcoholic, he miraculously continued his career climb. Clear of all drugs and drink, he has been more resolute than ever about his work. That guitar, together with his talent for setting his own poetry into songs, has been his salvation.

In five decades, Clapton has encountered the most demanding battles for life itself, spiritually as well as physically. That he has overcome those trials, and strengthened his gifts, testifies both to his resolve and to his innate abilities.

He's tough but tearful, self-critical but with an undercurrent of knowledge that he's very high on the list of the élite in contemporary music. Inspiring fierce loyalty but also criticism from all those around him, he frustrates and angers people with occasional lapses of sensitivity, and by his own admission, he is not very good at relationships.

To the millions of Clapton aficionados around the world, such blemishes are not merely superficial. They have provided the man's shape, his edge, and they have been central to his evolution as an autobiographical performer.

And what a tortuous trail his life continues to be. From his blighted childhood; through the epochal 1960s during which he was a key musical, social and cultural figurehead; on through the 1970s when he combated his own demons; into the 1980s and the consolidation of his peerless reputation; and into the 1990s as an international celebrity.

None of this could be predicted of Clapton, even as a great musician, at the start of his ascent in the early 1970s. The admiration of his work by members of the royal family; the use of his anthem 'Layla' for a television car commercial; the enthusiasm of the paparazzi to photograph him stepping out of a restaurant; the Grammys that joined the multitude of awards that line his walls; the hushed reverence that greets the mere mention of his name . . . this seemed unthinkable to the legions of Clapton followers who hung on his every note in the years before the air at his concerts became thick with perfume and before his sartorial climb into Armani and Versace.

Through all the hubbub of his trajectory, Eric has remained the zealous, incomparable guitar man while retaining an elusive aura of stardom around him. Above all else, his aspiration continues to be his earliest goal: to be the best guitarist in the world.

He can be modest when it suits him, and when I asked him if becoming the world's best player had been an early ambition, he reflected: 'No, I don't think I am. But I certainly aspire to be. Maybe we should all be careful what we want in life. Sometimes, we may get it. I had this *ideal* when I was young: to cross as many barriers as I could between the different types of music that existed. If I did that, and was good all the way, maybe I *could* become the greatest guitar player in the world. That seemed a good goal to set out for. What I learned along the road did me a lot of good musically, but has also been blinding. But, you know, that goal can only exist as an ideal. In reality, there isn't a greatest or a best guitarist. I hear lots of players I could mistake for myself occasionally. The most I could claim is that I am a good model . . .'

A biography of an evolving artist is, unavoidably, a snapshot at a time when the story is still unfolding. This portrait of Clapton took root when I accompanied him on an American tour in 1980. He was bashful about a book at first, saying his story had a long way to run (an understatement), but once the project was rolling, he demonstrated the self-analysis and candour that has marked his life. His ex-wife, Pattie, the crucial source of so much of Eric's inspiration, also spoke for hours about their relationship, and I thank her for her irreplaceable help.

My thanks are due to Eric's mother, Pat McDonald, and to his grandmother, Rose Clapp, who provided illuminating recollections of his childhood; to Guy Pullen, a friend from Eric's years as a toddler in Ripley, Surrey, and to Ben Palmer in Wales, one of Eric's close friends since long before his fame, who provided penetrating commentaries on the subject's personality.

Will Jennings, the American songwriter who co-wrote with Eric his cathartic and beautiful song 'Tears in Heaven', recalled that recording session with eloquence; Pete Townshend's insights into what makes his dear friend tick are always incisive; Steve Winwood spoke about his difficult period with Eric inside Blind Faith; Micky Moody helped me dissect the man's recorded work; Chris Stainton, the inspired keyboards player in Eric's band, applied his keen astrological mind to his boss's birth chart; Gary Brooker spoke of Eric as a fisherman and reluctant bandleader, and Paul Samwell-Smith spoke of the personality clashes that marred his relationship with Clapton in the Yardbirds all those years ago. Rex Pyke, who produced the film *Eric Clapton's Rolling Hotel*, provided interesting observations, as did Toby Balding, Eric's racehorse trainer.

Meg and George Patterson, who provided acupuncture treatment and 'open house' to Eric when he was at a low physical and psychological ebb during his heroin addiction, gave unstintingly of their memories, crucial to their portrayal of Eric at that time. Readers interested in a more comprehensive study of their methods should investigate their book *Off the Hook*.

In Paris, Alice Ormsby-Gore gave me hours of often heartfelt recollections of the years in which she and Eric lived together. Her exceptional memory for detail enabled Alice to describe their important relationship and I greatly appreciate her patience.

Roger Forrester, Eric's brilliant and super-protective manager, gave me practical help and penetrating observations, and authenticated many of the stories and anecdotes. I thank him for making this project possible from its inception. That king of British promoters, Harvey Goldsmith, who has been associated with all Eric's shows since a university dance in 1966, also gave his insights into the star's successes.

Tragically, Diana Puplett, Roger's secretary for twenty-seven years, died at the appallingly premature age of forty-two on 28 February 1994. That night, Eric played his 100th show at the Royal Albert Hall, London, in his series of annual concerts there that stretched back to 1987. Not merely through her longevity of service, but through her cool affability, Di was a widely loved woman who played an important 'backroom' role in administrating Eric's career. Her help and advice to me during the preparation of this biography was vital. A delightful, sincere woman, Di is greatly missed.

Alphi O'Leary, Eric's loyal tour assistant who has been by his side for twenty years, has witnessed the old and new Eric, loves both, and helped greatly with his observations.

Master record producers Glyn Johns and Tom Dowd provided important signposts of the man and the musician inside the studio; in Frankfurt the concert promoters Horst Lippman and Fritz Rau offered some amusing thoughts about Eric.

In New York, Virginia Lohle, one of the world's most

ardent and perceptive students of Clapton's art, helped this project with her insight. My thanks also to Susan Weiner in New York, Marc Roberty in London, the former editor of *Slowhand*, the Clapton Appreciation Society's magazine which ran from 1988 to 1989, to Tony Edser, editor of that magazine's successor, *Where's Eric!*, and to my editor, Helen Gummer, and copy-editor, Annie Lee, for their eagle eyes.

My thanks, as ever, to my wife Pamela and our sons Miles and Mark for 'being there'.

In talking to so many sources, I found deep affection for Eric Clapton and sheer wonder at how he has always managed to enhance his art despite life-threatening situations which would quash lesser mortals. When an earlier version of this biography was published in the mid 1980s, its British title was *Survivor*. Eric chastised me, jokingly, about the word's sombreness: 'It makes me sound like a war veteran!' he said. I pointed out that was exactly what he was. And if the description was valid ten years ago, it's an understatement now.

Ray Coleman
Cornwall, England
Spring 1994

ONE

THE TRAGEDY IN NEW YORK

CONOR CLAPTON was a very special son. All his adult life, Eric Clapton had craved fatherhood and when it came, as he passed his forty-second birthday, he plunged into the role with the same burning intensity that had marked every aspect of his journey to the stratosphere of music and stardom.

As the guitarist most in demand in the world, Clapton's career was still ascending when Conor was born on 15 August 1986. Eric was already an embattled survivor, having ridden a lifestyle on the precipice of disaster across three decades.

The birth of a son changed him perceptibly. It softened him. Friends talked of a different Clapton, one less concerned, as all artists must be, with his own mirror image. He was now anxious to take responsibility for the life of the boy who bore his name.

The father's love showed in his eyes. If, as it is said, they are the mirror of the soul, then Clapton's psyche had been profoundly changed by the arrival of Conor. The eyes of Eric, so often doleful, came aglow when he was close to his son. Travelling the world, he had less time in his company than he would have preferred, but communication was Clapton's business and his rapport with the toddler gained every time they came together.

Conor's mother, an Italian television actress and photographer, Lori Del Santo, ten years younger than Eric, had custody of their son, who had been born out of wedlock. Based in Milan, she, too, travelled frequently both to New York and to London, and though marriage was not on their agenda, the parents of Conor had a pattern of getting together with the boy as much as their busy lives allowed.

For parents of illegitimate children, there is sometimes the additional burden of impoverishment. Conor Clapton was among the fortunate. Not only did he enjoy a childhood and a future of financial stability, but in Eric Clapton he had a father determined to ensure that his son's childhood was not emotionally fractured, as his own had been. He, too, had been born illegitimately.

Eric Patrick Clapton was born on 30 March 1945, the son of Patricia Molly Clapton and a Canadian soldier stationed in England, Edward Fryer. Eric was raised in the two-up, two-down terraced house at 1 The Green, Ripley, Surrey, by his doting grandparents, Rose and Jack Clapp. Eric was born in their front room. His surname came from Patricia Clapton's father, Reginald, who was Rose's first husband.

Eric's parental lineage confused him. Eric's mother was sixteen when he was born, and as he grew up, he referred to her as his sister whenever they were in company. 'It saved us explaining the tangled web of relationships,' Pat Clapton reflects. Eric recalls: 'I must have been about six or seven, at primary school, and writing my name down as Eric Clapton, when I suddenly fully realized that my so-called parents were Mr and Mrs Clapp (his grandparents). All the other kids bore the same names as their parents. My feeling of a lack of identity started to rear its head then. And it explains a lot of my behaviour throughout my life. It changed my outlook and physical appearance so much.'

Solitariness blemished his early years, but crucially, it was to be the driving force of his life, and finally, his source of triumph.

The spring of 1991 was a heady period for Eric Clapton in what had already been an illustrious career. At the start of every year he took up residence at the Royal Albert Hall, London, for a series of concerts that lent majesty to rock. For two decades, bands had sought to pack the giant stadiums around the world and bask in the glory of statistics. But for many years Eric had a career based more on planned longevity than on the rock philosophy of packing in the crowds.

Clapton had preferred to operate a 'less is more' policy, as reflected in his music. From 1987 his spring concerts at the Royal Albert Hall had grown in stature. The 1991 season, the apogee of these ventures, spanned twenty-four nights. To boost interest and diversify such a lengthy residency, these were broken up into six nights with a four-piece band, six with a blues band, six with a nine-piece band and six with full orchestra. Even by his own exacting standards, this twenty-four-night marathon by Eric was heralded as a landmark. Uniquely creative in format, the series had put him in a buoyant mood when it ended on 9 March with the symbolic presentation to him of the original key to the Second Tier Box 77. 'We have had many stars at the Albert Hall,' the hall's chief executive said when making the presentation. 'Eric is *the* star'.

The concerts were followed by some recording sessions in London before Eric flew to New York to rendezvous with Conor and Lori. This was to be a father's glorious counterpoint to a triumphant concert season.

The last night of Conor Clapton's life brought him huge fun. On Tuesday, 19 March 1991, his father took him for a night out. The visit to Nassau Coliseum to watch the Ringling Brothers Barnum and Bailey Circus enthralled the laughing boy, who particularly enjoyed his first sight of the elephants. To Eric, his heaven-sent son was clearly growing in confidence and, in the past year, he had noticed a changing maturity. Their relationship was joyful, as Eric discovered the richness of a parent–child relationship which, he had often mused, had been missing during his early years. He was determined that he would never be an 'absentee father', despite the geographical problems posed by his world travels.

A perfect evening for father and son at the circus ended with Conor being returned to his mother's luxurious home at the Galleria, a condominium block at 115 East 57th Street, between Park and Lexington Avenues.

There Eric bade his son goodnight before returning alone to the nearby Mayfair Regent hotel.

'If there is one thing I care about besides my music, it is my baby son,' Eric had said a few weeks earlier. The passion that marked Clapton's life had, finally, found a natural release that carried none of the trauma of his first forty years.

It had been a life marked and marred by turbulent relationships and self-inflicted dangerous living. 'Life is like a razor blade,' he said to me once. 'I'll always walk along its edge.' Clapton did not believe in luck, but in destiny. Somewhere, midway into his career as a guitar hero, he sensed that his special gift as an artist had been handed to him. The musicians who played alongside him spoke of a deep spirituality which flowered eloquently when he picked up his guitar. Since his teenage years, his trajectory as an artist had never been in doubt.

His personal relationships were always more complicated. After his marriage to Pattie, the love of his life, had run into tensions, he had met Lori Del Santo at a party in Milan. She quickly fell pregnant. The first person Eric had told of the imminent arrival of his first child was Pattie, who had been unable to have children during their six-year marriage. For Pattie, Eric's impending fatherhood signalled the end of their marriage and they were divorced soon afterwards.

How incongruous his life seemed to have been as he left the mother of his cherished son that night in Manhattan. Just like him, the child was born illegitimately. Just like him, the child seemed to be shaping up to be a strong-minded person. Eric mused that Lori – by then ensconced with a new partner – indulged their son more than he wished, but she was a caring, good mother to an effervescent, sharp and sunny boy.

The day after the visit to the circus, blond-haired Conor should have gone to school. Lori said she kept him at home because Eric was due to take him to the zoo. By mid-morning, wearing red sweat pants, a blue top and blue slippers, he was scampering playfully around the duplex apartment. After playing upstairs in his room with his Ninja Turtles, he ran downstairs and began to play hide and seek with the babysitter.

Like so many children who live in skyscraper homes,

Conor enjoyed pressing his face hard up against the window of the sitting-room, and he had the attraction of the view from the 53rd floor, which gave a stunning panorama of New York's skyline. But suddenly, when the babysitter followed him into the sitting-room, she could not find him. Then Lori saw the window. Eighteen inches from the floor, the window, which opened inwards, was six feet wide, four feet deep. It was open. Conor was missing.

The jigsaw of the tragedy was pieced together. It transpired that the housekeeper had cleaned the window and left it open to air the room. Playfully, Conor ran past him and plunged some 750 feet and forty-nine floors to his death, landing on the tar roof of a five-storey building at 122 East 58th Street that houses the New York Genealogical and Biographical Society. He died instantly.

Eight blocks away in his hotel suite, Clapton lifted the phone to a call from a 'hysterical' Lori. 'She said that Conor was dead. And I thought: "Well, this is ridiculous. Don't be silly." I said: "Are you sure?" I mean, what a silly question, "Are you sure?" And then I just went off the edge of the world for a while.'

Speeding to the scene, by then teeming with para-medics, ambulance men and police cars, Eric was faced with the hard reality. Later, he would recall that he 'turned to stone' at the realization of what had happened; but he found the strength in the immediate aftermath of the death to console a distraught Lori, whom he described as 'a great mother who had been very close to our son'.

The wave of sadness at such a horrific death spanned the world. As fans flooded the condominium with letters of sympathy and flowers, Eric's close friend and manager, Roger Forrester, flew out to New York to comfort him, saying: 'Eric and Conor were very close, naturally. As soon as he wrapped up his recent concerts at the Albert Hall in London, all he could talk about was going to see Conor. The boy normally stayed in Milan with his mother but they went to New York to see friends or relatives.' Describing Eric as 'in a bad way', Forrester added: 'He called me up and he sounded so far away. He kept saying: "I can't believe it. I can't believe it. I can't believe that he's dead. He's my son, my only son."'

As the world awoke on 21 March to the front-page news that dominated all the media, the multi-faceted tragedy threw the focus on the bumpy life of Eric Clapton.

The nightmare for any parent of losing a child was unbearable enough. This particular tragedy was a pitiful accident. And the fact that the father was a rock superstar gave it a special dimension. He was no ordinary rock 'n' roller, either, but a gifted, much-loved artist whose work had stimulated millions. His life, long before this tragedy, had been a self-imposed obstacle course which he had been lucky to survive.

And people wondered. Could Eric Clapton bear it all? His body had, miraculously, survived years of drugs and drink, and he had bounced back strongly from the edge of self-destruction. Here, though, was a disaster that challenged his inner soul. Clapton was known to have periods of melancholy – how else could he produce such profoundly moving music that sprang from within? But this would surely be the biggest test of his life.

'Say it's not true,' implored Pattie Clapton, Eric's former wife and still firmly his friend, when she heard the news. 'This is horrific. My thoughts are with Eric.' His friends, ever loyal, rallied. Keith Richards of the Rolling Stones and Phil Collins were the first to make contact. Thousands of sympathetic letters arrived, both at the Manhattan address and at Eric's home in Surrey, England, among them letters from Prince Charles and the Kennedy family.

While those who did not know him well worried for his survival, his steely grit came forward to deal with practicalities. Shocked though he was, he decided to cope with the immediate arrangements personally. Conor's body had been taken from the Lenox Hill Hospital to the Frank E. Campbell Funeral Home at 81st Street and Madison Avenue, and Eric supervised plans for the funeral. Touchingly, he decided that this would be in Ripley, Surrey, the typically English village where his mother and grandmother still lived. Eric had been baptized there into the Church of England and so, too, three years earlier, had Conor.

About 100 mourners, including Pattie Clapton and George Harrison, who both arrived alone, attended the funeral on 28 March in the tiny Norman church of St Mary in the village so full of mixed memories for Eric. He sat in the front pew alongside Lori, facing the bronze and copper casket, as Steve Ferrone, drummer in his band, read the passage from St Mark, Chapter 10, which begins: 'And Jesus said, suffer the little children to come unto me.' The hymn 'Abide with Me' was then sung.

As they walked from the church to Conor's resting place beside a big yew tree and alongside the church's stained-glass window, the appalling sadness was emphasized. Amid the flowers, led by Eric and Lori's spray of tulips and jasmine, were wreaths and flowers fashioned into a guitar, a rocking horse, a football, a train, a teddy bear and a donkey from his mother. These were among the treasured items in the short life of a boy who had died nine days earlier.

The gravestone inscription that followed later was typical of Eric Clapton's strength through simplicity:

> Conor Clapton
> 1986–1991
> Beloved son
> Sweet child of
> infinite beauty.
> You will live in our hearts for ever.

In the weeks following Conor's death, questions were raised about window security guards. Two baffling issues were attached to the tragedy. Had it not been a beautiful day of spring sunshine, the window would not have been open; but since it was, a window guard should have prevented Conor's fall.

According to the New York City department of health, which has a window fall prevention programme, a law which began in 1976 established guards as compulsory if a child ten years old or younger lived in an apartment. Lease notices for tenants issued by the department state: 'Your landlord is required by law to install window guards in your apartment: if you ask him to put in window guards at any time (you need not give a reason), or if a child ten years or younger lives in your apartment. It is a violation of law to refuse, interfere with installation, or remove window guards when required.'

Public concern focused so strongly on the safety issue that in the months after Conor's death, hundreds of window security guards were installed in Manhattan high-rise apartments.

Two years after the death, Clapton moved courageously to help a recurrence of the tragedy for others.

He returned to New York and the subject of window security guards, and went into a television studio to tape a public service announcement urging people to ensure they had them fixed. Sombrely and heartbreakingly, the broadcast, first aired by MTV and later shown on other networks, reminded the audience that he had lost his son because of the lack of one.

How would he cope? How could he rationalize this, to survive such a cruel blow? No parent was equipped to deal with the death of their own child, and Eric seemed to be an especially vulnerable victim.

Two days after the funeral, Eric marked his forty-sixth birthday. For some twenty-five years, his life's journey had seemed a dangerous odyssey in which he had only just won through after adversarial experiences, many of them self-inflicted. This, though, was different. It was not the loss of a musician friend, but of his own son. Far removed from physical abuse like drugs or drink, this hit deeply at the inner reserves of a man known to be easily bruised by spiritual traumas. And could there be a bigger one than this?

Some feared he might weaken and revert to the crutch of drink and drugs, addictions which he had defeated. Others, who knew him better, were confident. 'He'll be OK,' Pattie Clapton said to me shortly after the tragedy. 'It's going to be hard for him, of course. But he'll come through it all in the end. He's a survivor.'

Among his first phone calls was one from another friend in the Rolling Stones, guitarist Ronnie Wood, who recalls: 'People said not to bother him, but I decided to blunder in. I reckoned he needed a friendly voice. He was amazingly positive and said: "I can't thank you enough for ringing. The main thing now is for me to take out my feelings on the guitar. I'm going to play better and I'm going to go from strength to strength."'

Wood says Clapton told him he realized nothing could bring Conor back, 'but I was at rest in my head listening to how he was going to deal with it. I asked him: "Doesn't it make you want a drink?" Eric replied: "That's the *very* thing I want. But just because I have these problems, I'm not going to give in. I'm going to work, work, work."' Wood could not but reflect on such strength, compared with the Clapton of eighteen years earlier, when Wood had been among the musicians who rescued him from his alcoholic haze, persuading him to appear at a landmark 'comeback' concert in London.

The loss of Conor was appalling to Eric not merely because of the nature of the tragedy, horrific though that was. The boy was credited, by the father, with having helped him turn the second stage of his life's journey into a positive new thrust. As he watched his son grow, in the last few years of the 1980s, Clapton was invigorated enough to shape a new chapter, renouncing drink, which had once again reared its head into his life after his first dangerous bout of alcoholism, some ten years earlier, had been cured. Conor had been, therefore, a lifeline, a creative stimulus.

What nobody could have predicted was the scale on which, this time, he would tilt the tables on disaster. He was to convert the darkest moment in his life into a monumental creative triumph. In doing so he would erect a fitting artistic tribute to his son. He would touch millions, and exorcise the tragedy, with resourcefulness and vibrant simplicity.

The magnificence of his artistry had always been that it stemmed from somewhere deep within him. There are those around him who do not know (and doubt if Eric can ever properly identify) how he ignites the music that comes from his soul.

What happened in the wake of Conor's death is that, once again, the man who scorched the rock landscape with 'Layla', a love song of blazing autobiographical fervour, returned twenty-five years later with another 'message song', this time one of heart-rending power, as a paean to his son. 'Tears in Heaven' moved all but the stony-hearted.

As always, Clapton had found both articulacy and refuge in his music.

At the inquest in Guildford, Eric told the court that 'no one was to blame' for the death of his son. He explained to the coroner how a cleaner, who had opened the window to the apartment, may not have been aware that Conor was there. 'I do not think anybody can be held to blame,' he said quietly but firmly.

Recalling his visit with Conor to the circus the night before, he said: 'He was in good health. He was very frisky, full of energy and full of life.'

Describing the scene at the apartment when he arrived twenty minutes after the accident, Eric said: 'It was very difficult to get a clear picture.' The first anyone knew of the tragedy was when Lori Del Santo, who had been downstairs, called Conor for lunch. 'She did not hear any answer. That is when she discovered the window was open.' Eric declared that he was in a state of shock when he arrived at the apartment, which he had visited four or five times before, playing with his son in the sitting-room or bedroom. The window the boy fell from was normally locked but did not have a guard.

Recording a verdict of accidental death, the Guildford coroner, Mr Michael Burgess, said Conor had suffered injuries equivalent to having been hit by a vehicle at 100 mph: 'The chances of him surviving were nil.'

TWO

THE SALVATION
OF MUSIC

THE TRAGEDY divided Eric Clapton's life and career. For two decades, he had been acknowledged as a peerless musician. His walk to the brink of self-destruction, and his triumphant survival, had strengthened his charisma. By the spring of 1991, a rising graph of record sales and a multitude of awards pointed to a glorious future. He was already a legend, before this crushing experience.

With the appalling nature of Conor's death, Eric was pitched into a notoriety he, and the world, would have preferred he had missed. Public grief for any parent suffering such a loss would have been intense; for Clapton, it stretched from the show-business community who had always held him in affection through to the New York cab drivers who had never met him but, like millions, felt strangely diminished on his behalf. And those who had followed the complexity of this particular father's character and history were fearful for his own psyche.

Public sadness was typified on the streets of Manhattan. A few days after the tragedy, Virginia Lohle, a devoted Clapton follower for twenty years, was walking and wearing a shirt bearing Clapton's photo as a show of faith. She was approached by a woman aged about eighty, shabbily dressed, probably homeless for she was carrying so many possessions. She looked at Virginia's shirt picture and walked over to her, to say: 'Oh, that's so *terrible* about Eric's little boy.' When an emotional equalizer of that nature occurs on the streets of New York City, the person at centre stage has moved beyond his established turf. Just as his old friend and sometime partner John Lennon met his assassin (and subsequent immortality) on the streets of New York, ten years earlier, so Eric Clapton suffered heartache, and fame of an unwelcome nature, from the same city.

Fate had decreed that Clapton was equipped to deal with almost any trauma. Only seven months earlier, on 27 August 1990, four of his colleagues had been killed in a helicopter crash. After a concert at East Troy, Wisconsin, a convoy of four flights left the venue. Eric was in one of the earlier helicopters, which took him safely to his Chicago hotel, where he went to bed. Next morning, he was awoken by a phone call from his manager, Roger Forrester, with the terrible news: the helicopter carrying guitarist Stevie Ray Vaughan, plus Eric's US agent, Bobby Brooks, his bodyguard, Nigel Browne, and assistant tour manager, Colin Smythe, had crashed in fog at Alpine Valley. All four were dead. Eric was silent at his loss of four valued friends.

There was something particularly cruel about the death of Stevie Ray Vaughan. The previous night, alongside two other players greatly respected by Clapton, Buddy Guy and Robert Cray, Vaughan and his brother Jimmy had jammed on stage in East Troy. And Clapton recalled how they had all been 'in awe' of the peaks to which Stevie Ray's playing had soared. For years, Eric had regarded him as a special friend and a great artist.

Like Eric, Stevie Ray had renounced drink and drugs abuse and had been 'clean' for three years, winning the respect of his fellow musicians. Clapton admired his playing enormously.

The deaths inevitably cast a shadow over the immediate itinerary of the tour. But, as always, Eric found resolution in his approach. He called a meeting of the whole touring party and asked for a vote on whether they should simply go home, or continue with the concerts. The general view was that if they cancelled the shows, and went home, the memory would be unbearable. So they pressed on to the next stop, a show in St Louis, Missouri. Eric was in shock, and says he could scarcely remember the words to some of his own songs. But it was a fitting tribute to lost friends.

Battered by the losses of loved ones, and particularly of a child in such circumstances, a person might be expected to need time to recover, contemplate, or simply grieve. The impact of the deaths of Conor and Stevie Ray Vaughan reminded Clapton of the fragility of life, he said, adding that each day had to be welcomed as a blessing.

Always, there had been at least two dominant aspects to Clapton's make-up. The artist deeply embedded in his soul contrasted with the hard-headed practical man, fully capable of focusing on the daily grind, and needing a routine. These twin peaks of his energy were to be his salvation. A new artist was about to be born and, just as in the past, whether writing spiritually about his emergence from three years of drug abuse, or about his passionate love for the woman who would be his wife, Clapton was to create his masterpiece from the ashes of his emotional torture.

In the immediate aftermath of the tragedy, music seemed remote to Eric. He went on holiday to his home in Antigua to recover from the role that had been forced on him, that of counsellor of others touched by the death: Conor's mother, Eric's relatives and friends. Eric had been so diverted by listening to others that he scarcely had time to deal with his own sorrow.

Music was not on his agenda in these early weeks. But he took on holiday with him an acoustic guitar and slowly turned towards his innermost thoughts. Simple songs recalling his memories of his lost son gradually came through. Different in texture from anything he had ever written, six titles including 'Circus Has Left Town' and 'Lonely Stranger' evoked a man struggling to come to terms with a new phase in his life. One song, in particular, would stand as an emotive piece of question-ing about that terrible day and the feelings that followed. Would you know my name, he asked Conor, if I saw you in heaven?

There had never been any shortage of work for Clapton. What his manager, Roger Forrester, knew had to be served up was an ever-changing menu of stimulating challenges. Regular tours of America, Europe and the Far East had been augmented in 1990 by an astonishing expedition to Africa, which included an open-air concert before some 80,000 people in Swaziland. Rather like the ground-breaking tour of Poland in 1979, it was very important to Eric because he had to prove himself before people less familiar with his status than those in the West or in Japan.

A fresh challenge was particularly essential in the wake of the loss of Conor. Not only did it have to fill the void, it had to offer a platform for what would inevitably be a new persona.

The answer came in the form of a film. Director Lili Zanuck pursued Eric to write the score for *Rush*, the movie version of a Kim Wozencraft book about a female vice officer who becomes involved with drugs. It was a story which touched Clapton closely; he was attracted by the determination not to glamorize narcotics, but to ensure that it was a meaningful, low-key documentary.

By the time Eric arrived in California in September 1991 to record the soundtrack, his mood of profound melancholy of earlier in the year had been replaced by a need for an intense workload. There was no self-pity. As ever, he was ready to pour all his feelings into his work; the man who had begun his musical life scrutinizing the blues of the black Americans now had ample reason to deliver his own pain in that same genre.

Clapton had written soundtracks for movies before, but that was in a different life. The drugs theme of *Rush*, and the backdrop of his recent nightmare, meant he was on foreign terrain. But there was familiarity in the friendly faces awaiting him to accompany his music, including members of his band: drummer Steve Ferrone, pianist Greg Phillinganes, bassist Nathan East and prominent keyboardist Chuck Leavell. The producer at the sessions at Village Recorders, Santa Monica, was another well-established Clapton associate, Russ Titelman.

One man who had never met Eric until then, but who was to figure importantly in Clapton's new anthem, had been known to Eric by name and reputation for ten years. Will Jennings, a Texan living in California, was a song lyric writer whose track record included 'One Day I'll Fly Away' (a huge European hit for singer Randy Crawford) and a pivotal album with his good friend Steve Winwood called *Talking Back to the Night*.

Although they had never met, Clapton told Jennings in the studio that he had always admired his work. His memory shot back ten years to the making of Winwood's album in Gloucestershire. Two Jennings lyrics, for songs called 'Help Me Angel' and 'Where's Robin?' (a song about Robin Hood which later became 'Still in the Game') were favourites, Clapton told a surprised Jennings.

'Eric had set himself a very heavy schedule as a catharsis to keep himself occupied,' Jennings recalls. They set about a song called 'Help Me Up', which eventually became the finale of the movie, before, as Jennings remembers: 'I was working on trying to get a couple of ideas going. And then, there was one particular place in the film that called for a ballad. Eric sat down with me and said: "I want to write something about my boy."'

Eric had decided the title, 'Tears in Heaven', and played to Jennings on his acoustic guitar what became the melody and the basis of the lyric. 'He had the whole first verse done, which is the heart of the song,' Jennings says. 'He asked me to help him complete most of the rest of the song.' It came quickly. 'It was very emotional. I had lost my mother a year before and was still mourning her, so there was an obvious parallel.'

Would you take my hand/if I saw you in heaven, Jennings wrote. 'For the last section, I was revising that as he was getting ready to record it. I was sitting in the control room in the studio, on the floor; we were writing on a deadline and there were many, many revisions to the final part of the song.'

When the lyrics fitted, the recording session was as simple and as moving as the song. 'It was so emotional,' Jennings recalls. 'Everyone was very subdued.' Almost all the studio lights were out. 'We were trying not to hear what he must have been feeling as he sang. It was absolutely naked, beautiful, a very rare experience.'

For Eric, the song was tearfully autobiographical. For the movie, it was largely an incidental track, with the main song, which had a similarly sensitive title, 'Help Me Up', arriving at the end. For many millions of listeners around the world, 'Tears in Heaven' touched a rare chord, demonstrating Clapton's anguish and sensibilities arising from his deep reserves of inner strength. When it eventually found its way on to the airwaves, 'Tears in Heaven' was adopted wherever grief involving a child was invoked, particularly in Britain for television programmes about the James Bulger murder case. The song was unexpectedly Eric Clapton's defining moment, lifting him far away from his achievements as a world-beating guitarist and singer. He was in a new league.

Immediately the 'Tears in Heaven' session had been completed, in December 1991, Clapton went to Japan. The seeds of this trip had been planted the previous year when, during his tour of the Third World and South America, Eric had repeatedly been asked by admirers about his old friend George Harrison. There has always been a curiosity about their jostling relationship, hardly surprising since Eric lured George's wife, Pattie, with 'Layla', his incendiary song of love and desperation that would stand as one of rock's finest moments.

Returning to Britain, Eric called up George as he often did. Curiously, their friendship had remained intact through the years, despite an ever-present undercurrent of tension based on history. Musically, though, they always meshed. Their styles were utterly different (George was from the rockabilly background and not the blues, Eric the reverse) but there had always been mutual respect.

Eric suggested to George that he might like to go back 'on the road' with him. There was, as ever, a practical reason. Clapton had, in his own words, the world's best band standing by waiting for something to happen, as well as a fine lighting system and a crew at the ready. They all needed the impetus of something different, and he knew that was also what George needed after a seventeen-year break from touring. George Harrison's previous tour, of the USA in 1974, had ended ignominiously. He lost his voice and was criticized for refusing to sing Beatles songs. The experience soured his attitude towards concert work.

Harrison prevaricated. Clapton assured him repeatedly that it was a natural event for him; he would have nothing to do except walk on stage to be supported by great musicians: all his regulars, including the gifted guitarist Andy Fairweather-Low and back-up singers Tessa Niles and Katie Kissoon would be there. After yes and no about five times, George was persuaded. The Rock Legends, a twelve-concert tour, arrived in Japan in December 1991. There was a solid reason for going to Japan before playing the US or Britain: the glare of the spotlight would be less focused, the level of critical observation less intense in the East, where adulation of such big names is less conditional than in the West.

The music was solid enough. Combining and

contrasting the powerful repertoires of two giants provided a wealth of strong material. George threw in a few Beatles songs, and they recorded a live album. Yet there was something truly bizarre about one aspect of their union: while Clapton sang 'Old Love' and 'Wonderful Tonight' and 'Layla', which were written for Pattie, George included 'Something', the beautiful ballad which he had written to her while he was in the Beatles. Rarely can two men have paraded so publicly their feelings for the same woman, whom they had both, at that stage, loved and lost.

If the stage smiles seemed to project harmony, the backstage atmosphere was tetchy. Friendship across the Surrey and Oxfordshire boundaries back in Britain was one thing; travelling together in Japan was another. Whose tour was it? Manifestly, the bigger star was Eric through the sheer weight of his music and longevity of his career. Yet George Harrison's presence represented a quarter of the best-known pop group ever. Known for his droll humour, George said to someone backstage in Tokyo: 'You can't talk to me like that! I'm an ex-Beatle!' Amusing it might have been, but more than one onlooker believed there was an ego problem.

Some members of the touring party could not wait to get back to Britain. Any thoughts that this momentous partnership might take to the concert venues of the UK and US were silenced.

The experience could be compared with the scene at any rock show in Japan. Whereas, in the West, barriers are erected to prevent over-exuberant fans from storming a stage, no such preventives are necessary in Japan. A piece of white tape is positioned, and no fan would dream of crossing it. The genteel audience respects, and politely applauds, from behind the white tape. A distance is established between artist and audience. So it was when Eric Clapton invited George Harrison to join his tour there. A barely visible barrier was in place.

Always sartorially conscious, Eric moved towards his forty-seventh birthday in 1992 with a new edge that was contemporary even for someone who had always absorbed style and fashion. His hair was close cut; his new round tortoiseshell spectacles had a designer stamp; his casual clothes bore the imprimatur of Armani and Versace.

Not surprisingly, there was a world-weariness in his face. His forehead was visibly lined, his beard greyer. Importantly, he seemed to have come to terms with enjoying material pleasures more than in the past, when what he described as his British working-class bigotry put him in conflict about enjoying the fruits of success.

In America, rock stars of his generation were lining up to appear on a cleverly conceived MTV programme, *Unplugged*. Stripping players bare of electricity, the show emphasized the creativity of the compositions and the unfettered artistry of the musician. For a man so anxious to stay in the fast lane, Eric surprised with his negative response when the idea of going on the programme was first put to him by his manager, Roger Forrester. Eventually, he was persuaded that his armoury of music deserved nothing less than such exposure on a TV series gaining respect as well as excellent audience ratings.

And so on 16 January 1992 Eric and his band entered the studios at Bray, Berkshire. Armed only with a Martin acoustic guitar, Dobro, gut string acoustic and a twelve-string acoustic, he sat astride the show's traditional stool to face an audience that immediately thrilled to the intimacy of the event. After the years of giant stadiums, and even the Royal Albert Hall, here was Eric in his more natural milieu, in the atmosphere of a small club. 'Well, are you ready?' Eric casually asks the musicians at the opening of the album that followed. Launching into a pretty instrumental, the crowd clapped along with 'Before You Accuse Me' before Eric rolled into the Big Bill Broonzy classic, 'Hey Hey', a foretaste of the blues emphasis that was to mark his future live work. His voice had acquired a new, gravelly resonance and if anyone needed reminding of his musical origins, here it was: his guitar work was as funky as that of any of his heroes. Next came the raw 'Tears in Heaven', uncluttered, questioning. Time can bring you down, time can bend your knee, he sang; it can break your heart, have you begging please. After his own 'Lonely Stranger' and a doleful treatment of the Bessie Smith classic, 'Nobody Knows You When You're Down and Out', there was a magical moment. 'See if you can spot this one,' Eric said with a metaphorical wink to the crowd as he launched into the unmistakable opening grooves of 'Layla'. Ripped from the familiar amplification, the song's audacious lyrics sprang to life.

What would you do if you got lonely, he says to Pattie. You've got me on my knees, Layla, begging darling please . . . he had tried to give her consolation when her old man had let her down; like a fool he had fallen in love with her. She had turned his whole world upside down. Would she please not say they would never find a way, or he would go insane. Often, the potency of this song's lyrics had been buried amid the flash of electricity and guitar pyrotechnics in the past twenty years. That night, Eric restated its function with a simplicity that may never be repeated. 'Thank you,' he said simply as the crowd erupted.

The rest of the show was vintage Clapton, pared down, heartful, and he seemed to relish the experience. 'Running on Faith' – 'Maybe I've been running on faith/what else can a poor boy do?' – he continued after 'Layla', in a song custom-built for his psyche. And the rest of the music was equally golden; his hero Robert Johnson's 'Walking Blues'; the spontaneous start to 'Alberta', in which he jestingly chides his musicians at the start – 'Hang on, hang on, hang on' as they might seem to be starting ahead of him; followed by 'San Francisco Bay Blues', the Jesse Fuller song that Eric converted to a good-time 'jug' band sound; the contrasting rural blues sound of Robert Johnson again with 'Malted Milk'.

And then, quietly, came the same guitar riffs that preceded 'Layla'. Unmistakably, here was 'Old Love', surely another lament for Pattie. His vocal is passionate as he recounts how he thinks of her: too much confusion in his head; it makes him so angry, he admits, to know that the flame still burns. With the delicate piano figures of Chuck Leavell, and Eric's shimmering, eloquent guitar solo, this performance would have eclipsed anything that night, had it not had to compete with songs like 'Tears in Heaven' and 'Layla'. Tender, angry, desperate, it presented Eric exactly as he is away from the stage: a man who had lived a life on the edge, survived to tell the tale, utilizing almost every nuance of his experiences in his art.

The amazing reality to emerge from *Unplugged* was that a man renowned for his instrumental supremacy had found an even more subtle instrument than the guitar with which to expound his art. His voice.

*

'Tears in Heaven' was all over the world's airwaves in 1992. From the moment he composed it, Eric had been anxious not to appear over-sentimental in the public view, but he took pride, also, in facing up to his loss and not running away from the outpouring of sympathy, which touched him. Whether he welcomed it or not, however, the public perception of him was heroic. Those who vaguely knew of him as a rock star who had renounced drugs and drink now viewed him differently. He was also a father, bereft, able to articulate emotions that touched millions.

A new artist had been born. Sales of the single rocketed in tandem with the album, which by Janury 1994 had sold fifteen million copies internationally to become by far Eric's most successful.

His crowning glory came at one of the entertainment world's most prestigious events, the Grammy Awards, in Los Angeles on 24 February 1993. For years, the 6,000 industry figures who make up the voters under the aegis of America's National Academy of Recording Arts and Sciences had wanted to honour Clapton, and now they had the perfect vehicle. But the extent of their accolades surprised him. Eric gained no fewer than six Grammys, including Best Song for 'Tears in Heaven', Best Rock Song for the twenty-two-year-old 'Layla', and best album for *Unplugged*.

Stepping up to the rostrum at the Shrine Auditorium for the televised awards ceremony, Eric was initially bashful. 'I think the other song, the Vanessa Williams one ('Save the Best Till Last', which kept 'Tears in Heaven' from number one) should have got the award . . . because it kept us out of the number one spot for about two months. But still, we're happy.'

But by the time he had arrived at the stage to collect

his sixth trophy, Eric had drawn on his natural composure for big occasions. Wearing his tuxedo and fashionable metal-framed glasses, he exuded dignity and humility. He waited for the long ovation from the audience to subside before saying: 'I'm very moved and shaky and very emotional. I want to thank a lot of people but the one person who I want to thank is my son for the love he gave me and the song he gave me.'

The show-business fraternity lauds success, but Eric's triumph struck a chord far more resonant than most. The world knew that, through the years, he had pushed himself to the very brink with drugs and drink. Having survived that, he had now demonstrated the true artist within himself, by shaping his music to commemorate Conor's life and death. Hitherto, he had been fêted internationally as the world's greatest rock and blues guitarist. Now, he was recognized by his own community, and far beyond it, as a gifted autobiographical songwriter. It was a night when some who had feared for Clapton's very sanity after the loss could only shrug at such a stunning conversion by the artist of a tragedy into a therapeutic peak.

Clapton is something of a paradox when faced with the limelight and the public adoration his profession automatically bestows. One aspect of his make-up enjoys show-business performance. Another belongs more to the purism of the jazz musician, stripping himself naked each night on stage or in the recording studio, pushing his music to fresh horizons and simply hoping his public will enjoy his journey. Fundamentally, he is a working musician whose oeuvre and swashbuckling personality, allied to a keen sensitivity in his playing, have struck a chord with millions.

That Grammy night, however, rammed home the

central truth about his entire life. He knows he is at his best when confronted with a monumental human drama – a problematic love affair, a private problem such as he had endured with drugs and drink, or the loss of a loved one. 'I seem to function best when I'm in a bind,' he said to me. 'In "peacetime", if you like, I'm not likely to produce my best work.'

Winning six Grammy awards was a spectacular achievement equalling the figure won by Quincy Jones in 1990 and by the late Roger Miller in 1965.

It did not end there. That summer of 1993, in London, 'Tears in Heaven' won an Ivor Novello Award as best film theme or song. And Eric was fêted by the British Music Industry. The Nordoff Robbins Music Therapy charity took the unprecedented step at its annual lunch of presenting him for the second time with its Silver Clef award for outstanding services to British music. Eric had befriended this charity for severely handicapped children, describing its work to help them through music as a 'source of great inspiration' to him. Making the presentation, Eric's friend Pete Townshend jestingly taunted Eric for wrecking his old classic 'Layla' with a 'bossa nova–karaoke version' on the *Unplugged* album. After a heartfelt speech by a parent of an afflicted child, Clapton addressed the charity's lunch at the Intercontinental Hotel. Touching the nerve of the charity, Eric spoke succinctly of his own therapy and his own life in one short sentence: 'I don't think I would be on this planet if it wasn't for music during the dark hours of my life.'

THREE

THE BLUES OF CHILDHOOD

THE ARTISTRY of Eric Clapton had its genesis in his blighted childhood. He marshalled his own destiny with an unswerving dedication to his youthful ideals, coupled with a steely will to succeed.

He wanted success and popularity, but never hankered for fame or notoriety. He aspired to individualistic achievement, but not what he saw as the treadmill of pop stardom, which called for one hit record after another. And though he was human enough to welcome the money that would come from reaching millions around the world, he did not want riches in order narcissistically to parade his persona, his mansions and his cars. Millionaire status simply gave him the freedom to live well and freely consider his next moves.

Above all, what he wanted was to live out a life as an artist on his own terms.

He reached his summit with a series of career moves that, with hindsight, can be seen to have been a brilliant strategy.

In his teenage years, Eric's unconscious policy, in the view of his friend Steve Winwood, 'was to transfer his art school background into his career as much as possible'.

'I could cry, listening to his blues,' declares his mother, Pat. A striking and gregarious woman, Eric's mother now lives in the village which gave her and Eric considerable heartache. And yet, she muses, the very pressure that he found as a child might well have contributed to his need for self-expression, and ultimately also to his genius.

'I knew from the moment Eric was born that there was no way I would have the opportunity to keep him, to bring him up,' says his mother. 'I shall never get over it, never lose the guilt. But I suppose that's the penalty I have to live with for having an illegitimate child when I was only sixteen.'

The scars of bearing such a baby in 1945 had a deep effect on Pat. Recalling her 'blond, really handsome baby', she talks of the whispering that permeated the traditional English village of Ripley at the news of the birth in the front room of her mother's home. And, she says, 'The minute he was born, I knew he wasn't mine. I knew that I wasn't going to get to have him.'

Eric's natural father was Edward ('Ted') Fryer, a well-educated soldier in the Canadian infantry, who was stationed in England during the war. He played blues piano around the Surrey dance halls, and Pat met him on one such evening in the summer of 1944. As their friendship developed she was attracted to him because, as a gifted artist, he shared her fondness for paintings.

Though he was christened Eric, her son became 'Rick' for life to Pat. The phrase 'love child' was unknown in those years, she reflects, adding: 'The locals were hard on me.' The space for father's name on Eric's birth certificate was left blank, and the implication that she did not know the identity of the father hurt Pat. The pressure on her was increased when, despite her fondness for Ted

Fryer, he returned to Canada and to his wife during Pat's pregnancy. This ensured that baby Eric would be raised in the stable household of his grandparents, Rose and Jack Clapp.

'Nobody wanted Rick to know he was illegitimate during his young days,' Pat says. 'It would have been awful for him, going to school with what in those days had more shame attached to it than now. But as the years went by, Rick told me that, when he realized he was illegitimate, that was one of the reasons he *had* to make a name for himself . . . to overcome his background and strive for something.'

As Eric went into the care of his grandparents, Rose and her bricklayer husband, Jack Clapp, another romance bloomed for his mother. Pat met another Canadian soldier, Frank McDonald, and at the age of seventeen she married him.

Settling first in Army quarters in Dortmund, Germany, and later moving to Canada with her husband, Pat fretted over her separation from her first-born. But there was at least the compensating reality that he was properly cared for by her mother and stepfather.*

'There's no doubt,' says Pat, 'that as a very young child he considered my mother and my stepfather to be his parents.' She left him to go to Germany when he was

---

* Pat and Frank McDonald had two daughters, Cheryl, born on 5 May 1953 and Heather, born on 27 September 1958. As well as these half sisters, Eric had a half brother, Brian, who died in 1974, aged twenty-six, the victim of a hit-and-run road accident while riding his motorcycle near his home in Canada. Eric, in Jamaica when he heard the news, cancelled his concert plans in order to be with Pat at the funeral. 'I was touched by that,' Pat says. 'I really knew that he cared about me as his mother.' Pat and Frank McDonald were divorced in 1982.

nearly two years old. 'I couldn't allow myself to love my own son fully because I knew I had virtually given him to my mother to bring up.'

Two factors worked against Pat returning to Ripley to see her son during her marriage. First, her absence in a foreign land in the years when travel was neither so easy nor so inexpensive; and secondly, that her husband Frank's devout Roman Catholic family would not tolerate the recognition that Frank's wife had a child born out of wedlock. 'Now, Rick knows I was in a hopeless position,' Pat says of those years of her absence. Eric's grandmother, cheerful, adoring of 'Rick', remembers: 'We just brought him up as our own but we had to be straight with him and tell him his real mother was away from England, and we told him when he was five, just before he went to school. Because children can be very cruel . . . He had to understand why my husband Jack signed certain forms as his guardian. We didn't have his name changed, or adopt him, because my daughter, if she wanted him back, was free to do so.'

Money was tight, and to boost the family income Rose worked as a telephonist at the time Eric was born, and later in a lemonade factory. 'It used to grieve me that we couldn't give Rick the same pocket money as his friends. Not that he had many. He was a lonely little boy, really. He didn't make friends all that easily. Very reserved. He was so shy.'

A fondness for animals was evident in the boy. He had an imaginary horse which he spoke of tying up for the night, and he had a collection of snails on the front doorstep. He loved Rose and Jack's black labrador, Prince. His biggest enthusiasm, though, was drawing. 'I used to give him a pencil and paper and he'd sit for hours and hours drawing,' Rose recalls. He drew in everything that came to hand, including her cookery books: car engines, men with verses coming from their mouth. Perhaps, Rose ponders, he inherited his interest in art from his father.

At five, Eric began as a pupil at Ripley Church of England Primary School. He was known as an exceptionally polite young boy in the tight-knit village community. In those years, long before its main road carried heavy traffic to trample Ripley's charm, it was a calm backwater, some twenty miles from London and eight from the nearest metropolis, Kingston-on-Thames.

'We drilled it into him,' says Rose, 'that he must have manners and respect.' A very old villager delighted her with the news that Eric doffed his school cap to him regularly, saying 'Good morning.'

At school, Eric immediately applied himself to work and did well in most subjects, excelling in English, faring poorly in mathematics. Art was clearly going to be his talent. At a mere six years old, he was encouraged by Rose to enter one of his best drawings in a local talent contest. He won first prize of a box of paints with his entry, a drawing of horses with cowboys. He was praised for his attention to detail, having surrounded the prairie with cactus plants. 'He's a very observant little boy,' a judge told a beaming Rose. Eric was particularly pleased to have defeated fourteen-year-olds in the contest.

As a cub scout and later a member of the 1st Ripley troop of the Boy Scouts, Eric quite enjoyed the team spirit, but he was not keen on the cap and uniform. A school cap was equally disliked; he wore it, Rose remembers, but never liked it.

'He was both an angel and a little devil, but quite a perfectionist,' remembers Adrian Clapton, Rose's son by her first marriage. Eighteen when Eric was born, he was

a soldier in the Royal Signals for the first three years of
Eric's life. But when he returned home for leave, he was
regarded by young 'Rick' as a brother. They developed a
good relationship. 'He was very pernickety and I remember being struck by his determination to do everything
well, even at that young age,' Adrian says.

In a strange childhood fetish, Eric grew his fingernails
literally half an inch long and flatly refused to allow
anyone to cut them for months. 'Rose wasn't allowed to
go near them. He had a hatred of anyone cutting his
nails.' Eventually, Sylvia, Adrian's future wife, was
allowed to shorten them occasionally.

Once, Guy Pullen, who would become a firm friend,
joined together with some of the other village boys in
shutting Eric into the public phone box on a hot
summer's day when the temperature was in the 80s. The
boys surrounded the box to prevent Eric leaving; ashen-
faced and shaky when he was finally released, Eric was
frightened by the experience. It was a kid's game that
went wrong.

When Eric was about eight, Rose asked him, as many
a relative had before her, what he would like to be when
he grew up. 'He said he would like to be a doctor, to
stop people from going to heaven. And then he thought
and said: Well, no, he'd like to be a vicar, because he
helps people to get there. I've never forgotten that. I
thought: what a strange thing for a child to say.' His
grandparents had never forced religion on to the boy,
but several people attest to his keen spirituality as a child.
It would be a central core to his adult personality.

The departure to Korea of her soldier husband gave
Pat the chance to return from Canada for nine months
to rekindle her relationship with Eric when he was nine.
Pat brought her six-year-old son Brian to Rose and Jack

Clapp's small house, and it was then that she realized that Eric knew he was illegitimate. She wept as Eric said to his half brother: 'You see that lady over there in that bed? She's *my* Mummy, too.'

On her seven-year separation from her son, Pat reflects: 'It must have been confusing for him when I arrived . . . I found I'd been kept hush-hush from him, which was understandable. He had to be protected from the truth. But it hurt me like mad.' She registered that her young son was 'very deep, a bit of a loner'. She stayed in Ripley a year before returning to Canada.

At school around this time, Eric's studies seemed to go awry. Rose received a letter from the headmaster inviting her for a talk. 'What's happened to Eric?' chorused his teachers, most of them confident that he had a strong grammar school future. 'This is a very important time for him and we think something is upsetting him emotionally. He should pass his exams easily but he seems unsettled.' The worry was that he had dropped academically to having only a borderline chance of passing his eleven-plus tests.

Teachers reported to Rose for several months about his lack of concentration. The situation at home was giving him problems. 'I remember being very traumatized at that time because it had come into my life that I wasn't who I thought I was,' Eric remembers. 'I was actually an illegitimate child from somewhere else. I found out about my Mum and my grandparents all being interchangeable. I had no idea what was real any more. I remember this all seemed to take place five minutes before I sat my exam. Of course, it was actually a year and a half prior [to the tests], but all that time just seems to have been compounded into me walking into this exam room and not caring, not wanting to be bothered with what people's assessment of me was all about. I was very angry, and I failed this exam.'

After the eleven-plus, Eric went to St Bede's Secondary Modern, Send, a school near Woking, Surrey. Academically, at that time, being consigned to a secondary modern rather than winning a grammar school place was reckoned to be a handicap, but for Eric the move was to prove a blessing in disguise. Finding comradeship in other boys who were loners was perhaps the most significant move of his young life. 'I actually made friendships with two other kids who were very much like me . . . I think it was like we had come from outer space and we didn't fit, didn't want to play sports, didn't want to do anything that smacked of normality. It was the first friendship I had that was to do with uniqueness and being in a minority.' The school move can perhaps now be seen as an early example of how Eric would often convert adversity into creativity. He was at the 'wrong' school – but he made it work for him.

Sport was a definite no-no for Eric – at seven stone, he considered himself 'a physical weakling, no good at games'. The nearest concession to boyhood leisure pursuits came when he bought a BSA air rifle and delighted at firing pellets at the door of the outside toilet at his home. His Uncle Adrian's method of chastising him for the damage was to throw bricks on top of its corrugated iron roof whenever the young Clapton went inside it. This irritated and scared his young nephew.

'When he was fourteen,' Adrian says, 'I got married and moved to Woking, leaving my pride and joy, a BSA racing bike, temporarily at my mother's house in Ripley.' Returning to collect it, he was furious to find that Eric had stripped it, repainted it, and changed the wheels. 'He said he was going to tour Britain by bike.'

At home, the boy's independence began to surface in small examples that were nevertheless significant to Rose, Jack and Adrian: nobody except Eric was allowed to pour the milk on to his Weetabix cereal at breakfast time, since it had to go into the dish from a certain angle. His early passion for perfection was evinced in the model-making which was Adrian's hobby. Eric was fairly good at this, but since his uncle outshone his ability, he discontinued the hobby, although he returned to it enthusiastically in later life.

School life at Send, however, became positive after the trauma of his identity crisis. Encouraged by the art teacher, Mr Swan, Eric finally zoomed in on a subject that aroused his passion. Most mornings he would take a drawing in to the teacher, who told Rose that her grandson displayed a unique talent and might well carve a career in that area. Responding to this news, Eric began sketching things around the house. Artistic expression was almost certainly going to be in his life at some level, all his friends and relatives believed.

His best pal during those years, Guy Pullen, the same age, grew up six doors from Eric's grandparents' home. They went to the same primary and secondary schools. In the same A-stream class together, they shared a uselessness at gardening and woodwork. 'We got the boring jobs together because we were no good, like putting compost on the roses or digging over the compost heap every week.'

In lessons, Rick, as Clapton quickly became to Guy, showed an early independence: 'He never thought we should help each other out. He never participated in sport, and that marked him out as different because the village had always been very enthusiastic about it, with keen, talented footballers and cricketers. We'd rope him into coming to matches but he'd vanish, fade away, and we'd see him later sitting out on the green with a guitar.' One concession to 'knockabout sport' came through friendly boxing matches organized by Pullen in the back garden of his home. They set up matches with proper gloves and a ring made from rope around the trees.

'He was basically a loner. The artistic thing was strongly in him from the moment Rose got him that cheap guitar. All the boys in the village really envied him, and when he got the Grundig tape recorder that was just too much.' Other boys were bemused by Eric's obsession with music. 'If another boy came up to him as he was sitting on the green, Rick would say "Hey, listen to this blues guitar." Then he'd try to emulate the sound and the notes, every day throughout the summer.'

The two boys would often go to the local cinema, which they called the Bug Hutch. 'We paid one and ninepence and always stood at the back, after sitting in the front or middle rows for the first few times and getting chewing-gum stuck in our hair from the kids behind.'

He was known for his generosity. If Guy or other boys visited his house and admired a toy, Eric would give it to them to take away. 'He's always been totally loyal and over generous to certain people, particularly old mates,' says Pullen.

He wasn't a boy who chased girls, either. Pullen recalls that Eric's first known date was with a local girl, Sandra Ploughman. 'But he wasn't exactly the local Romeo,' Pullen says. And although their friendship was solid, Clapton bore grudges. 'Once, we'd had a row. We were ten years old, it was his birthday party, but he didn't invite me. That's the sort of kid he was. He'd never forgive.

'He was cunning, a kid who manoeuvred himself into and out of situations. He'd stir up trouble, then walk away from it. Always avoided a fight.' The two sometimes clashed because Eric would not try his hand at games or support Pullen's enthusiasm for football and cricket. 'But I realized when I saw him play why he never did it. He had no ball ability whatsoever. Same with tennis. He was static. No timing. The ball simply went by him.' Later, though, Eric became a staunch supporter of Ripley Cricket Club and went to many matches.

Eric's grandmother loved music and played the upright piano in her house well. There was a wind-up, non-electric gramophone which Eric's Uncle Adrian commandeered to play his precious 78s of the period, mostly dance band records by Glenn Miller, Jimmy Lunceford, Lionel Hampton and Charlie Barnet. This was the music that Eric's mother loved and played, too, during her brief sojourn back at 1 The Green, Ripley. She enjoyed the big band swing of Benny Goodman and Harry James. Eric was particularly attracted to the melancholic tone of trumpeter Bunny Berigan playing the ballad 'I Can't Get Started'.

As a youngster he had been encouraged by Rose to 'do a turn', as she played piano when friends or relations visited at Christmas or on birthdays. Sitting in the bay window, the child would, when the curtains parted, sing simple songs such as 'I Belong to Glasgow'. A far cry from the music he would eventually embrace, it was his first taste of performance.

Like many thousands of other Britons in those years he became addicted to *The Goons*, a radio series featuring the hilarious comedy of Peter Sellers, Harry Secombe and Spike Milligan. Crucial to the show were the bizarre accents adopted by the Goons, which Eric, previously an introvert, enjoyed mimicking along with his friends, aided by the tape recorder with which they preserved each show to dissect. Eric proved a consummate mimic at age thirteen, and, as with most things he undertook, he honed his enunciation of the Goons' accents to near perfection.

That year, 1958, was also an important year for an infant called rock 'n' roll. As Buddy Holly toured Britain, and Elvis Presley, Eddie Cochran, Fats Domino and Gene Vincent became the urgent sounds on the radio, Cliff Richard launched his career with his début record, 'Move It', and the youthful revolution in music began. The years of adult domination of the hit parade charts by Frank Sinatra, Rosemary Clooney and Glenn Miller were about to be subsumed.

The new music was the talk of every school and the enthusiasm of most students. Eric listened intently to the music on the radio, but his examination of it was more intense than that of most listeners. One of his chief characteristics was that when he worked up an enthusiasm for something, he had to saturate himself with information on the subject. This new American pop music, he heard from radio announcers, had its roots in something called 'the blues'. He decided to investigate this strangely named source; even at that age, he did not like to adopt anything as 'second-hand' unless it was absolutely necessary.

For his thirteenth birthday, he asked Rose and Jack to buy him a guitar. They could scarcely afford it. But they took him to the best shop in the locality, Bell's at Kingston-upon-Thames, where amid the bewildering array of German Hofners and Scandinavian Hagstroms

Eric chose a Spanish Hoya. His grandparents paid for it by monthly instalments. 'I can see, in my mind even now, his smile on the way home,' Rose says.

A key statement of identity came next. Striving to find his way 'into' the guitar, he psychologically rejected what he would later describe as 'company music'. This meant the conveyor-belt pop sounds of perfectly competent but identity-lacking singers such as Doris Day, Frankie Laine and balladeers. They simply did not 'reach' him. And the guitar, he quickly found, was an instrument with which to communicate: everyone played it differently. Played at its best, it was able to become an extension of one's feelings. The notes, the feeling with which it was played had to be personally constructed.

The blues, that generic description for a wailing music he still had to discover, was lying in wait for him. It was also an apt phrase for the difficult years he had recently experienced. But all that was about to change.

After nearly two uneventful years at St Bede's school, Eric qualified to take the thirteen-plus exam, which was something new introduced in those years. This gave a student a 'second chance' to upgrade to grammar school, or be diverted to concentrate on a subject at which he excelled. 'I passed that in art and English, and because my marks were good in those two subjects I was sent to Hollyfield Road School in Surbiton, which had an art branch,' Eric recalls. 'It was a bit disturbing because I had just got settled in one school. I didn't want to go and it was an hour's bus journey every morning to the outskirts of London. I didn't see my friends any more. I had been completely uprooted. But almost immediately I found other people because in fact this whole place was about these people who didn't fit; and things got better, especially in terms of musical taste and musical comrades.'

Hollyfield Road proved to be his point of artistic growth. 'We did ordinary lessons like English, mathematics, woodwork and physical training some days. Then there would be three or four solid days of art alone. We worked with clay and paint and did still lifes and figure drawing. And we also had the bonus of going to Kingston Art School night classes.' For two years he studied the basic design course. He also began to mix with boys who shared his interest in music. Digging for more information about the roots of American pop, and the blues, he began to collect records by men who were then called Negro; to call them 'black' was considered an insult in those years.

The tremendous attraction of the blues to Eric was that it was always one man's voice, apparently crying out a message, sometimes of racial oppression, sometimes of poverty, but invariably of the human condition. He strongly identified with this *cri de cœur*.

'I felt, through most of my youth, that my back was against the wall and that the only way to survive was with dignity, pride and courage,' Eric told Melvyn Bragg on ITV's *South Bank Show* in 1987. 'I heard that in certain forms of music and I heard it most of all in the blues because it was always an individual. It was one man and his guitar against the world. It was one guy who was completely alone and had no options, no alternatives other than to sing and play to ease his pain.'

Though the origins of the blues are open to conjecture, the tradition was developed in east Texas and the Mississippi River Delta region during the first decade of the twentieth century. Big Bill Broonzy, a regular visitor to Britain and a riveting performer with an expressive, instantly recognizable voice, was Eric's first favourite. His Uncle Adrian recalls of Eric: 'I can see him now, in his room where there was a little Grundig Cub tape recorder with three quarters of an inch reel-to-reel tapes.' Trying to copy the sounds of Broonzy, 'Eric swore and cursed till he could copy the sounds exactly, from as many records as he could get hold of. He ended up with seven or eight of those reels full of his practising, with the sound of the house's two budgerigars tweeting in the background.'

Later, his career as a musician established, Eric said to me what he had insisted to critics who argued that a young white man from Ripley, Surrey, had no reason to sing the blues: 'I think the blues is more of an emotional experience than one exclusive to black or white, or related to poverty. It comes from an emotional poverty. The music I drew from came from an emotional deprivation. There could be poor white people and poor black people and they would make different music.

'Now, I didn't feel I had any identity, and the first time I heard blues music it was like a crying of the soul to me. I immediately identified with it. It was the first time I'd heard anything akin to how I was feeling, which was an inner poverty. It stirred me quite blindly. I wasn't sure just why I wanted to play it, but I felt completely in tune.'

But at the age of fifteen, Eric became impatient with himself on the guitar. Too many forms of music were trying to be expressed from his head to his fingers, and the frustration caused him to put the playing 'on hold'.

*

Eric's lifestyle began to change in tandem with his studies. At sixteen, after about two years at Hollyfield Road, he took his General Certificate of Education exams, achieving an outstanding A grade in art and an average pass in English. 'This didn't really qualify me for anything,' Eric says, since a more all-round pass level in other subjects should have augmented his stardom in art. He had registered from age nine the genius of Van Gogh – 'so primitive and yet so sensual and raw and strong and not abstract. I almost felt like I could paint like him.' And of course Picasso, who, as Eric recollects was 'starting to roar' in Britain in the 1960s, when his first exhibitions were taking place.

Art was certainly his best bet for a career. With thin qualifications, he decided to take a portfolio of his work to Kingston Art College. 'They did an interview and I got into the art school there for one year on probation,' Eric says. 'I didn't have enough certificates but they liked what they saw.' Students were expected to undertake a four-year foundation course.

But there was an unfortunate start to his life there. 'When they asked which side of the college I wanted to go into, Fine Art or Graphics, I said Graphics. I'd been slightly brainwashed by Rose and Jack that if you wanted to make a living at art, you had to be a commercial artist. And I was nodding my head to that at the interview. They said: "What do you want to be?" I said: "Commercial artist." So they put me into Graphics. And after the first couple of weeks there I realized I was in the wrong department. Because in the canteen I saw all the good blokes with paint all over them and long hair, and they were in the Fine Art Department! And all our lot looked like chartered accountants! So I really thought I'd blown it from the word go. I just then started getting more interested in learning the guitar and listening to music.'

In Ripley village, by then, he was known as something of a 'weirdo'. Since childhood he had always been known to have the best collection of toys: 'Rose and Jack did their best to spoil him, probably to compensate for the fact that he didn't have a real Mum and Dad around,' says Guy Pullen. Now, Eric Clapton was the only boy in Ripley with a guitar. 'It was certainly no rags to riches story from childhood,' Pullen says. 'But everyone remarked on him. He was the distant kid who was definitely a one-off, didn't join in. He wasn't a normal country boy. He had the tightest jeans, the longest hair, a dirty face. And eventually he sat alone on the village green playing guitar to himself. Oh yeah, he was certainly the odd one out.'

Art colleges were the wellspring of an extraordinary number of embryonic pop stars in Britain in the 1960s. John Lennon, Pete Townshend, and Kinks leader Ray Davies were among the many who found expression in art before responding to the clarion call of music as a future vocation.

Aside from a fundamental artistic leaning, the art colleges demanded a certain Bohemian temperament from those who were to enjoy them fully. Teenage expression in these post-war years could flower through the arts. The new urgency of rock 'n' roll music and its rebellious stance was a natural parallel attraction.

Life at Kingston Art College bestowed a maturity, a sense of self, in Eric. He took to wearing a beret, appearing like a beatnik, dating and living the freewheeling life that suited a guitar-playing troubadour. He began to hang out at coffee bars where the beatnik atmosphere was accepted and encouraged, 'making a complete idiot of myself' playing such songs as "Scarlet Ribbons", popularized by Harry Belafonte.

'I also found out about alcohol,' he says. 'I started drinking and the two seemed to mix up a bit there. I had a lot of personality conflicts and changes going on. I'd met girls and I had my first sexual experience around that time; a quite heavy confrontation-of-nature. I was deflowered by an older woman who really knocked my socks off. It couldn't have happened in a better way, in fact, but it was all tied in with drinking and hanging out with older people.

'Then I began withdrawing into myself again to try and re-evaluate who I was and whether I was going to be an artist or a musician, what was calling to me the strongest. I kept coming up with no answer, so I just floated.'

As a floater, however, he did revive his slightly tentative interest in the guitar. At home, Rose noticed that he was uncharacteristically proud of his art college uniform of maroon jacket and grey trousers. But his interest in art studies gradually became equalled by a consuming passion for the blues. When he stayed in for the evening, he would push his grandparents' patience to the limit by staying up until two or three in the morning, strumming the guitar, playing the blues records he had managed to get by artists like Leadbelly, Jimmy Reed, John Lee Hooker and Muddy Waters, and struggling to learn their chords with the aid of his tape recorder. 'Testing . . . testing . . . all night long,' Rose recalls. 'I can hear it now. I remember shouting down to him so many times: "Rick, are you coming to bed? Your father's got to go to work in the morning!" Eric's practising was even keeping the two budgerigars awake.

As beatniks did, he went through several changes in appearance. His hair was alternately long and short, he had a beard and then no beard. And he often carried with him the guitar in a case. He wore an overcoat and a very long brown scarf.

As sixteen-year-old Eric combined life at art college with an exploration of music, the music dominating the British clubs was traditional jazz. In Liverpool, the Beatles had returned from work in Hamburg and were slogging it out at the Cavern, where they eventually overthrew the jazz bands. In London, Clapton's search for his own niche in self-expression through music was helped by the splinter movement within the traditional jazz world.

To one side lay the Dixieland of Kenny Ball's Jazzmen and Terry Lightfoot's Band. Basically good-time, upbeat music, this found an audience of keen dancers in clubs like 100 Oxford Street, London. A more earnest, dedicated and academic crowd existed at Studio 51 in Great Newport Street, on the edge of Soho. This was the home of Ken Colyer's Jazzmen. Trumpeter Colyer disliked Dixieland music and fervently believed in recreating the insistent, heartfelt New Orleans music of men like clarinettist George Lewis and Kid Ory. Colyer's approach to jazz, more evangelical, more heartfelt and pure than any other in London, made him a father figure to young people looking for 'the truth' about jazz. At the interval, too, he led his skiffle group of guitars and washboard, interpreting the sounds of black American blues singers with spellbinding accuracy.

Clapton fell in with the crowd that went to the Colyer club and also the Duke of York pub, where music was made. 'The whole scene was very small and very, very exclusive in a way. If you knew all of these people they would probably fill up one room. They travelled from one place to another and it wasn't really an audience. It was a gang, a crowd. The musician wasn't looked at as a separate entity. He was just one of the crowd who could play: "Oh, that's Eric. He plays here. He'll play later if you like." It wasn't so professional then.'

It would be as much an evening out to be among friends as anything, 'And one of your friends was going to be playing,' Clapton says. 'One of the leading lights at that time was a guy called Wizz Jones who is still playing but works mainly in Europe and Germany. He was my hero because he was playing twelve-string guitar and songs like "San Francisco Bay Blues". It was the purest stuff that came out of skiffle.'

Clapton's addictive personality, which would later manifest itself in his obsessive behaviour with drugs, had begun in these teenage years when he took black dexedrine tablets. 'Dexys' were popular in the jazz club world and Eric was on its fringe.

At Kingston Art College, Eric was gaining confidence, playing guitar at lunchtime in the cafeteria. His art work declined in quantity during his first year at college and as he came up for review, Rose received two letters from the principal in quick succession. The first warned that Eric's volume of work was inadequate and unless he stepped up his output the college would have to seriously consider his position 'because he might be depriving someone else of a place here'. A few weeks later Rose and Jack were invited to the principal's office to be told that Eric would have to leave. 'He had not been putting in enough time,' Rose says. She believed he had been a truant. She, Jack and Adrian had been convinced that

Eric was 'up to something' when the time had come to renew his quarterly Green Line bus pass: 'He said something about not using the pass in the previous week and that was the first inkling we had that he hadn't been going to school every day.' Though she still believes Eric was banished from college because he was seeking out his friends to play guitar, Eric denies this.

'Not true! Where would I go? The only times I can remember going out of college were to spend the odd days in town [London] going to galleries, which I felt was part of my work as an art student. I'd go to a gallery for a couple of hours and then go to one of those cartoon cinemas to kill a little bit of time. But I couldn't be classified as a truant.'

Explaining the background to his ejection, Eric says now: 'At the end of my first year, simply because of my lack of interest and a lot of distractions (I was getting into the Bohemian, beatnik thing and not really working very much), I didn't have a big enough portfolio for them to think it was worth keeping me on. The stuff I did was good. But there just wasn't enough; they were judging by quantity. So I didn't make it. They booted me out, along with another bloke. Us two out of fifty, which wasn't too good.'

He was particularly aggrieved at being ejected from college because 'I felt my work at art school was very promising compared with the other students. Most of them in that department were mathematicians more than artists. What I was doing was creative and imaginative. I was shocked.'

'I used to wonder why he was so late home for his meal in the evenings,' Rose says wistfully. He had been to the record shops or playing guitar. 'I often gave him a good telling off. My husband was not the sort to holler.

But he made his point with Rick. He said: "You had your chance, now you've chucked it away."' A life in stained-glass designing, which was Eric's original choice, by now could not compete with the pull of music. Eric's grandfather said that to earn some cash and occupy himself during the day, Eric could go to Camberley with him as a bricklayer and help plasterers on the building sites. And that is what Eric sometimes did; his keen eye and flair soon showed in that work, too. 'Jack said he was an excellent worker – his perfectionism showed in the way he laid tiles,' says Rose. Eric grew to respect, and learn from, the work ethic of his grandfather as well as his craftsman skills.

There were signs of sentimentality in the teenager. When, at sixteen, he signed on as a postman to deliver the Christmas mail in the Ripley area, he returned from one round with £3 for Rose. It would help with the guitar payments, he said. Rose refused it, so Eric went out and bought her a bottle of perfume with the cash.

'I don't think he liked the work as a postman. He wasn't an energetic boy and the long round on the push-bike for the widespread area of Ripley wasn't much fun to him.' But he wanted the money! He bought her a vase for her birthday which she still cherishes.

And she remembers the days when she nearly went mad with the repetitiveness of his practising, once he had been booted out of art school and often stayed home all day. Her temper nearly snapped, but, as always, Eric was able to win her over with his quiet charm.

As the months passed, Clapton's dedication to music, particularly that with the pure touch of rhythm-and-blues, as it was then called, dominated his life. At his home, the same kind of scene was acted out throughout

Britain. As American popular music – and particularly the guitar – strengthened its influence on youth, exchanges like those between Eric Clapton and Rose were occurring between thousands of teenagers and parents: 'You're wasting your time on a thing like that,' Rose said to the seventeen-year-old Eric. 'It's a nice hobby, but not really a *job*.'

'You won't say that when I'm earning £200 a week, Mum,' Eric answered.

'I remember laughing out loud at him, and he looked hurt,' Rose recalls. 'Of course it was a difficult argument for him, at the time.' He was soon leaning on Rose and Jack to subsidize further his folly, part-exchanging his old acoustic guitar for a £100 electric model. Because he had demonstrated a willingness to work at the building site, Rose committed herself to the hire-purchase payments. 'If that's what you want to do, OK, but don't blame us if things go wrong. Stained-glass designing would be safer, wouldn't it?'

The word was out, in the pubs and at parties in the Kingston-upon-Thames area where aspiring musicians played: Eric Clapton was a rather special young guitarist.

With a career in art now difficult, Eric placed all his emphasis, interest, and serious study, on music. And Kingston Art College had provided an impetus for his first serious move into a band. He was friendly with a girl there who was dating Tom McGuinness, a bass guitarist who was instrumental in the formation of a new blues-based band.

Forty miles west of London, in the Oxford area, a fanatical blues purist, a pianist named Ben Palmer, was itching to launch a band to interpret the raw blues sounds of Sonny Boy Williamson, Little Walter, Muddy Waters and Big Bill Broonzy. Two of his early colleagues were Brian Jones, later to find fame with the Rolling Stones, and Paul Jones, who would later sing with the successful band Manfred Mann. No such fame and fortune or ambition fired Ben Palmer, who was content to preach the blues gospel with kindred spirits like Tom McGuinness.*

Palmer's group was launched in March 1963, at precisely the time the Beatles were releasing their third single, 'From Me to You', and going on tour alongside such quintessential 1960s British pop names as singers Helen Shapiro, Kenny Lynch and Danny Williams.

The Rolling Stones were together but it would be three months before their recording début in June 1963 with 'Come On'.

As Eric celebrated his eighteenth birthday, Tom McGuinness's girlfriend arranged for him to attend a rehearsal for the band Ben Palmer and McGuinness planned to call the Roosters. 'He joined the band there and then,' Palmer remembers of the rehearsal night in a Kingston pub. 'He was so good, obviously a natural, we didn't even have to discuss it.'

The Roosters lasted six inglorious months, playing the hip circuit of the Ricky Tick Clubs in Kingston, Windsor and West Wickham.

Clapton relished this baptism into a band whose members had musical integrity. There was a flourishing rhythm-and-blues scene in Britain at that time, its anchor the much-respected Alexis Korner, who played fine guitar in his group Blues Incorporated. Korner championed

---

* Tom McGuinness would eventually join Manfred Mann, and also formed a successful duo, McGuinness Flint.

and befriended the early Rolling Stones and was an influential evangelical figure to many young musicians. The music of this community was a far cry from the pop world of the day.

Inside the Roosters, Eric exchanged enthusiasms: around the clubs, before he joined the band, he had been singing such songs as Big Bill Broonzy's 'Hey Hey' and the Bessie Smith classic 'Nobody Loves You When You're Down and Out'.*

McGuinness and Palmer exchanged enthusiams with Clapton, talking about Bo Diddley and Chuck Berry, but while he understood their talent, that music was a little too modern in its approach. Eric was absorbing the simple, more primitive rural blues of artists like Furry Lewis and Blind Willie Johnson. Eventually, he decided, like many other future rock stars such as Robert Plant and Jimmy Page of Led Zeppelin, that the true giant of his chosen idiom was Robert Johnson, whose classic *King of the Delta Blues Singers* album had been released in 1961. Emotional, stripped bare, and challenging on every human level, the work of Robert Johnson was an inspiration to join that of his earliest mentors, Muddy Waters and Big Bill Broonzy.

With all its meagre pickings (a few pounds a night and sometimes free drinks for each player), the Roosters audiences, of about sixty people, were mostly discriminating. And for a teenager determined somehow to make his mark as a guitarist, the pace of life, the discipline of being collected by the band van at prescribed times, the

* Eric was able to draw on his immense knowledge of the blues by including these two songs on his album *Unplugged*, released in 1992.

promise of a faintly Bohemian lifestyle, all looked good to Clapton. And the Roosters' music had integrity.

Most important, though, were the nights on which he could hone his guitar playing with critical colleagues in the band and audiences who were talking about Eric's exceptional verve.

'It was immediately obvious that he was something that none of the rest of us were,' says Ben Palmer. 'And he had a fluency and a command that seemed endless. The telling factor was that he didn't *mind* taking solos, which people of our standard often did because we weren't up to it. I noticed immediately with Eric . . . give him a solo and he didn't care how long you let him play. He'd go *on* and *on* . . . until sometimes you'd have to stop him, to bring the singer back in. I knew from the very first that he was quite different from the rest of us in the Roosters. Coherent, lucid, fresh, powerful – and always *building*. He had a sense of dynamics quite remarkable for someone of his age.' He was also intensely serious about his playing, negotiating the repertoire with Palmer and McGuinness, the nominal leaders.

The Roosters petered out in October 1963, when Ben confessed one night to most of the band that he did not enjoy playing in public too much. He preferred rehearsals and his narrow horizons in music were too restricting, holding back the more ambitious players like Clapton and McGuinness. 'I was quite happy for it to end and to stop playing,' says Palmer. 'I couldn't see us ramming the Chicago blues down people's throats successfully or fast enough for my temperament.' The split of the Roosters was amicable enough, but a rock-solid friendship had formed between Clapton and Palmer. They were to become lifelong friends, partly perhaps because their paths diverged but mostly because their values and their uncompromising single-mindedness found an easy rapport.*

As teenage friends, Clapton and Palmer shared many days and nights living in a commune above a greengrocery warehouse at 74 Long Acre, in London's Covent Garden. Clapton was the only musician in a house which attracted a poet, a puppeteer, and occasional visits from actor John Hurt, then a student at the St Martin's School of Art. It was the time in Eric's life when he felt most free, drifting from band to band, and spending nights drinking cheap Algerian red wine with Palmer, who had by then given up playing in favour of working for the embryonic jazz record label Esquire, run by Carlo Kramer.

Eric's and McGuinness's move, after the Roosters, lasted a mere month, into the Liverpool-based band Casey Jones and the Engineers. Led by a young hustler named Brian Cassar, who had ridden the Merseyside beat group boom by forming a band named Cass and the Cassanovas, Casey Jones and the Engineers was Eric's most improbable band. In July 1963, with the advent of the Liverpool beat group bonanza, Cassar had touted himself around the record companies and picked up a one-record deal with Columbia. Casey Jones and the Engineers were an anonymous group of sessions musicians on the record. But when his manager insisted that 'Casey Jones' should do some concerts, Cassar had to hurriedly form a real band to back himself. He recruited four musicians, including Eric Clapton and McGuinness. They played Chuck Berry songs on shows

* Ben was to reunite with Eric three years later, as a road manager with Cream. Today, he is happy as a different kind of artist, wood carving at his home in Wales.

in Macclesfield, Manchester and Reading with 'Casey', then gave up abruptly. It was an unnatural musical marriage.

'By then I was learning so much so fast,' Clapton remembers. 'The thing that most inspired me was that I had found out how to play the "shake" that would make the sound of Muddy Waters' guitar part on "Honey Bee" when he goes into the verse. It's a three-finger triad that does it. I remember that as being the first major victory in my approach to guitar playing.'

After the diversion with Casey Jones, Eric returned to the pub and club circuit around Kingston. He played as much as possible, now hungry for experience, in small jazz clubs and anywhere that would offer a few pounds.

In a Britain then gripped by the mayhem of Beatlemania, the jazz scene still flourished but was splintered. Audiences eager for something fresh were identifying with rhythm and blues. The music needed a catalyst beyond the music to lift its popularity. The man of the moment was Giorgio Gomelsky. An experimental filmmaker who loved musical adventure, he had a particular love of jazz and the blues.

By early 1963, Gomelsky was running his own club in the rear room of the Station Hotel, Richmond. Two names who would eventually become internationally successful were featured there: jazz saxophonist Johnny Dankworth's band on Monday nights, and Sundays the Dave Hunt band featuring Ray Davies, later to lead the Kinks.

Gomelsky's biggest coup was in establishing the club, which he eventually called the Crawdaddy, as the place where the Rolling Stones made their name. And when the Stones stopped playing there, Gomelsky booked, as their successors, a group called the Yardbirds.*

The Yardbirds, originally called the Metropolis Blues Quartet, led by bass guitarist Paul Samwell-Smith, needed a guitarist on the departure of Anthony Topham, whose parents opposed his turning professional. Clapton was the only serious contender for the job, having acquired a strong reputation in the world of blues-based musicans. Keith Relf, the Yardbirds' harmonica player and singer, attracted Eric to a rehearsal. He fitted in immediately, strengthening a band that already had its sights on commercial success.

Relf had known Clapton at Kingston Art College, where they had tried to form a band together. The Yardbirds line-up Clapton joined was Relf, Chris Dreja (guitar), Paul Samwell-Smith (bass guitar) and Jim McCarty (drums).

This was Eric's first real experience of life as a 'communal' musician. The Yardbirds rented the top floor of an old house near Kew Gardens, where Eric shared a room with Chris Dreja. The two men were virtual brothers for six months, during which time Eric sharpened what would develop into a lifelong passion for stylish clothes.

His favourite hang-out fashion spot was Austins in Shaftesbury Avenue, London, where he often took Chris, advising him what he should wear. Clapton seemed to want to restyle his appearance every six months, from

---

* They were invariably called 'groups' in the 1960s. The jazz world had 'bands'. Only in the 1970s did the rock world start using the word 'bands'.

hairstyle to shoes, and had an unerring eye not merely for what was hip at the moment, but what would be correct in a month or more.

The obsessiveness that would always mark him was evident from his earliest days. He rarely took solos and stood behind his amplifier initially, perfecting just one riff. It was not until much later, in his stint with the Yardbirds, that he stepped forward to shine.

Contrasting with his serious application to music and his appearance, Eric had that eccentrically British custard-pie sense of humour. He enjoyed the cut-and-thrust of chucking things at his mates, pulling horrific facial expressions, bulging his eyes, wearing masks for a jape, spitting mouth rinse over the others in fun. He never minded, either, jokes that rebounded on himself. A still more bizarre stipulation, made by Eric when he joined the Yardbirds, was that he would have to have every Christmas free. He wanted to return to Ripley for a traditional time with his grandparents. The band hired a temporary replacement for him, much to his chagrin.

By then, Eric's natural mother had moved from Canada to Dortmund, Germany, where his stepfather, Frank McDonald, had been posted as an Army sergeant. Eric visited them with Rose and Jack. Mother and eighteen-year-old son still found it hard to confront their relation-ship. 'He looked at me; I looked at him. The knowledge was there but we both found it painful.' The immediate concern was the taboo of Eric's long hair inside the military area where Pat and Frank were living. 'We told Rick that before he could come into the Mess for a meal, he would have to have his hair cut. Rick had an army haircut, a crew cut, under great protest, but when he returned to England he made it appear fashionable. He went from the sublime to the ridiculous.'

Back in Britain, the Yardbirds were in the vanguard of the group explosion. Their musical credentials and aspirations were a notch higher than many other groups climbing aboard the Beatles bandwagon. But in the spirit of the year, such differences were blurred. For Clapton, it was essential, after the temporary experiences of the Roosters and Casey Jones, to be in a band that was making waves.

Now managed by Giorgio Gomelsky, the Yardbirds quickly acquired a cult following at the Station Hotel, Richmond. And there were visits to Liverpool to play the legendary Cavern Club and Newcastle upon Tyne for the club Whiskey-A-Gogo, where the Animals had been born. Travelling the country at last, Clapton was now finally on course for a career as a musician.

There was, however, friction in the group. It dated back to long before Eric joined the Yardbirds, and hinged on his dislike of Paul Samwell-Smith. Just before Paul's group the Metropolis Blues Quartet metamorphosed into the Yardbirds, the bass guitarist had played a session at the Crown, a pub in Kingston-upon-Thames, with Clapton among the audience. Paul decided to take a rare solo on a song called 'Papa Joe's Blues'.

Eric listened intently to the group he would soon join. At the end of the session he walked over to Samwell-Smith and said: 'Would you do me a favour?'

'Yes,' said Paul, anxious even then to keep on good terms with the guitarist everyone on the blues circuit was talking about.

'Don't play any more lead guitar solos,' Eric told him. Paul reflects with a smile: 'I clearly didn't have talent in that direction, and he spotted it.'

Once in the Yardbirds, such contempt increased. And it was not restricted to musical judgement. Samwell-Smith's taste developed into folk music and he loved the fresh sounds of Bob Dylan and Peter, Paul and Mary. With Eric's loyalty to the blues unswerving, the two men were on a collison course.

'Had I known more about the music I was playing, had I known more about the blues, he would have respected me more,' reflects Samwell-Smith. 'But he just didn't like my attitude and we did not get on well, which makes things difficult when you are shoulder to shoulder in the van from London to Liverpool. Eric regarded me as a snob, a lower-middle-class boy from Hampton Grammar School who was jumping on the blues band-wagon, and who had no right to lead the group *he* was in. And he hated the fact that I was not playing my instrument very well. I think that's what caused him to disrespect me. That, plus the fact that our manager told him, immediately he joined the group, that I was the leader and he must do exactly as I said. That didn't go down well at all. But I have no excuses – it's a shame we didn't get on!'

Clapton's memory of his aversion to Paul is cool and direct. 'I took an instant dislike to him because of several factors,' says Eric. 'He had such a very tweedy image. Then, he came from suburban *Twickenham* and he lived with his Mum and Dad and it was all so perfectly *normal* and *good*. He was such a good boy! I was much more into developing myself by hanging out with people who were more likely to be rebels, come from broken homes and were generally neurotic. Those kinds of people appealed to me more than Paul and his type. And on top of all that, he had a great love for folk music and white pop – Joan Baez and all that – and I was totally intolerant of that at the time. I came from the other end of the scale. It had to be black music in order to be valid. I mean – Paul liked the *Shadows*! I didn't.'

Yet Samwell-Smith's distance from Eric enabled him to judge coolly the man's make-up. While other twenty-year-olds were in a hurry to achieve fame, Clapton's aspirations were very different. 'He was certainly the best musician in the band, the most fluid, with that muscular connection that happens with great natural players between their brains and their fingers. He seemed to have a sense of *knowing* about his guitar playing. Talent, when it's that big, is so strong that even the possessor of it sometimes has to look at his fingers and wonder how the hell he's doing *that*. I got the feeling with Eric – he'd move to the front of the stage and take a solo, and we'd all know it was something special.

'Despite my own attitude to music, which was mostly commercial,' says Paul, 'I registered that Eric's attitude to it all was also very strong. He had definite great likes – people like B. B. King – and tended to be very exclusive. He wouldn't even join in a band conversation about the commercial stuff. And it really became a bit uncomfortable. When you're on the road travelling, that attitude isn't easy. He was . . . rigid. He'd end any conversation on music he didn't like, or on compromise, with something like: "Oh, it's gotta be *right* or what's the point?"'

Both the musicians and the audience would remark on Clapton's sense of design and fashion. While the other Yardbirds wore jeans and denim jackets, Eric arrived for one memorable show at the Star, Croydon, just outside London, with a crew-cut, smart shirt, neat, tight collar and Ivy League jacket. 'He never appeared ludicrous, just extraordinary,' recalls Paul Samwell-Smith. In those days when long hair was *de rigueur*, the audience gasped at the sight of the guitarist with neatly cropped hair.

Since the Rolling Stones were blues-based, Eric became a staunch admirer. In early 1960s Britain, fans were polarized between the Beatles and the Stones, whose recording career did not take off until a year after the Beatles had dominated the charts. When the Beatles went to the Crawdaddy Club on 14 April 1963, Eric was among the Stones' core audience, resenting the intrusive arrival of the guys from Liverpool. 'Everyone was very anti-Beatle because we were part of the Stones crowd,' he recalls. Later, the blues purist in Clapton was to resent the abdication, as he saw it, by the Stones who 'went Chelsea'. Clapton had always admired the guitar work of Keith Richards and has established a lifelong friendship with the Stones' original 'bad boy'.

Pete Townshend, then leading the Who to the top on the crest of the 'mod' look, remembers first seeing Clapton standing on a pavement in Ealing in 1964. 'He was waiting for a bus, like me, and he looked extremely smart and modish. He'd shaved all his hair off. We hardly spoke. Two weeks later I saw him at a clothes shop he went into regularly, Austins in Shaftesbury Avenue. They sold American clothes. We did have a short talk.'

But Clapton was aloof. 'Not many blues musicians in those days took the Who seriously,' explains Townshend. 'Although he was charming, he didn't treat me as if there was any substance to me. It was a bit of a one-sided affair. I'd never actually seen him play and I had no time for hybrid white blues anyway. I thought John Mayall's whole thing was stupid and Steve Winwood singing the blues was a waste of time.' (Eric had jammed regularly with Winwood's band, the Spencer Davis Group, at the London Marquee.)

'To me,' says Townshend forcibly, 'a London white performer trying to play blues music was a joke. I felt that what the Who had at least done was turn it into slightly more of our own urban form of music that depended very much on the lyrics. It seemed to me the blues was a very simple music form and it's what they sang about that counted.' How could a young white boy from Surrey sing or play the blues?

'So there was little basis for communication, although I thought Eric Clapton in those years had a sense of appearance better than most of the people he was hanging around with. He had a style. But musically, *he* felt superior – and I certainly did.'

'I equated my fashion-consciousness with the way modern jazz musicians looked,' recalls Eric. 'I always fancied myself as being part of an élite. That's why being a purist about my music was very convenient. Because being a blues guitar player was almost like being a jazz musician. In magazines like *Downbeat* there was always a page on blues, so I saw myself in that category. Not just an ordinary guitarist, a *blues* man! And I loved the idea that jazz musicians were very, very slick-looking guys. They were *always* clothes-conscious. And I was always keen on clothes, even before I played guitar. So it all fitted in well.

'The jazz musician's look had developed perfectly, for me, from the art college beatnik thing. Even the way I shaved, or didn't sometimes, it all went into being an art student and then a blues player.'

All the money he earned from the Yardbirds went on clothes. 'Ivy League suits, white socks, loafers, Levi jeans, or straight slacks and sports jackets with shirt and tie and tab collar. It was all very conservative.' It contrasted, though, with the shabby, careless look of many other musicians.

With his instruments, too, Clapton was totally organized, unlike some of the others. Says Paul Samwell-Smith: 'He knew exactly what he was doing, where they were, and if he needed another guitar he said so and by the next gig he'd bought one. He was always on time – once, I failed to turn up for a show and I remember he thought that totally unprofessional, unacceptable. He made me feel very bad about it. And of course he was right. He knew precisely what he was about and did it beautifully, without any fuss or trouble, regarding it as his work. He had a set identity . . . which the girls found attractive.'

The Yardbirds were flourishing on the club circuit, but it was a treadmill. The Rolling Stones were demonstrating that to survive and prosper, hit records were needed. Giorgio Gomelsky found that Decca Records did not want to take a chance on a second group too similar to the Stones, so he went to EMI, home of the Beatles, where the Yardbirds were signed by the Columbia label.

'I Wish You Would' backed by 'A Certain Girl' was their first single, and though it was no hit it spread the word and secured a television appearance. Their second single, 'Good Morning Little Schoolgirl', was Eric's idea but reached only 44 in the UK charts.

That year of 1964 ended with the release of their album, *Five Live Yardbirds*. An optimistic spirit pervaded the band, but Eric seemed restless. Compounding his dislike of Samwell-Smith was an unspoken realization that this group was being tilted towards the charts, and he had strayed from his first love, the blues.

A strong break for the band came when they were booked by Beatles manager Brian Epstein for *Another Beatles Christmas Show*, a season at Hammersmith Odeon, from 24 December for six nights (but importantly for Eric excluding Christmas Day). Low down on a bill which featured Freddie and the Dreamers, Elkie Brooks, Sounds Incorporated, Jimmy Savile and Michael Haslam, the Yardbirds tasted the full throttle of Beatlemania. Eric, their sartorial adviser, had the job of designing the suits for their stage apearances.

Eric had stepped outside the Yardbirds coterie by now, mixing with other musicians including Keith Moon of the Who, and going to clubs. He showed up for Yardbirds shows rather half-heartedly.

But the Christmas show alongside the Beatles was to bring him face to face with a man who would figure dramatically in his life. George Harrison, the guitar player in the Beatles, stood beside the stage as the Yardbirds appeared, noting the exceptional talent of Eric Clapton. And Eric did the same when the Beatles appeared.

'He was checking me out, and I was checking him out to see if he was a real guitar player,' Eric recalled later to James Henke in *Rolling Stone* magazine. 'And I realized that he was. But we came from different sides of the tracks. I grew up loving black music, and he grew up with the Chet Atkins–Carl Perkins side of things.'

'That rockabilly style always attracted me but I never wanted to take it up. And I think it's the same for him. The blues scene attracts him but it evades him somehow. He's much more comfortable with the finger-picking style of guitar.'

A mutual respect, and friendship, was born. The Beatles were kings of the pop world, ruling the airwaves and the national media. Six months before that first meeting the group had returned from America in triumph to make their first film, the zany *A Hard Day's Night*. On the set, George had met the stunning young model who would become his wife within two years.

As they chatted in the wings and in the dressing-room of the Hammersmith Odeon for the first time, neither Eric Clapton nor George Harrison could have had any idea that George's girlfriend, whom he had only recently begun to date, would be at the centre of the most tempestuous love affair for the two men, and a remarkable 'love triangle' that would be debated around the world for decades. George's girlfriend's name was Pattie Boyd.

FOUR

THE 'GOD'
OF CREAM

ERIC FELT distanced from the Yardbirds in the spring of 1965. His fifteen months with them had been a strong career move and the role of star guitarist had given him access to plenty of girls on the road. When the Yardbirds toured with the US group the Ronettes, Eric had a fling with singer Ronnie Spector, who later married the celebrated producer Phil Spector. But his blues playing convictions had somehow become derailed by a band that saw itself as joining the race for pop stardom. 'I needed to be true to myself', he said later. 'I am, and always will be, a blues musician.'

The Yardbirds had provided sporadic links with the blues, including memorable recording sessions accompanying American legends Muddy Waters, Sonny Boy Williamson and Otis Spann. Yet even these sessions served to emphasize to Eric that he was still an apprentice. Playing alongside such giants at such an early stage in his life, he felt intimidated.

With his Gibson guitar and spare but accurate solos inside the Yardbirds, Eric had gradually become the focal point, and was among the darlings of the British rock scene. Giorgio Gomelsky even gave him a nickname: Slowhand. 'He coined it as a good pun,' Eric recalls. 'He kept saying I was a fast player so he put together the slow handclap phrase into Slowhand as a play on words.' Eric enjoyed the tag.

But as the Yardbirds went into their recording session for their third single in March 1965, he came up against what would be seen as his most crucial move. At the Christmas Beatles show, Paul Samwell-Smith, who considered himself the leader, was given a song by a publisher who believed it would be their perfect new single. Called 'For Your Love', it was written by Graham Gouldman, later to be successful as a writer/performer with the Manchester band 10CC.

Paul loved it and worked on an arrangement including bongos, harpsichord and bowed bass. At the recording session, Clapton pointed out that there was scarely any room for him, as lead guitarist, to manoeuvre himself into the song at all. It was a moment of decision. Eric knew he had no future in a band that did not share his goals.

Samwell-Smith vividly remembers how Clapton came to quit the Yardbirds because the record was such a distance from his beloved blues. 'It just seemed so inevitable. He realized he had to leave. He was so unhappy. We were making our new single, which was not written by us, and that alone wasn't good news for Eric. The Yardbirds played the twenty seconds in the middle, the rhythm-and-blues bit. It wasn't a record, it was a production!

'Giorgio had come to us and presented us with the song and said: "Come on, we need a hit, try this!" And since I was steering the band commercially I agreed. I produced the record. In the middle of the making of it,

Giorgio got a phone call from Eric, very dignified, saying he was leaving. Nobody was surprised.'*

Eric describes the atmosphere in the Yardbirds at that time as 'a political thrust towards the top of the charts'. And he says: 'I didn't have any goal in that direction. It didn't appeal to me at all to end up on television and do cabaret and package tours. I was really happy doing the clubs with the following we got, and I think those fans wanted us to stay doing that kind of thing. So the more ambitious they got for the gelt, the less happy I became. I wanted out.'

Fame and money were not on his horizon: 'That never occurred to me. I just wanted to play the guitar and play it all the time. I didn't want to be lazy and laid-back and I didn't want the things that money would have bought. In those days, if you had a nice pair of jeans you were laughing.'

Eric says it was a decision by Giorgio to confirm Samwell-Smith as the leader of the Yardbirds that made his decision easy. A memo from Giorgio to the whole band piled on the discipline. He saw the professionalism they needed to convert a scruffy band into a tight working unit. 'Time is money . . . if you're late for rehearsals you will be fined . . . and if you have any queries about this, report to Paul Samwell-Smith or come to my office immediately,' said the memo.

Clapton says that was the breaking point for him. 'I went to Giorgio's office next day and said I don't like it and I'm going to leave. Instead of being upset, Giorgio said: "Good. OK, well, we're not really surprised. I

---

* Ironically, the B-side of 'For Your Love' was a blues instrumental, 'Got to Hurry', featuring Eric's best recorded work with the Yardbirds.

can't say I'm happy about you going, but we wish you well."'

When a music paper headline announced: 'Clapton Quits Yardbirds – Too Commercial', his uncompromising attitude became publicly known. 'It's very sad – I suppose he likes the blues so much that he didn't like it being played badly by a white shower like us,' said singer Keith Relf.*

If Gomelsky had not laid it down so forcefully that Samwell-Smith was the leader, a totally different route might have emerged for Eric. 'Keith Relf, the singer, was just as much a reprobate as anyone else, possibly more so,' recalls Eric. 'He and Jim McCarty were my soul-mates in the Yardbirds, if you like, and I used to enjoy going to parties and popping black bennies and drinking with them. As soon as I joined, I realized that Paul and Chris Dreja were too middle class for me. There was this two-way pull of people.'

He reflects on his seriousness as a musician. 'I took it all far too seriously. Perhaps if I'd been able to temper it, I might not have been so frustrated. I have regrets about my seriousness throughout my career. I still take it too seriously, in terms of relationships and being able to get on with other musicians. I'm far too judgemental, and in those days I was a complete purist. If it wasn't black music, it was rubbish.' The fact that 'precious' Paul Samwell-Smith was the boss was the final straw.

'Money never meant anything to me, because I've always been a bit of a scrounger. I've always managed to get by on other people's handouts. So when I quit the

---

* After moving on to bands Renaissance, Medicine Head and Arma-geddon, Relf died from electrocution at his home in 1976.

Yardbirds I fell on to the goodwill of my old friend Ben Palmer, who took me up to Oxford and gave me a roof over my head for a month.

'There's this big myth which says I locked myself up in practice there, but it wasn't true. I was simply trying to con Ben into making a blues record with me. I was just a purist, the music was all, but I certainly wasn't holed up in practice. I remember taking some money off a girl in Oxford who was very nice to me. I was broke. Oh, I was just a scoundrel.

'Being a bum, not even having a responsibility to a band, was far more attractive than security. I enjoyed having no ties for a while.'

Jeff Beck succeeded Eric in the Yardbirds. A dazzling guitarist, he was less committed than Eric to the blues and he integrated better into the band. The Yardbirds became, in fact, a breeding ground for several giant figures in rock, including Jimmy Page, who later achieved fame with Led Zeppelin. Ironically, Paul Samwell-Smith quit about a year after Eric, finding his niche as a record producer for such talents as Cat Stevens, Carly Simon, Simon and Garfunkel, Chris de Burgh and Murray Head. 'I began to appreciate Eric's guitar playing more when he left,' says Paul. 'From standing next to him on stage six nights a week, I suddenly saw him being hailed as a god. It was strange.'

Clapton announced his departure from the group two weeks before his twentieth birthday.

Looking back, Clapton's rationale for his lonely decision seems logical and clear, as it must have seemed to him at the time. 'I never did have my eye on fame as a pop star. When I listened to the radio at the age of ten, the blues was the only kind of music that I called "non-company music". The pop sound of the period, Guy Mitchell, Kay Starr, Frankie Laine, was well produced and well rounded. That was on the radio every day.'

Like so many British children in those years, he listened to a BBC programme hosted by Derek McCulloch ('Uncle Mac'). 'Maybe once a week as well as kids' music like "The Runaway Train", I'd hear something stand out – something by Sonny Terry and Brownie McGhee, for example. And it was so incredibly *personal.* So was Big Bill Broonzy. I caught sight of him in a television film clip and I was . . . mesmerized. I was anti-big-business music and here was this sound that was not from a company, or a band, but from one or two people. It was raw, primitive, and that's what I always preferred, in art or anything . . .'

It is thirty years since Clapton made that remarkable decision to leave the Yardbirds and concentrate on becoming a musician instead of a 'hit-making machine', as he called it at the time. Paradoxically, he has earned more adulation, for a longer period, than he might have gained as a butterfly of the 1960s. He's mature enough now to enjoy it, but he still feels troubled by the thought that he gained stardom for interpreting blues music that was not rightly his but belonged to black America. 'How strange, it seemed to me, to be worshipped! To be called a god when all I was doing was presenting a case, as it were, for the music I loved. I was just its *representative*! The reason I left the Yardbirds was simple: compromise became the order of the day.'

Quitting the Yardbirds was a boldly courageous move, but his departure to an uncertain future was unsettling back in March 1965.*

* 'For Your Love' scored a massive breakthrough for the Yardbirds,

THE 'GOD' OF CREAM 73

In Oxford with Ben Palmer, then working as a sculptor, and relaxing with other friends, Eric was enjoying the arty atmosphere when a phone call from London decided his future. John Mayall invited him to an audition for his authentic new blues band the Bluesbreakers.

Born in Macclesfield, Cheshire, in 1933, Mayall was the son of a dance band musician and had a firm reputation in the north of England as a blues pianist. His allegiance to the blues made him an automatic choice for Eric when he offered him a job only weeks after leaving the Yardbirds.*

Eric remembers: 'I was straight into his band without any problem. And as well as taking me into the band, he gave me a room at his house in Lee Green (south-east London), a tiny room, just wide enough for its narrow single bed. I stayed in there because I felt strange in the house: his family lived there and I didn't feel part of it, so I stayed in that room, practising and listening to John's vast collection of blues records.'

Mayall and Eric had a great rapport. 'He was very good in that he'd listen to me about music, one of the first people, apart from Ben, who did. We would listen to a lot of blues and pick songs that were right for the stage. He was easy company, and older than me, but keen to draw me out and find what I thought. It was most unusual, a very important band for me. I did flower a lot during my time with Mayall.' He also met Bob Dylan for the first time, starting a friendship that con-

_____

hitting the British charts at number three and reaching number six in the American charts in spring 1965.

* His colleagues in the Bluesbreakers were Hughie Flint (drums), later to join up with Eric's old friend Tom McGuinness in McGuinness Flint, and John McVie (bass), who would help form Fleetwood Mac.

tinues strongly. Dylan admired Mayall's work and the two men became friendly.

'Bob came down to jam when Mayall had this record out, "Life is Like a Slow Train Going up a Hill".' Clapton and Dylan got on well musically, although Eric was not at that time keen on Dylan's white-based folk music. He had been put off Dylan by the fact that Paul Samwell-Smith liked him. Later, Eric heard the *Blonde on Blonde* album and was totally converted to Dylan's music; today the two artists admire each other's work enormously.

'Inside Mayall's band, I was still a very moody character. In any situation, I've always found *something* that isn't right. In that band, it became John himself: my expectations of him began to rise. With a couple of the other members of the band, we started to gang up on John behind his back, muttering about him not being a good enough singer, being too flamboyant in his presentation. He went on stage bare to the waist.' In retrospect, though, the blues music, and the leadership qualities in Mayall, were a vital stepping-stone for Eric.

Mayall had a reputation not as a wizard keyboards player but as a gifted bandleader who acted as a catalyst for musicians who wanted to work vigorously. He ran his band almost along the disciplined lines of the jazz giants of yesteryear, Duke Ellington and Count Basie. Mayall demanded, and received, total dedication to the business of making music ... and he got it from such great talents, over the years, as Eric, bassists Jack Bruce and John McVie (later to help form Fleetwood Mac), and Hughie Flint on drums.

Joining Mayall, then, was for Eric as much a statement of intent as it was a move into the blues arena. Within a few months, he emerged strongly as a guitarist who had at last found his feet. Mayall recalls him as restless, evidently on his way to somewhere else. And one of the most remarkable periods of his life began as audiences recognized that he was indeed a special player.

Crowds began going to Mayall shows purely to see Clapton. They shouted 'Clapton is God!' 'Give God a solo!' 'We want more God!' For a twenty-one-year-old, even one who believed in his own ability, this was disturbingly heady stuff. Eric actually disliked the experience and that level of adulation. It came dangerously close to his being a pop star – and he preferred always to consider himself as a guitarist.

'My vanity was incredibly boosted by that "God" thing,' says Eric now. 'But it pushed me into myself a great deal. It made me very outspoken, because I got this false self-confidence, and then I realized I was talking so much rubbish to everyone around me. So I withdrew and became an introvert.

'I thought that if I was regarded as God then I had to be careful what I said. But I don't think I was mature enough in that period to reflect deeply on it, on the profound meaning of it all. I took it as a surface compliment and one that would probably fade.

'I became very cautious. I suddenly realized that people were very, very easy with their words. Then came a feeling of bitterness and sensitivity about what people said about me; a lot of it could, after all, be nonsense. So then I became very full of judgement about other people's opinions of me and what I played.'

But he did have a super-confident belief in himself that stopped just short of arrogance. 'I didn't think there was anyone around at that time doing what I was doing, playing the blues as straight as me. I was trying to do it absolutely according to its rules. Oh yeah, I was very confident. I didn't think there was anybody as good. The only person I ever met who was trying to be as good as me was Mike Bloomfield and when he came to England he bowed down to me straightaway. So I thought, well, that's that.' His sense of euphoria was high, but modesty kept his ego in check.

'It was only when Cream came together that I began to bend the blues rules. During my time with John Mayall, I stuck to the letter of that music as much as I could without keeping my own creativity down.'

An intoxicating year with Mayall sealed Eric's confidence. He voiced his disillusionment with Britain, his determination to settle in America where his music was born and thrived, and left us in no doubt that he saw himself as separate from the mainstream of British rock 'n' roll or pop.

'I don't think there will be room for me here much longer,' he said at the time. 'None of my music is English, it's rooted in Chicago. I represent what's going on in Chicago at the moment – the best I can, anyway, because it's difficult to get all the records imported.'

Eric said he was determined to get to Chicago, his 'spiritual home', as soon as possible. The Yardbirds had visited the city, and Jeff Beck, who replaced him as lead guitarist, had made a good impression. 'I gather it became Jeff Beck with the Yardbirds – the white Americans over there, who know what they're on about, dug Jeff a lot more than Keith Relf's half-hearted singing.'

He was certain, he said, that he would have to leave Britain. 'I deal in realism, nothing but realism, and the nastier the better. The buyers and sellers of records in England are not concerned with it. This is why I'm being driven out. Forming a blues band in England is like banging your head against a brick wall. Nobody wants to do it and certainly nobody wants to record it.

'This is the blues, this is true expression. I am contacting myself through the guitar and telling myself I have a power. I haven't a girlfriend or any other relationship, so I tell myself of this power through the guitar.'

Eric says now: 'I took it far too seriously. Perhaps if I'd been able to temper it, I'd have been happier as a person. I have regrets about that, and also about the fact that throughout my career I've taken everything too seriously. I still do. It's a strength, yeah, but it can also be a hell of a stumbling block in terms of relationships, like getting on with other musicians.'

His music and his often gritty personality have projected a positive portrait of the man. But in the mid 1960s, such self-analysis left him exposed to possible charges of pretentiousness. He was twenty-one at the time; it's possible that even Eric Clapton didn't realize how much his early years, before he became a musician, were to shape his determination and sense of isolation later.

Inside the Mayall band, Eric was again the stand-out player. He took with him from the Yardbirds a group of supporters of his work. The *Melody Maker* proclaimed him 'a knockout' with Mayall's band. A letter from a purist reader hoped the band would not 'sell out' to commercialism, adding that 'Eric Clapton is the best blues guitarist in Britain.' Yet, by contrast with his punctiliousness with the Yardbirds, Eric was not a totally reliable band member at that time, sometimes not showing up for appearances, or being late – to the consternation of the disciplined Mayall. This all added up, mysteriously, to his rebellious, outlaw image and, perversely, may have added to his reputation. While such casual behaviour was not natural, it reflected the laid-back mood of the mid 1960s; to rebel was to be hip and cool.

That move to John Mayall was to catapult Eric Clapton to the top echelon of British rock. It provided precisely the right environment for his individualism to mature. By the mid 1960s, virtuoso rock musicianship elevated players to the role of seers among audiences who believed popular music had powers of spiritual healing. Standing on stage almost motionless, with long sideburns, short hair, T-shirt and jeans, his appearance was unique. Almost an anti-star, he displayed no exhibitionism save the closed eyes and effortless solos that seemed to spring from within.

For all his dedication to blues guitar, there was still something of the wandering minstrel in him. Part of him still enjoyed the beatnik mentality and after four months with Mayall, it was time for something new.

The radical move he made was utterly out of character for a player making his mark so rapidly on a wide audience. Together with Ben Palmer and half a dozen other friends of Eric, made through his association with Ted Milton, a scheme was hatched to hire a double-decker bus to make an overland journey to Australia as travelling musicians. This idea collapsed but they did arrive by car in Greece where, for three months from August 1965, they busked as a band called the Glands. The line-up was Clapton (guitar), Ben Palmer (piano), Jake Milton, brother of the noted poet Ted (drums), Bernie Greenwood (saxophone), Bob Ray (bass) and John Bailey (drums). The fiasco of a trip was marred by work permit problems and overwork for Eric as they all tried to make enough money to survive. Wearily, they returned to London.

Though the blues scene in London had always flourished as an adjunct to the jazz world, it was now thriving as never before. The first wave of pop musicians who were serious about their art discovered, as had Eric many years earlier, that superficial pap could neither stimulate them nor maintain a career. Blues had depth, artistry, and a history. Honourable musicians of the calibre of Graham Bond, Alexis Korner and Cyril Davies, all of them the inspirations for the Rolling Stones in their earliest days, packed the clubs alongside John Mayall's Bluesbreakers. This vibrant scene into which Eric had pitched himself like a homing pigeon stood separate from either pop or jazz, but it certainly bore more affinity with jazz than anything. Musicians went on stage primarily to make statements via their music rather than to make a fortune.

Rather surprisingly, Mayall took Clapton back into his Bluesbreakers without recrimination. Eric had been sorely missed and he returned to the release of his first single with Mayall, 'I'm Your Witchdoctor', backed by 'Telephone Blues'. Featuring the new technique of feedback, this single, produced by Jimmy Page, was not a hit but it gained two rounds of applause. One came from Eric's grandmother, who for the first time realized Rick was a genius in the making, and the other from the *Melody Maker*, which considered the single 'a knockout up-tempo number'.

As he won a music paper readers' poll as Britain's best guitarist, the hottest soloist on the scene with his whirlwind of bending notes inspired audiences in the clubs who went to see him as the star of the Mayall band.

Now, for the hippest guitar slinger around, with an individualistic sense of style and direction, 'Clapton is God' slogans began to be painted by fans on walls and in London underground stations. As a guitarist he deserved every ounce of admiration. But such an elevation to the status of a deity embarrassed the guitar star. His ego was boosted but he did not know how to handle such adulation.

Now free of the Yardbirds, Eric seemed to feel a freedom to speak out. He had taken the job in that band, he said, because it felt 'cushy'. But he had been 'quite brainwashed most of the time. It was only when I got on stage away from all the hubble bubble that I suddenly realized I didn't really like what the group did or played. We became machines instead of human beings. I thought: if I'm going to become a money-making musical factory, I'll pull out. So I did.'

His purism caused him strongly to condemn white British pop. 'I feel the English are too rooted in rock 'n' roll and Tommy Steele. The stuff coming out of England now makes me puke. I'll be the first to put Chris Farlowe down. Everything you've ever heard Farlowe do has been done better and years before by Negroes. He can't hope to simulate what the American Negroes do. The Miracles and Ray Charles make their records commercial for the American white public to buy. Therefore by the time Farlowe and all have got the numbers, they're about third hand.'*

---

* Although Tommy Steele began his career as a pop singer at the famous 2 I's coffee bar in Soho, he was considered by other musicians to be more a Vaudevillian artist than a bona fide rock singer. Chris Farlowe, who scored a number one record with 'Out of Time', still performs successfully.

Recent adulation had obviously boosted his confidence, for he added: 'I'm not interested in guitar, sound, technique, but in people and what you can do to them via music. I'm very conceited and I think I have a power. And my guitar is a medium for expressing that power. I don't need people to say how good I am. I've worked it out by myself. It's nothing to do with technique and rehearsing. It's to do with the person behind that guitar who is trying to find an outlet. My guitar is a medium through which I can make contact with myself. It's very, very lonely.'

With those words at the age of twenty-one, Eric was outlining the foundation of his future.

John Mayall was the antithesis of a pop star, entrenched in his music, and something of a blues purist. Neither an outstanding keyboards player nor singer, he knew how to surround himself with outstanding talent that wanted to take part in building up the burgeoning movement to the blues, running in parallel with the thrust of the Beatles.

High-calibre musicianship was the essence of Mayall's band, and while personalities would naturally flower within it, Mayall placed great emphasis on the overall sound and texture of the music. It was a brilliant tactical move for Mayall to welcome Clapton into the band; and the perfect stepping stone for Clapton, who needed a firm anchor after the disillusionment of the Yardbirds.

Soon after he joined, in 1966, it was time to make the Mayall band's second album, their first studio session to follow the successful début of *Mayall Plays Mayall*. Coincidentally, the two men in charge of the studio for

the sessions were committed fans of blues and knew of
the formidable reputation Clapton had formed with the
Yardbirds.

The producer was Mike Vernon, a prominent blues
aficionado, and the studio engineer Gus Dudgeon who,
at the age of twenty-four, had been an ardent Yardbirds
fan and a committed 'Mod'. After eleven jobs in four
years, he had joined the wave of young men being
recruited by record companies to marshal the arrival of
new sounds, replacing the greying 'pop music producers'
of yesteryear.*

As Dudgeon sat in the studios of Decca Records in
Broadhurst Gardens, West Hampstead, awaiting the
arrival of Mayall's Bluesbreakers with Clapton, his enthusiasm and imagination was captured. Dudgeon had
watched Clapton's blossoming talent inside the Yardbirds, and the news that he would soon be working with
him in the studio was exciting for a young engineer who
had cut his teeth on such straight pop acts as Tom Jones,
Lulu, Marianne Faithfull and the Zombies. Although
these people were all good pop singers, Clapton represented classy musicianship.

Clapton was the first of the Mayall band to arrive at
the studio. 'He was an incredibly dapper young guy, very
cool, a designer Mod,' Dudgeon recalls. 'Very short,
spiky hair, long sideboards, very narrow lapels on his Ivy
League suit. Very cool!'

Clapton quickly demonstrated the same determined,
forceful streak that had caused him to quit the Yardbirds.
A guitarist arriving at the studio for his first session with
a new band might be expected to show a little diffidence

---

* Gus Dudgeon went on to become a respected producer of Elton
John's breakthrough album.

or even apprehension. But Gus Dudgeon saw a different persona.

'The studio was set up according to a well tried formula,' Dudgeon recalls of those slightly primitive years in music-making. 'Ahead of the session, the engineer got a simple piece of paper telling him what instruments to expect to be used on any session. Eric walked in, very charming, and asked me: "Where do you want my amp?" I pointed to where I'd set up the mike. He walked off in the opposite direction with his amplifier, a small Vox. I said to him: "Sorry, I meant over *there*", pointing to the mike area. He said: "Oh no, I've been this route before. I really want to play the way I play on stage, and you're going to set it up for a straight recording session. I want the amp a bit louder, set to six or seven."'

Clapton was not offhand, but decisive. 'I don't want it to be the way things have been in the past in recording session,' he continued, alluding perhaps to the Yardbirds. 'I really want to play pretty loud.'

Gus Dudgeon was worried. Mike Vernon then approached Eric, who reiterated to the producer that he was seeking a recreation of his stage work inside the studio. When Vernon confirmed to Dudgeon that the edict must stand, Dudgeon warned him that the move might well overpower the drums. Vernon repeated that Eric was 'determined to try it out'. The amplifier was duly placed a mere ten feet from the microphone.

The screaming guitar sound that came through into the control booth as the band warmed up dumbfounded Vernon and Dudgeon. 'What *is* he doing?' they said to each other. But as the session progressed, they both agreed that the dramatic input of the volume was 'nifty . . . this was a very raw, exciting, powerful club sound,' Dudgeon remembers. 'It was stunningly good, gave everybody in the studio a real buzz, and we were glad that he'd done exactly what he wanted to do. Because, loud though it was by the standards of those years, Eric was right. Mike Vernon and I looked at each other and knew something special had been done. When Eric came in and heard the playback, he said: "That's what I've always wanted to do."'

The incident immediately endeared Clapton to Dudgeon as a progressive musician who wanted to break some rules, take chances, and not confine himself to the boundaries of pop.

The resulting album, *Bluesbreakers*, featuring Eric on the cover reading the *Beano* comic, might not have carried the commercial clout of his old band the Yardbirds. But for Eric it was a kind of manifesto. Mayall was a great catalyst who hired, and attracted, the best musicians in the blues field, and Clapton was now gigging with credibility. The album reached number six in the British album charts and was an important word-of-mouth success as British bands like Savoy Brown, Chicken Shack and Fleetwood Mac achieved success with the blues.

'Eric was unquestionably the star of tomorrow,' reflects Gus Dudgeon of those years. 'He was always very charming, in no way egotistical. But determined. As a guitarist he was just extraordinary and as appearance-conscious in those years as he has remained throughout his life.'

Inside the Yardbirds, inside John Mayall, inside Cream, 'he was always to one side of them. He was the one with the big Afro hair style, the Afghan coat, the sense of style. I always thought he was a very cool guy. And I still do.'

*

In May 1966, the man who would go on to promote Eric Clapton's epochal concert performances in Britain began his long association with the guitarist then being hailed as a Messiah of Rock.

Harvey Goldsmith, who was studying pharmacy at the Sussex College of Technology, had started Club 66 to bring entertainment events on to the campus. When that succeeded, he became student rag committee chairman and social secretary, his pharmacy studies fading into the background. Soon he was producing shows for ten colleges in Brighton and along the south coast.

A jazz fan friend of Goldsmith's and fellow pharmacy student, who followed the scene at London's Marquee Club, tipped him off about the great guitarist, and Goldsmith booked the Mayall band for an appearance on 11 May 1966.

Goldsmith so enjoyed the world of pop that it would one day make him one of the world's major promoters, mingling with the musicians. Before the show, he attended Clapton's twenty-first birthday party at John Mayall's house. 'It was a very enjoyable, slightly strange affair,' he recalls. 'Someone was dressed up as a gorilla and I can't remember who it was.'

For the big day, posters appeared around Brighton:

Biggest rave of the year.
Rag Queen dance presents the fabulous American blues artist John Lee Hooker and the Machine.
London's current sensation John Mayall's Bluesbreakers with ERIC CLAPTON.
Jimmy James and the Vagabonds. Featuring the Rag Queen Contest 1966. Brighton Federation of Students Rag.
Top Rank Suite, Brighton. Admission 7s 6d.

The event was a great success. It was clear to the crowd that Clapton was on course to becoming a star. 'Absolutely obvious,' Goldsmith remembers. 'He stood out a mile.' Neither Clapton nor Goldsmith nor Mayall could have guessed that within three months Eric would finally be out of the band and into superstar orbit.

Although the Beatles reigned supreme that year, extemporizing musicians like Clapton often criticized them as formularized. Joining this absurdly snobbish chorus, Eric declared in 1966: 'Everything the Beatles have ever done is an absolute piece of engineering to play on people's neuroses: clever, subtle, brainwashing. The group and their songs are clever pieces of engineering. I'd like to say something about McCartney. I think he's a complete and utter blues singer. Where the others will pack it up some time and become estate agents or run chains of supermarkets somewhere, I think Paul will go on singing.'

A keen sense of identity separated Clapton from almost every musician on the London scene. His desire to re-invent himself, visually, with such accessories as spectacles and footwear, and his near-obsession with clothes, was as evident then as it became in the 1990s. A resonant style in his appearance, during his vital period with John Mayall's Bluesbreakers, added greatly to his mystique.

Just as in music he proved to be something of a sponge – soaking up all the work of players of calibre – in fashion, too, Clapton lifted the most impactful aspects from his peers. Bob Dylan had curly, frizzy hair, so Eric went and had his hair permed. His ballooning white bell-bottom trousers, purple shirts and sharp Italian boots made him one of the wildest-looking musicians of the psychedelic era, and later his friendship with the outlandishly dressed Jimi Hendrix was in keeping with his love of style. He became a regular face at the 1960s trendiest London boutiques, Hung on You and Granny Takes a Trip.

Steve Winwood, his close friend, points out that 'art *is* self-indulgent . . . He certainly always cared a lot about appearance from the first time I saw and met him.'

The Clapton of the psychedelic era moved, and spoke, boldly. His resignation from the Yardbirds, his move to the Mayall band 'because I could see integrity in its outlook', and his assertion of fashion consciousness, both on and off stage, marked him out to many players.

Winwood, whose magnificent voice powered the Spencer Davis Group of that period, struck up a friendship with him. Eric, he recalls, was by then rethinking the direction of his career. Winwood's group, based in Birmingham and with its roots clearly in the rhythm-and-blues camp, played on the same bill as John Mayall at Newcastle upon Tyne's Whiskey-A-Gogo club in 1966. Steve recalls being stunned by his first sight of the much-discussed Clapton on stage.

'There's no doubt that he was definitely something special, from that first moment I saw him. Very special. He had a finesse and artistry on display that no one else at that time, and since, could match. He had an energy. And I remember being struck by the fact that he wasn't particularly a technician.

'I later found, from working with him, that he is not a great student of the theory of music. But his knowledge of other people's music was always fantastic. We talked that first night a little, as young musicians do, asking about other players. He was a great instinctive musicologist – his knowledge of other people's music, especially black r & b, at that time, was enormous.'

As the two men spoke that night in Newcastle, it was clear that Winwood, too, distanced himself from the pop helter-skelter. Like Eric, he sought a career based upon the music of black America. Clapton and Winwood agreed to keep in touch, tacitly considering the possibility of working together.

'I visited him in London and I was living in digs when I came; Eric had very arty friends and this very arty flat in Convent Garden which I enjoyed going to for the conversation and red wine,' says Winwood. 'He was very much the existentialist at the time. Our only common ground, then and now, really, was music, but that rapport was terrific. We knew we ought to be working towards getting a band together because it was obvious, without either of us saying, that he was outgrowing John Mayall's band and I was looking for something to follow the Spencer Davis Group.'

Those were the rich days of 'sitting in', when musicians would enjoy drifting into another band's session and ad-libbing. The British bands that crusaded for rhythm-and-blues, including Georgie Fame's Blue Flames, Zoot Money's Big Roll Band, Manfred Mann, Alexis Korner's Blues Incorporated and The Graham Bond Organization, provided the powder for the explosion in rock music ignited by the Cream. At all-night sessions at clubs like Soho's Marquee and Flamingo and the Zeeta in Putney, Eric enjoyed occasional sit-ins with the Spencer Davis Group and many other bands.

The camaraderie generated in the long bar of the Ship pub, in Soho's Wardour Street, increased the talk between musicians of who was good and genuine and who was awful. It was like a rock 'parish', and the moustached, slightly menacing figure of Clapton, by now renowned, was surrounded by admirers.

'Sitting in' helped shape rock history, but still a definite loyalty prevented much interchange of players between bands. 'People leaving groups in those days was a dirty trick,' Eric recalls. 'I don't think it was particularly dirty for me to quit the Yardbirds – I was attracted by the big pop thing at first, and success, and the travelling around and the little chicks! I was seventeen. But, later, when you work in a more serious musical band like Mayall's, you don't quit unless there's a really good reason.'

Winwood continues the theme: 'The reason Eric and I didn't get together in the mid-sixties is because British musicians feel they are committed to their bands, whereas American players will mostly leave and join the next one almost on a whim and especially for money. I mean, I know so many American players who are playing in a band . . . and suddenly they're looking for something else to do.'

Clapton's timing, and rationale, had to be immaculate for a move from the hard-working and satisfying John Mayall Bluesbreakers. But 1966 was a year of great energy, inventiveness and excitement in the world of arts generally. Eric, aware of this, knew his time with Mayall was limited. The band was well run by a regimental leader, but Clapton believed John's confines were too narrow to hold his own aspiration as a guitarist. 'I just wanted to get further than that band was going, which was in the Chicago blues field. I wanted to go somewhere else, you know . . . put my kind of guitar playing in a new kind of pop music context.' The vibrancy of the period was contagious: he saw broader horizons. While the blues would always be the core of his playing, he could see himself planting the seed within a wider style. A new kind of rock 'n' roll, with a strong blues bias, its potential audience far wider than the club world, perhaps with a nod towards high fashion, and certainly with fresh lyricism, was needed to absorb Eric's energy.

Among the sitters-in on the club scene was an exceptional Glaswegian double bass player with a mercurial temperament. His name was Jack Bruce and he also played harmonica and sang with a well-respected band, the Graham Bond Organization. He passed the word on Eric's ability to the drummer in the Bond group. That band's great drummer, Ginger Baker, sat in with Mayall's band one night in June 1966. Baker had a faultless pedigree among musicians. Inspired by the jazz greats and in Britain by a futuristic jazz drummer named Phil Seamen, Baker rated himself at least comparable with the giants of American jazz drumming (Buddy Rich and Elvin Jones). There was a problem: his Anglo-Irish temperament matched his demonic intensity. And Jack Bruce was not exactly a placid Scotsman. And with Clapton, never a malleable musician, increasing his reputation for moodiness if things went badly on stage, the trio did not at first sight look good bets for a long marriage. Two forces drove them together to form Cream: their own ambition for adventure was the main reason. And big business clinched it.

Like bees in a hive, entrepreneurial pop managers were on every street corner in London in the mid 1960s, in the wake of the explosion of the Beatles (via Brian Epstein) and the Rolling Stones (via Andrew Loog Oldham). Record companies fêted them. But where Epstein and Oldham displayed panache in discovering and delivering original artistry in their groups, they lacked hard-dealing muscle and business experience. That ability, as well as an uncanny ear to predict success, came from Robert Stigwood, who was able to convince Clapton, Bruce and Baker to unite with the support of his financial investment.

Australian Stigwood had launched his own management company, RSO, after a period working on the staff of EMI. After running a music paper, *Pop Weekly*, he succeeded by launching the careers of hit singers John Leyton and Mike Sarne. Ten years ahead of the vogue, Stigwood had also launched his own anti-Establishment independent record label, Reaction, which was distributed by Polydor. Diversifying into the theatre, he managed such household names as comedian Frankie Howerd and Ray Galton and Alan Simpson (who wrote for Tony Hancock). With considerable verve, Stigwood envisioned Cream as a supergroup of musicians spiritually ahead of their time. Eric, Ginger and Jack found his confidence precisely what they needed at the moment they coalesced.

News of the formation of Cream did not immediately capture the imagination of the frenzied world of pop. The rhythm-and-blues scene watched expectantly as Clapton, the 'musician's musician', as he was now called, made yet another interesting move. While Ginger Baker had to leave the Graham Bond Organization, Jack Bruce was working with the successful Manfred Mann group, which was enjoying a hit with 'Pretty Flamingo'. The plan to launch a supergroup was exclusively reported by Chris Welch in the *Melody Maker* in a mere three-paragraph story on 11 June 1966.

This was a month before the group's second rehearsal,

in a church hall in Putney, south-west London. There was no indication of the band's name yet, and the news of the launch of the band read like this:

> A sensational new 'groups group' starring Eric Clapton, Jack Bruce and Ginger Baker is being formed. Top groups will be losing star instrumentalists as a result.
>
> Manfred Mann will lose bassist, harmonica player, pianist and singer Jack Bruce; John Mayall will lose brilliant blues guitarist Eric Clapton; and Graham Bond's Organization will lose incredible drummer Ginger Baker.
>
> The group say they hope to start playing at clubs, ballrooms and theatres in a month's time. It is expected they will remain as a trio with Jack as featured vocalist.

The official announcement came from the office of Robert Stigwood.*

With grand offices at 67, Brook Street, Mayfair, Stigwood had been booking John Mayall's Bluesbreakers. RSO, his organisation, housed several 'bookers' for such bands, including Roger Forrester, who would eventually assume Clapton's management and brilliantly steer Clapton's career.

The press release from Stigwood announced Cream's launch enigmatically:

> The first is last and the last is first, but the first, the second and the last are Cream. They will be called

---

* The record aspect of the deal was said to have given Cream a £50,000 advance for a three-year contract.

Cream and will be represented by me for agency and management. They will record for my Reaction label and go into the studios next week to cut tracks for their first single. Their debut will be at the National Jazz and Blues Festival in July when their first single will be released.

In the week of that news, Frank Sinatra was at the top of the record charts with 'Strangers in the Night', and the pop world was still gripped by the Beatles and the Stones.

As the time neared for a new Mayall album, Mike Vernon phoned Gus Dudgeon to break the news of Eric's departure. 'I was amazed', Dudgeon says. 'I'd worked with Ginger and Jack Bruce in the Graham Bond band and I thought it was very bad news.' Bruce and Baker were undoubtedly the cream of Britain's musicians but, having seen him in action at clubs like Klooks Kleek in Hampstead, Dudgeon was not alone in worrying about Ginger's volatility. How could his moods mesh with the sensibilities of Clapton and the well-known short fuse of Jack Bruce?

The triumphs, the trials and the exceptional chemistry of Cream, and particularly Clapton's role within a band that proved to be a watershed in rock's history, are recalled by Jack Bruce, an articulate and animated musician revered by his contemporaries. A music purist, he admires Eric's unique ability to combine adherence to his blues roots with a canny commercialism. That eye for self-projection, Bruce says, has never been one of *his* talents. But while he respects Clapton, relations between the two men have veered from distant and cool to affectionate.

Bruce is uniquely placed to paint a portrait of life

within Cream. He sang and wrote many of the songs, and assumed the leadership, he says, in the recording studio. On stage, he declares, Eric Clapton was the unassailable leader, 'because he was simply very much *happening* as a player and as a person'. The fractious relationship between Bruce and Ginger Baker, whose personalities clashed, with Eric in the middle as a hapless, often tearful, victim, made life in this great band as electrifying off stage as it was on.

'Great memories – it was a very special kind of time. There was a *feeling* among all musicians drifting around then that hasn't come again. I don't think I was quite ready for it, but I would be now,' says Jack.

What Bruce describes as an 'accidental, organic' partnership that generated Cream had begun in the most bizarre fashion. Ginger Baker virtually ran the Graham Bond Organization, in which he and Jack Bruce were key members. The communication between them was musically compatible but in human terms disastrous. 'One night Ginger fired me from the Bond band,' says Jack. 'He said I didn't fit. But I defied him. I simply kept turning up to each gig, and this went on for weeks. I refused to be fired!

'The next time Ginger and I were on stage, with me technically fired, at Golders Green (at a club called the Refectory) in London, his drums were too loud. I said "Shhhhhhhhh . . ." and he started throwing drumsticks at me, hitting me on the head. So I took my double bass, lifted it, and chucked it at him. That demolished that, and we were rolling around the stage fighting, and the audience was loving it. We punched the hell out of each other on that stage.'

After that, Bruce concluded that he had indeed left the Graham Bond group. He went on to join the bands of Manfred Mann and then John Mayall. He turned up at the Ricky-Tick club in Windsor for a jam-session alongside Eric Clapton . . . and found the drummer in the band was Ginger Baker.

The night went well, musically, with Bruce and Baker calling a truce on past battles. A few weeks later, Baker phoned Eric with the idea of forming a band. Clapton's reply was stunning to Baker: 'Well, yeah, OK, let's form a band,' said Eric. 'But only if Jack Bruce is in it.' He could not then have known, says Bruce today, 'that he had just mentioned Ginger's mortal enemy.'

Bruce and Baker decided to bury their hatchets. Here, after all, was the opportunity for a unit in which a superb bassist and an outstanding drummer pulled in the hottest, most talked-about guitarist in Britain.

If the whole idea was Ginger's, the surge of the band, the presence and the direction of it was shared by Clapton and Bruce, with Eric towering over them in personal magnetism. It was during his cynical period with Mayall, when he was poking fun at the leader's theatrics, that Clapton developed the spark that ignited the idea of forming his own band and which led to Cream.

'I first thought: well I can do this! You know, I can do what *he's* doing. And when John Mayall let me sing one song on his album, I thought, I can sing as well . . . God, I should get my own band! Who shall I get? And while I was thinking about this, Ginger came to see a gig, when I was with John, and asked me if I'd be interested in forming a band with him. So I thought, well, Ginger's a good drummer, Jack had once played with John Mayall for a bit and we got on very well. So I thought – a blues trio! And I would be the slick, front man, the Buddy Guy type, a white Buddy Guy, the guy with the big suit, baggy trousers, doing straight blues. The other two would be the perfect back-up. And this was typical of me. I often have all these mad fantasies in force, but never say anything about them. I just imagine that it's going to work out that way – without me having to do anything or say anything. So I never did. When we had our first rehearsal, that just went completely out of the window and they took over. Jack brought in the songs that he'd written and I just had to go along with it. Because it was very interesting and because Jack's songs are so good and the combination of the musicians was interesting, I found that I let my idea take a back seat and actually die in the end. My fantasy probably wouldn't have been very good anyway at that stage in my proficiency. And so from there we went to the concept of playing mad music, wearing mad clothes and having a mad stage set and all that. That dissipated too, because the music itself and the dialogue took over and that became enough.'

Adrian Clapton recalls driving Eric in his Ford 8 to a John Mayall appearance at the Plaza, Guildford, in 1966. Afterwards, when they adjourned to the Prince of Wales pub nearby, Jack Bruce and Ginger Baker appeared to discuss with Eric the formation of a new band. The venue for the first rehearsal was agreed: in the front room of Ginger's house in Neasden, London.

There was some early wild, enthusiastic talk by Clapton of calling the band Sweet and Sour Rock 'n' Roll. But the name was clinched by Eric in Ginger's house during that first rehearsal. 'He just came right out with it,' recalls Jack Bruce. ' "We're the Cream – that's the name of the band," he said, and we just said, yes. It was *right*. Eric always had this great knack for the right touch, the finishing gloss, if you like. I admire that in him. It has stayed right through his career.'

Clapton was faced, says Bruce, with an insoluble dilemma. While the promise of good music was powerful, he was sandwiched between two men who fundamentally loathed each other. 'Ginger and I never got on, ever,' says Jack Bruce. 'But perhaps because of the very pain of our relationship, we were the hottest rhythm section I've ever played in, and I've played with the best since then. Name the top drummers in the world, and I've played with them all. And yet . . . there was something between Ginger and me that was a *fire* burning. He brought out some amazing stuff in me. And he is a wonderful drummer. If you have respect for someone as a player, you set out to impress them.

'That's how it was between the three of us. Eric, Ginger and I wanted to turn each other on. We weren't playing for the audience at all. That's always a big mistake, a trap so many bands fall into. The only good music is when good musicians play for each other – for yourself first, for the other musicians second. And if the audience are there, they're quite welcome to listen. That was my philosophy, still is, and I believe that's what made Cream so *different* from the other rock groups. It was like a jazz band playing in a rock setting. And that's what frightened Eric about it. He doesn't have the roots I have in jazz. He has his own, different roots, which I respect. But coming from jazz, I loved the accidents, the limitlessness, the improvisation of the music. I think that's precisely what ultimately turned Eric off the Cream.'

Others were apprehensive about the musical cocktail. 'I was rather thrown by Cream,' says Gus Dudgeon, an admirer of all three players. 'I thought it was bizarre. Blues is supposed to be blues, jazz is jazz, and pop is pop; this had elements of all three, because there was an element of pop about it in the way they aimed their music at the charts with strong melody lines.'

Jack Bruce remembers that shortly after they were launched, Eric said he was sure they would 'never make it' as a live band. They would do well in the studio, but never achieve their goals on stage. 'I don't think Eric ever thought of it as a good group, but he was right when he said it was two bands. He led on stage, I led in the studio. But all the time, wherever we were, the atmosphere between Ginger and me made it impossible for Eric. So many times I'd have to go up to Eric and say: "Look, I'm sorry, it's no good, y'know, between Ginger and me". And he'd be in tears, or very, very down because of it.'

The rows were musical as well as personal. 'Instrumentally, Ginger didn't have the vision to see what I was trying to do. Eric was caught in the crossfire. I remember Ginger shouting at me across the stage somewhere: "You're playing *too busy*." He couldn't see that in a three-piece band, with no keyboards player holding down the thing harmonically and melodically, it was up to someone like me to do that. What has since become normal was being done by me in Cream. Ginger couldn't see that then. It was difficult, and not surprising that it created terrific tension.

'Once, in Copenhagen, we were in the car going to a gig from the airport and Eric actually burst into tears because of the slanging match between me and Ginger. It was impossible.' During another gig, Jack Bruce actually ran away. 'We used to travel around with very little equipment in America, and being the main singer I found it a great strain on the voice if there wasn't an adequate public address system. At one baseball stadium I said to Ginger: "Look, we've been given a hundred watts for the guitar, a hundred watts for the bass, and a hundred watts for the p.a." Nothing was miked in those days. I asked Ginger to get it improved but he just said, "No, we're not gonna do that." And I just got a taxi to the airport and bought a ticket. The roadies caught up with me and dragged me back, my feet not touching the ground. I was sitting waiting for the plane to take off and I went back. The sound was awful. You can imagine the atmosphere when I returned. But all these problems were part of Cream.'

The band took flight in the days before sophisticated sound systems enveloped rock and later gave birth to heavy metal. 'We were overworked in bad conditions with very often inadequate equipment, and the relationship between Ginger and me was one of constant bickering and dislike. It's a miracle that so much good music came out of Cream . . . but perhaps that's one of the reasons it did,' says Jack Bruce.

One man reacted to the launch of Cream with astonished delight. Up in north London, now heavily into wood carving and blissfully departed from the music world, Eric's warm friend from his first band, the Roosters, Ben Palmer, read the newspaper story with interest. 'Ah God, Clappers is starting a band!' he said to himself. 'This might be good.' Palmer mused that Eric had been unhappy with the Yardbirds, Brian Jones was dissatisfied with the musical route of the Stones, and Palmer didn't care for Eric's work in the Mayall band. With company like Bruce and Baker, though, Palmer thought there might be better prospects.

He phoned Eric: 'If you ever need someone to do

some driving, I'd quite like that.' Clapton arranged for his old friend to meet Robert Stigwood, the manager of Cream. Stigwood was concerned. 'Do you feel you can do this? I have to be sure you're serious, because I've invested a lot of money in this band ...' Palmer, believing that to be appointed a 'roadie' meant simply driving the band around, said yes, of course he could do whatever was needed.

'I must have impressed Stig enormously as a confident, competent road manager. In fact, I had no idea what was involved. Eric didn't think about it beyond the driving. He told Stig there was "absolutely nothing to worry about" with me.' So began the initial Cream shows, for what was then the exorbitant fee of £400 a show. But a big shock awaited Ben Palmer when he drove the three men, all feeling on the verge of a new life, up the motorway in the black Austin Princess for their first public appearance. Joyful and optimistic, they played records on the small car record player bought by Jack, and sang as the car headed to Manchester for the gig at the city's Twisted Wheel Club. Ben Palmer takes up the story.

'I parked the car at the back of the club and Eric, Jack and Ginger went in. I went off to the nearest pub. I thought I'd give them an hour and pop back to see how they sounded. I went back an hour later and all the amplifiers were still in the car. Ginger said: "You've been a long time. Is it all ready?" I asked him what he was on about. I said I'd not been long, just for a drink. "But you're the bloody *roadie*. You're supposed to set up our gear," boomed Ginger. I told him I hadn't a clue how to do it. I was totally out of my depth. I expected a fiver in my pocket for driving them, and "see you next week". I hadn't realized what I was taking on, having to build amplification equipment into a kind of architectural finish! I mean, in the Roosters, we used to put everything through two 30-watt amps which we carried like suitcases. This was something else.'

But when Palmer got involved in it, he became thrilled with the pioneering aspect of Cream. He learned to do the job properly, went on their first US tour and many others, and sealed his brotherly friendship with Eric. Another road manager of Cream, Billy Gaff, of the Stigwood Organization, would later emerge as manager of The Faces and Rod Stewart during his ascent to stardom.

There has never been a band with so much *gristle*, says Ben Palmer. And if anybody ever *stretched* Clapton as a musician, it was Bruce. 'On those long Cream numbers, when each played a solo, sort of answering each other over a period of three quarters of an hour, Eric was pushed by Jack as far as anybody pushed him. If Jack is bitter, it's because of the way his life has been. I don't think it's traceable to a jealousy of Eric. Jack's too big for that,' says Palmer.

Bruce, unstinting in his admiration of Eric, says he not only liked Eric, 'I *loved* him in the early days.' His memories of their great days of personal and musical brotherhood are punctuated by flashes of insight into Eric's make-up. He might not have realized it at the time, but Clapton was even then a rare survivor. Bruce remembers going with Eric to witness the squalor and horror of the youth of America high on acid in Haight-Ashbury, San Francisco, in 1967; he recalls the bleak look on Eric's face when Eric said to him what he still believes today: 'Black musicians start things . . . and white musicians make money out of it.'

'Eric is fortunate,' Bruce ponders. 'He's blessed with

a realization, a vision, of what's going to be commercially acceptable, on his level. But it's still musically good, which is why he feels OK about it. That's a very special touch, which I don't have. When I write songs, say even "Sunshine of Your Love", it never crosses my mind to relate it to commercial possibilities. Eric does, and I admire that. But in Cream we were doing fresh things and I've continued to do so, playing with the world's finest musicians. The difference between us is that Eric records and I don't any more . . . but his new stuff is just pleasant middle-of-the-road music.' (Bruce was talking to me in 1984.)

Chaotic, turbulent and exhausting though Cream was, it was a vital period for Clapton. As a group, they broke barriers, and were a significant part of the change in emphasis in popular music records from singles to albums. They made musicianship hip. But for Eric, above all, they saved him from the stagnation he felt in a Britain where there seemed little future.

'I was a loner when I reflected that America was the only place I could go to get anywhere,' Eric said immediately after joining Cream. 'I was really out on my own at the time, mentally. Now I'm with a band I really dig, I don't want to go to America – other than to see the place and find out what's happening. My whole musical outlook has changed. I listen to the same sounds and records but with a different ear.'

And, in a telling commentary on his own view of himself as an emergent star: 'I'm trying to listen from a listener's point of view. Whereas before, I'd always put myself in the guitarist's place, I now think it's the overall effect I must listen to. I'm no longer trying to play anything other than like a white man. The time is overdue: people should play like they are and what colour they are.

'I don't believe I've ever played so well in my life. More is expected of me in the Cream. I have to play rhythm guitar as well as lead. People have been saying I'm like Pete Townshend – but he doesn't play much lead!

'A lot of biased listeners say that all we are playing is pop numbers. In actual fact, closer listening reveals that none of us are playing anything that vaguely resembles pop, although it might sound deceptively like that.'

How did Eric think, at the birth of the group, that audiences would accept Cream? 'I don't believe we'll ever get over to them. People will always listen with biased ears, look through unbelieving eyes, and with preconceived ideas, remembering us individually as we used to be. The only way to combat this is to present them with as many facets of our music as possible. Some people might come to see Ginger, or to hear Jack's singing, or to look at the clothes I wear! Therefore we have to please them all – we have to *do everybody in*.'

Here, indeed, was a new Clapton talking. The air now filled, if not with compromise, with an awareness that a delicate tightrope could, and should, be walked to reach out for audience recognition – while not pawning any musical values.

Asked whether he felt in a period of transition, Clapton said, three months after the formation of Cream: 'Sure, I've changed. Jack Bruce has had a tremendous influence on my playing – and my personality. It's a lot easier to play in a blues band than in a group like this, where you've got to play purely your own individual ideas. You have got to put over a completely new kind of music. This needs a different image. Jack, Ginger and I have absorbed a lot of music and now we're trying to produce our own music. This naturally incorporates a lot of ideas we've heard, and we've all had. It's hard. It's original. It's satisfying. And it's worthwhile.'

By 1966, pop was beginning to be transmuted into rock, an album-orientated art form. Cream were among the barrier-breaking musicians who would turn the music scene on its axis. Their manager, Robert Stigwood, described their music quite deftly as 'commercial jazz', and at the band's major concert début at Windsor on 31 July 1966, Clapton, resplendent in his Cecil Gee smoking jacket, projected the sartorial elegance that would be visible for decades. The word 'rock' overtook 'pop' in the vocabulary of fans. Eric's playing demonstrated the blues, a familiar old music, in a modern setting.

Cream's début single, 'Wrapping Paper', had presented them as more like the Lovin' Spoonful than what the public finally came to expect from Eric, Jack and Ginger. But there wasn't long to wait before 'I Feel Free' pointed the way to the band's original style, with the guitar prominent. In his solo, Clapton's warm, bass-like tone (later christened by Eric his 'woman tone') progressed via a flick to the treble pick-up with his nimble fingers way up the fingerboard. This was not merely a solo, but a statement.

About that time, a series of EP records were released by Pye International in Britain demonstrating the talents of the black blues artists who recorded mainly at the Chess Studios in Chicago. One featured 'Spoonful' by Howlin' Wolf. Cream's version bore little resemblance to the original, and contained one of Eric's epic solos.

Fresh Cream, the band's début album, was awaited by musicians and fans with equal anticipation and went to number six in the album chart. 'Spoonful' had progressed from a simple Willie Dixon tune into a power-house of improvisation, with Jack Bruce's worldly-wise vocals and Ginger's percussive feel taunting the licks from Eric's Les Paul.

Now Eric was singing more. He and Jack had developed their own style of vocal interplay, heavy on the vibrato, with Eric's voice perhaps a little sweeter. On tunes like 'NSU', 'I Feel Free' and 'I'm So Glad', they harmonized like brothers, but when Jack spat out 'Spoonful', he gave it everything he had. The man's pungent personality came through.

Eric's songwriting talent did not really blossom in Cream. 'I wrote a few arrangements and riffs but I wasn't composing at all,' says Eric. 'But when it came to the time to make an album, Jack saved our lives. He'd come up with enough songs for the album, which meant that we were just about getting by. Ginger would kick up a fuss even at that. He'd argue that it was a co-operative band and we'd have to do two or three of his songs, as a kind of obligation. We did them to be fair to Ginger, but it was no way to keep a healthy atmosphere in the band.'

The massed limbs of Ginger Baker were in evidence on 'Toad', together with another instrumental, 'Cat's Squirrel'. Cream had by now shown us what virtuosity could do to a set of blues-orientated tunes. Next they would demonstrate what progression was all about.

The Yardbirds, with Jeff Beck in Eric's old role, had been involved in some earlier attempts at 'progressive rock', but that had come to a halt rather quickly when Beck left the group. Jeff's own style was never comparable to Clapton's, though they both shared a love for the blues. Eric retained the earthiness, Beck was flashier.

Once in Cream, Eric changed his chosen guitar from his familiar Gibson Les Paul to a Gibson SG Standard, a guitar with familiar pick-ups to a Les Paul but with a thinner, lighter body. His sound became more refined, a little less raunchy, but continued to have his cutting edge.

Disraeli Gears was the first 'real' Cream album: the band had become aware of their musical progression and Jack Bruce realized their capabilities in the studio. 'Sunshine of Your Love' was the ultimate example of the band's ability to produce its own sound and create a song that stands as a classic in the history of rock. It was revolutionary at the time, featuring heavy guitar and bass riffs plus an economical, powerful drum pattern coupled with an intense yet sparing guitar solo. Eric's 'woman tone' had arrived. Cream broke away from traditional approaches to rock and took full advantage of the artistic freedom then so prevalent, not just in music but in entire attitudes. Jimi Hendrix, taking the same stance to his music, projected himself on a more personal level. He was an experience, while Cream were a unit, but the similarity in ideals was certainly there, and Hendrix was also the leader of the trio. In forty-two weeks in the British chart, *Disraeli Gears* peaked at number five.

'Strange Brew', in contrast with 'Sunshine of Your love', found Cream paying homage to a blues master, Albert King. Along with Freddie King, he'd given authentic blues guitar playing a bit of 'beef', and Eric had obviously noticed. The inspiration from Albert's 'Crosscut Saw' was evident – Eric's actual cover version came much later. There were a couple of weird tracks on *Disraeli Gears*, such as 'World of Pain', which deals basically with the inherent sadness of a tree outside someone's window. But then these were strange days.

Eric shone through anew on 'Outside Woman Blues' and 'Tales of Brave Ulysses'.

Wheels of Fire, released in 1968, was probably the most representative of Cream's music. It showed the band at its best, both in the studio and in concert. Tracks like 'White Room' and 'Politician' were fine examples of their ability on a creative and recording level, while every other live recording showed off their individual talent as virtuosos. There was a light touch, too, with three most respected musicians singing about 'Pressed Rat and Warthog'.

Eric reached the pinnacle of his creative talents on *Wheels of Fire*. He played like a demon, not only as a soloist but as an accompanist. On 'Sitting on Top of the World', he took us to where he had left off in the Bluesbreakers. 'Spoonful' was an outrageous sixteen minutes and forty-four seconds of one of the best performances from any later sixties progressive rock outfit.

'Blues Ancient and Modern', as Eric Clapton described Cream after a mere three days of rehearsal, had their first major début in daylight the day after the club warm-up in Manchester. It was in pouring rain at the open-air sixth National Jazz and Blues Festival at Windsor on 3 July 1966.

The audience response was enthusiastic but not ecstatic. Among musicians, the vibrations were cynical. Three musicians with a very high pedigree were getting more advance publicity than many bands who had demonstrated their popularity to audiences throughout Britain; there was also great envy of the machinery surrounding Cream, fuelled by the entrepreneurial Robert Stigwood as manager and mentor.

Against that backdrop, and with the players clearly nervous, the début was a qualified success. Their extemporizing solo work, and Jack's affinity with jazz, scored with a crowd which applauded the improvisational 'feel'.

Eric enjoyed the vigour of it all but privately believed that British audiences would never warm to Cream. America beckoned, but not before the tenacity of the band was tested. For several months the trio achieved a chemical togetherness, travelling up and down Britain's first motorway, the M1, and learning the hard way. The business artillery behind Cream, however, had its sights firmly set on the US. In planning its exhausting schedule, there was a big ace: the three players, though still all in their twenties, were hardened veterans of the London club scene, revelling in all-night sessions. Little did they realize what gruelling days lay ahead.

The Clapton of the Cream period hardly smoked and never drank excessively. Both came later with a vengeance typical of his obsessiveness. Had he indulged himself during Cream days he would never have survived the punishing schedules that awaited the band in the US.

For young British musicians like these three, America was literally the promised land at that time. It was the birthplace of their inspiration, and Eric's spiritual Mecca. But the schedule that awaited Cream when they stepped off the plane in New York in April 1967 was more suited to a circus act than to three musicians seeking to extend their credibility.

The zany New York disc jockey Murray the K hosted a show at the RKO Theatre on 58th Street and Third Avenue. In this non-stop, fast-talking, fast-moving affair, the curtain went up at 10 a.m. each day. Each of several acts did just one song, in five shows a day. Cream were among the acts paraded by a beaming Murray the K to undiscriminating audiences: thirteen-year-old school-children on holiday formed the morning audiences, empty seats the afternoon, and adults in the evenings. Murray the K's *Fifth Dimensional Show*, so named because it ran five times each day, was perhaps the most soul-destroying show imaginable for a group hoping to break a pop image and the treadmill of chart-based performances.

The Who, with whom Eric struck up a firm friendship, were also on the bill, alongside Mitch Ryder and the Detroit Wheels, Wilson Pickett, Simon and Garfunkel, the Blues Project, and Jan and Dean. There were dancing girls and a daily film show on surfing. But Pete Town-shend remembers being jealous, underneath his bon-homie, at Cream's rocket to popularity; he resented their 'overnight stardom' compared with the Who's three-year slog to success.

Cream and the Who had one thing in common, though: they became totally disillusioned, especially when Murray the K said he could not pay the acts because he had lost £27,000 on the week. 'He hadn't bargained for our casual English approach and expected us to be leaping around doing a James Brown thing', says Eric. 'It just wasn't our show.

'The best moment came when we had these fourteen-pound bags of flour and eggs we were going to use on stage on our last night. But Murray the K heard about it and said we wouldn't get paid if we did. So instead we spread them all round the dressing-rooms. Pete Town-shend ended up swimming round in this dressing-room, fully clothed, in a foot of water when his shower overflowed!

'We took the actual show as a joke. There was no chance for Ginger to play his solo, and we had to use the

Who's equipment because we couldn't take any with us – there was none provided, as usual.

'The best musical times we had were in Greenwich Village. It was like an English Musical Appreciation Society. I sat in with a couple of the Mothers of Invention and Mitch Ryder at the Cafe Au Go-Go where Jimi Hendrix used to play. I liked the Village the most. The shops stayed open all night! I made a lot of friends there, including Al Kooper who played on a lot of Bob Dylan tracks.'

Life as a freewheeling musician, jamming and taking in the communal atmosphere of New York, made a big impression on Eric. 'New York's incredible,' he said while he was there. 'I'd love to live here. Everybody is so much more hip to the music scene. My taxi driver talked to me about James Brown! Can you imagine that happening in London?'

If the New York shows were a fiasco, San Francisco proved the turning point for Cream. The world capital of the hippie philosophy was uniquely prepared in 1967 for their kind of freewheeling rock. Like much of the West Coast sound, Cream's music, with its long, headstrong solos and assertion of individuality, proved the perfect backdrop for the marijuana smokers in the audience.

A major factor in helping Cream to happen in San Francisco was the visionary rock promoter Bill Graham. Eric told him they felt frustrated at not getting enough time to 'build' in their work. Graham's calculated gamble, knowing his audience would be enthralled anyway at having Britain's top guitarist on stage, gave Cream *carte blanche* to have an 'open-ended' programme. 'Go on and play and do it your way,' said Bill Graham, the first promoter to show such vision. 'If you want to play 'Spoonful' from night until dawn, do it. We've never done it before. We'll see what happens.'

For the next two weeks at the Fillmore, crowds went wildly enthusiastic. The good vibrations were contagious, wafting back to Britain, where Cream had scarcely had time to make much impact. At the end of it, Eric intoned: 'England could use a little more maturity. In San Francisco there is more encouragement and less competition from musician to musician. The scene in London thrives wildly, often because everyone is jealous of someone else's success. In the States you are encouraged. Everyone digs everyone else and they don't try to hide it. It seems the English market has been bred on immaturity. What they could learn from San Francisco is to be open-minded to what's *not* Top Forty, and grow up a little.'

He loved San Francisco audiences, 'the best anywhere. They're so obviously critical. Every little move you make, every note you play, is being noticed, devoured, accepted or rejected. You know you have to do it right. You do your best because they know if you don't. We seem to be a lot more popular in San Francisco than I'd imagined. I knew the Cream had been heard of through the underground scene but I didn't imagine we'd be this popular.'

Cream played on the same bill as Paul Butterfield's Blues Band and another band Eric rated very highly, Mike Bloomfield's Electric Flag. 'It's amazing that a band like Butterfield's can go to England and just die,' Clapton observed. 'It's not like that here, not competitive and jealous. I think English musicians are afraid that American music is too far ahead of them.'

The spirit of West Coast music and the philosophy of the players deeply moved Eric. When he heard that the Grateful Dead were playing a series of shows for nothing, he remarked: 'I'd never heard of anyone doing that ever before. It really is one of the finest steps ever taken in music. What the Grateful Dead are doing sums up what I think about San Francisco. There's an incredible thing that the music people have towards their audience – they want to *give*.'

After the Fillmore, Cream went on a gruelling coast-to-coast US tour lasting twelve weeks. Although nothing equalled the San Francisco experience, they were swept along on a tidal wave of popularity and respect; there were standing ovations in many cities. And back in London, where word spread that Britain had sent America a trendsetting band, readers of the *Melody Maker*, in their annual popularity poll, voted Eric Musician of the Year. Clapton ruminated that he had entered Cream as a blues guitarist and inside it he became a rock 'n' roller. He was not sure about the desirability of that, but was intoxicated by his success.

Cream returned home, triumphant. But, very ironically, they were so successful that there was nowhere they could comfortably play in Britain. The burgeoning campus concert circuit could not afford them; the clubs were far too small to hold a band with such a reputation – a club booking would disappoint many more fans than it would please. The band was at a critical crossroads. And they were increasingly at loggerheads. On several concert dates, the three men actually did not speak to each other, but just played and went their separate ways afterwards. At one Wembley show, Jack Bruce left midway through the show, and Eric and Ginger completed it. Now, the three insisted on travelling separately and staying not merely on separate floors in their hotels, but in three different *hotels*. They met up five minutes before the show, in the dressing room. The end of Cream was on the horizon.

They went off on a European tour, and their hit singles, 'I Feel Free' and 'Strange Brew', and best-selling albums, *Disraeli Gears* and *Wheels of Fire*, had given them great self-confidence. The public saw a band on a perpetual adventure, apparently finely balanced, too: Jack's soulful singing and harmonica wailing, Ginger's explosive drum solos and Clapton's shimmering solo work on tunes like 'Steppin' Out'. But that title was more accurate than anyone could have known at the time: the band that promised so much was indeed stepping out from itself. It was difficult enough to adapt to hit singles, adulation and big money but the non-stop aggravation of battling personalities clinched the decision to find a way out.

Clapton was the first to want to split. 'I've had enough. I'm leaving,' he would say to manager Robert Stigwood, in person and by telephone, on many occasions. Eric's irritation at the acrimony within the band, the constant bickering between Bruce and Baker, reached a peak in Europe. Stigwood always managed to paper over the cracks and repair the problem temporarily. Cream were, after all, a vital backbone of his show-business empire. He needed the money they were generating to subsidize his investment in other long-term properties, like the Bee Gees.

In personal terms, too, Eric was changing. Uncharacteristically, he allowed the rapid fame to seduce him into behaving like a pop star, almost crossing the division between musician and idol. With his ever-present shades, monstrous collection of fashion rings around every finger, leather jackets, colourful shirts and menacing, drooping moustache, he now lived in a rambling studio apartment at the Pheasantry in the King's Road with his girlfriend Charlotte Martin, a model, amid an 'artistic commune' which included Martin Sharp of the London 'underground' magazine *OZ*.

Eric had met Martin Sharp, an artist, in London's Speakeasy club and shortly afterwards the two men agreed to share the accommodation at the Pheasantry. Chelsea was the happening part of town at the time; soon after Eric had moved in, Charlotte Martin joined him. (She later married Jimmy Page.) The Pheasantry was a perfect backdrop for the Clapton of that period; its residents or habitués included Germaine Greer, who was writing *The Female Eunuch* in a room there, writer Anthony Hayden-Guest, and the prominent music and art world personality David Litvinoff.

Says Eric: 'I remember thinking the music wasn't going anywhere. We were just ad-libbing all the time, not planning any changes. It first hit me when I heard the Band's album, *Music from Big Pink*. I realized we were already out of date and there was no way of trying to get the other two to move forward. I thought, if only we had a keyboard player, or could play a bit differently. What I should have been was more satisfied with what we had, instead of wishing for more of other influences. It was incredibly difficult. I felt I wanted to change Cream but it wasn't up to me. I wasn't the leader of the band and I didn't know how to change it even if I could persuade Jack and Ginger. I was frustrated. That's why I faced up to a split.'

The non-stop verbal lashings between the other two finally clinched it. 'Their anger was so vicious. I'd never experienced any words like it. It never reached blows in my presence, but the language, the venom was so powerful that it would reduce anyone to tears.' During the European trip, Eric was, in fact, tearful about the friction. 'I was a stripling of a lad, remember. It really got to me. This was a big band going out of anybody's control. Between Jack and Ginger, it was pure love–hate.'

What probably also lay at the root of Eric's discomfort in Cream were the utterly different musical backgrounds from which the three men sprang. Jack Bruce, born on 14 May 1943, was a multi-instrumentalist, an ex-student of the Royal Scottish Academy of Music, who went to London in 1962 as a capable cellist, electric and upright bassist, harmonica and piano player. He became immersed in the thriving blues and jazz scene, playing with Alexis Korner's famed Blues Incorporated and the Graham Bond Organization before impressing Clapton in John Mayall's band.

Pete 'Ginger' Baker had a similarly structured background in a world of music more 'legitimate' than the casual beginnings of Eric Clapton. Born in Lewisham, London, on 19 August 1939, Ginger had begun as a fourteen-year-old trumpeter with the Air Cadets. Two years later he had transferred his allegiance to drums and then moved through several prominent traditional jazz bands in London – the Storyville Jazzmen, Acker Bilk's Paramount Jazz Band and Terry Lightfoot's Jazzmen – before spreading his wings into modern jazz and the blues. For a period, he was the resident drummer at Ronnie Scott's world-famous Soho jazz club.

Having renounced the Yardbirds for their brazen commercialism, Eric believed that with two mature colleagues he need have no fears. But he reckoned without the reality of the music business: despite Cream's visual and musical trendiness – they were, like their friend Jimi Hendrix, pioneers of psychedelic fashion – Cream had quickly been put under great pressure to make a hit single. Jack Bruce and his lyricist partner Pete Brown, who were together to write some of Cream's best songs, came up with 'Wrapping Paper', a superficial if catchy effort which did not reflect the band's real style. Nevertheless, it reached thirty-four in the British charts in the autumn of 1966 and was followed by the more aggressive 'I Feel Free', on which Eric dominated with a vibrant solo indicative of what was to come. That single rose to number eleven in the British chart.

'Wrapping Paper' is an excuse for a twelve-bar blues. That's all it is – a good tune, very commercial, with the sort of feel that represents *us*,' Eric explained at the time. 'We do exploit this kind of feeling, but we retain the beauty feel as well, all the time we play. Although we might play a number very loudly, and it might appear violent, in fact the tune and lyrics are very sweet.'

With two hit singles and a much acclaimed début album, events had moved too rapidly for Cream during that heady flower-power year of 1967. They went to America for the Murray the K concert season, and while there recorded some tracks for their second album, *Disraeli Gears* (the title was again Eric's, a stream-of-consciousness notion gleaned from a cyclist who boasted to him about his machine's uniqueness). The American tour that year was immaculately timed for the turned-on generation, the flowing solos allowing Cream's heavily stoned audiences to turn off their minds, relax and float downstream. The band were not ready for the tumult but their egos were handsomely fed at last.

By the autumn, with the release of that second album, the warring factions within the trio were already simmering, but such was their momentum that they knew they had a band that was perfect for its time. Martin Sharp,

Eric's Chelsea flatmate, who had designed much of the controversial magazine *Oz*, gave the cover of *Disraeli Gears* such a stunning psychedelic impact that it might serve for ever as Cream's most telling memento: a glorious fusion of pink, turquoise and green imagery, with peacocks symbolically preening beneath the cut-out faces of Baker, Bruce and Clapton. Musically, the album was equally urgent, featuring 'Strange Brew' (their third single, which had been a moderate hit) and 'Tales of Brave Ulysses', which Eric co-wrote with Martin Sharp. Also on the record was 'Sunshine of Your Love'. It was the clincher for a band which had soared so quickly, and went into the top five in both the American and British album charts.

But as that period of achievement neared its end in 1968 it was obvious to Eric that, despite some fine gigs, Cream could not continue. Of Jack and Ginger, he says now: 'I was outside them. They couldn't agree on *anything*. The vibe was horrible. It had even begun at the very first rehearsal, where I thought up the name. We weren't rehearsing, just *talking* about the rehearsal, when it turned out that Ginger had leaked the news of the band's formation to a newspaper. Jack flew off the handle. They were into one another's throats at that first meeting.'

Eric's first public sign of disenchantment and frustration came when he announced that Cream would not make any more single records. 'The main reason is that we are very anti the whole commercial market,' he told the *Melody Maker*. 'The whole nature of the single-making process has caused us grief in the studios. I'm a great believer in the theory that singles will become obsolete and LPs will take their place; singles are an anachronism.'

That was a musician's statement of exceptional prescience in the late 1960s. He continued: 'To get any good music in a space of two or three minutes requires working to a formula, and that part of the pop scene leaves me cold. I hate all the rushing around, trying to get a hit. As long as the pop scene is geared to singles a lot of people will be making bread who shouldn't be making bread.'

It was at that point, he says, that he finally sat down and said to himself: 'OK, I own up. I am Eric Clapton, a guitar player, and now I'll just stop mucking about and make my career under my own name.' The idealism of the musician would remain, but the belief that he could submerge his stance into that of a sideman would have to disappear from his thoughts.

'We were fighting success, but it happened against our will. It really did. We were desperately trying to be jazz musicians and lived that life and role. I fought success because I could see the traps and pitfalls. When Cream became acknowledged as virtuosos, that's when the rot set in, because we started to believe it, and became very cynical about success.' It had to end, he declares.

Musically, he enjoyed it while it lasted. 'It worked like a jazz group. We started with a theme and improvised on it, and because there were only three people, as long as we got back to the same place in the tune at the same time, it was OK. You can't do that in a band structure where there are more than three people. So it worked pretty well and we all bounced off each other on stage in an interesting way.

'But we worked too hard and we didn't get a chance to sit and reflect on where we were going or what we could do to change, to keep up with what was happening, musically, outside us. We were cocooned, on the road for seven months of the year just doing the same old stuff. We were still improvising, but in a repetitive way. Towards the end of the Cream's life there was a great revolution taking place, led by the Band. And when we all opened our eyes to that, we found ourselves miles off course. And we made the Goodbye album by Cream with all of us trying to establish a new face for the group. By then it was too late.'

The front cover design of *Goodbye*, the farewell album from Cream (which topped the British chart) showed just how Eric had viewed the band: as a *tour de force*. There they were, looking happy – if a trifle bizarre – in grey silk suits and matching grey shoes, bowler hats and canes – vaudevillian rockers! The music inside was a fitting farewell.

In the surprisingly short space of less than three years Cream had given some stunning performances, through the exceptional chemistry of three musicians who came together at the right time.

Clapton remembers Cream with both affection and regret. 'It was very intense. I don't meet many people with that kind of intensity any more, with that serious musical intention.'

On Christmas Eve, 1967, Eric, Jack and Ginger trailed wearily back into Heathrow Airport, London, after another tiring American tour. They were hardly speaking to each other, so dismal was their relationship. Although they had many commitments, including a return to Chicago just after Christmas, the band was doomed. 'It was,' says Eric, 'just a question of how and when we could split, not whether we should do it.'

Musically and personally, Eric felt at sea. The band

had lost direction. The route taken in the company of Bruce and Baker had strayed too far from what Eric regarded as his natural blues playing. 'I got really hung up. I tried to write pure pop songs and create a pop image. It was a shame because I was not being true to myself.' The same warning bells that had rung in his ear when he walked out of the Yardbirds only two years earlier had pulled Eric back from the precipice of musical dishonesty.

There was another aspect to it which only onlookers, rather than Clapton, Bruce or Baker, could see. Cream had been conceived as a coalition, an improbable scenario for such a visible musician as Eric. Baker and Bruce, ostensibly the rhythm section to Eric's lead role, were never going to be satisfied with being subjugated. The beauty of Cream was that it contained three gigantic talents; the weakness that threatened its survival was that not one of them was allowed to obscure another.

Cream had peaked in San Francisco, Eric declared. 'From then on, we all went on such huge ego trips.' Making it so big in the States had proved 'a big bang in the head'. The three men were exhausted, he said, and needed privacy and independence from each other. 'I want to perform contemporary blues. With the Cream, solos were the thing, but I'm really off that virtuoso kick. It was all over-exposed. We died the death from playing too much.'

They had also become a money-making machine, selling millions of records and catapulting the three men into a lifestyle hitherto undreamed of. Their final six-week American tour, which began in October 1968, earned $650,000. Yet his reputation was spreading; around the world Eric in particular was discussed by all other musicians with almost hushed reverence. He struck up a promising partnership with George Harrison. The Beatles had stopped touring and George was busy producing albums by such fine artists as Jackie Lomax for the Beatles' idealistic Apple label. Eric played guitar on that session, and even played on one of Harrison's Beatles songs.

In the post-psychedelic haze of London, 1968, a new breed of confident musicians had emerged. The survivors of the pop explosion that had erupted five years earlier had absorbed the rich tapestry of sounds that had come from America. Eric had been utterly bowled over by the dynamism of Jimi Hendrix. The two men had cemented a friendship after Hendrix had jammed with Cream in 1966 in a London club, and the Hendrix Experiences's first booking was supporting Cream at the Central London Polytechnic. Musically and in personality, Hendrix was the embodiment of all Clapton strived for: the American delivered fiery modern blues and his swashbuckling but sensitive personality melted all who met him. Hendrix had style, passion, and a keen sense of self, yet he was palpably shy. Eric felt a strong empathy with him.

From America's West Coast, the rock revolution had thrown up a fascinating cross-section of styles and players who interested Eric and opened his mind to new formulae of bands: the Mothers of Invention, the Grateful Dead, Buffalo Springfield and the Lovin' Spoonful. Cream had been singing 'I Feel Free'. Now Eric intended to implement the phrase.

Attempts by manager Robert Stigwood to keep the group together failed. Said Eric: 'Our management have come to realize that unless we are allowed to do what we want to, we can kick up a bigger stink about it than them.' The farewell concert at London's Royal Albert

Hall on 26 November 1968 sold out all seats within two hours and a second performance was added. As they played, Jimi Hendrix went on television to say Cream's farewell was a sad day for rock 'n' roll; he dedicated a song to Eric, Jack and Ginger.

In a highly emotional send-off, fans climbed on to the stage and showered Eric in confetti. They played three encores, and their programme favourites like 'White Room', 'I'm So Glad', 'Sitting on Top of the World', 'Crossroads', 'Toad', 'Sunshine of Your Love' and 'Steppin' Out'. And the meteorite that was Cream had fallen to earth. Few bands had combined such innovative music with the role of signposting rock's future.

But Eric was pleased it was over. His reputation as a guitarist and as an intelligent songwriter was now legendary. The security of a lot of money gave him the cushion of freedom. And his appetite was whetted for new ventures.

If the Beatles had dragged pop out of the fifties, then Cream had progressed it into the sixties and beyond and were instrumental in changing serious music fans' thoughts from pap and frothy singles into imaginative solos and inspirational albums. For students of Clapton's guitar, and for those who had deified him, the result of the readers' poll in *Disc and Music Echo* in 1968 provided a smile. In the Best British Musician category, Eric was voted into second place, behind Hank Marvin of the Shadows. In third place was Jimi Hendrix and fourth was George Harrison.

The memory of Cream is strong enough with Eric, but for millions, particularly in America where their impact was colossal, he will for ever be remembered as part of that splendid trio, just as Paul McCartney will always be 'ex-Beatle'. Eric has mixed feelings about the historic aspects of it, and living with it is a millstone around his neck.

'I look at it both ways. Looking back, I really enjoyed it and a great deal of life during those three years. I met great musicians and I learned a lot. On the other hand, we started a ball rolling which I don't like being responsible for – people say we started the heavy metal thing, which is quite an indictment! But Cream *had* to fizzle out. It was the first time I'd felt really disappointed, though. I had been glad to be out of the Yardbirds situation, with John Mayall I'd been pleased to be moving on to something new. With Cream, at the time I felt disillusioned. I felt then that I'd wasted three years. I now know better, but at the time I was down.

'There were times when I felt like I had the right direction, but I never felt confident enough to take the initiative from the other two, because their musicianship was more experienced. In Jack's case, and Ginger's too, to a certain extent, they had a wider scope. They had played jazz for money, you know, they had literally *done* it on the road. I felt that maybe they were more entitled to know what was right and wrong. But if we were going to do a blues song, then I felt pretty confident, I knew how to do it. So there was the introduction of material too that I would be responsible for. But other than that, I wouldn't tell them how to try to play. I'd have to leave it to them.' Cream certainly did not prepare him at all for band leading.

To Eric, Cream seemed to last for an eternity. He remembers that he had quickly tired of the role of mediator preventing Bruce and Baker from fighting. 'I managed to be in the middle of them and my mellowness, my delicacy in some of the situations, probably stopped them from actually tearing one another to pieces.

It might have been because of their concern for me, or because I was the youngest of the band. And I was also helping to make the band. They didn't want to lose me. At first, I had a great time. It was only towards the end that I started seeing the faults as being a reason for ending the band.'

Eric's verdict on the musical frustration that forced the end, as well as the bad chemistry, is succinct. 'Instead of growing, we used the same material on those long tours. We played the same stuff over and over again and really worked ourselves into a hole embellishing it all. And that, in the end, becomes very hollow. There was no core left at the end of it. We were just empty.

'There were a lot of telephone conversations taking place, transatlantic, with Robert Stigwood. We were calling him for different reasons. Jack was calling him because of Ginger, Ginger was calling him because of Jack and I was calling him because of both of the other two! I was getting the most favour from Stigwood. He was saying in so many words, "You're the one I pick. So if you don't like it with them any more, don't worry, I'll look after you. I'll take care of *them* later. But you've got big things ahead of you, so if you want to break the band up, don't worry about it, because we can go somewhere else." I was getting a lot of strength from that dialogue, enough strength, probably, to break the band up!

'We all loved one another in a way. That's the heavy thing! I remember having a reunion with Jack and Ginger in the mid-seventies at my home. The three of us met in London in the office by accident and tore the place apart and came back to my house flying – really flying – on cloud nine. Took acid and just started talking. It was a summer's day, people were arriving – like they sometimes do in a country house – and we were out there, sitting on that terrace, in chairs, facing the same way, the three of us, almost as if we were expecting people to come. And people were arriving and sort of walking round the corner, down round the side of the house, walking round there and stopping, as if they were approaching a *court*. And this buzz was coming off of us. Ginger would get up and address whoever it was. It was amazing, just bizarre, and the three of us were like an unit like that. One of us would take care of one angle, one would take care of another angle, one would address the remainder. It could happen again. If you put the three of us in a room, we would immediately find our level and function on it perfectly. Very strange. We haven't changed that much. Jack's still basically the same, Ginger's still basically the same and I'm still basically the same. Those two fought like dogs, but the triangle made it work.'

Reporting from California in November 1968 on Cream's final US tour, Judy Sims wrote in the British pop weekly *Disc and Music Echo* – 'The imminent break-up of the group seemed to make them closer and tighter. They were so good, so together, that when they started playing "I'm So Glad", some of the more restrained viewers were close to tears. The performance [at Anaheim] was marred only by a large group of younger fans who stormed the stage, thereby ending the performance prematurely. Clapton is freshly shorn with straight hair once again and looks very good indeed.'

For years after the demise of Cream, relations between the trio were strained. But by the 1990s, their friendship was rekindled and Eric included several Cream songs in his repertoire, notably 'Sunshine of Your Love', 'White Room' and 'Badge', to the delight of his audiences.

*

While Cream were disintegrating, it occurred to Eric that if they added a keyboard player they might be able to reassess their music outlook, and perhaps continue with a fresh approach that would also curb the clashes of personality within the band. 'That person, to me, was Steve Winwood. I thought if he joined Cream, it would be great, so I went looking for Steve after Cream broke up. And we hung out in each other's houses for several months, playing together and having a good time. Then Ginger joined and we looked for a bass player, and suddenly we were taking ourselves too seriously. We were nudged into the studio, nudged on to the road, and I nudged out when I saw Delaney and Bonnie. I was slipping out of the back door, really.' Looking back, he saw that decision as consistent with everything he had done up to that point.

'I'd left the Yardbirds because of success, and Cream ended as a direct result of its false success, or what appeared to me to be a hypocritical form of success. So with Blind Faith I wanted no more to do with success. I wanted to be accepted as a musician. Derek and the Dominos was what that was all about. We went on tours of England when nobody knew who we were. We played to punters who came to see what they thought was probably a local band. And it was great, because they were knocked out by the fact that we were good. We had no expectations to live up to, and no trappings. So that succeeded for a while.' But he says that because some members of the Dominos were 'younger than me and from the hills of America, the money went to their heads and that all went wrong. It's the same old story . . .'

In the prelude to Cream's split, Eric had several times met Steve Winwood, then part of a successful band, Traffic. Steve and Eric exchanged confidences: there were deep-rooted personal and musical differences within each man's band. 'Neither of us believed the difficulties could be resolved,' recalls Winwood. 'We both knew Cream and Traffic would split. One day, Eric came down to the house in Berkshire where I was living and we had a play. I said it would be nice to try to get back to the old feeling when he jammed in my first group, the Spencer Davis Group. He said: "Yeah, I think we should form a band." And that was it. It had been a long time coming; we both hoped we'd be free of our bands one day and it happened naturally.'

Winwood says that Clapton described Cream to him that day as 'too self-indulgent'. He believed they had strayed too far into the area of jazz-rock. He wanted to play more songs rather than leave each player virtually undisciplined. Only three months after Cream's farewell concert, by February 1969, Eric and Steve had agreed to partly form a new band. 'Eric named it Blind Faith because that's exactly what he had in the project,' recalls Winwood.

The first idea was to be a trio, like Cream. Just as the two founders of Blind Faith were casting around for a likely player, Ginger Baker arrived at Winwood's house. 'You need a drummer,' he said. 'Look, I can play pretty good. There aren't many people who can play better than me.' Clapton was now in a quandary. True, Baker was a majestic drummer. But he didn't want him in his new band. As well as the danger of clashing personalities, he told Winwood, he was looking for a change of scenery in his musicians. And two former members of Cream would leave Blind Faith wide open to accusations that it was Cream Mark Two.

But Winwood did want Baker in the band. He was mightily impressed by Ginger's dynamics and persuaded a very reluctant Eric that the music would benefit. It was to be, as Clapton had predicted, the single biggest factor in sealing Blind Faith's fate. The public did see it as a reincarnation of Cream. As the ballyhoo grew surrounding the formation of a 'new supergroup' (which included two ex-Cream men, one great singer who came from Traffic and the respected bass player Rick Grech from the band Family), Blind Faith had a lot to live up to.

Blind Faith's only major British appearance was a free concert in London's Hyde Park on 7 June 1969. Among the crowd of 150,000 were scores of eminent rock stars, curious to see Clapton's new guise. Mick Jagger and Marianne Faithfull were backstage and, as a gesture, Blind Faith played the Rolling Stones song 'Under My Thumb'. The band's music was subdued and bore little resemblance to that of any other band; Eric smiled happily when one voice from the crowd beneath the stage boomed out: 'It's not Cream, Eric, it's Blind Faith. Play what you like!'

The band was judged with cautious optimism by most of the cognoscenti. The big achievement of the day, reported London's *Daily Mirror* in an editorial, was: 'There aren't many countries where 100,000 youngsters could get together so peacefully and give the police no real worries . . . [it was] one of the most remarkable and amiable gatherings of young people ever seen in this country.'

Within the band, the storm clouds already loomed. After a spectacular response from a crowd of 20,000 at their first New York concert at Madison Square Garden, Blind Faith ran into controversy in the US in July 1969.

American record dealers who saw the cover design of their début album described it as 'obscene and salacious' and said they would refuse to stock it unless it was redesigned. The cover showed a naked eleven-year-old girl holding a silver spacecraft. As reaction against the picture grew in America, the Robert Stigwood office in London was told that 70 per cent of American record dealers had decided against stocking the album, so a fresh cover was essential. Faced with advance orders of a quarter of a million for the album, there was little choice; a new, acceptable cover showed a harmless picture of the musicians in Blind Faith, a stronger sales pitch anyway in view of the fact that it featured two-thirds of the mighty Cream. A note included with the album said that buyers could obtain the original, controversial, sleeve on request from the record company, Atlantic, who released the LP as planned in Britain.

Eric faced questions all the time about why Steve Winwood was allowed to dominate the band. 'I think he's the most talented guy in the group, and as a result he deserves to be out front,' Clapton invariably answered. 'But we're not just backing him up. We all play an incredibly big part.' Other factors, however, quickly militated against the band. As they went on the road, it looked like the clashes between Baker and Bruce in Cream might be re-enacted by Clapton and Baker in Blind Faith. And, finally, in America, according to Winwood and Clapton, the fate of the band was obvious.

A combination of greed for the big money that was around, plus a lack of material – astonishingly, this band could only play for just over an hour without running short of original material – sowed the seeds of the band's demise. In America and in Britain, many members of the audience were Cream or Traffic fans; faced with the easy applause and constant demands for Cream or Traffic favourite songs, and their lack of other material, Eric and Steve succumbed to the easy option. The band became exactly what they had hoped to avoid; a mirror image of their previous groups. And because they were so rapidly thrust forward, they did not get the time to reflect on their musical identity or produce enough new songs to sustain it.

'The management and the record company joined our own greed,' says Winwood, looking back on it. 'You can't really blame them or us. There was a multi-million dollar time bomb out there. We wanted to work, so we said: "Oh, let's go and earn the bucks!" There were pressures left, right and centre to go out and earn the money. Never was there a moment to develop the character of the band. Who would let a million-dollar-a-week potential in a band sit around and rehearse? It's understandable. And we thought it was more sensible to go out and work rather than sit around. We decided to make our mistakes in public. But when it came down to it, we failed because we couldn't resist requests for the hits. Ginger did a drum solo and they thought it was Cream, so we chucked in an old Cream song, then I put in a Traffic song, and the identity of the band was killed stone dead. If you have 20,000 people sitting out there and you know you only have to play one song for them to be on their feet, you *do* it! We were only human. But that was the end, really, when that began.

'Soon there was a realization that this was a bit of a cop-out. We should have started Blind Faith by insisting on playing 1,000-seater halls. There was serious pressure on us not to do that because it would be a retrograde step. And our egos might have been a bit of a problem . . . Eric had been playing 20,000-seater halls around the world and Traffic had done pretty big shows, too. That was the root of our unrest – the audiences, the planning, and the fact that we didn't get away from who we had been before the band began.'

Eric agreed with Steve that Blind Faith lacked an identity. But there was a more deep-seated reason for his conviction that Blind Faith was doomed from the start. 'Steve couldn't see it this way, but when Ginger walked in, I lost interest. I was freshly grieving from Cream and I wanted no more part of Cream again. I found Steve and he was loose. The pair of us were living in the country and we were developing lifestyles which were very similar. Steve would come here, or I would go to his Berkshire cottage and we'd do some dope. We'd play and hang out for days on end without forming an idea of what we were doing – just enjoying one another's company. And then somehow word leaked to someone to someone to someone . . . and the next thing I knew, Ginger was knocking on the door. Now I love Ginger very much, but at that time I didn't really want him around! But I didn't have the heart to say no.

'And then Ginger took the reins because Steve and I were both so laid back! We were in no hurry to get anywhere, whereas Ginger could see . . . zoom the bucks. So could Robert Stigwood. Before we knew it, we were into the harassments of making a record and with a tour lined up which we weren't ready for and had no desire to do.'

Blind Faith became, to Eric, Son of Cream – and he says: 'I was looking for a way out, subconsciously, from the minute we hit the road. And Delaney was there . . . so I jumped straight into that Delaney and Bonnie Bramlett band scene for a while.'

Just as America had been the scene of the demise of

Cream, it also proved the country where Blind Faith's coffin was nailed. 'Look, this is ridiculous,' Eric said to Steve after one show. 'It's a successful group all right, but we're getting applause for all the *wrong stuff*. It's not the group we planned, is it? It's Cream stuff and long drum solos!'

Winwood's theory with hindsight is that, despite the collapse of Blind Faith after only a year, Eric gained enormously from the experience. 'In a way, the jump from being inside John Mayall to being the star of Cream was too big. He wanted to learn a little more about what happened in between for a musician . . . that role of accompaniment. I think he learned that role inside Blind Faith, whatever our failures. But we didn't even have to talk the end of the band through. It was perfectly obvious to Eric and me on that tour in America that it couldn't last. As we had put the band together, so we just split it up. In fact we didn't split formally. We just drifted away . . .'

As throughout his life as a musician, Clapton had absorbed the experiences of the period like a sponge. 'Inside Cream, I felt I had to live up to something all the time. With Blind Faith, I didn't. The audience did, but I didn't! In Cream, on those long solos, I found I was repeating myself night after night. There never seemed any time to stop and think. I was totally exhausted in Cream. The only thing that doesn't change is that I'm changing all the time. The consistency of my character is that I'm a paradox. The only thing you can count on in me is that I'm going to keep changing. And that I'll always be playing guitar, five and twenty-five years from now.'

He added that while he might have proved himself to many thousands of listeners, he had not proved himself to himself. He felt restless again. 'Looking back,' reflects Steve Winwood, 'it's obvious that Blind Faith, just like the Yardbirds and John Mayall, was a stepping stone for Eric. He was just moving from band to band, taking lots in each time, but it was all leading for certain to where he is today. Eventually, he could not remain a member of any band. He'd have to go solo.'

Clapton weathered strong criticism over his handling of Blind Faith. Many fans and musicians thought he had appeared too subservient to Winwood, and should have assumed the leadership more aggressively; he was, after all, the bigger name. But Eric wanted different things from the band. He was not ready for the leadership job at that stage. 'It's easier to be led than to lead . . . I felt very insecure sometimes inside Blind Faith, and that was my own hang-up that had to be cured in its own time.'

Fights in the audience had also marred the band's American tour. In the worst scenes, in New York, Los Angeles and Phoenix, Eric reported that 'the crowd came prepared for the fact that there would be cops there, and were prepared to be bugged from the start. Their main thing was to heckle the cops. The cops replied with violence. Our main thing was to appease them both. And that had nothing to do with being a musician. That's being a politician. The violence happened everywhere we played. Partly because of that, we played too loudly, which is the very thing I wanted to avoid with Blind Faith.'

But at least two satisfying aspects of the American tour had been the band's album jumping to the top of the charts . . . and the money which came from playing such big venues. The band might have failed to fulfil Clapton's hopes, but behind his biblical beard and thinner frame, the man who returned to Britain was more mature as a twenty-four-year-old, robustly confident of his future as a musician who could take his time before making a new career move.

FIVE

THE DRUG
OF 'LAYLA'

ERIC CLAPTON in 1969 was hardly the archetypal, hedonistic rock star. Although big money was flowing in from record sales generated from the Cream tour of America, he was still more concerned with self-exploration. As a musician he would emerge, within the next twenty-five years, as unquestionably the most industrious 'jammer' in rock, performing on hundreds of other people's records for pleasure, stimulation and essential camaraderie.

As he celebrated his twenty-fourth birthday, though, it was time to put down roots after all the years as a troubadour living mostly in flats. Not surprisingly, he chose a beautiful twenty-roomed mansion a few miles from Ripley. Occupying sixteen acres and bordering National Trust land, it cost Eric £40,000 (expensive in 1969), and with its ornamental ponds, deer in the fields, donkey in the garden and even an observatory and swimming-pool, it certainly carried Eric's imprimatur of style. The teenager who had aspired to be a stained-glass designer had a perfect eye when choosing his home. 'I fell in love with it immediately on my first look,' said Eric, who saw a photograph of it in the magazine

Country Life. Built in 1910, the house had an Italian architectural look. Redecoration of the house, in which the artistic Eric took a lot of interest, proceeded during the first year of Eric's residence there, during which he was generally alone.

Yet there was no smug self-satisfaction about the man as he moved in. 'I feel as if I have achieved nothing,' he said quite seriously, as he sat in his living-room. Nearby, his collection of twenty guitars disproved that, but in the aftermath of Cream, Clapton resisted the headiness of triumph. Experiences counted most in his life, then as now. 'I've got miles and miles to go,' he continued. 'I have covered a lot of ground as far as material things go. They're only possessions, things to make me more materialistic. I'm trying all the time to make music that satisfies me and everybody else. That is very hard to achieve because you can rarely make completely satisfying music.' He said he listened to his records 'only when they are new. To study what's wrong.'

The transformation from a determined, struggling blues guitarist, who had sometimes slept rough on railway stations after missing the last train home, to a superstar's grandeur, had happened very quickly. Cream had delivered him to the top in materialistic terms, even though the band had lasted a mere two years. Clapton has always found essential adaptability easy. Others found the opulence of his new home hard; on their first visit to the beautiful house, Eric's grandparents cried. They found it very difficult to grasp the changed lifestyle of the vulnerable boy they had raised in their modest terraced house. Quickly, Eric reassured them that if the surroundings had changed, he was the same man. One of the first of his many gifts to Rose and Jack was a six-week first-class world cruise.

By that year of 1969, the euphoria of the decade's pop revolution was subsiding. The Beatles, in disarray after the death of their manager Brian Epstein, began arguing about their future and John Lennon stepped out with Yoko Ono. Eric's music continued apace at this period of non-alignment with a band of his own. A telephone call one night from Lennon asked Eric if he would go, next day, to Toronto to guest with John and Yoko Ono's Plastic Ono Band at a big rock festival. The infectious enthusiasm of John soon persuaded Eric to join them at Heathrow Airport on 13 September 1969. They had no repertoire and actually rehearsed on the plane. 'It was a great gig. We did an hour of solid rock; numbers like "Blue Suede Shoes" and "Dizzy Miss Lizzy",' says Eric. He had great affection for Lennon, which was reciprocated. After the Canadian show, John said that the Plastic Ono Band was his successor to the Beatles and Eric was vital to it. He wanted Eric and the others in the band, particularly the fine bassist Klaus Voormann, to go on a concert tour. Eric's empathy with Lennon was based on Clapton's simple belief: 'He was sincere.' The murder of John in New York in 1980 devastated Eric.

Eric reflects on Yoko's controversial singing: 'Yoko has the same effect on people as a high-pitched whistle has on a dog. Her voice is spine-chilling, very weird. John and I played some feedback guitar while Yoko was singing. I think she was amazing. Her style of singing requires a technique, like anything else. If you try it, after ten minutes your voice will break. She is doing something unique – it has never been done before. She doesn't really need a backing but it's more entertaining to work with a foundation. The drummer just sets a beat but he can go into very abstract rhythms if he wants to. Toronto

Sept. 29, 1971

Dear Eric & the Missus,

I've been meaning to write or call you for a few weeks now.
I think maybe writing will give you and yours more time to think.

You must know by now that Yoko and I rate your music and yourself very highly, always have. You also know the kind of music we've
been making and hope to make. Anyway, the point is, after missing
the Bangla-Desh concert, we began to feel more and more like going
on the road, but not the way I used to with the Beatles - night after
night of torture. We mean to enjoy ourselves, take it easy, and
maybe even see some of the places we go to! We have many 'revolutionary'
ideas for presenting shows that completely involve the audience - not
just us 'Superstars' up there - blessing the people - but that's another
letter really.

I'll get more to the point. We've asked Klaus, Jim Keltner,
Nicky Hopkins - Phil Spector even! To form a 'nucleus' group (Plastic
Ono Band) - and between us all would decide what - if any- augmentation
to the group we'd like - e.g. saxs, vocal group, they all agreed so far -
and of course we had YOU!!!! in mind as soon as we decided.

In the past when Nicky was working around (Stones, etc.) bringing
your girl/woman/wife was frowned on - with us it's the opposite, Nicky's
missus - will also come with us - on stage if she wants (Yoko has ideas for
her!) - or backstage. Our upermost concern is to have a happy group in
body and mind. Nobody will be asked to do anything that they don't
want to, no-one will be held to any contract of any sort - (unless they
wanted to, of course!)

Back to music. I've/we've long admired your music -. and always kept
an eye open to see what you've been up to lately. I really feel I/we can
bring out the best in you - (some kind of security, financial or otherwise
will help) but the main thing is the music. I consider Klaus, Jim, Nicky,
Phil, Yoko, you could make the kind of sound that could bring back the
Balls in rock 'n' roll.

Both of us have been thru the same kind of shit/pain that I know you've
had - and I know we could help each other in that area - but mainly
Eric - I know I can bring out something great - in fact greater in you
that has been so far evident in your music, I hope to bring out the same
kind of greatness in all of us - which I know will happen if/when we get
together. I'm not trying to pressure you in any way and would quite
understand if you decide against joining us, we would still love and
respect you. We're not asking you for your 'name', I'm sure you know
this - it's your mind we want!

John Lennon was a great admirer of Eric Clapton's work. After persuading
Eric to take part in the Live Peace In Toronto concert in 1969, John and
Yoko Lennon continued their theme of unity among musicians with several
other plans. One involved a band including Clapton which would be filmed
while on a world cruise. The idea reached fruition but Lennon and Yoko's
long letter to Eric, reproduced here, provides a fascinating insight into the
mood of that period.

Yoko and I are not interested in earning bread from public appearances, but neither do we expect the rest of the band (who mostly have families) to work for free - they/you must all be happy money wise as well - otherwise whats the use for them to join us! We don't ask you/them to ratify everything we believe politically - but we're certainly interested in 'revolutionizing' the world thru music, we'd love to 'do' Russia, China, Hungary, Poland, etc.

A friend of ours just got back from Moscow, and the kids over there are really hip - they have all the latest sounds on tape from giant radios they have. 'Don't come without your guitar' was the message they sent us, there are millions of people in the East - who need to be exposed to our kind of freedom/music. We can change the world - and have a ball at the same time. (of course we'd work Europe. U.K. USA too.)

We don't want to work under such pressure we feel dead on stage or have to pep ourselves up to live, maybe we could do 2 shows a week even. It would be entirely up to us. One idea that I had which we've discussed tentavely, (nothing definite) goes like this:

I know we have to rehearse sometime or other, I'm sick of going on and jamming every live session. I've also always wanted to go across the Pacific from the U.S. thru all those beautiful islands - across to Australia, New Zealand, Japan - wherever, you know - Tahiti - Tonga- etc, so I came up with this.

How about a kind of 'Easy Rider' at sea. I mean we get EMI or some film co., to finance a big ship with 30 people aboard (including crew) - we take 8 track recording equipment with us (mins probably) movie equipment - and we rehearse on the way over - record if we want, play anywhere we fancy - say we film from L.A. to Tahiti, we stop there if we want - maybe have the film developed there - stay a week or as long as we want - collect the film (of course)we'll probably film wherever we stop (if we want) and edit it on board etc. Having just finished a movie we made around our albums 'Imagine' & 'Fly' - it's a beautiful surreal film, very surreal, all music, only about two words spoken in the whole thing! We know we are ready to make a major movie. Anyway, it's just a thought, we'd always stay as near to land as possible, and of course, we'd take doctors etc, in case of any kind of bother. We'd always be able to get to a place where someone could fly off if they have had enough. The whold trip could take 3 - 4 - 5- 6 months, depending how we all felt - all families, children whatever are welcome etc. Please don't think you have to go along with the boat trip, to be in the band. I just wanted to let you know everything we've been talking about. (I thought we'd really be ready to hit the road after such a healthy restful rehearseal.)

Anyway, there it is, if you want to talk more please call us, or even come over here to New York. We're at the St. Regis, here til Nov. 30 at least, (753-4500 - ext/rm. 1701, 1702, 1703) all expenses paid of course! or write. At least think about it, please don't be frightened, I understand paranoia, only too well, I think it could only do good for you, to work with people who love and respect you, and that's from all of us.

Lots of love to you both from,

John & Yoko

John & Yoko

was tremendous fun.' Lennon gave Eric, on Apple Records writing paper, five drawings in lieu of payment for the Toronto show. They were typically witty and Eric has them framed.

A short drive away from Eric's new home, George Harrison lived at Esher, Surrey, with his wife Pattie, whom he had married on 10 January 1966. A bond between Eric and George had built up since their first meeting at the Yardbirds Christmas Show five years earlier. Sharing an apprehension of pop stardom, they were in the vanguard of a breed of dedicated young musicians who would significantly shape rock's future. George had co-written with Eric one of Cream's best loved songs, 'Badge', and even played on the record under the pseudonym 'L'Angelo Misterioso'.*

There was no regular woman in Eric's life as he embarked on a somewhat solitary existence in his new home. As he drove his new Ferrari across to George and Pattie's home regularly for dinner, a fateful future for the trio of friends began to develop in Eric's mind. 'I went to Esher several times,' he recalls, 'and every time I left, after a nice time with George and Pattie, I remember feeling a dreadful emptiness.' He was falling in love with the wife of one of his best friends. That emptiness was 'because I was certain I was never going to meet a woman quite that beautiful for myself. I knew that. I knew I was in love. I fell in love with her at first sight. And it got heavier and

---

* This classic rock song got its inexplicable title accidentally. Eric arrived at George's home and read the word upside down on George's notepaper. He congratulated him on the enigmatic title, 'Badge'. But he had misread it. George had written a word as a musical expression: 'Bridge'.

heavier for me.' Pattie was unaware of Eric's feelings at these dinners for three. For Eric, it was to develop into his magnificent obsession.

As Pattie Boyd, one of Britain's top models of the 1960s, she had rocketed into the headlines when she became the girlfriend of George Harrison during the filming of the Beatles' film *A Hard Day's Night* in 1964. Pattie had first achieved a modest degree of fame as the Smith's Crisps girl in television advertisements. The producer of those commercials, Richard Lester, hired her to appear in a brief scene in that first film by the Beatles, which he was producing. On the set, Pattie began a romance with George and they were married two years later. Pert, infectiously smiling and with the flowing blonde hair almost mandatory for the models of that era, Pattie was born in Somerset on 17 March 1944, the daughter of a fighter pilot and the eldest of six children.*

Pattie moved with her family to Kenya between the ages of five and ten. Back in Britain, after her boarding-school education, she moved to London and took a job training at the Elizabeth Arden hairdressing salon. Her modelling career began almost accidentally, after she washed the hair of a woman magazine journalist who asked her if she had considered becoming a model. A photographic session followed.

She had first set eyes on Eric when he played a concert with Cream at London's Saville Theatre on 2 July 1967. Sitting with George and the other Beatles and their ladies in a box, Pattie recalls thinking he 'looked absolutely

---

* Pattie's sister Jenny, also a prominent figure on the 1960s scene, helped launch the Beatles' boutique Apple; was the inspiration for Donovan's song 'Jennifer Juniper'; and married and divorced Mick Fleetwood of Fleetwood Mac.

wonderful and played so beautifully'. Later that night, the owner of the Saville Theatre, Beatles Manager Brian Epstein, threw a party at his home at 24 Chapel Street, Belgravia. It was the first time she met Eric, a remote figure but a celebrated musician held in awe by his peers. 'I was surprised by how alone Eric looked at that party,' says Pattie. 'He was terribly reticent, didn't talk to anybody or socialize.' It was that very quietness and his 'rather mysterious' behaviour amid the party babble that intrigued Pattie. 'There was an aura around him which set him apart from the others. Definitely.'

As Eric consolidated his friendship with George, his obsession with Pattie increased. In a bizarre method of attracting Pattie's attention, he dated her eighteen-year-old sister Paula for three months. 'My mother was absolutely furious that Paula at that age was living with this pop star,' says Pattie. 'I wondered why he'd done it, but it became obvious later.'

Eric tried another ploy. From his home, he telephoned Pattie at Friar Park, Henley-on-Thames, to where she and George had moved in 1970. 'I asked her if she knew any models that might be on the loose because I didn't have a girl at that time,' says Eric. 'She said she'd think about it.' Pattie remembers: 'I actually did have a girl-friend who wasn't going out with anyone at that time, so I phoned Eric back and said I'd bring her along to the studios the next night.' At London's EMI recording studios, George Harrison was recording his blockbusting triple album *All Things Must Pass*, and Eric was playing guitar on it.

'Eric was so rude to my girlfriend. I could hardly believe it. She had never met a musician before and she was shocked beyond belief. He ignored her or made fun of her throughout the evening. She just disappeared – I never heard from her again.' Eric's language had offended her; and his immature posturing had also irritated Pattie, who was embarrassed for her friend. There was a reason for Eric's uncharacteristic tension. Next day, Clapton phoned Pattie again. 'Look, I didn't really want you to find me a girlfriend. I meant *you*. I really need to see you. Can I come over and talk to you about it?'

'I was hot and cold all over,' remembers Pattie. 'I said: "Look, I'm married to George, and it's difficult."' Eric says: 'Even when I blurted it out on the phone, I could sense she was flattered and pleased.'

'There had been amorous beginnings to it all,' Eric says. 'I went to Friar Park, or she came to parties here, and we made eyes at each other, had a few cuddles and whispered sweet nothings. What I couldn't accept was that she was out of reach. OK, she was married to George and he was a mate but I had fallen in love and nothing else mattered.' But, musically, there was always complete harmony and an edge of competitiveness between Harrison and Clapton. Only Eric knew that the healthy friendship might be threatened by his love of his friend's wife.

'I'd set myself up to fall,' says Eric. 'It was an impossible situation. Nobody ever steals a Beatle's wife. It's not *on*. They'd become very big Establishment figures, had been awarded medals as Members of the British Empire and here was this rogue banging down the back door. It was an impossible situation for Pattie to cope with, or for me to cope with. I'd actually gone out of my way to find a good enough excuse for me to hit rock bottom.'

Says Pattie: 'I couldn't believe the situation he'd put me in. I thought it wasn't right . . . and after that bad experience with my friend when Eric annoyed us, I thought it was destined to end. Then a letter came, addressed to me at Friar Park. Tiny, scrawly handwriting, unsigned, it said, "I need to see you and I love you." I showed it to George and told him some nutcase was writing to me; I had no idea who it was from. Next night, Eric phoned me and asked if I'd got his letter.' She stuttered a 'yes', but reaffirmed the complications and problems about being able to do anything about it, even if she wanted to. George Harrison was a man of intensity too; he had written the pretty ballad 'Something' about Pattie and it has proved his most popular composition, with more than 150 cover versions. She was therefore quite used to being sought after. But Eric decided to increase his own pressure by using one of his strongest assets: an eloquent simplicity in the use of words. His directness, his command of English, has always run parallel with his articulacy as a musician.

He invited her to meet him platonically from time to time during her marriage to George. During one meeting Pattie remembers that she and Eric 'went to see a beautiful film called *Kes*. Afterwards we were walking down Oxford Street and Eric suddenly said to me: "Do you like me, then, or are you seeing me because I'm famous?" I answered: "Oh, I thought you were seeing me because *I'm* famous!"' Both laughed because each meant what they said. Eric, she reflected years later to me, always had difficulty expressing his emotions to her 'which is why he puts his deepest thoughts into songs'. In perhaps the most profound remark ever made to sum up Eric Clapton, Pattie adds: 'He's incredibly romantic, to the point of visualizing his life as a novel.'

Meanwhile, away from the music world, Eric's coterie of friends from his Chelsea flat years were to stay constant. One, in particular, was to be a pivot of his romantic life.

Ian Dallas recommended the interior designer David Mlinaric to Eric for the planning of his new home. Mlinaric was starting to make his mark in his sphere and has since become a respected figure who went on to design interiors for British stately homes and castles. 'At that time,' Clapton says, 'there was a set of aristocratic hippies who were all into a sort of gypsy way of life.' Eric fell in with this set, which included the antique dealer Robert Fraser, a close friend of Keith Richards and Mick Jagger. When Mlinaric went with Fraser to Eric's home for the first time, he took with him the sixteen-year-old daughter of Lord Harlech.*

Her name was Alice Ormsby-Gore, a tall, willowy girl born on 11 April 1952. She had been attracted to Eric when they met at a party in Glebe Place, Chelsea, during November 1968. Visiting his home as part of the interior design team, she sensed a chemistry between them and felt Eric reciprocated it. 'I asked her if she was free . . . at sixteen years old!' Eric says with incredulity at himself. 'I had other girlfriends around, but no one steady.' After 'a very innocent courtship' for about a year, Alice moved in with Eric. So began, for them both, years of traumatic, life-threatening seclusion.

Alice moved into his home in March 1969. But when Eric began the two-month liaison in December 1969 with Pattie's sister Paula, Alice moved out. They reunited but their relationship quickly turned stormy. Alice feels now that Eric's treatment of her was insensitive; she was,

---

* Former British Ambassador to Washington and president of the British Board of Film Censors, Lord Harlech was one of Britain's most respected peers. He died in a car crash in 1985.

after all, then only seventeen and he was twenty-five. In April 1970, Alice left to spend the summer alone in Israel while Eric's house assumed the air of a commune, with the players in the band that would become Derek and the Dominos living in and taking it in turns to cook. The air was thick with drugs. And Clapton gave full rein to his passion for Pattie. During Alice's absence he wrote the pleading song to Pattie that would forever stand as one of rock's most intense anthems of love.

Ian Dallas, who was at that time becoming a Sufi to embrace the Muslim faith, had been enamoured of a book called *The Story of Layla and Majnun* by the eminent Persian writer Nizami. The story's sensitivity and intensity correlated precisely with Clapton's make-up and made a strong impression on him. In Arabic, 'Layl' means night and Majnun means madman. The man, Majnun, falls hopelessly in love with the unavailable Layla, and her non-availability in turn drives him to madness. The story is filled with vivid poetic descriptions of the girl to a degree similar to Eric's obsession for Pattie:

> To look at, she was like an Arabian moon, yet when it came to stealing hearts she was a Persian page. Under the dark shadow of her hair, her face was a lamp, or rather a torch, with ravens weaving their wings around it. And who would have thought that such overwhelming sweetness could flow from so small a mouth?

> Is it possible then to break whole armies with one small grain of sugar? She really did not need rouge; even the milk she drank turned into the colour of roses on her lips and cheeks . . . and she was equipped with lustrous eyes . . .

The name of this miracle of creation was Layla. Whose heart would not have filled with longing at the sight of this girl?... He was drowned in the ocean of love before he knew that there was such a thing. He had already given his heart to Layla before he understood what he was giving away. And Layla? She fared no better. A fire had been lit in both – and each reflected the other.

And:

... Nothing can ever extinguish the love for you in my heart. It is a riddle without a solution, a code which none can decipher. It entered by body with my mother's milk to leave it only together with my soul, of that I am sure ...

... Love, if not true, is but a plaything of the senses, fading like youth. Time perishes, not true love. All may be imagination and delusion, but not love. The charcoal brazier on which it burns is eternity itself, without beginning or end.

... Oh, who can cure my sickness? An outcast I have become. Family and home, where are they? No path leads back to them and none to my beloved. Broken are my name, my reputation, like glass smashed on a rock; broken is the drum which once spread the good news, and my ears now hear only the drumbeat of separation.

In his passion for the girl, Majnun 'no longer knew what was good and what was evil and could not distinguish the one from the other. Through every tent rang out his cry: "Layla . . . Layla."'

Eric wrote the song at his home. 'The words and the music [percussionist and drummer Jim Gordon helped] came very quickly,' he recalls. He planned and wrote the song with a ruthless, romantic determination that it should reach Pattie and declare, fully, that he needed her.

LAYLA

What will you do when you get lonely
With nobody waiting by your side
You've been running and hiding much too long
You know, it's just your foolish pride.

Layla, you got me on my knees, Layla,
I'm begging darling please, Layla,
Darling won't you ease my worried mind?

I tried to give you consolation;
When your old man had let you down.
Like a fool, I fell in love with you;
You turned my whole world upside down.

Layla, you got me on my knees, Layla,
I'm begging darling please, Layla,
Darling won't you ease my worried mind?

Let's make the best of the situation
Before I finally go insane.
Please don't say we'll never find a way
And tell me all my love's in vain.

'I remember writing the song, finishing the album with the Dominos, and then having to go back to record the vocal part of "Layla",' says Eric. 'We'd finished all the other tracks, so I invited Pattie's sister Paula to come and hear me sing "Layla" for the first time. When she heard that vocal, she packed her bags and left my home in great distress. Because she realized it was about Pattie and that I'd been using her, I suppose.'

By now, the Dominos were no longer living at Eric's home. The band had moved to a flat in South Kensington. Visiting the theatre in London with Robert Stigwood, to see the play *Oh! Calcutta!*, Eric spotted Pattie across the theatre – and George was not present. Clapton swapped seats with a stranger sitting next to her. 'And after the show, I took her off to the Dominos' flat for the night.'

Clandestine meetings at Eric's home followed. He played her the whole of the *Layla* album and gave her the book which inspired the song. 'When you do that to a woman, their emotions get so confused by your own presence that they hear it but they don't receive it properly. I remember her saying she took it as a great compliment, but who can say what was going through her mind? I've always found that when I've written songs for Pattie, it gets too heavy for her to cope with.'

Pattie remembers: 'He played "Layla" to me two or three times. His intensity was both frightening and fascinating, really. I was taken aback. It was a very powerful record. I hadn't read the book, although I'd also been given it by the same man who had presented it to Eric. I recall Eric telling me that I had to read it because he identified very strongly with the leading character. I was puzzled; flattered, shocked, amazed. I knew his feelings were strong for me, but I had no idea it would run to him writing a song for me.'

It attracted Pattie to him, initially at least, and they had an affair, in which Pattie made occasional visits to Eric's house. 'But I felt terrible guilt. He kept insisting I should leave George and go and live with him. I said I couldn't. I got cold feet. I couldn't bear it.'

Pattie became so tense and worried about the situation that she stopped seeing Eric. At what she told him must be their final encounter at his home, he applied dramatic emotional blackmail. 'I told her that either she came with me, or I hit the deck. I actually presented her with a packet of heroin and said: "If you don't come with me, I'm taking this for the next couple of years." And I did. I put dreadful, dreadful pressure on her but I couldn't help myself. I really could not visualize life without her. Well, the pressure from me must have been so great that she went back and closed herself back into Friar Park and George.'

In the wake of Blind Faith, Eric's career followed a jagged if eclectic path. As if to exorcize his past role as other people's 'God' inside Cream and Blind Faith, Eric virtually buried himself as a sideman. He appeared in the never-seen Rolling Stones *Rock 'n' Roll Circus* film; he jammed with the greatest players in a supersession at Staines, just outside London (jazz multi-instrumentalist Roland Kirk, blues guitar star Buddy Guy who would become a firm friend, guitarist/drummer Buddy Miles, guitarist Stephen Stills and others); and he guested on George Harrison's hugely successful triple album, *All Things Must Pass*.

He went on tour with Delaney and Bonnie Bramlett, the gifted husband-and-wife team whom he had first seen in America when touring with Cream, and who had opened the concerts for the Blind Faith tour. On the road, Delaney and Bonnie and Friends seemed like one long jam-session, with some of the cream of American musicianship inside the band: Bobby Keys and Jim Price (horns), Carl Radle (bass) and Jim Gordon (drums). George Harrison chased them for the Beatles' Apple label, and for about a year, among the top rock musicians, they were the most fashionable name around.

People began to mutter darkly that Clapton was submerging himself alongside others too much, particularly on his first solo album. This bore the title Eric Clapton, but most of the songs were co-written with Delaney. Only when he was allowed to stretch out on his own, in a song called 'Easy Now', with a light, appealing vocal, did his identity come through.

Even deeper moves into solitude followed. Next, Eric decided to try to go on tour incognito as Derek and the Dominos to test the reaction of audiences in small clubs throughout Britain, who were not expected to guess that the leader was famous. Here was another identity-seeking move. The musicians were the same as Delaney and Bonnie's good-time boogie unit: bassist Carl Radle, organist Bobby Whitlock and drummer Jim Gordon. The music was good, if unspectacular, and the grassroots return to the club circuit achieved what Eric wanted.

But the disguise was a failure: everybody knew it was Clapton playing games. His record company, wanting maximum publicity, even showered 'Derek is Eric' badges on the music industry. By the time the band hit the road, people were talking and writing about 'Eric Clapton's new band, Derek and the Dominos . . .'

On the afternoon of 18 September 1970, Eric was wandering around London's West End and went into an instrument shop. On the wall hung a left-handed Fender Stratocaster guitar. Eric bought it on sight, as a gift for one of his dearest friends, Jimi Hendrix. That same night, Eric went to London's Lyceum Ballroom to see a show starring Sly Stone. Jimi was expected to sit in a box opposite Eric's. Clapton took along the special Stratocaster. But Hendrix was not at the concert; next day, Eric learned that he had died that night.

'I was heartbroken. We had a very close, intuitive friendship. People weren't so demonstrative in those days, so we didn't go around saying "I love you man", but the sad thing is that we both acknowledged that we'd be around as musicians and friends for ever and so we didn't have to rush to talk about anything. We never had the serious conversation we both wanted, but there was a great empathy.'

The two men had spent magical jam-sessions together in Greenwich Village during Cream's tours: 'We'd virtually take over a club for a guitar duel, then move on for a jam to someone's house. Great days.'

It had been a mere nine days before Hendrix's death that, preparing the Derek and the Dominos album (*Layla and Other Assorted Love Songs*) Eric had performed Hendrix's song 'Little Wing'. Analysing the rapport between them that never fully reached a deep friendship, Eric says: 'We were both similar at the time, both very, very shy. Yet at the same time we both recognized how far away from the rest of the musical community we were and how much we wanted to be more that way. And so there was an acknowledged brotherhood and feeling of spiritual akin-ness which you could detect but wouldn't mention.'

The rock world bitterly mourned the loss of an original, shining star whose work, like Clapton's, was rooted in the blues. Although Hendrix's death was linked with drugs, the London inquest recorded an open verdict. It was stated that there was no evidence to suggest Hendrix had been a drug addict or that he had been depressed. Medical evidence showed that death had been caused by inhalation of vomit due to barbiturate intoxication. Eric, badly hit by the death of an inspirational musician, nevertheless did not attend the funeral. He feared that it would be a 'showbiz event'. Throughout his life, Clapton's mourning for close friends or relatives has always been very private and swift. But that should not be misconstrued as heartless; it is his own way of handling his grief.

After Jimi died, Eric felt 'very, very angry'. He says: 'Nobody could be blamed, but I felt incredible fury. I just had this terrible, lonely feeling. I loved Jimi, and his music, and I'd played with him ... and because everybody was talking about him, I'd keep running into these young kids playing guitar like him, saying to me "Have you heard this one? I can do a Hendrix." It made me feel sick. I just turned away from them and said to myself: "Forget it, mate. It's all been *done*."'

Eric's awe of Hendrix's work was summarized in an interview he gave to London's *Q* magazine in March, 1994. 'If the cards were down I would have to admit that, even then, what I was doing was just nowhere compared with what he was doing. But I kidded myself along that we were on a par.' This is a combination of modesty and heresy, characteristics Eric often uses to keep his ego checked. Superb though Hendrix was, his acrobatic panache was not comparable with Clapton's articulacy and soulful verve, when set free as a guitarist and, later, as a singer and songwriter.

Six weeks after the death of Jimi Hendrix, Derek and the Dominos were on tour in America when a phone call from Robert Stigwood gave Eric the news: his grandfather had been taken to a clinic in Guildford with suspected cancer. Clapton cancelled a press reception for his new group and flew home; Jack Clapp died shortly afterwards, aged sixty.

'It was a traumatic experience,' recalls Eric, 'mainly because of what it did to Rose. Not me so much, because I'd departed from Ripley and I felt my role in their situation was more of a benefactor than anything else. But my love had always been there, very deeply, for Rose. I was very broken up for her when Jack died. My caring was purely for her and not for me, in a cold sort of way. From my early teens, I felt I'd established a way of being, and thinking, and staying, *alone*. I severed all my home ties when I went to live with John Mayall. I had no real attachment to Ripley in my late teens and early twenties. I felt gratitude to Rose and Jack for raising me, you know, but little more. But when Jack died, it cut me up for her.'

It would be too simplistic to say that Eric plunged into his long, silent reclusive period after those two deaths. But it is certain that they contributed to the deep-seated soul-searching that was affecting him. Aged twenty-five, with the world at his feet, he went home and closed the door. From the end of December 1970 until the beginning of 1973, the only time he ventured out

with his guitar was for the all-star Concert for Bangladesh, organized by George Harrison, at New York's
Madison Square Garden on 1 August 1971. The attraction of playing with a band of old friends, including Bob
Dylan, was a contributory factor in forcing Eric out of
hibernation. But his playing at the concert was unsteady.
The miracle was that he was on stage at all. I attended
the concert and remember thinking that Eric had, in a
sense, achieved what he wanted: he had become a
sideman in a band of stars, yet the New York audience's
applause for him was loud and clear. The world was
unaware that Eric was passionately in love with the wife
of the ex-Beatle who had lured Eric on to that stage.

Eric's descent into the long, three-year darkness of hard
drugs and silence will haunt him for ever. He and Alice
were barricaded from the world. He and hundreds of
other people both close to him and distant will always
attempt to explain why and how he became a recluse at
his home, insulting and rejecting his dearest friends and
relatives. Eric is both the best and the worst expert on
the subject; the wide-eyed, alert Clapton of today looks
back on the period as an essential – if dangerous –
diversion. He wanted to enter the tunnel in order to
come out the other side, triumphantly. He had to ape
the habits of some of his blues heroes. He *had* to
experiment and over-indulge himself in drugs, he says,
for several reasons: as a kind of heroism, to push himself
to the brink and to emerge having proved to himself and
others that he could survive; because the rock lifestyle,
the headiness of Cream and fame, and the fashion of
drugs in the late 1960s had endorsed it; because of his
unrequited love for Pattie Harrison, as she was then,

married to Beatle George. These things, compounded by the deaths of people close to him on different levels – his grandfather and guitar star Jimi Hendrix – seemed to hammer home to Eric at that time the pointlessness of rock stardom. But he greatly regrets the loss of time spent in a heroin vacuum.

By contrast, Cream had been a reasonably clean-living band. 'We were incredibly hard-working and, apart from the occasional acid trip and the mild drugs, we were certainly not a group of doped musicians,' says Eric. 'We worked more in the old jazz tradition, I guess; living for the next gig.' He ponders the big question about why he felt the need to go so far down the road with drugs. American musician Leon Russell and George Harrison once went to see him when he was 'smacked out of his mind' on heroin. 'Leon was angry. He demanded to know what the hell I was doing and the only answer I could think of was to say I had to go into the darkness to find out what was in there, and I didn't know what light meant.

'There was definitely a heroic aspect to it. I was trying to prove I could do it and come out alive. At no time did I consider it being suicidal or a shutting down on life. The rejected love affair, the apparent non-availability of Pattie, was certainly a factor. I had to prove to myself that I could do this thing on my own – that I could forget Pattie, survive, and come back from the dead. I still functioned, even though it was not in public. I mean, I had a box full of cassettes at the end of that period. There was me, playing guitar, and I hadn't remembered doing them at all. But I'd been churning out the music; some was usable later . . .'

The road to heroin addiction began almost accidentally. In 1970, with Blind Faith an unsatisfactory memory, the whole of the Derek and the Dominos band lived at Eric's house. 'We played music twenty-four hours a day and then we'd stop and go to sleep, whatever the time, and to live this kind of life, you tend to want a stimulant. We were taking all kinds of mild drugs: marijuana and acid and uppers and downers, and cocaine. And that's where the heroin came in, because the dealer we were usually getting the coke from was insisting that we buy a little bit of heroin with it, because that was his stock-in-trade as well, and he couldn't off-load it. So he said we'd have to buy a gramme of coke and a gramme of heroin as well.

'No one wanted to go near the heroin. And from being close to other musicians I knew it was dangerous. But the problem was that I had a drawer with most of the drugs in, and this pile of heroin was building up and up. And so, one day, I just became too curious for my own good. And I liked it. I was a quick learner. I didn't puke. In fact, I thoroughly enjoyed it and I thought, well, this isn't so bad. When it wore off, I didn't feel too bad either, and so I did it for maybe a year, very infrequently, also doing lots of coke and lots of other drugs and drinking as well.' The heroin habit grew, though. 'It became once every two weeks, then once a week, then two or three times a week, then every day . . . so it was insidious. It crept up on me without me really being aware of it.'

All the negotiating with drug dealers was done by Alice, something she now regrets. 'I remember when we went to New York in 1971 for George Harrison's Bangladesh concert, I was desperately running around that city trying to score some heroin for Eric. And I remember thinking how stupid it was for me, even then. I did that for him, and for myself, for three years. It was probably childish to be over-protective, but I thought it helped him not to have to face the full horror, himself, of scoring his own heroin supply. It might have been better, I can see now, to let him do it and learn the difficulty of it firsthand. Then he'd know, like I learned, the degradation of the dealing. But then, you see, Eric's able to give himself into other people's hands for a limited spell of time, and give himself *totally*, if he thinks it will tide him over a problem. If it hadn't been me doing the scoring for him, it would have been someone else.'

As the Dominos drifted apart as a working unit, and one by one left his house, Eric and Alice sank deeper into an addiction to heroin. The cost was high, financially as well as in human terms; before long, Eric was operating a 'cover-up' system with his office. The hundreds of pounds he was getting from the office, legitimately, was not enough to buy heroin, since he was spending about £1,500 a week on it. Gradually, he began pawning his precious guitars, through the drug pusher.

At his home, throughout Eric's period of addiction, the phone rang continually and nobody answered. For two years Eric was seldom seen, even by his close friends and relatives. The word was out that he was ill, heavily into drugs, or just wanted retirement from the dizziness of being hailed as the world's greatest rock guitarist. All three theories were correct.

His old friend, Ben Palmer, back in wood-carving but surprised at the lack of postcards which used to arrive from a 'normal' Eric, decided to visit Clapton Towers, as his home was nicknamed, to find out why the phone was not answered. 'I had no experience of drugs and wasn't prepared for the vehemence. I went in virtually saying: "Well, Eric, you're not going to live long now. You're going to die soon." I felt impotent, but he was furious that I had even broached the subject.

'It was the worst experience I'd encountered. I saw a man who was very dear to me, and he was clearly killing himself. I felt I had no part to play and I also felt guilty at not having gone down there before, when he began with drugs. Eric had *always* been lonely as a man, even though he had good friends – but nobody, dare I say, like me who went back a long way and he knew loved him as a bloke instead of as a famous rock star. I felt terrible guilt that I'd not been around to stop him going down. I probably couldn't have achieved that, but I'd have tried. First time I went to his home, I couldn't even get inside. No reply from the front door. I knew he was in. Second time, Alice opened the door, but Eric made me feel like an intruder. I've since heard this is a typical heroin user's behaviour. Very antisocial, very cross with anyone who's straight.'

The guilt caused by his deflating of one of his closest friends touches Eric's conscience. 'The surprising thing about heroin,' says Eric, 'is that you believe you can make yourself invisible. The minute your eyelids begin to droop, there is no one else in the room. You may be in a room full of people, and they may be concerned about you, but you neither care nor feel anything about them.

'Yes, I do remember the situation Ben describes. I can see him now, coming down the drive, and presumably he'd come all the way from Wales. I think I was on my own, upstairs, and I was stoned on smack. I was annoyed he'd come to see me because he required a me that wasn't there, a straight me, a compassionate me, a friend. He wanted to see his old friend, and his friend wasn't here. And I was desperately ashamed of this. So I hid upstairs while he stayed for a long, long time. By instinct,

I knew he stayed downstairs for hours and I couldn't face him. I've lived with the guilt ever since and always will. Even though it was a small thing, I now realize what that rejection meant to Ben. Actually, it's amazing that I can think back and remember that shame, because heroin should have blotted that out as well. But it doesn't. People can look at you with fear, concern and pity . . . and their grief means nothing to you, because you feel all right, you're in this shell. You don't need anybody. All you need is that powder.'

Eric never injected himself with heroin. The survival instinct told the inner man that injection was the most slippery route of all. But heroin in powder form, for inhaling, costs much more than that bought for injection. 'Heroin,' Clapton continues, 'feeds on the nerve centres that make you selfish. You don't take the drug because you're selfish, but you do become selfish because of it.' Eric credits Alice with steering him away from any possibility of injecting heroin, but she says categorically: 'I don't think Eric would have injected; it was available a couple of times, but Eric would have said no.' The danger was always there, though, she emphasized: there could be no guaranteed avoidance, because the need for a heroin supply was a 'twenty-four hour preoccupation. When you know it is not around, you are in so much pain.' Even if Eric had tried the needle once or twice, 'he would never had become habitual with it,' Alice asserts, 'because he is a survivor.'

Another unwelcome visitor to Eric's house was his mother, Pat. Visiting England from Germany, where she lived at the time, she too was puzzled by the hermit-like behaviour of her son. She went to the house, got inside, and sat talking to Alice in the kitchen for several hours. Eric, upstairs, did not feel he looked physically presentable enough to meet his mother. 'I cried a bit on the way back to Ripley,' says Pat. 'I thought he was killing himself, and what could I do? I sat for hours and hours and hours waiting to see him. But nothing.'

It was tough, too, on Rose. He visited her infrequently during the two years, and when he did occasionally arrive, with Alice, she could not believe her eyes. 'He'd stand in the doorway, looking tired out. "Hi," he'd say. It didn't seem like Rick. I thought, Oh God, he's drunk. Then my daughter said: "Mum, he's on drugs. I can see it in his eyes." I used to really pray, get down on my hands and knees and say my prayers for Rick. I tried to talk to him once when he came round here with Alice. He just laughed, and that made me feel a lot worse.'

'Most of my family guessed what was going on, but Rose didn't,' says Clapton's Uncle Adrian. 'Those of us who went to see him, like his mother Pat and me, felt aggrieved because every time we arrived Alice would say sorry, he's upstairs in bed asleep.' Eric occasionally made the effort to visit Rose, who had by then left Ripley for a house in another Surrey village, Shamley Green. 'I saw him there a few times,' recalls Adrian Clapton. 'We knew he wasn't well. He was in a vague dream most of the time. It was sad to see him like that.'

The relationship between Pete Townshend and Eric Clapton has always been musically grudging but personally respectful. Eric liked the Who, but it wasn't strictly his kind of music. Pete's early view of blues playing by white people was cynically dismissive. 'I thought that young British white boys emulating black American music was too funny for words. So I always felt a bit superior, and Eric felt a bit superior to me, I believe, in the mid 1960s.' Still, they were both articulate and committed, and a kind of trust developed. 'During the psychedelic period we started to see quite a lot of each other because of the atmosphere that prevailed in London,' recalls Pete. 'We were mixing with a lot of the same people. We socialized a fair bit and went to see Pink Floyd a couple of times together because we both had a passion for Syd Barrett. Then we got a bit closer during the Murray the K show in New York, when the Who and Cream were together on the bill. But in 1969, after Cream finished, he disappeared completely from my life.'

One year later, the two men met when Derek and the Dominos were recording at the Olympic Studios in Barnes, London. 'It was strange. He obviously had some cash-flow problem, because he was *selling guitars*. Actually *selling guitars* to people who would buy them. [Eric denies this.] Then I heard why – from Bob Pridden, the Who's senior sound man, whose wife went to school with Alice Ormsby-Gore. Bob said Eric had a drug problem. That's why he was selling guitars, to raise ready cash to buy dope.' Townshend had no such problem. He had renounced drugs in 1967, in favour of the spiritual teachings of Meher Baba, who reached out to Townshend in the way that the Maharishi Mahesh Yogi's transcendental meditation had briefly captivated the Beatles.

Clapton's guitar-selling incident preceded his three-year period of seclusion. Townshend would be the last to claim that he alone pulled Eric back from the precipice – 'The only person who can stop a person being a junkie is the junkie,' Pete says forcefully. But while Eric was down, he was one of the few visitors allowed access to Eric's home. Townshend was appalled by the indignity of the slope down which Clapton was sliding. And by now, Pete, always a conscientious spokesman on the force of rock, had witnessed the rapid death toll of old friends: Rolling Stone Brian Jones, Beatles manager Brian Epstein, Jimi Hendrix, American singer Janis Joplin, and too many others.

In late 1971 and throughout 1972, Townshend endured what he describes as 'the terrible strain of seeing what was happening with Eric and feeling pretty powerless'. Townshend had never used heroin; he had 'a couple of belts' at cocaine, which had done nothing for him; but he knew enough of heroin addiction to realize that Eric was in a deep mess.

'I was having to answer hysterical phone calls from Alice practically every night. She always wanted me to go over there. It was an hour and a half's drive, and always at awkward hours of the night. When I got there, usually she just wanted to explain what was happening. Eric would be asleep somewhere and she would be running around hysterically. What was worrying her, what she needed to talk about, was that she was giving Eric all of her heroin supply, most unselfishly. And then she was having to deal with Eric's extremely selfish outbursts accusing her of doing the *reverse*. He kept alleging she was keeping the best for herself.' Alice, emphasizing that she handed over her supply to Eric, said to me, 'When you love someone, you do . . .'

'It was a typical junkie scene,' Townshend continues. 'It was despicable. But even through all that, you know, I got to like and love them both very much. It was the first encounter I'd had with heroin addicts. I wasn't prepared for the lies, I wasn't prepared for the duplicity . . . but even through all that, I decided they definitely seemed to me to be worth the effort.'

Says Alice: 'I always thought Pete was one of the most extraordinary, intuitive and intellectual people around. I needed him so that someone besides me could see what Eric was like in his attitude towards me'.

Eric and Alice were together for about four years before and after his brief association with Paula Boyd, but Eric says, 'Three of those were spent under the influence of heroin, and Alice and I never communicated at all – only to have an argument. And although we had some good times, I'd never describe it as head-over-heels in love. All the time I was with Alice, I was mentally with Pattie. My love for Pattie began almost the first day I saw her, and grew in leaps and bounds.' His brief fling with Pattie's younger sister, Paula, he reflected to me later, 'really was a case of a surrogate Pattie in my mind. Alice was really on the rebound, when I was waiting to build up some plan of action to get Pattie.

'But it was a very solid, good, working relationship. Alice understood me very well and I understood her. We worked together to be happy. In spite of the fact that a good amount of the time we were stoned, we still managed to function together as a couple. We had a very good rapport. She's a very intelligent girl. The one thing that kind of kept us apart was her low estimation of her abilities, which I always find difficult to deal with in other people. If people have a low opinion of themselves, I get very short-tempered. Because I often think that it's a front or that it's an adopted stance to gain attention. And often it isn't, obviously. It's deeply based. But I've never got any patience with that and that was one thing that kept us very distant.'

Alice agrees that her lack of self-esteem infuriated Eric

so much that it created a barrier. But she does not concede that their relationship was not a love affair. 'I can't go along with him on that,' says Alice. 'Maybe because I was only seventeen I wrongly thought of it as mutual. My extreme youth made any rational analysis of the situation impossible.' Whatever Eric's verdict now on their relationship, Alice declares, 'I was in love with him, most definitely.'

Soon after her return in the autumn from her Israeli holiday, by which time the Dominos spree was over, Alice took on all the shopping and cooking for the house. She recalls that she was 'subliminally' aware that Eric was thinking of Pattie for a great part of her time with him. 'When he first fell in love with Pattie, he was very open to me about it, but as the years went by he was very quiet on the subject.' But Alice remembers realizing that Pattie was still very much on his mind.

It would be wrong to think of Clapton's three-year self-imposed monastic existence as that of a junkie incapable of assessing what was happening. 'Mentally, I was totally aware of what was going on, what I was doing to myself, and I was not lying in bed all day long taking H.'

Alice recalls that Eric often rose at four in the afternoon and casually played his guitar most days. They were not a reclusive couple for the entire three years: 'We went to London quite often, and made weekend trips to Rose at her home not far away and Eric would enjoy a game of badminton in her garden. It wasn't all sitting at home getting full of smack. We were both completely aware of ourselves, and he was very aware of how the house looked.' They even flew, at Pete Townshend's invitation, to a Who concert in Paris in October 1972. 'Eric's condition was much more worrying to outsiders than it was to him. I could see that he knew he was all right and going to come through it all. But anyone seeing him would think he was on the road to being finished. That was the difference,' Alice says.

One afternoon in 1972, Pete Townshend received a surprise phone call from Eric asking him to the house. He had an eight-track recording studio, he said, and he wanted Pete's help in completing some work he had begun with Derek and the Dominos. 'They'd done four or five tracks, which we sat and played through, but they weren't quite *there*,' says Pete. 'My job was to try to revive his interest, engineer, produce, finish the records off. But by the time I got there, he was very, very unwilling. He vacillated tremendously. He gave me all sorts of excuses. He sent me off to write lyrics for the songs, look for new material – anything to stop me doing what he knew should be done.

'Then he took me into the little sub-sitting-room, the room where he used to listen to short-wave radio all night and where I'd sat with him on many occasions for hours and hours, talking.' Eric's only real diversion during his two years of 'retirement' had been making models of aeroplanes and cars. But such was his condition that he had trouble focusing his eyes on the intricacy of the work.

'Finally, in that little room, he announced it to me: "Look, I'm a junkie. That's why I'm having such difficulty."

'I answered: "Look, I *know*" – and Eric was flabbergasted.

'"God, did you *know*?"

'"I know," I replied, "that's why I came down here so often – to try and help you get active again."

'"Oh God," said Eric, "I thought I was hiding it really well."'

He seemed, recalls Townshend, dismayed that *anybody* knew – mostly because his dignity had suffered.

Eric's manager, Robert Stigwood, played what Clapton considers to have been a role of 'discretion, wisdom and benevolence' during the three years of addiction, during which Eric hardly moved out of his house. 'He had been a very big part of my life and career. He was the mirror we looked into when we went to him with the Cream idea, and he said yes, it would work. I love him as a man, and he must have known me well to handle my drug period so carefully. He stayed totally in the background and made sure I got enough money so that I didn't end up selling all my possessions, or hit the streets. I made very open appeals to the office for money, which was obviously for drugs.' Eric says that Stigwood did not visit his home once during his smack period.

Lord Harlech, Alice's father, also played a particularly supportive role. Eric recalls: 'He'd appealed to Alice many times and I think he'd tried to appeal to me, but he was a perfect gentleman and a sweet human being. He did write me a threatening letter which must have cost him a great deal. It said that if I didn't either leave his daughter alone or give up the drugs and make sure that she gave up the drugs, he would turn me in to the police. And for someone like him to say something like that must have required a great deal of effort. Then, after that, he was very supportive. He was always the kindest man. We got on very well.' Eric visited him twice to discuss his situation and also went to see Alice's sister, Victoria, in Wales.

Lord Harlech masterminded the major step towards public rehabilitation. He asked Townshend to put together a concert in London which would benefit a charity which he, Lord Harlech, supported. Eric would be persuaded to take part, as a major return to work; it would be the ultimate cure.

Pete remembers that Eric was particularly cooperative when the idea was put to him that he should appear at a special concert at London's Rainbow Theatre on 13 January 1973. Ten days of rehearsal were arranged at the house of guitarist Ronnie Wood, at Hampton Court, Surrey. Many people believed Clapton had not touched his guitar in two years. Despite Eric's pretence, the players – in fact most of the music industry – suspected that he had been in a private hell. Villagers near his home said he had not been seen for more than two years.

Eric's ability to tune himself mentally into disciplined rehearsal work surprised Townshend. 'The drugs were flowing very freely among the musicians, and I think Eric upped his intake of heroin – he stopped trying to substitute it with other things, which he had been doing to try to pull himself round. But his togetherness was a surprise and a great pleasure to see . . . He was very, very strong, authoritative and confident,' says Townshend, 'and when anybody voiced any doubts, like "Oh God, how am I going to remember all these chords?" he'd say: "Oh, don't worry, it's easy, you know. They're simple songs." Somebody said: "This song isn't going to work live," but Eric was positive in attitude. "Yes, it *is*," he'd say. "Don't worry. It's going to be *good*."

'He retained his dignity for the rehearsals. We were all very impressed. The only pushing I had to do at the rehearsal was of Steve Winwood. He came the first day, played beautifully and Eric was absolutely inspired to have him around. Everybody was. He was an important catalyst. Second day, he didn't come.' Townshend, furious, berated Winwood on the phone: 'Listen, if you don't want to come, don't, but don't piss us about. Get over here now, or tell us all to fuck off. We can take it either way . . .' Townshend says there was stunned silence at the other end. 'Maybe I'd taken a sledgehammer to crack a nut, but Steve does have to be bullied. Anyway, he came back.' Winwood's presence was crucial to Clapton's continuing confidence.

The word was out for the concert: Clapton's comeback after two years of hibernation which people would not discuss was going to be tense. Could he still play? What would he look like? There was an all-star turnout for the band of young veterans: Clapton, Townshend and Ronnie Wood (guitars), Rick Grech (bass), Steve Winwood (keyboards) and Jim Capaldi (drums). Harvey Goldsmith was the promoter. In the audience sat George Harrison and Ringo Starr, Elton John, Rory Gallagher, Joe Cocker, Jimmy Page and Ahmet Ertegun, whose Atlantic Records had championed Clapton through happier times.

Backstage, the tension and worry by the organizers was palpable. Five minutes before the start of the first show, Clapton had not arrived. Robert Stigwood said to Pete Townshend: 'Pete, pray.' Townshend recounts the story:

'I said: "No, Robert, *you* pray. He's your artist."

'Robert said: "Look, if I pray, He won't listen."

'So I went out on the stairs alone at the back of the Rainbow and I said, twice: "Please God, make Eric come before the show . . ."'

That morning, Eric had woken up thinking he had lost his voice. But it was sheer nerves; he knew too much depended on his arrival that night. One minute before the start of the concert, he arrived with Alice. Breathlessly, Stigwood asked him why he was so late. His white suit, which he hadn't worn for two years, needed letting out, said Eric. He had to wait for Alice to get out her sewing machine and let out the waist of his trousers. Clapton had gained quite a lot of weight during his addiction. 'I ate like a horse, mostly junk food and chocolate, especially.' On stage, his waistcoat buttons would not meet.

The security arrangements were intense as the crowd leaving the first show met the second house crowd. Even Eric's mother had trouble persuading the backstage officials who she was. A mighty roar went up when a confident Eric, showing none of his nervousness, took the stage. From the opening wail of 'Layla', it was evident that Clapton was not going to be a passenger in an all-star band. When Winwood sang 'Nobody Knows You When You're Down and Out', Eric played a solo that almost wept with emotion. They drew powerful applause for Jimi Hendrix's beautiful song 'Little Wing', and played other Cream, Traffic and Clapton solo songs. During the much-loved 'Let It Rain', one of Eric's strings broke, but he ploughed on relentlessly, the string swinging from the neck of his guitar. At midnight they played 'Key to the Highway' and 'Crossroads', an apt title and song to match the occasion, and they encored as the show had begun, with 'Layla'. On every level – creative, organizational and as an event packed with emotion – the Clapton comeback was a triumph. Inwardly, though, Eric hated every moment of it . . .

because it was just a 'showbiz occasion' such as he usually shunned.

Addicts of any kind of drug stand in a doorway at a certain moment, and have to decide whether to retreat and continue with their habit, or whether to step out of the doorway into the daylight. The Rainbow Theatre concert did not cure Eric; he was still addicted to drugs when he went on, and came off, the stage. But it was a powerful axis on which he could think about reshaping his life. The performance had renewed his confidence in his ability to play. From the stage, above the applause, Eric said of Townshend: 'Thank the man who got me to come up here because I wouldn't have done it without him.' Eric says now: 'Pete has been very close, and I owe him a lot. The reason for that is that he really took a lot of time to help out, because he thought I was worth it, and I didn't think I was. He gave me faith in myself again.'

Townshend, though, is typically analytical about his role in Eric's return. 'He knew it was not something I'd done for him alone. He knew it was something I'd done partly for me, and partly for the dignity of the British music industry. That's why, quite rightly, he's never got down on his hands and knees and thanked me. He knew I'd get lots of credit in time, and that all I'd done was respond to a bit of a crisis. I don't pretend to have been any more humane, caring or compassionate than any of the other people involved. There was Lord Harlech; Alice, who we all realized later on had practically given her own life through using any substitute for heroin that she could lay her hands on, rather than deprive Eric of any of his drug. There were so many other people in the background . . .'

In the audience at the Rainbow sat Paul and Linda McCartney. 'I hope his touring plan comes off,' Paul said later. 'He played fine at the Rainbow, but touring would be the best thing for him. It will make it all less precious from the "We are coming to witness a legend" thing and change from "We are coming to witness a legend" into "We're going to see a band", and it makes it much nicer. I do think Eric needs to play in public a lot more, just to kind of ease up the pressure. At the Rainbow, the compère came on and said: "He's here!" Yes, we knew he was there; we'd come to see him!'

Eric believed that, musically, he had lost nearly three years of his life. But soon after he saw daylight, he found the pile of cassettes at home on which he had recorded some of his idle strumming. One song, particularly, which ended up as 'Give Me Strength', demonstrated both the turmoil and the faith within Eric during his lost period.

GIVE ME STRENGTH

Dear Lord, give me strength to carry on.
Dear Lord, give me strength to carry on.
My home may be out on the highway,
Lord I've done so much wrong,
But please give me strength to carry on.

All Eric's and Alice's friends knew that several urgent moves were crucial if they were to gain permanent advantages from the initiatives taken by Lord Harlech and Pete Townshend. First, Eric would have to be willing to undergo a medical cure. Secondly, a split from Alice would be essential if both were to survive.

Alice has kept the letter from her father to Eric in which he pleaded with Clapton to seize control of his drugs problem before it was too late. Written in August 1973, Lord Harlech's letter ran:

> I love you both so much that I cannot bear to see what you are doing to yourselves. For all that you can do and all you can have in your lives, please let me help you . . . you can paint and draw art, you can travel the world. Look what you have before you. I will probably never know how much courage it will take, dear Eric, but for your own sake, please do it.

The sincerity of the message from this man whom he admired enormously struck home with Eric, but he was addicted. He was inhaling a minimum of two grammes of heroin a day, sometimes double that amount – an extremely large quantity. He drank very little, perhaps wine with dinner, but physically he was in no state to respond instantly to David Harlech's supplications. By February 1974, he knew he was plunging back down in the abysss. Heroin was costing him incalculable sums and he was drifting aimlessly, squandering his resources and his talent. His financial mess was exceeded only by his physical state. He sat around for days, weeks, months on end, eating vast amounts of the chocolate which addicts crave. He vanished upstairs when anyone arrived. Nobody, particularly his family and best friends, was allowed to see him at his worst.

Lord Harlech moved determinedly. Eventually, Eric arrived at the Harley Street home of Dr Meg Patterson. The quietly spoken doctor, a no-nonsense Scot with a medical degree from Aberdeen University, a Fellow of the Royal College of Surgeons and holder of the MBE for outstanding medical work in India, seemed an unlikely guru for Eric Clapton. Many requests for him to go and seek treatment for his heroin addiction had been stonewalled: the obstinacy of the addict, combined with guilt and Eric's inborn suspicion, made him reluctant to offer himself for help. After the Rainbow 'comeback' concert, a full year passed during which Eric virtually retreated into his old habits of seclusion and addiction.

An unusual feature of Meg Patterson's treatment was that she practised neuro-electric therapy, as she called it, a new form of acupuncture in which electric current penetrates the ear lobes. The doctor's memories of her first encounters with Eric and Alice are insightful into the mind of Clapton the addict. First, Meg said she would have to establish whether Eric was willing to be treated; a time was set for Eric, then twenty-eight, and Alice, then twenty-one, to visit the Harley Street home and base where Meg Patterson lived with her husband George, who worked with her, and their three children. Meg and her husband had little idea of Clapton's fame, having only recently returned from ten years in Hong Kong.

Predictably, Eric and Alice were half an hour late for their evening meeting with Meg. 'Drug addicts are nearly always late,' says Meg. 'And they're usually so terrified of even thinking about treatment that they always come full of their particular drug. And, to some extent, unless they've got their drug, they can't behave normally. So, of course, they were stoned on arrival at my home.' The couple found refuge from their fear by playing on the floor with Meg and George's two sons, Shane, twelve, and Lloyd, ten. 'Taking drug addicts into a home where there are children is one of the most therapeutic things you can do,' says Meg. 'The children treated them as if there was nothing exceptional about them, and they were at ease very quickly. So we chatted . . .'

Over a cup of tea, Meg explained to Eric and Alice the concepts of her treatment. 'I told them the techniques were still fairly rough. The only stimulator I had at that time was one that was made in Communist China but which I'd bought in Hong Kong. At that time, I was also still using tiny acupuncture needles. They were applied, I told them, into the saucer-shaped hollow, the contour, of the ears, on a little clip. The Chinese stimulator I used on Eric was about ten inches by five inches by two inches deep. You could carry it in your hand, it is connected by wires to the clips, which I'd invented myself. It was like a clip-on earring. But because there was a needle in it, I could still only use it for at most an hour at a time, three times a day.' It wasn't painful, but not comfortable either: no night treatments were possible, because 'you couldn't sleep with that thing stuck in your ear,' says Meg. The nights, therefore, tended to be very bad, because they received no treatment at all.

Guardedly, Eric agreed to a next step after Meg's exploratory conversation: she told him she would have to move into his home with him for an extensive week of treatment.

The first problem came from a nurse who accompanied Meg to Eric's home: an evangelical Christian, she began preaching at Eric and Alice, who nearly ejected her and Meg on the spot. After she had been reproached by Meg, the nurse stopped preaching. 'The first day we were there, things were very tight. But I think Eric realized we had gone there with a genuine desire to help, and he became more open and responsive. Initially, he had been very very cautious indeed towards us.'

Alice loved Eric so deeply that she was giving him as much heroin as she could get hold of. To compensate herself for the heroin she was missing, she was drinking heavily: at least two bottles of vodka every day. Meg's first demand was tough: Eric and Alice would have to stop using heroin immediately and totally. 'All drugs were banned from the start of the treatment,' she says. 'I knew there was no heroin in the house because I saw Eric and Alice scraping among the fibres of the carpet to see if they could pick up a few grains. We had the cooperation of Lord Harlech, and Eric's manager Robert Stigwood, who said he wouldn't give them any money to buy it; Eric and Alice didn't have to leave the house to do anything.'

Eric loosened up in conversation with Meg and her husband George, who went down to the house to reinforce her efforts. 'He was desperate, and wanted to try to cure himself,' recalls Meg. Two days after the nurse had tried to lecture him on Christianity, Clapton said to Dr Patterson enigmatically: 'You know, I was converted to Christianity a few years ago . . .'

Eric bared his innermost soul to George Patterson, especially when they discussed religion. This was when Eric revealed that he had become a Christian some years earlier; a Scots-born disc jockey whom he had met in America had converted him. The disc jockey had travelled on a concert tour of the US with Clapton for several months and Eric was particularly grateful that he cared enough for him, and his spirit, to travel with him and nourish his desire to embrace a faith. Eric's friendship with the man, and acceptance of his conviction, was dented when they went together to a New York music business party. Part of the man's Pentecostal beliefs dictated that whenever the spirit moved him, he had to

Above and previous page: A boyhood visit to the seaside; joining the
Yardbirds on stage at London's Marquee in 1964. (*Eric Clapton Collection*)
Honing his craft with the same band; and shaping his facial image that same year.
(*London Features International*)

With his grandmother, Rose, who raised him, outside her Ripley home.
(*Eric Clapton Collection*)

Back with Eric in the Surrey village where she gave birth to him: his mother, Pat.
(*Eric Clapton Collection*)

Above: A moustached Eric upon joining the band in 1966 that was important in shaping his attitude, John Mayall's Bluesbreakers. (*Melody Maker*)

Left: Eric leads the way on a Cream clothes-shopping spree in London with Jack Bruce and Ginger Baker. (*Star File*)

Cream's farewell: Eric at the final concert of the trail-blazing supergroup, Royal Albert Hall, London, November 1968. (*Barrie Wentzell/Star File*)

At a party at London's China Garden restaurant in April 1974, Pete Townshend continues his encouragement of Eric to return to concert work. (*London Features International*)

Left: The recluse: a rare photograph of Eric during his years of silent addiction at his home in Surrey. (*London Features International*)

Opposite page bottom right, and above: With Pattie Boyd (before their marriage) and manager Roger Forrester, Eric prepares for his massive 1974 comeback tour in America. (*London Features International*)

A proud moment for Eric as he joins his lifelong hero and friend, Muddy Waters, at a Chicago concert in 1979. (*Paul Natkin/Star File*)

A sombre visit to the tomb of the unknown warrior during Eric's unhappy visit to Poland for concerts in 1979. (*Chris Horler/ Camera Press*)

say prayers, there and then. At that party, he announced: 'I feel God wants me to pray.' An irreverent rock star chipped in: 'I feel *I* want to pee.' At which point, Eric's 'guru' lost his temper and stormed out. The incident was a major turning point for Eric: he felt that if God could not hold on to a committed believer in that situation, he was no longer so sure of his own wavering faith.

Within a couple of days of Meg and her nurse moving into his house, Eric was opening himself up to her as well. He clearly realized he needed treatment but his customary guardedness, and Meg's inhibition at being in his home for the crucial early stages, made the beginning difficult. Eric baulked at Meg's first instruction that they cut out all drugs immediately. 'Eric's physical condition was getting worse,' says Meg.

'I make all my patients stop taking drugs totally and immediately. Neurotherapy is so different from just coming off the drug that within two or three days the addicts' minds are so clear that we can start our psycho-spiritual counselling.'

There was a fear that Eric might sell his last guitar to get cash for dope, but Meg and George became alerted to this just in time. Says George: 'It was agreed that the symbolism of selling that last guitar would be so import-ant ... life would be finished and he would commit suicide.' No money, no dope and no guitar would be too much. Within three days of Meg's arrival, Eric had changed from desperation for heroin into formulating a new attitude: 'I will do something about my condition.' He drank a little brandy and whisky, but his mind stayed clear. Alice, however, leaned increasingly on neat vodka.

Eric denies that sales of guitars were ever on his mind, despite the recollections of George Patterson and Pete Townshend. Says Eric: 'There were so many guitars here, getting on for two hundred downstairs and in storage, that selling my last guitar would have been out of the question. I recall some talk of selling one of my four cars. That would have made more sense, because selling guitars wouldn't have produced enough money.'

When he eventually conquered heroin and 'saw daylight' in 1974, the full irony of his financial needs during those years came before him in a bizarre discovery. For years Eric and Alice had opened none of the mail arriving at the house. When Pattie moved in in 1974, she discovered 'mail everywhere, with lots of brown envelopes containing about £5,000 in out-of-date cheques'. Eric had not touched any of the letters arriving at his home during that period.

The days were long but Eric busied himself making models. The nights were complicated. 'Neither Eric nor Alice could sleep,' recalls Meg. She and George decided, five days afer she had taken up residency with them, that complete separation of Eric and Alice would be essential if both were to benefit. With some persuasion, Alice went off alone to a clinic for individual treatment, and Clapton went back with Meg and George to their Harley Street home.

There, Meg took delivery of the first model for her self-designed stimulator. But there was an early hitch: before leaving his home, Eric had, unknown to Meg, taken a large dose of methadone, a liquid substitute for heroin. Then came a technical problem: Eric, who was negative and passive all the time, told Meg he had felt no current from her new machine throughout the first day. Alarmed, she traced the fault to a broken wire. Within half an hour of giving him proper treatment, he felt better after a day of being violently ill.

'We check a patient's pupils all the time, and his pupils

were large so I knew he couldn't have had heroin,' she says. But she had not reckoned on Eric's slipping methadone into the mansion. 'Whether they kept it as a fallback I don't know, but I didn't find out until much later that they'd got it. That did set him back a bit, but apart from sleeplessness and his craving for the drug, he responded well to the treatment.' Eric stayed with Meg and George for two weeks, sleeping in the same room as their two young sons on a fold-down bed.

'His sleeplessness was so bad that sometimes I did give him a sleeping pill, which I almost never do because addicts have such a tolerance for drugs that you have to give them a huge dose to make them sleep. So you're in danger of overdosing. Mercifully, he had my two sons with him as supportive company, but he was so utterly passive. One day, in my consulting room when I was seeing other patients, I said: "Eric, could you just make coffee for yourself this morning because I'm so busy?" And he said: "Meg, I don't know how to *make* coffee." He wasn't fibbing. There was nothing there but passivity.

'He wasn't interested in life at all. But it was very strange: the children stimulated him. He would play toy soldiers with the children and spent hours talking to them about music, playing records to them. He even brought up some of his records and tapes and took the boys out and brought them the first rock records they ever possessed. He came to life with the children, but not with anyone else.'

One day, the inquisitive Pete Townshend arrived to visit Eric. He asked for a demonstration of Meg's stimulator and after half an hour he said: 'Yes, this really is doing something for me. I really feel the effects of this.' To which Eric replied: 'It's funny that it's affecting you, yet it doesn't do a thing for me.' So while Pete was there,

Meg told Eric: 'It's time for your treatment.' Eric connected the stimulator to his ears and within twenty minutes was sound asleep, snoring. Because of his night-time sleeplessness, Eric often fell asleep during his machine treatment.

'We tried very hard to ban alcohol,' Meg continues, 'but we had alcohol in the kitchen and you couldn't watch Eric day and night. George and I were busy and Eric was often around on his own. The only time he really had a lot was when George and I had to go out and we left him with our young sons to look after him. We weren't out for long and we had given them our telephone number . . . but Eric had wandered through to the kitchen and had quite a lot of whisky to drink. Poor boys – by the time we got home, Eric was so drunk that when he wanted to go to the bathroom they had to take him, holding an arm each. Eric and the boys were both upset about it afterwards, but this is all part of the experience.'

Inside a month, the week at home followed by slightly more than two weeks at Harley Street with Meg and George, Eric had withdrawn from his heroin addiction. Just before Meg Patterson concluded that he was ready to leave her daily care and return home, he shattered her with an eyeball-to-eyeball statement: 'You know, Meg, even though I'm cured of my heroin addiction just now, the moment I leave this house I'm going to go back on it again.'

She begged him to rethink his attitude. 'Eric, it's as if you're in a prison just now, and you're seeing things from inside your own prison. All I'm asking you to do is come out of your own prison and view it from the outside instead of the inside.'

Eric plucked up courage and said: 'All right, I'll go on with it.' And almost as quickly, he contradicted himself: 'I just can't live without it.' That day, the craving was really bad. 'Look, Meg, I feel that I've just . . . there's something I feel urgently, and that is . . . I've got to feel what heroin is like, again. Already it's so confused in my mind. You know, if you don't let me try it, I'm going to go out and get it somewhere. I've just got this compulsion. I've *got* to try it again.'

Meg says: 'I felt he was at the stage when he would walk out if I didn't let him have it. Remember, I had to balance things the whole time. Treatment of Eric was very difficult at that moment. I said: "All right, Eric, go ahead. Phone the dealer and get some." Eric replied: "Meg, when you were out of the room I phoned the dealer and he wouldn't give it to me."'

This, says Meg, was most unusual. 'Dealers usually come running to give anybody the drugs, because they want the money. But Eric explained to me that the dealer was a very good friend of his and he'd said to Eric: "I'm not going to give you any heroin unless I have Meg's permission." So I said, "All right, I'll phone your dealer."

'So I phoned him and he brought one dose of heroin to my house. Which Eric took. And after that, there was no more problem. He said: "Yes, it was good." But they always say that, those who have done this with or without my permission. In fact, it's always been without my permission. Eric's the only one I gave permission to have a dose.'

Meg Patterson explains that she was partly calling his bluff in allowing him to have a dose, and partly applying logical psychology. 'I felt he really would walk out if I didn't give in on that point. I couldn't be sure, anyway, that he was going to stop taking heroin for ever. You just live one day at a time with addicts. And you get used to the fact that they are liars. I knew that one dose might slow down the process of withdrawal because he was setting himself back again, chemically. But at that point, the greater danger was that he would walk out.' Her method worked, for later, after his initial enthusiasm, Eric said to Meg: 'Well, it was good, but it wasn't like it was before. OK, I'll go on with the treatment.'

Meg has no doubt that if he had not gone for treatment, Eric would have killed himself. 'The impression I got from him was that he was surprised he hadn't already killed himself, but he just hadn't had the courage to do it.' It might not have been heroin that would have killed him, unless he overdosed. 'But Eric had already almost killed himself,' says Meg, 'because in his own effort to come off heroin, he's taken a very large dosage of Mandrax, which is a powerful sleeping pill and a particularly dangerous one. It is banned in Britain now, although you can still get it in America. He very nearly died from that large dose. And I'm sure that either by doing something like that, by overdosing on a more dangerous drug or actually overdosing on heroin, he would have killed himself.'

Significantly, Eric had taken with him to Meg's clinic his acoustic guitar. He told Meg and George he had not touched it for the three years of his drug isolation. This was untrue; but he might not have realized just how much the guitar had helped him pass the time during those long, hard days of heroin-induced torpor. More importantly, his triumph over heroin during his time with Meg heralded another tough crisis inside his head.

Eric firmly believed that through heroin he had lost all his talent, and also all his friends. 'He started strumming his guitar, and whenever he started I used to stop whatever I was doing just to listen to him. Just his strumming was so exquisite, so beautiful. But he really was in a spiritual trauma,' says Meg. 'Part of my treatment was very much instilling in him the will to live. It was desperately difficult. He'd lost all the confidence in his creativity'.

It fell to Meg's husband, George, to deal directly with the mental torment inside Eric that followed the successful departure of heroin from his life. George found himself face to face, night after night, with a man empty and defeated. George Patterson had studied the world's religions, and worked as a missionary and preacher; he had travelled throughout China and Tibet before meeting Meg in India and joining forces with her. He had studied occultism and parapsychological phenomena – and had worked as a journalist for thirty years. 'As far as talking to Eric Clapton went,' says George, 'it was merely a one-to-one situation for me. Here was someone with problems related to how he coped with life. When he said "What's the point of living?" he was talking to someone who had been asking that question for forty years.'

With Clapton, however, there was a difference: Eric said he only wanted to live if he could make music. If he couldn't make music, life offered nothing for him. 'He didn't feel his music was there any more. This was compounded by a guilt complex. Another level of his problem was this: he said the greats of music, who got into the same problem as him, chemically with alcohol or drugs, when they reached the place he was at in life, killed themselves. Jimi Hendrix had died, Janis Joplin too. Charlie Parker, the jazz player, had done it and some of the others in early rock had also done it in their own way. So Eric had a kind of professional as well as a personal guilt complex. He rationalized that their deaths must have come because they felt the same as he did. Artistically, they had exhausted their experience and there was nothing else to give, he said.

'That's the message he gave me. I rejected it on several levels. Ever since I went to China I had moved among people who took drugs . . . opium, especially. You learn never to trust them, ever, anywhere. They're all liars. Totally. Meg is more gentle and better natured than me. I learned the hard-headed way. So Eric to me was just a liar. And I can deal with liars. So when we got talking about it, I knew his argument wasn't strong. I began probing.'

To try to rationalize his negativity, Clapton said drugs had entered his life as a cumulative effect. Three years previously, when he began, he seemed to be losing his gifts and he took more and more drugs to try to stimulate himself and bring back his creativity.

'But when he took drugs and then played back his performance on tape, when he listened objectively, he realized his performance was not so good. So he became increasingly despairing, and this led to tension and contradiction.' The only exception was the performance of 'Layla' by Derek and the Dominos when the band were stoned out of their minds.

'That was the only time he ever thought that under drugs he performed better than when he was not on drugs.' The sheer animal-like power of that song, containing as it does Eric's passionate cry to Pattie Harrison to listen to his love for her, would anyway cloud any objective judgement of his performance.

Put simply, Clapton was telling himself – as many jazz musicians before him – that drugs would improve his performance. The reality was that they didn't; that factor, and the consequent distrust of drugs, caused the problem fermenting in his mind.

'It was all tied up in a mesh of personal guilt, and nothing was clear in Eric's mind. Fear certainly came into it. He had been trying to justify his indulgence to other people as well as to himself. Underneath his conviction that drugs were good for him was a suspicion that this was wrong, so he had been trying to repress that conviction. My conversations with Eric, every day, every night, were on the basis that I knew, and I knew that *he* knew, that the rationale of drugs being good for creativity was bullshit. So when I talked with Eric, I hammered away at that point: "Hey, you know, I don't *believe* you. You *know* you're not doing as well with drugs!"

'I said no aesthetic gift ever came from nothing. It comes from a spiritual experience. I argued that the art produced by Charlie Parker, Beethoven, Bach, Haydn and Mozart came from a spiritual tension, and *never* from a chemical, like a drug. It never did and never will. It might give a whip to a horse, but all it does is give a spurt to something that's already there.' Gradually Patterson's cogent argument won through.

The departure of drugs had stripped away Eric's inhibitions so much, and he spoke so honestly to George Patterson during those two weeks, that it's possible he will never recapture that moment of transparent soul-bearing. Repeatedly, Patterson hammered across his point to Clapton that art and talent came from the spirit, the suffering, the aesthetic, and not from chemical input.

'He'd lie to me about his background, he'd evade everything. But I knew there was much to come from him,' says Patterson.

Clapton led Patterson to believe that the circumstances and events of his early childhood underpinned his problems with drugs. 'His illegitimacy had an impact on him and he felt embarrassed that other kids might get to know about it, or even that he felt they did know. So he withdrew more and more. In fact, he concentrated more and more on learning and he learned music by listening to it. Basically, this was the big thing in his life that had produced various reactions. There were three: one was that he hated his mother; the second was that he wanted to be the best blues player in the world; the third was that he wanted to lay as many women as possible – he wanted to lay a thousand women.

'Now about this statement on his mother – I said the most significant statistic was that all addicts had a bad relationship with their father, or the father was non-existent or weak. That's how his statement came about – I said this meant the mother took the role of the father and became domineering or indulgent.' Eric became fascinated at the unfolding of all this. Nobody had ever talked about or dealt with his feelings, or his parental relationship.

'I said: "As far as I'm concerned, this is where true Christianity comes in, or true religion. It's not a question of whether you become Pentecostal or whether you forgive your mother. That's where healing starts. You hate your mother, but what do you want to do? Lay a thousand women? But with every woman you lay, it will be worse. You get more distant from a real relationship because you're laying them for the wrong reasons – hate, not love. You'll end up not knowing what a relationship is.' (Before his liaison with Alice, Eric's associations with girls throughout his late teenage years had been concentrated mostly into the years when he was with the Yardbirds. Most had been short-lasting physical flings. His confused attitude to women had been gnawing away at him ever since he had realized his dual loyalty to his mother and his grandmother.)

Confronted with George Patterson's cold, hard facts, Eric bristled. He put up some resistance to Patterson's argument, and said he still could not find a way of dealing with the suffering he had endured as a child. The next stage of Patterson's persuasion process advanced this theory: Eric's music had nothing to do with his technical ability to play guitar, or compose, or, with taking heroin. It was what Eric did with his suffering that would be transmuted into his work. 'I told him the biggest composers in the world had always been the people who had the least in the world. The Jews painted and sang. Why? Because they're always under persecution. They, and others, develop the capacity to survive under it. Mozart produced the greatest stuff under persecution. Beethoven too, and he was deaf. It's the spiritual quality of how you cope with suffering that does it.' Eric pondered that one long and hard.

These deep conversations, with Eric conceding very little but listening attentively, took place as George Patterson prepared the evening meal in the kitchen at Harley Street or when Eric was lounging around between treatments. Eric still couldn't sleep and it usually fell to Meg to talk to him at night when he wanted company and conversation. He tended to wake after four hours' sleep. One night, Eric tapped on George and Meg's bedroom door and George opened it. Eric told him he had been having a 'black scene' alone in his bedroom and could not sleep. Sitting on the side of the bed, the two men talked about religious beliefs and George Patterson confessed his own scepticisms. Then he added: 'God has just told me to pray with you.' Open-eyed, he said prayers with Eric while Meg went out to make hot drinks and offer Eric a sleeping pill. He refused. 'OK,' said Eric. 'Where do we go from here?' Patterson's reply was simple and direct. 'There's you and your guitar and there's God. I can only think of two lines: "Lord, for tomorrow and its needs I do not pray, Give me, dear Lord, give me strength for today."' Paterson said he knew of no other solution to life than that. A pensive Eric retired to bed on that note.

Next day, Eric spent hours strumming his guitar. George and Meg noticed him crying. 'He went inside himself, just strumming, never playing a song.' After that night marked by a prayer, Eric was particularly quiet and emotional. Soon afterwards, he went back alone to his Surrey home. Meg and George noticed that the man who had arrived on their doorstep several weeks ago with a world-weary shuffle and a slight stoop now looked more positive. If he wasn't exactly radiant, he had at least responded to their medical and spiritual treatment extremely well, and the future looked more hopeful. Still, the Pattersons knew better than to predict that all his problems were over. 'Dealing with addiction,' they point out, 'you're dealing with underlying resentments and bitterness and hatred. You have to pick your way through a minefield of insincerities and deceits. The chemical is the least important, by about 49 per cent to 51 per cent, and you cannot deal with the person at all until they are detoxified and thus deprived of the excuse of a distressed mind or body.

'The excuse all addicts use is that they can't get it

together – too much pain, a thick head, stomach pains or sweats, you know. We have to eliminate that. After three days of treatment, they have an ice-cool head because they are allowed no drugs. So we strip away the façade and then they hate themselves for having lied!' Eric's fertile mind had become bored at Harley Street. 'Drugs had filled his mind for so long, now his mind was crystal clear he needed to get back to activity,' says Meg. She sent him away with a portable stimulator machine so that he could continue his treatments. He insisted, against Meg's wishes, on her giving him some sleeping pills, and off he went. He told the Pattersons he needed to find somewhere to recuperate.

Eric's rehabilitation, planned by Lord Harlech and Meg Patterson, called for a month of farming near Oswestry under the eye of Frank Ormsby-Gore, Alice's brother. 'I drove myself there and took my acoustic guitar,' recalls Eric. 'I was very unfit, and very low in spirits and the agreement was that I would semi-work, according to my condition.' But he struck up an immediate friendship with Frank. 'We had a lot in common in terms of taste, and intellectually we were on the same wavelength.' On a less intellectual level, they also went to the local pub and got drunk several times. 'I came straight off heroin into drinking. It was essential. Woke up most days with a hangover, and Frank said that if I didn't want to work, that would be OK, but I couldn't stay around too long in that case.'

As a motivating therapy, the Welsh experience worked perfectly. Frank set an example as a hard worker and within days Eric was up at dawn. 'He was running a farm which barely managed to break even,' Clapton recalls of Frank. 'It was all manual labour, with hardly any machinery. So there was a load of hard work to be done, mucking out and baling hay, chopping up logs, sawing trees and God knows what. It was up to me to pull my own weight. And within a month I was very fit, brown from windburn and ready to take on the world. All that time, I had a guitar and I was playing.' He took occasional breaks most days, went back to the farmhouse and played and sang – 'dreaming up ideas of the kind of record I'd come back with'.

Alice, meanwhile, had entered a clinic for treatment of a different kind. 'They had come to the conclusion that not only was she suffering from drug addiction but alcoholism as well. Whereas I was a more simple case of just drug addiction. She stayed in the clinic after I came out of Meg's.' Eventually, Alice joined Eric in Wales. Eric says: 'We tried to form an understanding friendship again but we were told by Meg not to sleep in the same room together, not to start any emotional relationship right away because it could turn us back into what we'd been.' In fact, the medical instruction to freeze the relationship with Alice only confirmed Eric's personal decision.

Alice says she believed then that their separation was temporary and physically essential while she underwent detoxification. After the farm experience and her own treatment, however, Eric and Alice returned to his home together, although it was agreed that it would be a temporary arrangement. During the three years of addiction, Eric had hardly mentioned Pattie to Alice. 'Pattie was dormant, almost dead, in my mind during those years. But as I gained consciousness again, she came right to the forefront. And I told Alice of my passion and determination to see her. I'd go and see Pattie and tell Alice I'd been to see her.' The final separation from Alice was 'painful'.

Touchingly, Eric sent as a departing gift to Meg Patterson the gold spoon which he had worn around his neck most days for the past three years: it was the spoon from which he had sniffed heroin. With it came a simple hand-written message: 'Thanks, Meg. I won't be needing this.'

Today, Eric looks back on his three years as a drug addict with mixed feelings. He can rationalize what led him down the road, but feels remorse and regret at the loss of time, the wasted years and the self-deception in which he told himself he needed to do it for his art's sake.

He had begun on black dexedrine which led to marijuana and red wine which led to cocaine which led to heroin: 'Something like that,' he told London's *Q* magazine in March 1994. 'They all introduced one another. For me, there is nothing that is not addictive.' Surprisingly, he added: 'I don't have anything to say to people who take drugs. It's all their own business. I'm not a person who says: "Say No!" You have to do what you have to do.' But on other occasions, Eric has stressed that he, and other survivors, were fortunate to have a craft to return to. The implication in this is that a drug-user faced with a vacuum in his or her life might not be so consciously spurred to control it.

'I conquered drugs,' says Eric, 'through my own wish or will to survive, with the help of Meg Patterson and her husband and family. They gave me love, and I found that was the medicine I needed as much as, if not more than, the actual acupuncture which she was practising. Mine was a totally self-centred way of getting better. It's very irresponsible. I do think that if I hadn't jumped off the path into the mire, I may have had a fuller career at this stage. It would have been a lot different. I do think that there are gaps in my life which needn't have been there, and drugs took a lot out of it. Although I carried on functioning. And who's to say that I couldn't have become even better, if I'd been practising, or if I'd been concentrating on making music or working with other people, or building healthy relationships instead of indulging my own pain?

'I don't believe you play better under dope. I think it helps you to perceive it in a more pleasant way, but that's because you perceive everything *else* in a more pleasant way. If you put me in a kind of laboratory situation, with drugs and then without drugs, and made me play two identical pieces of music, or even ad-lib or improvise over a certain amount of time, I would not be able to say that one is better than the other, or even different. It's just that when you're on drugs, your *perception* of what you're doing is far more rose-coloured. That's all.'

Alice remembers Eric's self-justification for embarking on the role of a martyr. 'He repeatedly said that to play the blues, which was his music, you had to *be something*. Long before we took smack, he would talk about the great jazz musicians, and his favourite bluesman Robert Johnson, living the right kind of lives to create his kind of music. So yes, it was definitely an act of heroism to go down that road and find out what it was like.'

Alice has her own views on Eric's battle with drug abuse, and subsequent victory. 'As it was with heroin, so it was with drink: Eric always waits for the other person, or in this case it was the other article, smack or alcohol, to make a mistake. In the case of heroin, the drug's failure for Eric was not to live up to his expectations in helping him create some work of genius, or help him towards some profound recognition of life. So when heroin did not provide any answers, he could kick it and say, "I've conquered it! I've won. Because I've met heroin head on and I've come out on top and I can *still create*!" So yes, heroin was a major reason he went down the road. Because deep inside him, he knew that he could find the way back.'

Clapton says he never took drugs with his mind on suicide, even at his lowest ebb: 'I don't believe I ever did. I don't think you go to the brink unless you actually want to end it all. I think as long as you're enjoying life, no matter what you're using to enjoy it with, you've still got a chance of survival. I don't remember ever, during that period, feeling so distressed that I wanted to die. The thing about heroin is that it makes you feel *good*. It looks terrible to everyone else and you *look* like you're dying. But in your little shell, you feel great. The only trouble is that if you're mainlining [injecting], then you can die from an overdose, but if you're snorting it through the nose, as I was, it's difficult to actually injure yourself *fatally*. You do your liver and everything a lot of damage, but that can be repaired. The biggest problem you've got is the addiction itself and how to break it.'

Alice is adamant that Eric was never in danger of killing himself with drugs. The real danger, she maintains, is that he might have killed himself in a car crash, or in an accident in the house, as a result of slow reactions or over-confidence. Alice says his driving was appallingly erratic during his three years of addiction: 'His driving really was frightening. I distinctly remember removing the rotor arm from the Mercedes once or twice, to immobilize it so that he couldn't drive it away from the house.' Inevitably, that provoked another argument between them.

'No, there was never any question in my mind of his being close to death, or suicidal, or at death's door from drugs. There was a totally different certainty, to me: that he would *survive*. Everything pointed to that. If anything depressed Eric during our time together, it was me, and what he saw in me and kept on hammering across to me . . . my low opinion of myself and my lack of confidence and self-respect. *That* brought him down much more than the drugs.'

On injection, Eric says: 'No, I never did. I did, at one point, ask to be injected, because I was going through heavy withdrawal . . . but it was denied and that was by Alice . . . and I think that was very clever of her really to see that that was a big step. And once you took that step, you were in a lot of trouble.'

'I don't think Eric would have injected,' says Alice. 'There was never a complete guarantee, because of the junkie's twenty-four hours-a-day, seven-days-a-week, three-hundred-and-sixty-five-days-a-year preoccupation with wondering and worrying about the supply of the next dose. And when you fear it's not going to be around, you're in so much pain you just want to die. On a couple of times it was available by injection I said no for Eric, but he would have said no anyway. He hates injections of any kind, and he'd never have become a habitual injector of heroin.' Confirming Eric's recollection that she steered him away from the needle, Alice adds diffidently: 'Yes, I urged him not to. Because I knew that it would have been a very different and dangerous slope.'

Throughout the three years, he was eating fairly abnormally: 'Oh yeah, very heavily. I was overweight. Mainly junk food and sweets . . . chocolate, because that all goes along with any kind of morphine addiction. And so I was bloated, quite grotesque, really. I was not healthy, but not unhealthy.' Eric's assessment of his condition may be an overly positive one.

Paradoxically, while he was mentally introverted during his years of addiction to drugs, Clapton retained his sense of sartorial pride. He continued to amass hundreds of shirts, shoes and suits and Alice recalls that on most days he was 'meticulous, almost fanatical' about his appearance. 'He would change his whole outfit up to three times a day, just to sit around the house. He was potty about how he looked and loved the exercise of changing his clothes.'

On Christmas Eve 1974, Eric threw a small party for his family and friends. When he got up to dance with his grandmother, he said: 'Rose, I have a confession for you . . .' He was about to tell her of his drug addiction, and his renunciation of dope, when Rose interjected: 'I know Rick. I know all about it. Don't you ever do that to us again.'

'Don't worry, Rose, I won't.'

Clapton is realistic when he talks of his lucky escape from heroin addiction and when asked for his advice to potential heroin users. 'I had a craft to go back to from the word go. I was sure that I would come out the other end and that I was having a kind of holiday. And Alice obviously recognized this too: it never looked to her as if I was getting anywhere near a danger zone. And I never felt that way, because to me, it was incidental to being a musician. Really, taking heroin never became my life. It was a very heavy habit, but it was a case of: "Well, I'm a musician, and this is what musicians do." It took over and it was an illusion for me to think that I could get away with it. But I did.'

His message to today's drug-users is based more on

practicality than on a lecture. 'If you have no root to hold on to that will get you through, like being a great writer or being a great bricklayer or a great musician or an artist or *whatever*, as you were before you considered getting involved with it, then you obviously cannot do it, because it will kill you. Unless you are really sure you can make it with something else in life, you can't look to heroin. I was absolutely lucky.

'And despite the fact that neither I nor Alice thought that I was close, I may have been close a couple of times. I might have got killed in a car crash or an accident at home ... so really, it's not just a question of having something like a career to hold on to, either. That's a good way of looking at it idealistically, and made sense from my standpoint. But obviously heroin can kill you in many different ways, even if you are taking it for the first time.'

Meanwhile, Eric had to face the reality that 'Layla', stunning anthem to win Pattie, had manifestly not, so far, worked. George and Pattie Harrison had surprised Eric by visiting him in Wales during his therapeutic month of farming. The couple made the journey as a gesture of friendship, to encourage Eric to return home fighting fit. But Clapton told Alice bluntly that he wished Pattie had arrived without George. It was a remark that dampened the dying embers of Eric and Alice's relationship. In Wales, Eric also told George and Alice that he was in love with Pattie and that he sought her as a partner. But the woman he wanted remained at the side of her husband in Oxfordshire. There were problems in that marriage, and unknown to Eric she had been thinking of him. But even the romantic character of Pattie could not then contemplate escaping the net around her. She remained loyal to George.

After that Welsh trip, Alice left Eric's life. Both of them realized that a complete split was essential if they were to reject the danger and degradation of the past. But they stayed in touch with each other and Alice had a firm friendship with Rose, who enjoys her company. Alice remembers her birthday every year. And Eric invited Alice to his fortieth birthday party at his home.

Eric lost no time in informing his manager that he was fit enough to make a comeback album. His much-discussed wall of silence, and his return to work, merited a party, Robert Stigwood decided. In April 1974, a rock world that considered Clapton at best to have retired, at worst to be on a long self-destructive bender or worse, was invited to the China Garden restaurant in Soho. With less than a few hours of notice by telephone invitation, dozens of journalists and radio and television people poured into the party, alongside friends of Eric including Elton John, Pete Townshend and Ronnie Wood. Looking bronzed, Eric arrived from his home by chauffeured Rolls Royce. Enthusing about his return to work, he spoke of a plan to go to Miami to record with US keyboardist Carl Radle and other musicians whom Carl had organized. 'I want to record again; I'll also be doing a tour of America. And later on some dates in England.' His warm smile and suntan showed no sign of his worrying isolation at Clapton Towers.

'We just wanted to have a raving party to celebrate Eric's return to work,' Robert Stigwood announced, before the event moved to his palatial home at Stanmore, Middlesex where it raged until 5 a.m.

Eric Clapton's return from the precipice of death to his flowering as a genius of blues music is a dramatic story of renaissance. If proof were needed that his music stemmed from his soul, it came when he returned to studio work to record his 'comeback album'.

Within a few weeks of convincing himself, and everyone around him, that he was 'clean', Eric was on a plane for Miami, Florida. There, in a month of free-flowing creativity, his rebirth could be judged from his resonant vocal work: he found a real bluesy voice to join his plangent guitar. He knew on his return home that he had to get busy, and quickly. He went straight into Robert Stigwood's office and asked him to book him a studio. He also asked particularly for the fine producer Tom Dowd to be booked with him. The result was Eric's biggest-selling album to that point.

Incredibly, in only two and a half weeks, he recorded the album which still stands as one of his finest: *461 Ocean Boulevard*, named after the address of the house in which the musicians lived. It proved a turning point in his life and career, overflowing with a new ingredient – his voice. Eric agrees that his new timbre came from a new, clearer, inner consciousness.

Gone, now, was the experiment of Cream, the stoned intensity of Derek and the Dominos, the blues purist of John Mayall's Bluesbreakers, the unwilling puppet of the Yardbirds. Now Clapton's identity shone through for the first time. The vocals carried a resonance and maturity.

Stigwood had, all along, been a staunch believer in

Eric's talent and his will to survive. He needed little convincing by Eric that he was totally serious about a comeback, and wanted to make an impact. But neither man could have guessed that it would be an album carrying such weight. And Eric had no prior hint that the musicians who would be assembled for him would have such empathy with his new style. The line-up was begun when Eric telephoned Carl Radle, his friend from Derek and the Dominos, and Carl put together the band with the help of Tom Dowd.

Eric was therefore working with a completely new band apart from Carl Radle: guitarist George Terry from Florida, and, from Oklahoma, keyboardist Dick Sims and drummer Jamie Oldaker, and, together with keyboardist Alby Galuten and the excellent duetting vocalist Yvonne Elliman, the musical empathy they provided for a fragile Eric was obviously perfect.

It was not all rock 'n' roll, but the rich ballads, 'Let It Grow', 'Please Be with Me' and 'Give Me Strength', were handled in a manner that only a blues musician could have conceived. 'Give Me Strength', one of the first songs Eric had written after receiving treatment from Meg Patterson, carried its own pathos. It begins with Eric playing a sensitive slide figure on Dobro (an acoustic guitar with a built-in resonating speaker hidden behind a metal plate). The soul-searching vocal indicates quite starkly the torment he has just been through, and with the bittersweet sound of the Dobro, it is a very special lyric and music.

There is more evidence of his slide playing in 'I Can't Hold Out Much Longer', an Elmore James classic which was an old favourite of Eric's, and there is the first hint of Eric's love of the music of Bob Marley with his jaunty version of the reggae king's 'I Shot the Sheriff'. The song became a big hit for Clapton, and a perennial particular stage favourite.

Culturally and commercially, Clapton's adoption of 'I Shot the Sheriff' proved important to the US. It rocketed up the Billboard charts, hitting the top spot on 14 September 1974. As well as providing Eric with his only American chart-topper, it sparked the arrival of reggae in the US, providing the springboard for Bob Marley and Peter Tosh and other acts. For such a comeback album, the choice of producer was crucial, and Tom Dowd drew praise later from Eric. 'He watches your moods and sees when, for instance, you're in a creative mood. Then he'll try and pump the best out of you. And when you're not, he'll let you slide. He doesn't force you to do anything.' In the years ahead, Clapton would come to regard Dowd as his father figure in the studio.

Eric did not drink particularly heavily during those sessions. He was acutely aware that so much was at stake, and he seemed inspired by fresh musical company. But a cripplingly long concert tour followed. It re-established Clapton's musicianship and credibility. But it was so exhausting that he needed some kind of prop. Brandy was his answer. 'When I came off drugs,' says Eric now, 'I was left with a huge vacuum, a huge hole, which I couldn't fill because at that time my belief in anything other than myself wasn't really very adequate. The only way I could fill it was with booze. So I went from one vice to another. I stopped taking drugs but went for the drink, and like everything else in my life, I did it one thousand per cent.'

Confidence and determination, combined with shyness and diffidence, had always been in his make-up. When he left drugs behind, he simply found that their absence fuelled an emotional turmoil inside him. A superficially 'up' person, powered by nervous energy and still discovering fundamental truths about himself at the age of twenty-nine, Clapton took to that most punishing of institutions which all rock musicians love to hate: the American Road.

The twenty-six week, coast-to-coast tour, on which Eric was accompanied by the same musicians who had made the album such a triumph, would have been hard on the stamina of a fit man. Eric Clapton and his Band, as it was now named for the first time, were booked to perform at the nation's biggest sports stadiums with between 60,000 and 70,000 in the audience at most venues sometimes for two performances each night. The 461 tour, as it was called, had been masterminded by Robert Stigwood. He had invested in Cream and had a strong affinity with Eric, who liked and admired him. Eric and all of Stigwood's artists of the period, who included the Bee Gees, were regular visitors to his home at Stanmore, Middlesex.

Working for Stigwood, as agent and broker, at the time of Cream's formation, was Roger Forrester. Although the two men worked well together, their characters were utterly different: Stigwood was the entrepreneurial, persuasive stylist moving ever onward; he would amass a fortune by his entry into the movie world. In 1994 he re-presented *Grease* (his original production) on the London stage, with great success. Forrester, a hard-headed, practical, hard-nosed, assiduous, gruff businessman, was also a dedicated enthusiast of Clapton's, going to nearly all his shows. When Stigwood told Forrester of the multi-million-dollar, record-breaking American tour to follow the 461 album, Forrester opposed the idea. He regarded it as both greedy and physically unhealthy for Clapton to be plunged into such a gigantic schedule, so soon after returning from death's door.

Forrester argued strongly but lost the battle; Stigwood was still Eric's manager and had the final word. But it was probably the last decision about Eric's career that Stigwood made. By the time a triumphant Clapton returned from America, Stigwood had delegated all decisions about Eric's future to Forrester. Within a few years, Stigwood's management contract with Clapton lapsed and, in 1979, Forrester became Clapton's official manager, having been associated with him for twelve years.

Their relationship now is intuitive and brotherly. Tough, waspish and conspiratorial in manner, Forrester is super-protective and admits that he has often been over-defensive of Clapton, reassessing his moods, his tantrums, his abilities and his capriciousness almost hourly. This most extraordinary manager–musician relationship is essential, says Forrester, because for many years he was dealing with a man impossible to predict from day to day, sometimes from hour to hour. And he attributes much of the problem he inherited to the 1974 American tour.

'Fantastic pressure was put on Eric, and many of the problems inside him amassed from that tour,' says Forrester. 'Eric was keen to get back to work and proved it by recording that *461* album so quickly. It could have been done in an even shorter time, he was performing so well and at such a speed. But the tour was another thing. He leaned on the drink, and that caused major problems later on. Eric's never been that ambitious, to want to play the major halls across America flat out like that. Eric has always been lazy. When he had to face those big stadium audiences every night, it wasn't natural for him. He'd stopped all that with Cream and suddenly – here he was again, straight out of a three-year problem as a drug addict, into these big halls. It was all too much.

'For him to return to the studio was enough; he needed six months' rest to find himself again – and then he should have gone into the 3,000-seater halls instead of the 70,000 capacity stadiums.'

'When I got back from the farm in Wales,' reflects Eric, 'and the rehabilitation from heroin, I felt I could take on the world. Unfortunately I picked up a bottle at the same time. All the musicians and friends were using a pint glass. So I felt I *belonged* in the same little club. It was comfortable. I felt no compulsion to stop. It was full road work on that tour and I have great, great memories of it. I remember I was so drunk on some stages that I played lying on the stage flat on my back or staggering around wearing the weirdest combination of clothes because I couldn't get it together even to dress properly.' He caught conjunctivitis from singer Yvonne Elliman – 'I did half the tour with no eyes, too. But mostly, it was full-tilt drinking, morning till night and after the show. And I don't regret it at all. It was essential for me, as a kind of release.

'From my side, looking back, it all seems like a series of steps rather than a severe turn to the right or left, or an upward or downward movement, which is how a lot of people must view it. By 1974 I'd been absent for a long time. I went into the studio, but not with any earth-shaking ideas. I just had a couple of songs I'd always liked, like "Willie and the Hand Jive", a Robert Johnson song, and a couple that I'd written.' The producer, Tom Dowd, was partly a coach and mentor in the studio, patient and painstaking but quickly sensing the rich mood that Eric was generating from his voice, his soulful playing and the texture of the song material. 'It seemed to me a bit of a hotch-potch as we made it,' says Eric. 'When it was finished, I liked it. And now in hindsight, it is a great record. But at the time, it never seemed to me that much of an earth-mover. It was just coming out of hiding . . .'

His confidence, he said, never left him: 'I still had that, even throughout the drug taking [Meg Patterson disputes this], but there was something missing in terms of an emotional or spiritual yearning. That was killed, or muted, by the heroin, which makes you believe in yourself to such a degree that you don't need anybody else. After a couple of years, the awful feeling of not needing anybody else becomes so important that if you stop taking the heroin, you're faced with an awful pain of shame and guilt, with the terrible reality of how many people you've turned away from your door, of how many loved ones you've neglected, simply because of your own desire for comfort. And that's what I was left with when I was weaned off the heroin . . . this awful pain, but also a great amount of joy at being able to *feel* the pain. Being able to cry, which had been denied me for so many years because I didn't want to, didn't need to, with that drug. And so, coming off heroin, I turned around from being very introverted to being very extroverted. Suddenly, you want to be part of the world again. Be loud and noisy!'

Eric says his love of Pattie, and the turbulent frustration at her rejection, was partly responsible for his descent into heroin addiction during the three years from 1971 until 1974. 'Not Pattie herself, as a person, but as an image, she was my excuse. That was the catalyst, a very big part of it. It was a symbol, my perfect reason for embarking on this road which would lead me to the bottom.'

During the three dark years, Pattie telephoned Eric's home a few times. Always, the phone would be answered by Alice; Pattie did not then pursue a conversation with Eric, but hung up the phone. The word was out, anyway, that he was very ill. That both frightened and worried her. Pattie's lifestyle with George was far removed from such abuse of the body. Harrison was deeply involved with meditation, and members of the Hare Krishna sect were regular visitors to his home. Pictures of Indian gurus adorned the walls. Pattie sympathized with this philosophy – it was she who originally introduced the Beatles to Transcendental Mediation via the Maharishi Mahesh Yogi, thus beginning an important aspect of the psychedelic period. But the non-stop, daily vibrations on the same theme from George and the endless stream of philosophers tired her.

While Eric says Pattie's non-availability was the catalyst which gave him a reason to plunge, Pete Townshend has a more positive theory about the heroin period. 'If anything kept Clapton alive throughout that whole period, it was the *possibility* that he might just achieve the impossible. He'd elevated it to a Layla and Majnun relationship, to the level of a spiritual fusion. Here was Pattie, this hopeless target, married to one of the Beatles, endlessly wealthy, snatched out of the world by George into a kind of pop royalty. And for Eric, she was an unachievable. On top of this, he knew and liked George, so it was like falling in love with your wife's sister, or close relative. It wasn't done. And that depth of fantasy was so important to Eric. There was a warm air between George and Eric that could not be breached, particularly in this way. I'm sure the very fact that it was such a *maudlin* desperation got through to Eric's inner psyche, during the heroin period, when nothing else did.'

When Eric came off heroin, the events leading up to his eventual capture of Pattie were as theatrical as the scenarios that had punctuated his four years of unrequited love. He set about renewing contact with her with a streak of determination which surprised everybody except himself. He decided there would be no clandestine relationship this time. Direct action was essential. 'She had become very disillusioned with George. It became clear to me,' Eric continues, 'that if I could somehow arouse her enough, there was a chance I could get her to live with me.'

At a party at Robert Stigwood's home in Stanmore, Eric grasped the initiative. Knowing George and Pattie would be there, Eric went straight up to Harrison and said: 'I'm in love with your wife. What are you going to do about it?' Eric continues: 'George said: "Whatever you like, man. It doesn't worry me." He was being very spiritual about it, and saying everybody should do their own thing. He then said: "You can have her and I'll have your girlfriend," who was Cathy James at the time.

'I couldn't believe this! I thought he was going to chin me. Anyway, Pattie freaked out and ran away and got into her car. Suddenly she was in limbo and I think it was at that point that she became disillusioned with George. So I don't think I stole her, because I did tell him straight away. Pattie was very upset and it all suddenly became very foreign. I imagine George must have been very upset too. But that's crazy! If he didn't want her to leave him, he shouldn't have let me take her.'

Eric's brutal frankness at least had the redeeming quality of honesty. The party ended amid some tension, George and Pattie driving away, symbolically, out of his life. Or so it seemed.

Eric's next ploy was to lean on his old friend Pete Townshend as a kind of foil. A recording session for the film *Tommy*, in which Eric played the part of a preacher, ended at eleven o'clock one night. Leaving the studios, Eric said to Pete: 'Let's go and see George out at Friar Park.' Townshend declined; he wanted to get home to his wife Karen. But Eric persisted: he had no car and needed a lift. 'Please come with me – I know George really wants to see you.' Townshend said the trip was impractical: Eric might be stranded out there without a car because he intended to leave soon after taking him there. Clapton said that was OK.

Townshend takes up the story. 'George, Eric and I sat talking for a while. Then Pattie came in and said hello, looking stunning. She was very bright and intelligent. A couple of Indians were walking around the house and George was talking very interestingly to me. It was the first real conversation we'd had and we found a lot of common ground, particularly in the area of mysticism. Anyway, many hours passed, with George and me talking. Eventually we went out and Eric and Pattie were in the big hall, talking. She made us some soup, George went back into the studio he has at the house, and Eric came up to me and said: "I need about another hour." So I said: "What?" He said: "I need about another hour before you go."

'Well, I went back and kept George occupied for

another hour. Then I thought no more about what they were up to. I got in my car, alone, and drove home. I decided they could all sort this out between them. I later realized that what I'd actually been doing was keeping George busy while Eric talked Pattie into leaving.'

Townshend, hearing of the outcome of that night a few days later, reflected to himself on Eric's iron determination. 'I recall thinking how determined Eric was to face up to what he wanted, and how ruthless he had been in achieving that. I also wished he'd let me into it a bit earlier, what he'd been up to. But I didn't feel used. I felt honoured. He did two remarkable things: he actually straightened himself out from being a junkie, and then he went out and made his fantasy happen.'

Pattie recalls: 'After that night's conversation with me at Friar Park, Eric went on his American tour with the band that had made the album *461 Ocean Boulevard*. Shortly after that, I decided it was all over between George and me; he didn't seem to worry whether I left him or not. So three weeks after Eric's visit, I went to Los Angeles to stay with my sister Jenny, who was married to Mick Fleetwood at that time. While I was there, Eric telephoned me and asked me to join him on tour. I joined him in Buffalo.'

American audiences were feverish in the summer of 1974 at the return to live concerts. 'Such was the aura at the Philadelphia Spectrum that it only needed Mr Clapton to strap on a Sunburst Fender Stratocaster for an audience of 20,000 to leap from their seats in acknowledgement of his past glories,' wrote Chris Charlesworth in the *Melody Maker*.

That long tour marked the actual union of Eric and Pattie. When it ended, they went to Jamaica to combine recording work with a brief 'honeymoon'. While there,

Eric heard from his mother that his half-brother, Brian, had been killed in a motorcycle accident, so Eric and Pattie flew to the funeral in Canada. For Pattie, it was a difficult and delicate entry into the Clapton family circle.

Swiftly after the *461* album and the tour, Eric was hungry for a return to the studio, and with the same line up of musicians he cut songs in Kingston's Dynamic Studios that would become his new album, *There's One in Every Crowd*. This featured a number of guests including Bob Dylan, who duetted with Eric on 'Sign Language'. Also on that track was Robbie Robertson, the outstanding guitarist with the Band, who had so inspired Eric and legions of other players earlier with their futuristic album *Music from Big Pink*.

Returning to Britain with Pattie provided him with a solid home life, but having a pub very close to his home accelerated his drinking habits. When Pattie moved in with Eric, he warily asked her if she liked the house and its design. 'He was very conscious that Alice had left her stamp on it and was worried what I'd think,' says Pattie. 'But it was fine. I loved the house and being with him. We had a jolly time setting up the home together. It was not a problem for me, despite his worry.' Sharing an interest in fashion and colour-blending, they were perfectly matched and friends considered them the perfect couple. Eric was elated at having attracted Pattie; it might have been a combination of this celebration and the vacuum left by quitting drugs that caused him to embark on his next dangerous journey, along the alcoholic road.

By the end of 1974, Roger Forrester told Eric that for tax reasons he had to spend a year out of Britain, so Eric and Pattie rented a house on Paradise Island in the Bahamas. 'It was a base for making money,' says Clapton, 'but it was a beautiful spot, and virtually a year's honeymoon for Pattie and me, although I did some work.' From that base, he did an Australian tour. Alone, he went to the US to join his band. Because Pattie had a London conviction for possessing marijuana she was not allowed into America, so had to go from the Bahamas to Australia via London. Changing planes at Anchorage (where she was not allowed beyond the transit lounge), she spotted Eric and ran up behind him, clasping her hands across his eyes. 'Guess who?' said Pattie. Clapton was overjoyed at the sight of her, but was frustrated in his attempts to ensure they flew out from Anchorage together. An even greater irritation followed: once in Australia, Pattie was barred from entering New Zealand because of her drugs bust, so she missed that part of Eric's tour. A furious Clapton vented his views in radio and newspaper interviews. Life as a Beatle's wife had virtually marooned Pattie. 'Going on tour with Eric was so exciting because that had never been allowed when I was with George. Wives were not allowed to travel with the Beatles because of security. The Beatles were heavily protected. So this sudden new life with Eric and his mad antics was great fun, an absolutely fantastic and completely new world to me.'

Surprisingly, Clapton and Harrison's friendship survived the long episode, and still does. Even in 1971, during a peak of Eric's frustration, George had been able to persuade Eric to go to New York to appear at the Madison Square Garden concert in aid of Bangladesh. Eric is full of praise for George's laconic humour, which helped defuse the situation, after his initial pique.

'I think the world of the man,' says Eric. 'His adaptable wisdom for any situation, his wit and his humour are a great source of inspiration for anybody who knows him. That helped us all through the split-up. He managed to laugh it all off when I thought it was getting really hairy. I thought it was tense, he thought it was funny. George, Pattie and I actually sat in the hall of my house and I remember him saying: "Well, I suppose I'd better divorce her." And I said: "Well, if you divorce her, that means I've got to marry her!" In black and white, it sounds and looks horrible. But it was like a Woody Allen situation.' That conversation was in 1975; George and Pattie's marriage was dissolved on 10 June 1977 on the grounds that they had lived apart for more than two years.

For Pattie, changing partners was accompanied by a welcome switch in the tempo and style of her life. 'I felt more earthed at Eric's home than at George's and there was something magnetic about Eric,' she says. 'I felt as if I was losing my identity when I was with George. It was all too exclusive and unreal. I was getting a little lost inside that.'

She knew of Eric's work from a special perspective. George Harrison had been fascinated by Cream. 'In every way,' Pattie says, 'the Beatles were very exclusive, almost a royalty of the pop world. And we very rarely listened to other musicians' work. The Beatles were totally absorbed with what *they* were doing. So any other band had to be very special before the records were played in the house.' But among the records played by George were Cream albums and he soon recognized Clapton as a great guitarist. Pattie became very familiar with the *Fresh Cream* album. Once she was by Eric's side, he indoctrinated her into the blues, playing her his records by the old masters and light-heartedly quizzing her about the singers and songs to strengthen her knowledge.

Pattie's love for Eric grew, but nothing could have prepared her for the years that were about to envelop her. 'After the spiritual life with George, within a few weeks of going to live with Eric I seemed to be surrounded with mayhem.' Clapton had hit the bottle. 'I drank like a fish, too,' says Pattie. They were releasing much of the tension of the five years when their future had been uncertain. 'We were leaning on each other,' she says. 'It was jolly good fun but we were quite hopeless for each other a lot of the time.'

Eric denies that taking to drink was a triumphant celebration of achieving his goal of getting Pattie to go and live with him. Within a few months, Courvoisier and lemonade became his regular drink. Pattie says he was not a pretty sight. The Courvoisier and lemonade routine was, then and forever, traceable to one simple truth about him: he has an addictive nature. Once tasted or experienced, any activity has to be repeated.

'Some of the time I was an accomplice, then I backed out,' says Pattie. 'I thought one of us should be sober some of the time, so I was. I found him very hard to live with. He expected me not to care about his drunken friends lying all over the house. Sometimes he'd even bring drunken strangers back from the pub – tramps, who he insisted should not stay out in the street but should stay the night with us!

'A lot of people were abusing him, encouraging him to drink so they in turn could carry on drinking. And there was another nasty element: some people enjoyed watching Eric get so drunk. They thought it was great to see someone with his reputation, so brilliant with the guitar, behaving in a sloppy, drunken, almost idiotic manner. I despised that. And sometimes I didn't even have to be sober to see it.'

Paradoxically, Eric was able to work consistently, although Roger Forrester worried increasingly about his condition. At home Pattie found him tetchy: 'Little things annoyed him. He had about two hundred shirts, and he'd go absolutely berserk if I couldn't find the one he wanted that day. He'd describe it in absolute detail and I'd find him one similar. That wouldn't do.'

He sought comfort in free-spending and amassed loads of clothes. 'He had no idea about money whatsoever and never wanted to know what anything was costing. He adored his huge collection of shoes but treated them badly, scuffed them, which I got cross about. I got worried about his failure to see any value in money. Making money from my career in modelling clothes and shoes has made them more valuable to me.'

The friction between them was not helped by his decision that all women should be banned from concert tours. Clapton agrees that this was part of his chauvinism. But he explains that too many bands suffered from the mere fact that wives and girlfriends did not necessarily get along together. And putting warring women together on planes, in hotels and dressing-rooms made no sense. Eric's regular absences on world tours left Pattie feeling lonely and isolated; she, too, leaned increasingly on drink.

'I would always make a point of asking if I could go on tour, knowing that I wouldn't be allowed to,' says Pattie. 'He always said he was working and there were no ladies on the road. So when people asked me, I always turned the phrase into: "I haven't been invited." That sounded much better than, "I'm not allowed to go . . . I've been told to stay at home!"'

She regarded Eric as a chauvinist: 'But Roger Forrester is as well . . . and the combination of the two was very strong. They egged each other on.' She did not fight Eric's decision: 'In an argument you do need a leg to stand on . . . and I didn't think that I had one. Because he *was*, after all, working. For me, the travelling would just be something pleasurable to do. He saw me as a potential distraction. There was no point in arguing.' During the whole of his heavy-drinking year of 1979, Eric fastidiously kept a diary in which he wrote, drew cartoons and confessed his innermost thoughts and observations around the world and at home. One of several diary references to his ban on women on the road reads: 'I play better when Pattie is not there to watch me. I wish I could understand that, too.'

Although she accepted the ban, Pattie was hurt by what she considered to be Eric's thoughtless desertion. 'He's not one for using the phone much so he wouldn't ring me, either, while he was away on tour. That was very disturbing for me, when the tours lasted for about six weeks. I'd seen some of the American concerts, and the sight of the candles being lit by the audience at the end was very thrilling on that first tour I went on. Such a different experience from hearing a record. But no, I saw nothing after that 1974 tour when he travelled the world. And I felt very cut off.'

They had little social life even when he was home. 'He doesn't like restaurants. He feels trapped. His idea of eating was to do it as quickly as possible and then leave. Even when we had friends for Sunday lunch, he'd be the first one to leave the table and go and watch television. He couldn't understand the rest of us sitting round the table for another hour after eating, just talking.' Eric's eating habits, including an obsession for eating food while it is burning hot, stem from his childhood. His grandmother produced the food for her husband first, who sat eating in total silence, and then Eric and Rose would sit and eat their meal quietly too. Eating, to Clapton, was in those years, a functional operation, not a social occasion. That changed dramatically as Eric became a highly visible socialite of the 1990s.

The eminent actor John Hurt, who had by now become a firm friend of Eric, told me he recognizes part of himself in Clapton. 'If we are going to do something, we overdo it. There's a certain love of danger in both of us and that's always been apparent to me in Eric's work. The *danger* is what makes it electric. It follows that the person making that music has to live on the edge just a little bit. There is a self-destructive streak in both Eric and me which I've always known about. And it's always been getting on top of it, keeping it at bay, which has helped Eric survive and got him through the worst brandy period. He is a survivor.'

Clapton once told Pete Townshend that in order to be able to play at the level of some of the great black blues musicians, he felt he had to experience life at that level. 'And he was prepared to undergo that for music. And that's why Eric allowed himself to go down. So that he, and virtually he alone, could pull himself back.'

Eric also enjoyed the social aspect of visiting the pub, he recalls. 'There was always enough drink in the house. I didn't need to go there; but I enjoyed being at the bar.' The drinking spree was also rooted in his desperation for a busy social life. Reunited with all his old friends in Ripley village, he took up residence on many nights in the Ship with Guy Pullen, his former school pal, and Sid Perrin, a friend of Eric's mother with whom he struck a rapport. Describing the period, Pullen says: 'It was lunacy. We'd spend the night drinking then go over to Eric's home for snooker. It was one long party.' Cards was another game he played, with Eric not being a good loser. He was, however, a successful arm wrestler: 'I used to take on anyone,' he recalls, 'and I was quite good at it, through sheer determination.'

Summing up his worst three years of drinking, from 1979, when he was consuming up to two bottles of brandy a day, Eric says frankly: 'My mind had gone so far that if I didn't have double vision I was worried. I saw two TV sets, all the time two of everything. And if I didn't then I'd have to have more drink to perpetuate that double vision. Because it was *secure*.'

SIX

THE ADDICT

BY 1970, AWARDS lined his walls. In a mere five years since making his bold statement to quit the Yardbirds, Clapton was one of the world's most respected rock musicians. For three successive years he had won the title of Top British Musician and Best International Guitarist in the readers' poll of the *Melody Maker*. The headiness of such success put many artists of that period into a self-inflicted decline; creatively, as well as physically, they found it hard to live with acclaim and riches.

Clapton's descent into drugs and later alcohol never represented a renunciation of his vocation as a musician. During his period of self-imposed exile, he picked up his acoustic guitar only sporadically, for throughout his life he has maintained that playing should be a shared experience. But when Clapton was playing, he was the most active musician on the planet. After the demise of Blind Faith, he plunged into recording sessions for myriad artists in Britain and America, including Howlin' Wolf, Stephen Stills, the Crickets (the group that once backed Buddy Holly, an early enthusiasm of Eric's), the Rolling Stones, Buddy Guy (a blues player whom

Clapton maintains has been consistently underrated) and for George Harrison's breakthrough solo album *All Things Must Pass*. He particularly enjoyed touring several times with Freddy King.

A highly developed sense of élan, both in his work and in his lifestyle, continued into the new decade. The cover on the 1970 album called *Eric Clapton*, his first solo outing, portrayed a serious-looking young man lounging on a chair, his Fender Stratocaster guitar between his legs and a couple of apples near by.

Among students of his work, the Fender Stratocaster sound was not really associated with Clapton. Apart from a brief flirtation with Fender Telecasters and the odd Gretsch in Yardbirds days, he had always been a Gibson man. Moving to a Stratocaster affected his music, with less emphasis on the heavy, block-chord, riffy solo playing Eric had made famous in the Cream days. Now came a tighter, more melodic approach. It was a definite American influence.

Three songs endured from that début solo album. 'Blues Power', with its autobiographical theme, remains one of Eric's favourite standards by himself; 'Bottle of Red Wine', though its title would become contentious to Eric as the years passed, demonstrated his ability to play a shuffle; and the fervour of 'Let It Rain', today an enormously popular song with international concert audiences, was aglow with passion.

But while his identity crisis went off at a tangent with the launch of Derek and the Dominos, the album was a full frontal assault. The album *Layla and Other Assorted Love Songs*, released in December 1970, brought back the elongated guitar solos from Eric, missing since Cream days, coupled with a fabulous collection of original material and a couple of blues classics. Clearly induced by the wafts of dope that permeated so many records of the period, and also by Eric's unrequited love for Pattie when he recorded it, the Layla album carried a sensual, emotive quality and stands today as masterful and inspired.*

Clapton had retained the same rhythm section used on the *Eric Clapton* album, christened them the Dominos, renamed himself Derek, and added the spectacular guitarist and slide specialist Duane Allman, who had made such an impact with the album *Idlewild South* which showed off his original slide guitar style on 'Nobody Knows You (When You're Down and Out)' on the *Layla* album. It complemented Eric's solo playing, never getting in the way, while adding a rich colour to this old blues standard.

'Bell Bottom Blues' oozes emotion, from the heartfelt lyrics to the beautifully sensitive solo in which Eric slips in a few chime-like harmonics, a technique that the Band's Robbie Robertson had started to perfect. The Clapton–Robertson appreciation society had begun. So had the one with Duane Allman, and for a while the two men's names were linked inextricably.

Duane was a Clapton fan who had developed his own distinctive guitar style in an incredibly short period. Like Eric, he was a naturally inventive player, with a blues feeling. There's a track on the Duane Allman 'anthology' album, released after his death on a motorcycle in 1971,

---

* Although it was recorded in 1970, 'Layla' had a chequered history before Eric clinched it as a signature song on his 1974 'comeback' tour of the USA. He had played it only a few times live before then, including his performance at the Rainbow, London, in 1973. It reached only fifty-one in the USA Billboard chart in 1971, but in the summer of 1972 returned to the charts at number ten both in the USA and in its UK début.

called 'Mean Old World'. It came from the *Layla* sessions and features Allman and Clapton duetting on acoustic slide guitars. This was Eric's first embrace of the slide technique, and Duane was partly responsible.

'Key to the Highway', which has remained in Eric's repertoire, was live, loose and lovely. Overdubbing throughout the album was kept to a minimum, and there was not a synthesizer in sight. The title track, 'Layla', is still considered by many to be rock's perfect love song, a fascinating combination of soliloquy and *cri de cœur*. Almost overnight, the power and delivery of the song transformed Eric Clapton from the guitar-hero syndrome into a singer-guitarist-songwriter of world stature. Eric has told me that this performance of 'Layla', performed in the studio under the influence of various substances, was the only time he believes drugs to have allowed him to free himself of all inhibitions and produce a piece of work superior to that which might have come from him without drugs. But then, the subject of 'Layla' was a drug in itself, and the message in his mind transcended the music.

Coming in at seven minutes and ten seconds, 'Layla' was probably the most produced track on the album, Eric's scorching guitars weaving a compelling pattern that vied for urgency with his tortured vocals. With Duane's heavenly slide playing on top, the tune seems to find peace with itself just as the listener feels it's all over. Bobby Whitlock's piano leads into a lamentful finale with Eric and Duane crying out to each other through their instruments.

Partly because of the inspirational title and also because of the company he kept, Eric's playing on the *Layla* album was incredibly eloquent. Some inner force, together with the talents of Allman, Jim Gordon, Carl Radle and Bobby Whitlock, meshed with Eric to set a new musical standard for the 1970s. 'Why Does Love Got to Be So Sad?' steams in with Duane exercising his fingers without the aid of a slide, and 'Little Wing' was a celebratory tribute to Jimi Hendrix. Eric duets with Bobby Whitlock, who had a hand in writing six of the tunes. The density and soaraway vocal by Clapton on the provocatively titled 'Have You Ever Loved a Woman?' helped make *Layla* one of the greatest rock/blues albums ever recorded.

As Derek and the Dominos opened their British tour at Dagenham on 1 August 1970, Simon and Garfunkel's *Bridge Over Troubled Water* topped the British chart, with the Beatles' *Let It Be* second. The Dominos ran from May 1970 until April 1971. Throughout the crisis provoked by Eric and Pattie's association and the birth of the song 'Layla', relations between Eric and George remained cordial. This remains, although Eric says there is perhaps an underlying, unspoken tension. At the time of his split with Pattie, George took a rational view of a mercurial situation, saying that if the marriage was to end, then it was at least good that his wife was going with someone as intelligent and worthy as Eric Clapton.

Musically the two men continued their respect. George's role as concertmaster in a charity concert to aid Bangladesh refugees, on 1 August 1971, was to be his finest hour as he recruited such luminaries as Bob Dylan, Clapton, and Ringo Starr to the show in New York.

That show at Madison Square Garden marked his last stage appearance for two years. He went home, closed the door, and began the long, heavily publicized period with drugs in his life. Now, he looks back on it as a method of anaesthetizing himself from reality. At the time, it was simply an addiction that embarrassed and disheartened those around him.

Eric's capriciousness in love, his brandy-for-breakfast routine, and his chauvinism, combined with his provocative treatment of Pattie, led to their surprising first separation just after Christmas 1978. It had been an appalling holiday, Pattie continually berating her lover for being drunk, for not eating, and in one sharp aside to him, calling him 'cold'.

On 7 February he wrote irritably in his diary: 'It's becoming increasingly hard to find anything in this house. We've got so many records, so many tapes, so many photographs, so many books and so on and so on, and none of them are where you'd expect them to be. Everything seems to be in the last possible place you would expect it to be. Madness. I will have to get out of here soon so that the house can get itself straight again. The whole play gets a bad or untidy influence from me whenever I'm here too long ... [later] Had a row with Nello and pulled her hair. I stand accused of being cold. My feeling is sometimes too strong to be controlled but that don't make me a cold person. There are a lot of frayed nerves around here and we've got to beware of pointing fingers at one another. I don't know what's on Nell's mind and my pride prevents me from coaxing it out of her. I shouldn't have to, at this time, before a grand-slam tour. I am like a caged animal. Even I don't know what I'm going to do next. How can I expect to know, by instinct alone, what she is up to? Anyway, humble pie is needed all round.'

The next day's entry began: 'Today has started as

strained as the day before ended. And you can't go on blaming it on the stars.' After documenting a petty argument with Pattie over who had lost the keys to a window when a cleaner arrived, Eric wrote: 'A definite state of détente exists, and then, just as suddenly, it disappears. I will never understand the female gender. But it's certainly a relief when everything, for no apparent reason, is all right again.' He ended the day's entry euphorically, implying that he and Pattie had made up. 'Such a night . . .'

The social butterfly inside Pattie was now finding pursuits outside her home. She had become friends with two young model twins, Jenny and Susie McLean. When Jenny visited their home one day, Pattie insisted she stayed overnight because it had become so late for her to drive back to her Hampstead home. By the time Pattie got up next day, Eric and Jenny had gone out together, first shopping and then to a pub. Pattie decided to visit her sister.

Returning that afternoon, she found Jenny McLean and Eric sitting 'very closely together on the sofa'. Says Pattie: 'I started to talk to her and then Eric said: "Can't you see . . . I'm in *love* with this girl? Can't you see that I'm talking to her and I'm courting her?" I was so shocked, I couldn't believe it. This was nearly five years after he'd pursued me, and after all that had happened. I was so shocked I carried on talking to her. Then it sank in, so I rushed upstairs, shaking. I thought, how *can* he suddenly change like this? I thought he loved me, that we were having a nice relationship. I downed a few Valium which I don't normally do, and phoned my sister and she said I should go and stay with her.' By early evening, in the dark and pouring rain, Pattie walked, confused and stumbling into bushes, up the drive to be met by her sister – also named Jenny – in her car.

When she apprehensively phoned Eric two days later, he asked where she was. 'I'm not telling you, but are you still with *her*?' said Pattie. He replied: 'Um . . . yes.' Pattie says: 'I just couldn't bear it.' She phoned some friends in Los Angeles, Rob Fraboni and his wife Myel. Fraboni had been a producer respected by Eric for his work on the seminal album *Music from Big Pink*, by the Band, which made a huge impact on Clapton in 1966; the two men had become firm friends, with Fraboni visiting his house frequently when he was in Britain.

Flying to Los Angeles, Pattie was in floods of tears. The stewardess said she would have to move to the rear of the plane to avoid upsetting other passengers. 'I was *so* heartbroken. I didn't know what to do with my life and thought I might start a new life in America. I had no intention of returning to England.'

Meanwhile, Eric had begun a tour of Ireland with his new band. His diary contained several references to his desire for Jenny McLean, 'Sweet Jen', who visited him there. 'The gig was great and sweet Jen flew in to make the day perfect. We talked and talked about our respective wounds.' Noting that Pattie ('Nello') had gone to America, Eric showed some contrition about forgetting her birthday. 'I am a bad man and I think the world better roll on without me for a while, anyway. All in love is fair.'

Three factors played a part in the reunion of Eric and Pattie: the first, probably, was fate; the second, Eric's modesty in failing to acknowledge his fame; and the third, Roger Forrester's instinct to gamble and determination to win. Between the Irish concerts and the

American tour, Clapton visited Roger's home for a game of pool. Casually, the manager said to him: 'You want to be careful with this girl Jenny, Eric. Someone will take a photograph of you and you'll be in the papers.' Eric, often apparently unaware in those years of his value as a news item, replied: 'Don't be silly, who wants to put *my* picture in the paper?'

Forrester insisted that he could ensure that Eric's picture appeared in the national papers next day, if he wished to. Eric, riled anyway because he was losing the pool game, said: 'No way. Ten thousand quid says you can't do that.'

Forrester walked to the phone and called Britain's top newspaper gossip columnist, the *Daily Mail*'s Nigel Dempster. Forrester said: 'Rock star Eric Clapton will marry Pattie Boyd in Tucson, Arizona, next Tuesday.' Eric went home, convinced he had won £10,000; Forrester sat up all night waiting for the paper to slip through the letterbox next morning. To his astonishment the story appeared.

An enraged Clapton hurtled in his Ferrari to Forrester's Mayfair office as soon as he woke to the news of the story. Roger was on the phone, but Eric stormed in, wrapping the cord around his neck and hitting him over the head with the phone. How dare he assume the right to make a personal decision for him? Eric was livid at being put in an impossible situation.

'Really', said Forrester, calming him down, 'you have to decide whether you want to be with Pattie or not.' By now, Eric's brief affair with Jenny McLean had ended and he was morose about the messy situation he had caused. Forrester told him it was time either to marry Pattie or to make a clean break and be free. Eric was totally confused about his next action; *en route* to

London, he had been congratulated on his imminent marriage by his regular petrol pump attendant and a pub landlord. He was warming to the idea but was furious with Forrester.

'Yeah,' said Eric when his temper subsided. 'I want to be with Pattie but now, because of your stupid behaviour, she's gonna read this story in the paper before I've even proposed to her.'

Not so, said Forrester. Retrieving the phone, he dialled Rob Fraboni's home in Los Angeles. Pattie was not in; she was down in Malibu recovering after a sushi dinner with lots of wine on the beach the night before. Fraboni told Eric he would drive out to see her with any message.

Arriving at Malibu, Fraboni found a tired, hung-over Pattie and walked her out on to the balcony of the house in which she was staying. She was exhausted. She had a nervous rash all over her body and had not yet had her daily trip to the acupuncturist which cleared it.

'Doesn't the ocean look beautiful today?' Fraboni began.

'No, Rob. Nothing looks beautiful with the kind of hangover I've got.'

Fraboni then read out, from the back of an envelope, the telephone message from Eric to Pattie. 'Please marry me next Tuesday in Tucson, Arizona.' Eric's message added that if she refused, 'she was to get on her bike'. Fraboni would be the best man.

Predictably, Pattie's first worry was what had happened to Jenny McLean. She phoned Eric. 'He said she was no longer with him,' says Pattie. 'I asked why it had to be so rushed and Eric explained the bet with Roger and the story in the *Daily Mail*. I said: "How cheap. You should really pay your debts. I can't marry you under these conditions."' But romance won the day. Finally, with tears of joy, Pattie said yes. Once off the phone, she realized she had only three days to buy a wedding dress, have the blood test for rubella essential for non-residents marrying in America, and get to Arizona.

The day before the wedding, Eric and his party flew in. They checked into the same hotel as Pattie and her girlfriends Myel Fraboni and Chris O'Dell. Pattie was certain there would be a hitch because nothing would persuade Eric to have his blood checked with a needle. He had a horror of injections. The problem was solved by having a Clapton lookalike, Larry McNeny, from Tulsa, who worked with Eric's musicians, going to have Eric's blood test, taking with him Eric's passport. Next, Eric went to the registrar's office to get a licence, and was followed by journalists and an official who stopped him on the steps as he walked away with the licence. 'Excuse me, you have to pay, Mr Clapton.' Eric had no cash with him and his friends found a few dollars to hand over for the licence fee. It was 27 March 1979.

Six local churches had been booked by Roger Forrester, in an attempt to throw the local press off the scent. The wedding took place at Tucson's Apostolic Assembly of Faith in Christ Jesus. Eric and Pattie followed the tradition of not meeting until they reached the altar; in her mind she flashed back to the memory of the last time she had seen him, snuggled up to another woman. Two identical rings had been bought for the bride and groom by Nigel Carroll. Eric and Pattie were married by the Rev. Daniel Sanchez.

'The service was super,' says Pattie. 'The Mexican preacher was lovely and the roadies and the band looked wonderful in powder blue tuxedos with black piping, some in pink suits, and all with sneakers on.' Rob Fraboni

→ <u>WE ARE WED</u>

tuesday

27
MARCH

i married well today, hurray,
it was a beautiful wedding. and i had
a really bad case of nerves until i met
the priest, who put me at ease straight
away ~ amazingly must in fact. all of
what he said to us came off right, all of
his heart, and then he refered to his
bible, we got married, in the sight of God.
i will tell you more about it later
when my pen is working. about midday.

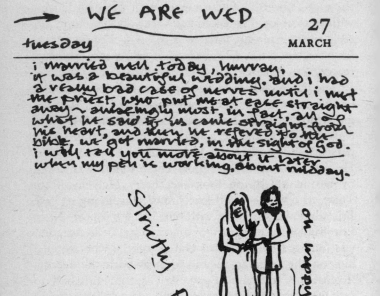

Strictly private

he hidden no

count your blessings
one by one ~ EC

the bash was unbelievable ~ what more
can i say ~ God bless our wedding ~

Diary entry by Eric on the day he married Pattie.

was the best man, Roger Forrester gave Pattie away, Alphi O'Leary and Nigel Carroll were the ushers. Ben Palmer flew in specially for the wedding.

Back at the hotel, the reception satisfied Eric's custard-pie humour by ending in a cake fight. Next night, an elated Clapton began his forty-concert American tour. Appearing with him was one of his greatest musical idols, and a great friend from the Yardbirds years, the legendary blues singer Muddy Waters.

Although Eric was by far the bigger attraction, he felt humble alongside the veteran, and honoured by the fact that Muddy wanted to open the show for him. One night, backstage, someone handed Eric Muddy's guitar to hold for a few moments. Clapton refused to touch it, explaining that it was no ordinary guitar. Owned by Muddy, it had an aura and demanded special treatment. 'Touching that guitar is absolutely taboo for me,' said Eric.

All seemed sweetness as the tour opened, and the newly-wed guitarist performed beautifully, kicked along by a swinging band: Albert Lee, Carl Radle, Dick Sims and Jamie Oldaker. Such was Eric's euphoria that when the tour reached his wedding city of Tucson, he sprang a surprise on Pattie, insisting she join him on stage. Then, taking a leaf from the show-business performer beneath the cool rock 'n' roller, he sang a song to her.

The song was 'Wonderful Tonight'. He had written this most direct, poignant song to her in 1976 and still considers it 'the most perfect love song'. Simple, profound and born of true passions, it was written, fittingly, in the same sitting-room of the house where he had written love letters to Pattie during her marriage to George Harrison.

They were preparing to go to a party one evening. 'I was waiting for her to get ready,' he recalls. Not knowing how long he would have to wait, as he stood on the landing outside their bedroom, he said: 'Come *on*! Are we ready to *go*?' Pattie was busy trying on dresses.

'Within five minutes, I was down here (in the lounge) and I'd written the song. As a love song, I think that's one of the finest going, much more so if I think about the song than if I think about me doing it. I've done my versions, live and studio, and I still think that they're scruffy. But the sentiment is so simple, so honestly loving, that it's a great love song.'

WONDERFUL TONIGHT

It's late in the evening
She's wondering what clothes to wear
She puts on her make-up
And brushes her long blonde hair
And then she asks me, 'Do I look all right?'
And I say, 'Yes, you look wonderful tonight.'

We go to a party
And everyone turns to see
This beautiful lady, that's walking around with me
And then she asks me, 'Do you feel all right?'
And I say, 'Yes, I feel wonderful tonight.'

I feel wonderful because I see the love light in your eyes
And the wonder of it all
Is that you just don't realize . . . how much I love you.

It's time to go home now
And I've got an aching head
So I give her the car keys
And she helps me to bed.
And then I tell her, as I turn out the light,
I say, 'My darling, you were wonderful tonight,
Oh my darling, you were wonderful tonight.'

Self-deprecatingly, he adds that it was fortuitous that he completed the song so quickly before Pattie was ready to go and then headed for the party. 'By the time I got home I was too blind drunk to remember [the circumstances that motivated the song]. It was a blackout in the end.' Later, he conceded that there was a degree of subtle irritation built into the lyrical theme. As a generally punctual person, he often erupted when he was kept waiting unduly, and that factor formed part of the air of affectionate resignation in the song.

As he sang 'Wonderful Tonight' to her on stage in Tucson, Pattie turned crimson with embarrassment. Meant as a sincere tribute to his lady, the moment was almost too much for Pattie to take. 'She loved them, you know,' Eric says of his intense compositions that celebrated his passion for her. 'Difficult to know what she really is feeling. One always gets the impression that, although you could see she was getting a kind of tingling feeling from it, it was slightly embarrassing, too. An awful pressure, which I can imagine it would put on a person. If it was done to me, I would feel very obligated in a way to live up to this person that's being written about.' Some years later, when their marriage became rocky,

Pattie remarked to Eric that, on reflection, she had not felt strong enough to be put on the pedestal he had erected for her.

The crowd loved the sentimental occasion at Tucson as he introduced his wife. But thankfully for her and for those in the Clapton entourage who sensed an 'over-the-top' event, she was not called upon to go on stage again. Receptions everywhere were ecstatic. A beaming Pattie stood in the wings as the tour made its way through Albuquerque, El Paso, Dallas.

And then she was floored by a shattering decision from Eric. He told her that he wanted her to go to Los Angeles and collect her baggage and return to England. Mentally re-aligning himself with an established rock band ethic that precludes women from travelling with bands, Eric wanted to concentrate on his work. However much he loved his wife, her company was a diversion. He wanted to regain his focus.

'I was awfully upset,' Pattie says. 'He obviously wanted me to become the little housewife. Anyway, I did as I was told. I wasn't happy because I love New Orleans and was looking forward so much to going with Eric to that city, the next stop.'

That curious dichotomy of the incandescent lover and the working musician had collided to establish a fragile bridge between him and the person he had just sung to on stage as 'this beautiful lady . . .'

Back in England after a triumphant tour, Eric and Pattie threw a huge wedding party for relatives and friends. It developed into a major occasion for musicians, too, with such notables as Mick Jagger, Jeff Beck and Lonnie Donegan attending. Three ex-Beatles – Paul, George and Ringo – joined in the jam-session in the marquee. Informed of the event later, John Lennon told Eric by phone from New York that he would have been there if he'd known about it. Had he done so, that would have been the only time all the Beatles had played together since they split amid such bitterness nine years earlier; it would have been the informal reunion that the world is still craving fifteen years later, even though it's fourteen years after Lennon was killed.

After the fireworks display and the revelry and the jam-session, there was a sad scene, a commentary on the callousness of all the musicians. Alone among the players, Jack Bruce approached the music of the night with his usual intensity. Playing bass, he improvised with tremendous imagination on old rock 'n' roll songs like 'Johnny B. Goode'. But the rest of the band didn't want to treat the session so seriously. They ostracized Jack. In the early hours of the morning in the chilly tent, Bruce was the lone musician playing.

'The others couldn't take it,' recalls Ben Palmer. 'They treated him *so* badly. He was really playing an advanced form of rock 'n' roll, probably the sort of music Cream would have played if they'd lasted. But they all moved further and further away from him, leaving him in the marquee. And Jack came off the stage broken. He sat in my lap and cried. He had nothing to say and nowhere to go.' Three hours later, the house was empty and Jack was still there, with a drunken hanger-on. Eric had gone to bed. Ben Palmer persuaded a depressed Jack Bruce to go home.

All the crowd from Ripley were at the party . . . Pat and Rose and Sid and Guy and many others. Eric had put them at ease for the big day, writing a message at the bottom of their invitation cards: 'To the Ripleyites: you don't have to bring a present if you don't want to.' The most original gift came from Guy Pullen on behalf of the villagers: a tin of mock turtle soup. It was an affectionate reminder to Clapton of his roots: 'When he was a kid living with Rose,' says Guy, 'we all remembered him sitting after dinner with a ring round his top lip after drinking mock turtle soup . . .'

To the musicians and other friends and their respective families, Mr and Mrs Eric Clapton epitomized a couple in perfect harmony. Eric had secured the woman of his dreams and Pattie's enjoyment of his music pointed to near perfection in marriage. Their honeymoon was in Kingston, Jamaica, the city whose reggae music Eric so admired. Among those who regarded the marriage as a fairy tale come true was Pete Townshend. 'They'll grow old very graciously together,' he predicted.

Eric continued his drinking and his extensive travelling as his career intensified and he sought more and more refuge in work. He wrote another simple love song to Pattie, 'Pretty Girl', and despite the pressures of great periods of separation when he was abroad, he believed all was well.

But when he was at home, the obsessive streak that dominated him sent him scurrying for hobbies that would take his mind away from alcohol. 'I went strongly for fishing, and that's a very anti-social hobby,' he says. He and Nigel Carroll had become active members of the Ferrari Owners Club, and Eric and Roger Forrester were rabid supporters of West Bromwich Albion football team. His guitar plectrums, often a source of his ribald humour, carried messages to possible thieves: 'THIS IS MY FUCK-ING PICK. E.C.' And as a further identification, his support of West Bromwich carried his imprimatur: UP THE BAGGIES.

Eric's home life appeared passive, but his creativity during the years of heavy drinking was surprisingly high. Later, he would say how much he regretted the 'lost time', during which he could have enhanced his career so much faster. This statement alone belies any theory that he is casual about his work. He is fiercely professional, dedicated and ambitious. But the quality and quantity of his work in that period has provided aficionados of Clapton with a rich harvest.

In the autumn of 1975, the album *E.C. Was Here* carried all the flaws of a live album, but demonstrated that Eric in concert was a far more relaxed artist than the sometimes taut, self-conscious studio singer and guitarist. Reacting to the input of the players around him, on a stage, was far more stimulating than the controlled atmosphere of a studio.

His spirituality was evident in the song he had so touchingly performed at his 'comeback' concert at the Rainbow Theatre, London. 'Presence of the Lord', one of the earliest recorded examples of his songwriting and the only Eric-written song on the Blind Faith album, sounds almost autobiographical.

> I have finally found a way to live
> Just like I never could before
> I know that I don't have much to give
> But I can open any door.

No one could relate to the blues, and absorb that art's sensibilities, without an inner spirituality, and Clapton is best described as a man of God who does not actively practise a religion. 'I was brought up Church of England with a loose, average religious education,' he says. 'I always did feel there was some kind of destiny preordained for everyone. But I felt, and feel, that the choice and conscience is up to the person. I always felt bad when I knew I was doing something wrong, therefore I believe there is something other than my own momentum in charge. It always felt bad to go against the grain. And I put that down to God!'

In his wedding album, he wrote: 'Dear God, Bless our marriage, Amen.' And at the end of every tour, he hugs every member of his band and frequently says: 'God bless.'

An unnerving quasi-religious moment occurred when Clapton gave a concert in Jerusalem in 1979. A girl fan ran up to the stage and threw a rose to him, which accidentally hit him in the face. In his dressing-room later, Eric looked at the cut on his forehead and saw that it had turned into a cross. He was shaken by the sight. 'I knew I should never have played rock 'n' roll in this place,' he said.

He told some members of his band that he prayed sometimes. He is superstitious, never putting shoes on a table or walking under ladders. 'I take my superstitions to ridiculous extremes,' he says. 'If I'm waiting for something, I count to thirty and if it hasn't happened by then, something's wrong. On the phone, I let a number ring out a number of times and if they haven't answered by then, it's a bad sign and I hang up.' Palmists and tarot card readers have not attracted him, however. Superstition of a more human kind carries over into his work: 'Just as I leave the dressing-room or walk near to the stage, Alphi [O'Leary, his tour assistant] is on hand.

And he always says the same four words before I walk out: "Have a good one." If he isn't there to say that, well, it doesn't throw me completely, but I do wonder.'

Most of 1976 was spent working in California. Eric continued his apparently insatiable enthusiasm for joining recording sessions by friends, playing alongside such artists as Joe Cocker, Ringo Starr, Kinky Friedman, Stephen Bishop and Corky Laing. He also attracted Bob Dylan to the session at Shangri-La Studios, Malibu, to contribute the song 'Sign Language' to the album that would become *No Reason To Cry*, released in August of that year.

The album's enigmatic title was matched by the texture of the album. The blues rang out on 'Double Trouble', originally recorded by Otis Rush, and 'County Jail Blues'. 'Innocent Times' was beautifully sung by Marcy Levy, a regular collaborator with Eric. Members of the Band (Robbie Robertson, Garth Hudson, Richard Manuel and Levon Helm) guested along with Dylan, Ronnie Wood of the Stones, and Pete Townshend. It was a highly musicianly album, but as far as fans were concerned, perhaps less accessible than most Clapton music. Enjoyable though it was as a kind of musicians' super-jam session, it lacked a focus.*

*

* Eric considers it 'one of my favourite albums – good groove, voice improving,' as he told Marc Roberty, author of the indispensable book *Eric Clapton: The Complete Recording Sessions 1963–1992*. His industriousness in the laid-back Malibu atmosphere is confirmed by Eric's statement that he 'cut something like twenty-five tracks in three weeks out of nowhere . . . it was just like falling rain'.

In the seven years of Eric's drink problem, those close to Clapton found him as prickly on stage as he was when he left the concert platform and hit the bottle. He was particularly vulnerable when fans in the audience received heavy treatment, as they did once in Austin, Texas. 'Without those kids,' says Eric, 'I'm out of work.' So when the security team in front of the stage at Austin began billy-clubbing exuberant kids, and spraying Mace on their faces, as well as on Clapton's own crew, the guitarist took dramatic action. He laid down his guitar on stage, stopped the band, and walked off. When the confrontations between the security men and the fans had subsided, they returned. But to all those around Clapton, and the promoters, it was a sharp warning, from a superstar, that he would not play at any price.

Surprisingly, Eric's drinking years did not colour his judgement of others, or his decisiveness, or, crucially, his ability to play. 'But I was on automatic pilot most of the time,' he says now. On stage, or when he rationalized his career to himself and even to his guardian Roger Forrester, Clapton was lucid, cool and objective. Chris Stainton, joining him near the end of his drinking period, found him a 'natural bandleader, whatever he says'. Stainton observed immediately that Eric 'loved or hated, people or things, cities or countries – everything. There was no in between, no shade of grey.' The total definition in Eric made for a leader who knew a bad audience, or a bad night's playing, and did not want, or expect, to be bolstered by false persuasion to the contrary.

Fifteen years of performing had given him an ability to judge an audience quickly. Stainton recalls casually saying to Eric after one European concert: 'Good one tonight, Eric.' Eric snapped back: 'Nah, it wasn't. It was like playing to a load of fucking corpses.' The quality of his music, and that of the musicians, was lost in the absence of Eric's more important 'fix' – the warmth, the instant response, the empathy of the crowd.

Only twice did drink seriously affect his playing. Both concerts were, strangely, in a country he loves, Japan. He had stopped drinking but sneaked back on it that day when nobody was with him. He thought he was able to have an occasional drink, but his body rejected it and he went on stage with a combination of pain-killing tablets and too much Cognac inside him. He played a whole solo a semitone out of tune. His musicians and the road crew cringed, but he survived, blissfully unaware that although he was hitting the right notes, the key was wrong.

Chris Stainton, a veteran of rock who saw service in Joe Cocker and Leon Russell's bizarre Mad Dogs and Englishmen tour, views the Clapton drunken walk along a tightrope with a glance back at his own drugs problem. 'What happens is that *you* think you're playing better, but you're not. You're usually coming out with a load of rubbish. I think there was a little bit of the culture of jazz and the blues players he idolized. So many of the black players Eric loved used to get through a bottle of Scotch before they went on stage. So maybe there was a bit of that romance in it for Eric. I know, from experience, and Eric does now, that if you want to deal with music properly, you must do it straight.

'But the determined, stubborn streak inside Eric makes for a very complex attitude to drugs, and drink, and that's why he went right to the edge with both. You know, he actually had to be at the point of death, looking the angels in the face, before he gave up. Now he's kicked everything, I know he will never, ever go back to it. He's a survivor.'

Eric's odd sense of humour and practical jokes have often been at odds with his seriousness as a man and as a musician. Once, he pushed his jokiness too far even with loyal aides like Roger Forrester and Alphi O'Leary. On tour, Forrester knocked on Eric's hotel room to be told from the other side by a mocking Eric, sleepy from brandy: 'Oh *go away*! I'm not going *on* tonight. Don't feel like it.' Forrester and O'Leary literally smashed the door down, thinking Clapton meant it ... to find him ready to go to the concert.

At the local pub, O'Leary called the joking Eric's bluff one night. Under the influence again, Eric began systematically kicking Alphi under the table. O'Leary, whose physical size and strength does not invite argument, said: 'Eric, if you do that once more, I shall take you outside and knock the shit out of you, whoever you are. You're not a big enough boy to kick me.' Clapton turned to his other drinking friend and said, 'I think he means it.' He stopped, knowing he had pushed the joke too far, and not wanting to take issue with the six-foot three-inch giant body of a sober O'Leary.

Another dangerous confrontation came in the Bahamas after O'Leary had hired a Toyota car and a playful Clapton snapped off all the chrome fittings and placed them inside. Then he jumped up and down on the roof. 'Now,' recalls Alphi O'Leary, 'he could say he paid the hire car money, but that wasn't the point. He was treating me like a moron. I didn't want to drive around in a car looking like trash. I picked up a paving slab and threw it at him. It missed him by half an inch and shattered on the floor. He said: "You're mad." I said: "Fair's fair, Eric."'

Eric went through a period of winding people up, seeing how far he could push them. 'I'd never been used

monday

nelly saw me pouring myself a double brandy and lemonade about mid morning (while she was talking to her mother on the phone) and gave me the evil eye at which point i promptly slipped over and spilt my drink all over fridays page!... explanation over..... glyn called and has invited us for a drink at the parrot, could it be he has heard about john astley coming to japan to record us?.... we shall see....

Self-conscious diary entry from Eric.

to that,' says O'Leary. Deep down, though, Alphi O'Leary has massive respect and love for his boss. 'He's sincere, there's a ton of love and tears inside him, and he really is a god of the guitar.' Talking to fans at stage doors around the world, Alphi O'Leary is convinced that many really do idolize Clapton as a seer.

Among those who saw the unhappy years of Eric from close quarters was Gary Brooker. The ex-leader of Procol Harum, the group that ran for ten years from 1966 and recorded the international psychedelic anthem 'A Whiter Shade of Pale', bought a pub, the Parrot Inn, two miles from Clapton's house. The year was 1976, bang in the middle of Eric's drinking years.

Clapton and Brooker had first met in the sixties. Cream were playing 'Strange Brew' and Procol Harum 'A Whiter Shade of Pale' on television's _Top of the Pops_. Later, Brooker's band toured America in the footsteps of Cream, and he says they were 'staggered' at the breakthrough Cream had achieved.

After Eric had wandered into Brooker's pub one night to find him behind the bar, the two became friendly. Two years later, when Procol had ended, Gary had gone solo as a singer-songwriter-keyboardist. Eric asked him if he wanted to join his band, complementing the rocking piano work of Chris Stainton.

'The day he asked me to join, I saw that he had a problem,' says Brooker. 'He said he wanted someone strong in the band.' Brooker's role was to be twofold: as an experienced bandleader, he was expected to help knock the band into shape and take some of the leadership responsibilities from Eric; and he was also to help Clapton emerge from the shroud of bleary boozing.

'Eric's condition was very worrying,' says Brooker. 'Often we'd get drunk together, but I was surprised that he'd flake out, or be drunk many times in addition to the ones when we had a drink together. And he'd crack up, in tears. I tried to get to the bottom of what it was . . . and Eric would say things like: "Oh, I just want to play the blues." This wasn't just the drink talking, it was something very deep that was troubling him. It was distressing.'

Brooker tried to convince Clapton that part of the problem was that his musicians at that time – Chris Stainton, Dave Markee (bass guitar), Albert Lee (guitar) and Henry Spinetti (drums) – didn't behave like a *band*. 'We should all get together more often, get to know each other,' said Brooker. A stiff attempt to do so, a formally arranged jam-session in the barn of Brooker's home, did not ignite; the others failed to understand why Gary had been brought into the band in the first place. 'I think the others revered him, and didn't mix, whereas he'd enjoy coming round to my hotel room, or me to his, at eleven in the morning for a chat. He seemed removed from the band and I don't think that helped.'

In a vivid recollection of the days when he saw Eric behave emotionally, Gary Brooker says: 'There were tears in his eyes on some occasions. He'd say to me: "I'm cracking up." He didn't like what he was doing to himself but he couldn't get out of it. He said it was such a slow process, winning himself round to saying: I don't want to be this person any more. It definitely seemed to hurt him to realize he was ruining himself.' The worst periods, predictably, were when there was no concert tour on the road, no album to prepare, and consequently no responsibilities to work. Clapton always performs best, as a person, when he faces the prospect of putting himself through the hoop. 'The other time I saw Eric cry was when we all went to see the film *ET* in America. There wasn't a dry eye among the whole band,' says Brooker.

Eric is capable of darting in and out of firm old friendships and sustaining them, despite lapses of time. Although he is quick to jettison hangers-on he meets on the road, and also inside the community of music, cherished friends are dear to him. Among them are Chas and Dave. The Cockney singers, who have won great popularity in Britain for their lively singalong music, first saw Clapton when he played with John Mayall's band at Cook's Ferry Inn, a pub in Edmonton, North London in 1966. But their friendship did not blossom until the mid 1970s, and eventually they opened the concerts on Clapton's British tours.

'He's a genuine, honest geezer and what he likes about our music, and us,' said Chas, 'is that we're unpretentious.' Eric's admiration for Chas and Dave's knockabout, knees-up style surprises some, but their warmth, professionalism and good-natured fun is precisely what Eric likes.

But they had a sharp reminder one night of his competitiveness. Most nights, they had invited guitarist Albert Lee to join them for their finale. After a few nights, Clapton started niggling away at Chas and Dave: 'It's always, "Come on, Albert", and never "Come on, Eric,"' he said petulantly. Chas and Dave thought he was joking, but he definitely was not. He thought Albert Lee was getting the heroic treatment. Chas and Dave had thought Eric, being the star, would not want to join in their spot. 'But he was genuinely choked, and it surprised us,' says Dave. They did bring Clapton into their set . . . and Eric gave Chas a banjo, which he treasures.

'Don't give it away,' Clapton warned him.

'Nah, I wouldn't part with it for Paul McCartney's songwriting royalties,' Chas replied.

The strong bond that links Chas and Dave and Eric is a fundamental love of the blues for its simplicity; Clapton has sung along with them often on the Huddie Ledbetter classic, 'Goodnight Irene'. But Eric's manager hates him doing it, believing it reduces him to the level of a pub singalong. Most times they meet, he tries to bribe Chas and Dave with £5 each not to get Eric involved in the song.

The simple spirit of that old song, and Eric's affinity with such genuine, unaffected characters as Chas and Dave, is important in understanding the man. In matters of hard commercial decisions, when a giant audience or his next album is under consideration, Eric will listen to advice and often accept it. For years, he allowed his concert running order to be devised by his manager, unusual for such a stubborn artist. His affection for Chas and Dave and their music reflects one of Clapton's most endearing characteristics: a refusal to believe in the remoteness of stardom.

This isn't easy. His home is littered with trophies that tell him he is a giant among musicians. While Clapton tries so often to walk away, or submerge his status, the awards feed his ego. There's his hat-trick of awards, for three consecutive years from 1967, as Top Musician in the *Melody Maker* readers' poll; the Gallery of the Greats award from *Guitar Player* magazine; three awards from *Playboy* magazine for his guitar work, including a Hall of Fame nomination; the prestigious Best Electric Blues Guitarist award from *Guitar Player*; Britain's Silver Clef award (twice) for services to music; even the award as Britain's Best-Dressed Man in 1970.

From his years with Cream particularly, Eric had learned how to balance the serious aspects of life on the road with zany interludes. 'Ginger and Jack's humour was vicious but we did have some really funny times and, despite the atmosphere in the band, there was a lot of comedy,' Clapton says. 'Once, we all climbed Ben Nevis together and the hilarious running back down it, chest-high in gorse [they had parked their car and dropped acid] will stay in my memory for ever. There were some crazy times as well as hard ones – like going to the office and tearing the place apart, just for a lark.'

Eric's penchant for Monty Pythonesque humour stayed with him when he launched his own band. 'When he came back off the tours, lots of people asked each other for Clapton stories,' says Pattie. 'With great glee, they'd want to know what pranks he'd got up to on the road and how many practical jokes he'd got away with.

People eagerly awaited his return from other countries because he was such a source of amusement.' Eric enjoyed the role people had cast for him. 'He enjoyed being the bizarre hero,' says Pattie.

Against the backdrop of superstardom, Clapton believes the best method of surviving the high mortality rate, either personal or professional, among top players is to refuse to be derailed from fundamental values. He loves to keep contact with other musicians. For many years, Eric boosted the sales of dozens of other people's records by his presence and his name on the label. But he hated being exploited, or having his friendship used for gain. He eventually decided to surprise some people by seriously asking for a token fee – to be paid in cash. The 'working man' ethic prompted that. And when, occasionally, he sells some of his guitars, he instructs that they should be sold anonymously so that they cannot fetch inflated prices on resale as 'Eric Clapton's guitars'.

Eric's ability to remain 'one of the blokes' and his easy-going accessibility to genuine Surrey village people were exemplified just after Christmas 1977. The Round Table, an organization which raises money for charity, was wondering what to do for the annual Valentine's Day dance. The 7,000 people of Cranleigh enjoyed four events a year in the village hall. They wanted something different from the traditional old-time dancing, raffles, fancy dress or cheese-and-wine parties. When the Tablers were in committee, one member, Roger Swallow, suddenly said: 'What about Eric Clapton?' The idea was greeted with howls of derision. Eric Clapton, live, at Cranleigh Village Hall? Forget it! But Swallow thought it was worth a try: he wrote to Eric.

A few days later, the phone rang in Swallow's office. 'Hello, it's Eric here. That dance of yours – I'll do it.' After recovering from the shock and his suspicion of a practical joke, Swallow asked how much he wanted as a fee to appear.

'Nothing, but there's just one thing. It's got to be strictly under the counter,' Eric answered. This puzzled Swallow, 'because in my business, "under the counter" means a hefty back-hander, if you know what I mean. But I quickly discovered that what Eric meant was that he wanted no publicity at all.' Clapton and his manager were so insistent on this that they told Swallow that if a newspaper got advance news, he would not do the show. It went ahead.

Eric even rehearsed at the village hall for two days in the week before the concert; he took a great interest in how much money could be expected, and how it would help re-equip the Cranleigh Cottage Hospital; and he brought an old friend, guitarist Ronnie Lane, formerly of the Faces. The music was laid-back, the hall packed with 350 people, ardent Clapton fans at the front, and soberly suited Round Tablers at the rear. Pattie Clapton and Katy Lane, flouncing around in scarlet and black French dresses and white petticoats, did an impromptu can-can which prompted the locals to dance and Eric to christen the ladies 'The Harlots'. Eric hit his musical peak with a great blues, 'Alberta, Alberta', his stylish instrumental phrases evoking a call-and-response technique between his superb vocal and his guitar. He was in a loose mood for the whole evening, feeling no pressure. The night raised £1,000 for the hospital and was described by Eric as a 'good 'un'. The mood of the evening was summed up after Eric and Ronnie Lane had harmonized on 'Goodnight, Irene', like a pair of mates fresh out of the local boozer. The audience joined in. As Eric left the hall, a young fan shouted out: 'Eric, do "Layla" or we won't have you back again!' It was the one song Eric didn't feel like doing that night.

The big arenas around the world are important 'career moves' in pleasing the people, but major artists always yearn for the intimacy of the clubs that first generated their love of playing. Eric became immersed in blues jam-sessions at Gary Brooker's Parrot Inn; Gary played piano and brought along some distinguished musicians, including saxophonist Mel Collins, violinist Darryl Way and guitarist Mickey Jupp, for evenings which were dedicated to blues music. 'We had a hundred and fifty people in at £1 a head, food included,' says Brooker. 'The amplification was small, and Eric sat down behind the pillar and seemed at his happiest. It sounded very similar to what a little Chicago club might have been years ago.' The tunes, too, rekindled Eric's deepest affections: golden oldies by the Coasters and Chuck Berry and Elmore James material.

The Parrot Band, as it has become known, played half a dozen nights at the pub before Eric decided a sense of style was called for. It was just like the scruffy old days with the Yardbirds. He phoned Brooker and asked what uniform they should wear that night to replace the casual look that was gaining too much ground. An air of formality was essential, Eric said, and he would wear a white dinner jacket and a black bow tie. That night, almost in return for their professionalism, they decided that the profits from their work should not go entirely to charity. They each earned £50, and the face of Eric Clapton was alight at the sight of the ready cash.

The camaraderie of pub life, as well as the music, strikes at Eric's heart. 'Real people,' he says simply. He greatly prefers it to the private-aeroplane-and-limousine life of world tours. On the road in the US, he once became so cynical about the similarity between the journeys, the cities and the halls, that when people asked where the next night's show was he had a set reply: 'Anywhere in America.'

After his world tours of such anonymous, massive stadiums, Eric enjoyed the earthiness of the final venue of all his British concerts. For many years this has always had to be at the 1,500-seater Guildford Civic Hall, a few miles from where he was born and from where he lived. The Guildford finale was very much a case of the meteor returning to earth, with his mother Pat, grandmother Rose and other local people cheering from the balcony. As a regular appearance for a player of his stature, it was for years a unique tradition and, with the vibrations of the occasion strong in his mind, Eric often played his most breathtaking solos. Promoter Harvey Goldsmith stopped the Guildford finales only in the 1980s, when Eric went to live in London.

'He's always prepared for women to reject him,' Pattie says. 'He is the classic blues player. He understands loneliness.' And he needs love. While 'Wonderful Tonight' is Clapton's most popular song, particularly requested by women, 'Layla' remains his most significant favourite of his compositions in that genre. He loves its urgency, its rock 'n' roll bite. 'Because while "Wonderful Tonight" is a pure love song that can be applied to any couple, and many people do, I wrote "Layla" specifically about Pattie and me. It was my open-heart message that I was in love with her and she knew it couldn't be about anyone else. I just couldn't visualize a life without her.'

With 'Wonderful Tonight' and 'Lay Down Sally', plus other songs written while he was on the road, Eric was anxious to get into the studio. Before these two potential classic Clapton compositions, plus the J. J. Cale song 'Cocaine' could go on record, Eric received a phone call from Pete Townshend, who with his guitarist friend Ronnie Lane was preparing an album called *Rough Mix*. This was being produced at the Olympic Studios, Barnes, in February 1977 by the eminent producer Glyn Johns.* When Townshend told Johns that he wanted to have Eric Clapton play one particular instrumental, the producer was negative. 'I had no ambition to work with him. I really didn't like him very much, because of his habits.' Johns had the 'greatest distaste' for junkies, and as an experienced record man he loathed their unreliability in the studio.

However, Johns remembered his early experience of working with Eric fifteen years earlier (with the legendary Howlin' Wolf on 'the London Sessions') and he always admired Clapton's work tremendously. Working with him again, after his history of addiction, was still not attractive, but when Eric guested on dobro on several Townshend–Lane tracks, Glyn Johns was surprised. 'I found him absolutely delightful and the overdubbing he did on dobro was astounding. I'd never heard anything quite like it; the emotion he put into his work was impressive and I saw a side of him I'd never really been aware of.'

* Glyn Johns has an immaculate pedigree as a producer. Beginning as an engineer on records by the Rolling Stones, the Faces, the Who and the Kinks, he went on to produce landmark albums by Led Zeppelin, the Beatles (*Let It Be* and half of *Abbey Road*), Bob Dylan, the Eagles, John Hiatt and Nancy Griffith. In 1994 he produced the reunion album by Crosby, Stills and Nash.

When the Townshend–Lane sessions ended, Eric asked Glyn if he would produce his next album, which became *Slowhand*. 'I said absolutely, because I'd seen a side of him I wasn't aware of before,' John recalls. Establishing himself as a disciplinarian in the studio, Johns noted that Eric responded well: 'He did mess me about a bit and when he did, I hauled him up. Eric in those days always saw recording rather like going to work, "clocking in", and was rather resentful of that. It was a case of "Suppose we've got to do some work now." You couldn't ask him to pick his guitar up. You'd have to push him into it. He'd rather be doing anything than picking up his guitar. However, when he did pick it up and was ready to play, you had better be ready to record instantly because what came out of him was amazing. And you didn't have too many cracks at it, because he'd soon be off again. I didn't mind that because what most people take several hours to achieve he would do in five minutes.'

'Wonderful Tonight', which would become a celebration and centrepiece of his compositions for ever, took nine takes to meet Eric's demands when they recorded it on 2 May 1977. To the public it finally touched, the song and the rest of the album seemed to mark a rejuvenated Eric, with no signal that he was in the middle of a drink problem. Battling successfully in Britain against the prevailing trends of disco, New Wave rock and punk, the *Slowhand* album, featuring Clapton's songs 'Lay Down Sally', 'Mean Old Frisco' and his dramatic reading of the J. J. Cale song 'Cocaine' (forever a stage favourite), provided a solid, optimistic statement from him. With his favourite guitar, the Blackie he had personally built, in his hand to the exclusion of most other instruments, the *Slowhand* sessions hit a winning groove, abundant with songs that went on to be perennial specials with his fans.

Though he usually responded well to Johns's instructions, 'he was capable of all manner of moods: stroppy, bossy, and the sudden realization that it was his show, after all'. He could even convert his fury to creativity. Once, recording the song 'The Core' for the *Slowhand* album, Glyn chided Eric for poor effort in overdubbing a guitar solo in the middle of the song. 'I had a go at him and he completely flipped, lost his rag . . . and played the most amazing solo as a result of his anger.'

The producer's assumption of a headmaster's role was a running joke. 'One day he came to the studio with an explanatory "Sorry Eric's late" note from Pattie! He was like a naughty little boy going to school. That summed Eric up during that period. Pattie was like his Mum.'

In awe of Eric's talent, Glyn Johns soon had to reverse his apprehensions about getting together with him. He became fond of Eric and the two men socialized. Johns knew Pattie well from two standpoints: he had produced Beatles records when she was married to George; Johns's brother Andrew was married to Pattie's younger sister Paula; and, since Glyn lived not far from Clapton's home, he would often ride his horse round there to drop in for coffee. And there were dinner dates.

Johns observed 'a man who was quite lonely, suffering from all kinds of pressure from commercialism, which I don't think he knew how to deal with because of the state he was in'. Pinpointing Eric's lifelong demeanour, which encourages people to feel sorry for him, Glyn Johns adds now that he 'fell for that one, hook, line and sinker'. Clapton's multi-faceted make-up includes an exterior demonstration of a lost soul who needed to have his own way in every compartment of his life. This caused people to indulge him. Glyn Johns was to embark on that route with the purest of motives towards Eric, but with a fatal result eventually for his own role as producer.

How Eric could draw upon the artist within his soul during this dark period for him, physically, is a puzzle to many observers. Pattie, when asked if she saw his music as a true reflection of his personality, replied thoughtfully: 'No, I see him as two separate people. He has a conscious mind working on a day-to-day basis and the other side is the unconscious mind of the artist, with the ability to tap into a different side of himself in the same way that anyone does when they dream. The unconscious mind has a universal consciousness and a natural insight and knowledge and Eric as an artist can connect with that.

'His day to day living is on a conscious level. It's very different from the artistic side. His daily personality is not reflected in any of the songs he writes.' It was curious for her to have lived with someone who, when sitting quietly, had 'all sorts of fantastic melodies going through his mind'. He tapped into a very private source for that, she believed.

The people around Eric have become familiar with his idiosyncrasies. He is adamant that, when on tour, there should be no crowds, particularly hangers-on, in the dressing-room, and he insists on sharing the room with his band. 'He likes simplicity, but he draws a line,' says Roger Forrester. 'He won't tolerate inferiority. He certainly notices when things are not right.' Clapton does not lose his temper often. He tends to allow a situation that irritates him plenty of time to correct itself before blowing his top. On an American tour, for the first two weeks he contained his irritation that the audience was held back by security men from advancing towards the stage until the final two songs, 'Cocaine' and 'Layla'. 'It was the same scene every night,' says Eric. 'But in the dressing-room after a couple of weeks, I did explode to Roger Forrester that it was so artificial that the audience was seen to be released at the same moment in the show every night. It's the only time I can remember really losing my cool. The falseness, the predictability of every show really got to me.'

Although Eric appears casual before a show, the inner man is more tense than he might admit. Walking towards the stage, he has often told his manager that he didn't feel like playing. 'Oh, I just feel tired . . .' Forrester, escorting him like a trainer with a boxing champion, knew how to work him up. 'Listen. West Brom just lost, six-nil.' Clapton would get into such a steaming temper, either with the news or with Forrester's 'winding-up' ploy, that he would go on stage and play better because of the tension. Only his crew knew the sign, at the end of a show, that Clapton had not enjoyed his performance, or rated the audience as unresponsive. For some years, to symbolize a bad gig, Eric held up his guitar to the audience with the back of the instrument facing them.

After several years, Clapton told Forrester he hated his backstage technique of telling him when it was time to go on stage. It was a corny method: 'That's it, Eric. Let's go on stage . . . ready to *go*.' Finally, Clapton announced to Roger: 'Look, for five or six years, I've *never* liked you walking into the dressing-room telling me, it's time to go on stage, Eric. 'Cos I'm waiting for you to walk in through that door and my tension's building up. It's like you're preparing me for the gallows! So don't do it!' Forrester's solution was to arrange, world-wide, for a special coded knock-knock on the door as the signal to *him*. Then he would say slowly: 'Ready when you are, Eric.'

It's often said that the real man emerges from the drunk. If that is true, then the Clapton of the late 1970s was an exhibitionist trying to escape from the sentimentalist. Many rock musicians revelled then in wild behaviour, destroying hotel furniture and causing mayhem as an immature means of attracting attention. Clapton, enjoying his alcohol but not in the top league of hotel wreckers, was still a hazard for those around him on world tours. The child inside him had a ball.

His most horrific and dangerous moment came one night twenty-six floors up at the Rainbow Hilton Hotel, Waikiki Beach, Honolulu. A drunken Eric, stripped to the waist, and clutching a samurai sword given to him during a Japanese tour, climbed perilously round the balcony into the next-door suite of his drummer, Jamie Oldaker, who was in bed. Down below on the street, a woman called the police, petrified at the sight of a man with a sword in his hand, dicing with death. The drummer recognized the drunken Eric, but by the time Clapton had walked out of the room into the corridor, there were three Hawaiian policemen moving up to him, with guns aimed straight at his head.

It was like something from an Errol Flynn film. The youngest cop recognized Eric, but the two older policemen hustled him down to the hotel lobby. 'You can't arrest *Eric Clapton*!' said the young one. 'Do you want to bet?' asked the angry older cop. Eric put a cigarette in his mouth but they took it from him and snapped it in two. The drama ended after Roger Forrester suggested the police should give Eric a heavy talking to and leave it at that. 'And that's how it finished,' says Forrester. 'The police did say he'd risked certain death. Three people had been killed attempting that balcony walk before. It was a sheer drop. He was very lucky to be alive.'

Capriciousness and unpredictability had been an easily identifiable trait in the man, and everyone involved with a Clapton pursuit became resigned to this reality: it would proabably not outlast his initial enthusiasm. 'I plunge into everything full tilt and then hope to level out,' he says. Luckily, he could apply this to his addictions as well as to his more frivolous diversions.

In 1975 he began his flirtation with the turf as a racehorse owner, buying Pattie a horse as her Christmas gift. He was going to call it Layla's Song, but at the last moment changed it to Bushbranch. Although she won five races, they were low-category races, but the horse whetted Eric's appetite for more involvement; he had always taken a lively 'punter's interest' in horses. With a prominent trainer, Toby Balding, who runs stables in Hampshire, Eric bought a filly for £500. Named Via Delta (a pun on the US airline) by Roger Forrester's secretary, Diana Puplett, the mare was literally a soaraway success: she won twice as a two-year-old, had a fine three-year-old season and finally, in 1979, brought Eric his finest turf hour, winning the Fortnum and Mason trophy at Ascot, with prize-money of £9,000. In tweed suit and trilby hat, Eric attended Ascot looking every inch the dapper racehorse tycoon, beaming happily at cameramen recording his surprising entry into the world of racing.

Within two racing seasons, Via Delta was sold because, in the words of Toby Balding, 'we had an offer we couldn't refuse for her to go to Oman'. After winning Eric about £28,000 in prize-money, she was sold for £50,000. Toby Balding believed and hoped that the success would encourage Eric to invest in bloodstock. There was even talk of Eric keeping some fillies at his Surrey home. But the idea was dropped when it was realized that staff would be needed to look after the horses.

When Via Delta was sold, Eric turned to his wife for an inspirational name. His next horse, called Nello (his nickname for Pattie), won at 25–1 at Leicester. Then came Ripleyite who, in Toby Balding's judgement, 'didn't win us as many races as its ability warranted'. Ripleyite, on which all Eric's friends were persuaded to gamble, won a race at Goodwood as a three-year-old, the Brighton Cup as a four-year-old, and ran second many times. He was eventually sent for sale to America. On the strength of selling him, Eric invested in two young horses, Vague Melody and Shagayle. Balding says he has often 'tried to involve Eric with a fairish capital expenditure'. This was decisively resisted by Clapton, who wrote his trainer a letter:

Dear Toby,

Thanks for your letter. At this rate, I'll be lucky if I cross my own path. Let's race her against good class with a high prize rider up, just for the race. Give me a bell as soon as you can. All my love to you and yours, Eric Clapton.

P.S. Bugger all this long-term investment nonsense. The football season starts in a couple of months.

Eric immersed himself in the subject of racing. He showed a good grasp of the technicalities of training and ground conditions; he 'picks up things about horses very quickly,' says Toby Balding. 'He absorbed the language and the thinking behind racing and his enthusiasm at the races is enormous. But it's just another interest.' Among the jockeys, there was often competition to ride a Clapton-owned animal. 'He doesn't see enough of the horses to get emotionally involved with them as we do,' says Balding. 'He's businesslike enough to realize that when we get a good financial offer for a horse, it has to be sold. But he obviously enjoys horses and racing, which has a certain poetry for him. He attends races for the atmosphere, the physical thrill of it, and the pleasure of winning. And he loves betting.' Balding says he had hoped for a greater commitment from Eric in the horse-racing world, but was thwarted partly by Forrester, who decided it was a bad business enterprise for Eric. To get Roger involved, Eric bought him a horse for Christmas. But Gold Saint did not prove a winner. 'The only real argument I had with Eric's team,' says Balding ruefully, 'was that all the money we got from Via Delta, instead of being spent on yearlings, had gone on buying Eric's smart new Ferrari . . .'

Eric Clapton's most ardent admirers had been hard pressed to defend him when, in the summer of 1976, he made a remark that was construed as racist. In unrehearsed remarks from the concert stage in Birmingham, he plummeted to the depths of bad taste in the opinion of many people.

At that time, the immigration of blacks into England was an explosive topic. Enoch Powell, MP had warned against unrestricted immigration, and Birmingham was a particularly sensitive city for Eric to touch on the subject. Eric called out to his audience: 'Do we have any foreigners in the audience tonight? If so, please put up your hand . . . I think we should vote for Enoch Powell.'

It was a highly inflammatory, off-the-cuff remark, particularly as it came from a musician whose inspirational sources were black. The music community was aghast. Partly as a result, a movement called Rock Against Racism was formed in Britain. At the time, Clapton was unrepentant. 'I think Enoch is a prophet. His diplomacy is wrong and he's got no idea how to present things. His ideas are right. You go to Heathrow airport any day and you'll see thousands of Indian people sitting there waiting to know whether or not they can come into the country. And you go to Jamaica and there are adverts on TV saying "Come to lovely England."

'I don't think Enoch Powell is a racist. I don't think he cares about colour of any kind. His whole idea is for us to stop being unfair to immigrants because it's getting out of order. A husband comes over, lives off the dole to try to save enough to bring his wife and kids over. It's splitting up families. The government is being incredibly unfair to people abroad to lure them to the promised land where there is actually no work. Racist aggravation starts when white guys see immigrants getting jobs and they're not. Yeah, I'm getting a lot of stick for what I said, but so did Enoch. He was the only bloke telling the truth for the good of the country. I believe he is a very religious man and you can't be religious and racist at the same time. The two things are incompatible.'

Eric recorded few regrets about his remark, for he regards Enoch Powell as having predicted a mounting problem. Recalling the events leading up to it, he says, 'We had travelled up to Birmingham from London, where I think an Arab made some kind of remark to

Pattie in the lobby of the Churchill Hotel. And I was incensed when I looked round and saw all these Arabs and all the signs in Arabic. I began thinking: what the hell is happening to this country? And I was drunk at the time. But though it's a horrible thing to have to admit, I think he's been honest. Every now and then you'll hear a voice that isn't pandering to what people want to hear, uncomfortable for the masses. Then I think you've got to take notice of it. Enoch Powell had a lot to risk by saying these things. He can't have done it for pure gain. But I never believed that I, as a rock musician, had any particular right to make speeches.

'I think rock stars and musicians have got a very good angle on some parts of the sociological ethic, in terms of what is harmonious. but all too often their ideas prove to be based on fantasy.'

Rock Against Racism responded forcefully to Clapton's self-justification. 'Before Eric Clapton opens his mouth he should not only understand the facts but also the political climate in which he makes his statements. And as a popular musician he should exercise that responsibility,' the organization stated. Enoch Powell, it declared, had 'never said anything with the welfare of the ethnic minorities in mind'.

Eric faced heavy bombardment, too, from readers of the *Melody Maker*. One wrote: 'It seems impossible that Eric Clapton, a man who owed his inspiration and career to black musicians, cannot see the racial bias in Enoch Powell's ideas of "repatriation" and his ignorance of the implications of such a policy reflects a surprising lack of sensitivity and tolerance towards other people.' Another taunted Eric that years of heroin use had 'finally rotted Eric "Slowmind" Clapton's brains . . . he thinks religion and racialism are incompatible? The Incas or the North

American Indians would be glad to hear that. But of course they can't because their races were wiped out by religious men.'

Support came from a reader who wrote: 'Without doubt, Clapton echoes the feelings of most of the people in the street. Most people with any sense reject the stupid violence of the National Front and feel sympathy for immigrants. Nevertheless, the average working man does not want all these immigrants in the country.' The letter praised Clapton for his 'courage and convictions'.

Clapton's publicly aired views on race taught him that rock and politics are uneasy bedfellows: 'I'd always continue to speak out if I meant something from the heart, but John Lennon must have fancied himself as Lenin, a great thinker, when he said the Beatles were more popular than Jesus. It's really dangerous territory, and those days of mixing rock and public speech are over. I'm not gonna be clammed up, but if you have some sort of name, you have to be careful not to say things loosely. I think that next time, I'd have to mean something from the bottom of my heart to speak out on a controversial issue.'

Garrulous he might have been, but he was redeemed from criticism, in the eyes of many, by his guileless honesty. Whether it was traceable to his addiction is debatable, but in the 1970s and early 1980s Eric Clapton stopped short of show-business preening.

For manager Roger Forrester, however, running Clapton's career presented a continual challenge. 'The only certainty,' he recalled, 'was that Eric would be in a permanent alcoholic haze.' During this period he walked into his manager's office regularly and declared: 'I'm retiring. No more tours. I've had enough.' Forrester, used to such mercurial moods, wore the resigned look of a man who had heard it before . . . but this time, perhaps, just perhaps, Eric meant it. 'OK,' he would say. 'I'll put everything on hold.' Next day, Clapton would ask for details of his next session or tour. Planning his diary more than a week ahead would be a gamble. Forrester tended his star with the consummate skill of one who has been down the alcoholic road himself, but he was by then a non-drinker. The method he chose of keeping the Clapton creative flame alive was to generate stimulating activity that attracted Eric's attention through its originality and unpredictability.

One of these experiences was the making of a documentary film as Eric and his band toured Europe alongside his inspirational hero Muddy Waters in 1979. That alone was a thrill, with Muddy throwing down the gauntlet to his youthful counterpart. Eric expressed his humility quite touchingly, recalling how, the first time he picked up a guitar, he had tried to replicate Muddy's bell-like tone on 'Honey Bee'.

'Muddy Waters was the first blues man to get down to me, really into my soul. He has always made me feel this was the end of the road, as good as it could get. I listened later on to B. B. King, or Freddie King, or Buddy Guy and many other great players. There was this element of showmanship, of commerciality, of learning, still going on with those people. When I heard Muddy for the first time, I knew that was *it*. That was the final statement of blues music with no dressing, and that has remained my opinion all my life. No one was better.'

Touring Europe alongside Muddy was therefore humbling for Clapton. 'It was a treat, but also a severe test of my integrity. He was a man who had stuck to his guns all his life in his music. Every time I went off track during my part of the show, and played a quote from something, something melodic or even classically tinged, I got pangs of guilt. Because I felt that he was watching, and I was being untrue to my art. So at the same time as it being a great privilege and pleasure to be with Muddy, it also made me very self-conscious, in a positive and constructive way.'

Muddy had an outlook, too, that in retrospect seems to have set Clapton on a musical course for the rest of his life. 'He kept hammering it home to me that there was nothing wrong with being a blues musician. He said a guitarist didn't have to be *appealing*, to play the biggest halls and sell the most records, to play well. I can never thank Muddy enough, really, for spelling it all out to me, that blues playing is beautiful, because it's from inside yourself.'

Eric first met Muddy in 1966, during his period with John Mayall. The American singer came to do a British tour with Otis Spann. When Mike Vernon of Blue Horizon Records persuaded them to go into the studios in London, Eric was among the musicians asked to work as a sideman. 'Muddy paid me a lot of compliments and I took an immediate shine to him as a man. From then on, we kept in touch. Not only as a great musician, but as a person, he was one of the greatest, sweetest. We teamed up for tours and he took me under his wing, told me I was his son, gave me little clues or guidelines about what I should be doing and what he liked to hear me do. He was very instrumental in forming my correct identity as a blues musician.'

Eric was petrified at being outclassed by Muddy's power of simplicity. Once, when the blues master opened the show, and the crowd was ecstatic, a dejected Clapton gave everyone backstage the feeling that it would be impossible to follow such a performance. Muddy sensed Eric's feelings. Next night and every night after that, he seemed to temper his own show and came off smiling at Eric. 'I've left 'em for you, Eric,' he said, smiling. What Eric never knew until the tour ended was that on most nights, Muddy stood in the wings watching Clapton's show, saying: 'Whooo, boy, whooo!'

In the early 1970s, when Eric became confused about his direction, Muddy's wisdom prevailed. Eric remembers, 'I was starting to worry about being limited to performing as just a blues player. I started to write more varied material to get out of what I regarded as the trap of being just one kind of guitarist. But Muddy re-inspired me, made me realize that to do just one thing well was enough. You see, when I listened to other guitarists, I went through a spell of trying to get flashier, like the younger guys. But I kept coming back to Muddy and the first music I had heard. Always, the maturity of his music got through to me. And although I still struggle to achieve it, that belief in pure blues is now deep rooted in me'.*

Roger Forrester's super-protective role came into play forcefully during these dangerous years for Clapton. 'Roger was very concerned about outside people having an interest in an artist he wanted to control,' says

---

* Muddy Waters, born McKinley Morganfield in Rolling Fork, Mississippi, on 4 April 1915, died in 1983, two years after his second marriage, which Eric and Pattie attended in Muddy's Chicago home. Roger Forrester and Ben Palmer also went to the wedding. 'He had a heart condition,' recalls Eric. 'The road probably did it to him more than anything, as well as worrying about his band.'

promoter Harvey Goldsmith. 'And Roger is a control freak. Roger was a father figure. I'm pretty convinced Eric wouldn't be in the position he's in today without Roger there; he really nurtured him through, unselfishly. There was no ulterior reason, no power trip, because Roger is basically someone who shines when he's in the background. He's not a front person. He works at his best when under pressure and when nobody knows who he is. That's when he's at his best ... and most mischievous.'

In the mid 1970s, Goldsmith was managing Van Morrison, with whom he worked alongside Robbie Robertson to put the Band's project 'The Last Waltz' together. Through that, Goldsmith became friendly with Bob Dylan. When Goldsmith debated with Dylan the six-night concert series at Earls Court, London, and what should follow it, the Blackbushe Festival idea was born. 'We talked about the idea of doing that open air show,' Goldsmith remembers, 'and Dylan said to me: "If I'm going to do this, there's only one guy I'd like to work with and that's Eric Clapton. What do you think?"' 'It's done,' Goldsmith replied, knowing it was a perfect match. The result, a triumphant festival attracting 250,000 to the Hampshire event on 15 July 1978, was another round in the mutual admiration between Dylan and Clapton.

Eric's affinity – as musician and friend – with Dylan, one of the artists he most respects, has curious origins. When Eric was a Yardbird and Dylan was making his first impact, his genius as a songwriter was touted to Eric by none other than that band's bassist Paul Samwell-Smith. 'That fact put me off,' Eric smiles. But later, once he had left that band, his Chelsea flatmate Martin Sharp continually played Dylan's seminal album *Blonde on Blonde*. And

Clapton was hooked. Dylan and Clapton met several times, in America and in Britain, as members of the rock fraternity, and eventually made guest appearances on each other's albums, Bob on Eric's *No Reason to Cry* and Eric on Bob's *Desire* album.*

'We do have a special communication and I think it's because we're both basically shy,' says Clapton. 'In a room full of people, or in a recording studio, we seem always to be the ones who like to remain quiet, so we veer towards each other.' Rather like his bond with Jimi Hendrix, his understanding with Dylan is intuitive rather than spoken. It has resulted in some outstanding open-air festival appearances featuring the two stars. In Germany that same year, 1978, a major event was staged in Nuremberg on the field built by Hitler for his rallies and speeches. The heavy irony of the event was not lost on any of the musicians. As Clapton remarked at the time, here was a major Jewish singer and songwriter peacefully entertaining a crowd of 80,000, in sharp contrast with what had happened on the same spot four decades earlier.

The Nuremberg concert was promoted by two men who had a unique connection with Clapton dating back to 1963, when he was in the Yardbirds. Horst Lippmann and Fritz Rau came into rock, like so many promoters during the 1960s, because the jazz musicians they usually worked with flirted with the rhythm-and-blues scene in which Clapton and the Yardbirds were working.

Lippmann was the very first record producer Clapton

* On 16 October 1992 Eric went to New York to guest in the star-studded celebration of Dylan's thirtieth year as a recording artist. In the concert at Madison Square Garden, Eric performed alongside Bob on 'Don't Think Twice, It's All Right', 'Love Minus Zero' and 'My Back Pages'.

met. He went to record the American blues singer Sonny Boy Williamson at the Richmond Crawdaddy Club in 1963, but became particularly impressed by the young man playing lead guitar alongside him. The music was dear to Eric's heart: the raw, compulsive sounds of such blues standards as 'Smokestack Lightnin'', which he would later convert to his own style. But Lippmann recorded the songs and released them as singles; they sold so poorly in Germany that he was not motivated to continue an interest in the Yardbirds.

With Fritz Rau, Horst's connection with Clapton came much later. They first presented him on tour in Germany with Delaney and Bonnie. Again, they saw Eric as a band member rather than a leader. But as the man's career gathered fresh momentum, his popularity in Germany soared. Interestingly, Eric developed a particularly strong bond with Lippmann and Rau, which they believe is because of their roots in jazz. To many people, including actor John Hurt, Clapton is not a pop or rock star but a modern jazz troubadour. Echoing the views of so many, Fritz shakes his head in disbelief at Eric's guitar work: 'One note from him is worth twelve from anybody else.'

At the time of the Dylan–Blackbushe liaison, Eric was going through a severe identity crisis which was accelerated by his heavy drinking (he took the stage at Blackbushe drunk and played on autopilot). In the middle of making a new album, with Glyn Johns again the producer, Eric turned in some strong performances, but the producer felt it was 'not so exciting as *Slowhand*, which had fantastic material. For *Backless*, there was not the material available and we ended up cutting two or three songs Dylan had sent him. They were good but the whole album didn't have the flair or variety of *Slowhand*.'

Rhythmically, *Backless* carried the stamp of the backing musicians Eric had now nicknamed the Tulsa Tops: Radle, Terry, Oldaker and Sims. It was an album of deceptive power and raunch, featuring the upbeat 'Tulsa Time' and 'Tell Me That You Love Me' and the more romantic, softer approach of 'Golden Ring' (which Eric rates the best on the album) and 'Promises'. That song, a perennial favourite on British radio, proves that, given a powerful country-styled song, Clapton's voice is very comfortable in that idiom, coming close to the relaxed style of his friend Don Williams. For the concerts of the next few years, 'Tulsa Time', a near-country song, was the opening choice.

The title *Backless* was an affectionate commentary on Dylan's eagle eye, on and off the stage, at the Blackbushe show. Eric remarked to several musicians that the master had omnipresent eyes surveying the entire cast and was uncannily knowledgeable about what every musician was doing. Since Dylan appeared to have eyes in the back of his head, he was considered by Eric 'backless'. The album's handsome cover carried a neat reference to Eric's favourite football team. Draped at the far end of the settee on which he is pictured was his West Bromwich Albion club scarf.

The first time the film director Rex Pyke met Eric, in the London office of Robert Stigwood in the late 1960s, Clapton was doing an impression of Richard the Third. Pyke, former consultant at the Royal Opera House and Royal Ballet, had worked with such giants as Nureyev and Fonteyn. He immediately decided Clapton was a natural. 'He's a born actor,' Pyke reflected. 'I'd love to make a film with him.'

Pyke struck a friendship with Forrester and, as the years passed, the two men decided that Pyke might hold a key to enlivening Eric's career, moving it away from the traditional tours and albums. Fresh momentum was needed, as Eric and his American band planned a six-week European tour.

The result was the filming of *Eric Clapton's Rolling Hotel*, shot as Clapton and his band travelled from London to Paris to Hamburg and all the major European cities in three train carriages. Complete with a chef who tore off to the local market to buy fresh food at each stop, the train was leap frogged by the road crew while Eric and his musicians japed and talked.

It was a refreshing change from the usual air transport. Robert Stigwood visited Eric's show in Paris, and a backstage encounter, captured on film, showed Eric trying to 'interview' his former manager. 'Right . . . now's the time for some questions. There are a lot I haven't dared ask and here they all are,' Eric said to him. Confident from drink, Eric went on to assert, good-naturedly but with a serious undertone, that Robert had used the money earned from Cream to finance the Bee Gees.

Robert deflected him: 'This isn't the right time to talk about this. We should speak about this another time.' But Eric pressed on: 'Don't go away,' he urged the cameraman and Robert. 'This is my film and I want it in it.' Like several other items, that episode was cut from the finished film.

The impromptu moments of the film produced its cutting edge. From the opening sequence, in which Clapton sings unaccompanied 'Bye Bye Blackbird', to his moving tribute to his old friend Jimi Hendrix ('I don't want anyone to see me crying,' he says at one point, full of emotion), the film had some compulsive insights into Eric and those around him.

There was Eric recollecting the story of Layla and Majnun and his inspiration: 'They could never marry and he went raving mad, and split for the desert and started hanging out with the animals . . .' Pattie is captured on film saying: 'He [Majnun] spoke to the birds, used to sing to the trees. And it just drove him totally crazy. It is a very, very beautiful and delicate love story.'

Eric: 'This was the way I was feeling about Pattie at the time. Because there was no way I was going to be able to take her away from George, without hurting George and without breaking up someone else's home, you know. So that was it. That was my comment. And she was Layla and I was Majnun.'

Pattie: 'Just the first few chords make me melt. If you ever hear something that pulls your heart and your soul strings, it does that for me.'

After Eric describes Roger Forrester as 'probably my closest mate', his manager defines his role and adds: 'I think that I am over-protective. But it's a hell of a job to strike a happy medium.'

To Rex Pyke, three non-music aspects of Clapton's personality surfaced in the film. He described his acting ability: 'Terrific! He can do perfect imitations. He doesn't do Laurence Olivier doing Richard the Third but he does Spike Milligan doing Laurence Olivier doing Richard the Third. And I was astonished to find that he could recite from *The Caretaker*, playing all the roles like Donald Pleasance and Robert Shaw.'

Secondly, Clapton demonstrated exceptional ability as a calligrapher. 'He would take an empty book,' Pyke recalls, 'and copy out maybe ten poems and it would make an absolutely beautiful present for anybody. It interested me to find that he had more talent than that which he was famous for. And thirdly, he is actually a man with no secrets. He writes an open diary, through the day, and he leaves it on the table. Anybody can read it and there are very personal, very intimate and revealing things in it.' Eric's policy in making his inner thoughts public was that the reader ran a risk, in reading it, in finding that he/she had been recorded, not always in complimentary observation.

Although some excellent footage of Muddy Waters was captured, the magical possibility of Eric and Muddy playing together eluded Pyke. 'They both had such admiration for each other. They each kept saying the other party wouldn't want it to happen. I kept saying: "Listen, I've spoken to Eric. He's as embarrassed as you are. Come along. It might happen, it might not. But at least come with your guitars and be in the same room." And they always used to treat each other fairly formally, which is a shame. Eric would creep on to the back of the stage and just be hiding amongst the p.a. stack to watch Muddy. But he would just creep off at the end, not to allow Muddy to see that he was watching.'

Eric Clapton's Rolling Hotel was shown to critical acclaim at London's National Film Theatre. But in spite of its revelatory content, or perhaps because of that, it was never shown nationally. Eric's insistence that his work contained a great deal of influence from Bizet was one fine moment. So was his statement that, when on stage, he watched the exit door areas for the unnerving prospect of seeing people leaving his show. But too many moments of tension made the film untenable as Forrester faced the daunting task of ensuring that Eric survived such a dangerous period. One such example was Ben

Palmer's insistence that Muddy should have had the facility of being on the train rather than on the band coach, because he was suffering from bronchitis. Ben's compassionate pleas met no response. The concerts filmed showed Eric performing well . . . but his speech was slurred and there was too much evidence of his bad physical condition. *Eric Clapton's Rolling Hotel* remained, though, a flawed but fascinating glimpse of Clapton's weakness and indifference during that year. 'Musically, I was not pleased with anything I came up with,' he says now. 'I was doing the gigs, but just pressing the buttons.'

In the late autumn of 1978, Clapton invited Glyn Johns out for a drink in the pub lethally situated at the top of his drive. 'He said to me: "I don't know if I want to be the front man any more." He was deadly serious, and wasn't pulling a "feel sorry for me" number,' Johns remembers. 'I said: "Look, cock, you've been in this business for years and years and years. You have earned the right to whatever the bloody hell you like."'

When they entered the recording studio, it became clear that Eric had genuinely tired of his role as the focal star, the engine-room from which came the songs, the decisions, the lead guitar. Whether the alcohol was blurring his self-image is unclear, but he certainly wanted less visibility.

Glyn Johns's receptiveness to Eric's frame of mind came naturally. 'I see my role as a producer as being there to represent the artist in the true sense of the word. I'm not making an album for me. Of course I have a responsibility to the record company who are paying for the sessions. But my first responsibility is to the artist,

Wonderful tonight: the exceptional romance. (*Eric Clapton Collection*)

Pattie and Eric at their wedding reception in 1979, and leaving afterwards in a limousine. (*Eric Clapton Collection*)

Left: Gone fishing: Eric prepares for action. (*Pattie Clapton*)

Above: Lori Del Santo with Conor, appearing on Italian TV shortly after the baby's birth in August 1986. (*Star File*)

Eric with his lifelong friend Keith Richards of the Rolling Stones. At the International Music Awards in New York in May 1989, Eric presented Keith with a 'Living Legend' award, while Clapton was designated The Most Valuable Player. (*Bob Gruen/Star File*)

Eric and George Harrison at JFK Airport, New York, on their way back to London after their concerts together in Tokyo in 1991. (*Star File*)

A keen cricketer, Eric taking his place in a show-business team.
(*London Features International*)

Above: A night out with Lori Del Santo in London. (*London Features International*)

Left: Conor, looking sharp in his Armani sweater, not long before the tragedy of his death in New York. (*London Features International*)

Above: Taking the spotlight with a friend: Eric joins Bob Dylan at the latter's 30th anniversary tribute concert at Madison Square Garden, New York, 1992. (*London Features International*)

Right: With model Naomi Campbell at the Rock 'n' Roll Hall of Fame ceremony, Los Angeles, 1993. (*London Features International*)

Left: Stepping out on a shopping expedition in London with actress Julia Smith. (*London Features International*)

Below: Reunited in Los Angeles, 1993: Cream (Eric Clapton, Ginger Baker, Jack Bruce), after their induction into the Rock 'n' Roll Hall of Fame. (*London Features International*)

Facing page: An abundance of historic blues songs formed the core of Eric's 1994 season at London's Royal Albert Hall. This photograph was taken at his 100th concert at the venue since his annual season began there in 1987. (*Virginia Lohle/Star File*)

Above: Facing his
ardent fans at the
Royal Albert Hall,
January 1994.
(*Linda Leismer/
Star File*)

Right: Wailing: a
classic shot of
Clapton, deep into
his music. (*Steve
Judson/Star File*)

and what goes down has to be true to them, a fair representation of what they are at that moment. That's what making a record is supposed to be, in my opinion.'

As the music unfolded under this philosophy of freedom for the artist, people in the Clapton camp voiced concern. They felt a more decisive, commercial stamp was needed. Johns's belief that he was making the correct psychological move for Eric, allowing him to be the member of-a-band, backfired. The session at Olympic, Barnes, was cancelled, the record aborted, and Johns was fired – 'by Eric at the end of the day, but I'm sure it was Roger Forrester's decision,' Johns states.

What they wanted, Johns says, 'is someone who was not sympathetic to what Eric was trying to achieve. I was very bitter about the way I was treated but now I see more realistically that Roger was making a cold, calculated decision based on the survival of Eric's popularity. The fact of the matter is, he has been a brilliant manager for Eric Clapton, without question.'

What irked Johns, however, was that he took the blame for the reality that Eric had hit a non-productive period. 'He didn't write many songs and wasn't in a very good frame of mind. So it was far easier for them to turn round and say: "It's Glyn's fault, we'll fire him," than it was to say: "Eric, this is on your plate, you've got to deal with it." It was perfectly normal behaviour. And if it enabled Eric to carry on in a better way, that's fine. If the artist has a hit, he's been brilliant. If he has a failure, it's the fault of the producer. It comes with the job.'

SEVEN

THE CURED MUSICIAN

'I DON'T like the Clapton legend thing. I don't want the right to go on stage and get a standing ovation for what I've done in the past decade,' Clapton said as the 1970s neared an end. Consumed by self-doubt, the inner man surfaced in a particularly emotional diary entry on 20 February 1979: I realized today that I am a very nervous and bitter man. I've been reviewing some of my records to help Nell [Pattie] put together a programme for the tour and I felt it come through the music . . . God bless all, I'm scared stiff and I don't know how to deal with it yet. I know I'm good, but good enough for you? I drink too much and I lie, mostly to myself, I write this to you because I need your help. All I know is your gift and you can have it back any time you like. You see, I lie. Dear Lord, please give me strength to stop drinking all the time and please grace my hands with the beauty that we all know. I am yours, E.C.' Two days later came a short entry summarizing the whole day, and what was to be a continuing problem surrounding his forthcoming tour: 'A lot of trouble today,' wrote Eric, 'concerning the itinerary clause about no women on the road. Still not much done.'

'I'm just now starting to feel the effects of middle age,' Eric said to me, as our car left Warsaw to begin a 250-mile journey for the next concert in November, 1979. 'It's just hitting me that I can't still do all the things I used to do every day when I was twenty-one or twenty-two. Then, I'd easily do two shows a night and an all nighter. Now, that schedule would grind me to a halt.'

The visit to Poland, among the first by Western rock musicians, was yet another diversion from tradition for Eric, organized by Forrester in an attempt to spirit Eric away from his self-imposed torpor. With photographer Chris Horler, I had flown into Warsaw to see a major rock star in a unique setting behind what was then the iron curtain of Communism.

'It's time for guys like me to ease up a little bit,' Eric continued. 'Rock's not like jazz, like the old Count Basie bands, where they could grow old playing the same charts. Rock's emotionally and physically draining because you're constantly trying to invent something new.'

The previous night, before 3,400 people in Warsaw's Palace of Culture, Clapton had mesmerized an audience which knew of his reputation but had precious little evidence: his albums had been available only on the 'black market', though his nickname was used by young fans familiar with the *Slowhand* collection. Polish critics, twelve years after Britain had deified him, were still writing 'Clapton is God'.

Before this short East European tour, Clapton had last worked 'the road' in America on a forty-seven-city trek which had exhausted him the previous February. His sartorial simplicity in Poland seemed to cause a smile among the locals: he looked typically British in a tweed suit, white shirt and sober tie. For the show he wore jeans. Most of the front seats at the Palace of Culture in Warsaw were occupied by civic dignitaries, their friends and their relatives. They sat stony-faced, clapping politely, for a show which discerning Western ears would judge as magnificent. Their stiffness had a bad effect on Eric. 'I need optimism and feedback from my audience to play well,' he explained. At the American Embassy later that night, the organizers recruited some cheerleaders to attend the second concert. American Army personnel, waving The Stars and Stripes, led an impressive demonstration of enthusiasm, and the band played one of its finest sets.

Eric had gone to Poland with a new all-British band. Showing that even through his bleariest two-bottles-of-brandy-a-day haze he would decisively protect his career, Eric had parted company with the Tulsa musicians who had previously accompanied him on the US tour, and hired the high-pedigree British guitarist Albert Lee. 'When he joined the band,' Clapton told me, explaining his love of its British profile, 'it showed me that although American musicians may be closer to some of the music, they are not necessarily the right kind of people to play in a rock band and keep company with. You know, just because they've heard the latest James Brown or live next door to so-and-so . . . it means nothing when they have to get up and join a band and play together. They have what I'd describe as a discographer's attitude to music-making and that doesn't suit me.'

Joining Albert Lee came Dave Markee (bass guitar), Chris Stainton (keyboards) and Henry Spinetti (drums). His hair shorn, his mood buoyant, Clapton warmed to the tightness of this new line-up with infectious enthusiasm.

'Half-way through the last American tour I realized the Americans were not on the same wavelength as me and I decided to form this all-British band. It's a joy. There's no cynicism. In this band, there's a really good atmosphere of a family. Though it sounds as corny as hell, it's true.' There was a jocular sideswipe at Lee, with whom Eric got along famously: 'Course, Albert's bone idle, but we have to put up with something!'

Even through this period of difficulties about which he and his manager had not 'gone public', Clapton showed an iron resolve to protect his own legend, while trying hard to debunk it. 'My responsibility is to the other members of the band and they help me keep my feet on the ground,' he told me. 'The legend? Well, it's blown up out of all reality. It would be easy to float up like a balloon and believe in all that, but I have a reality check with the lads. I still keep in mind the fact that I have a responsibility to them. More than anything to do with a legend, I'm a member of a band with the next gig to think about.'

But surely he accepted that thousands regarded him as a catalyst, a superstar figure . . .?

'Yeah, but I find other people's vision of me that way disappointing. They shouldn't be satisfied with what they've heard about me, but about what they hear on my next album or my next gig. I'd rather have a cold reception for playing badly than be applauded for what I've done in the past. I find that whole thing totally ethereal.

'I'd like every audience at my gigs to be impressed with the quality of the music rather than applaud the Clapton memories. That was the whole thinking behind the Derek and the Dominos idea. Lots of people didn't know they were coming to see someone with a reputation, and it worked. I want credit where it's due rather than just credit – or just take away the credit when it's not justified. You can get so lazy living on your reputation.'

At a Warsaw press conference, he was asked about his days with John Mayall and the Yardbirds, and dealt with all the memories in good humour. Later, reflecting on his early years, Eric said to me: 'Blind Faith failed because it was a co-operative group. That never seems to work. Ginger [Baker] and Stevie [Winwood] started bickering at a very early stage and I knew it was doomed. Then I was charmed away by the Americans, Delaney and Bonnie. Another mistake. This time – British is proving best.'

Warming to the subject of the newer rock musicians, he said that, whether he was a legend or not, he and his friends from the sixties got older, and they were being forced to take things easier. 'Keep touring, sure, but you just find you can't do the scenes of many years ago. That's for the younger bands. The fact that the new wave of rock is pushing at the door really hard means that we've got to grind on and on if we want to keep our reputation. And I really do want to earn my reputation in the future. Really, I've made enough money and paid my mortgage, so I don't *have* to do it. But I need to do it for my self-respect.'

The last word captured the imagination, and he pondered it for a while as he lit one of the forty Rothman filter cigarettes he would smoke that day and every day. 'The new wave's great,' he continued, eventually. 'But I'm not gonna let these new wave musicians see me off. I don't see myself retiring and lots of players from my period should feel the same. I treat a lot of the newer musicians with respect and all I ask in return is respect from them. The rock scene needed a kick and these young kids came along and gave it. I'm under no illusion. I couldn't provide that kick, as I'm not the vigorous, youthful person I was ten years ago.'

Always determined to be trend-conscious, he sang the praises of the Police and the Specials. 'They both sound so strong and vibrant and they really know where they're going. I reckon the new wave's the best thing that's happened for years; it's the future.' Curiously, in a separate interview, Clapton was contemptuous of Brian May, the guitarist in Queen – a strange criticism of a player who at least offered the virtue of musicianship compared with the posturing of some of the trendy acts supported by Eric through the years. It often seems that he feels the need to be *seen* to be contemporarily aware. (In later years Eric spoke enthusiastically about such acts as Prince, the La's and Björk.)

After seven hours of hard motoring through storms, our car finally aquaplaned into the mining city of Katowice. There, the night's concert at the 8,000-seater stadium was to prove a dark contrast with the exultant atmosphere of the previous night's Warsaw show. The atmosphere was immediately tense as the strong-arm methods of the Polish police viciously suppressed the audience's enthusiasm. Fans went wild with excitement as the band swung into 'Tulsa Time', 'Lay Down Sally', 'Wonderful Tonight', and Albert Lee's thrilling solo on 'Country Boy'. The problem was that the young Poles, turned loose in the liberating atmosphere created by such a British rock superstar, lost their inhibitions in scenes never before seen in the town. And the police and security guards overreacted, literally hurling teenagers

over security barriers on their way to being frogmarched
to the exits. It was a brutal experience. From the stage,
Clapton saw beneath him exuberant rock-starved fans
being sprayed with face-freezing Mace by police determined to quell their enthusiasm.

Fans hoisted each other in the air and shared embraces
as Eric played on, 'Blues Power' and 'After Midnight'
being followed by 'Knockin' on Heaven's Door' and
'Tipitina'.

Eric's personal stage crew, led by the burly Alphi
O'Leary, clashed with the Polish guards in a futile
attempt to stop their violence, but to no avail. At the
interval, Roger Forrester told the authorities that Eric
could not play the second house under such violent
conditions. He needed a guarantee that for the next
concert, the security guards would be removed and/or
their strong-arm tactics would not be repeated.

When this request was denied, Forrester told them
that Clapton could not perform at the second show.
Tense and dangerous scenes followed. The band's public
address system was smashed in the hubbub of bitter
arguments and accusations by both sides. Forrester was
told he would have to forfeit fees for both concerts
(£1,000 a performance) before being allowed out of the
country. He finally agreed the next day, signing a form
of release at Warsaw airport, before hustling Eric and the
band aboard a Lufthansa flight to Frankfurt, en route to
Tel Aviv for the next leg of the tour. The Polish
authorities were not merely angry at Clapton's cancel-
lation of the second show. They were menacing and
threatening, and an air of real danger permeated the
departure from the hotel and the drive from Katowice to
Warsaw.

For Eric, the visible repression of kids in front of his

stage had been a bitter experience. He was tearful, backstage, as he said: 'How can I play when I see kids right in front of the stage, underneath me, being pushed around by the men from Sainsbury's?' (A sardonic reference to the overall-clad heavies dealing out tough treatment to youngsters rushing the stage for a closer glimpse or touch of a Western musician). 'Anywhere else in the world, we could help the kids by telling them to cool it. But here, I'm powerless because of the language problem and because the authorities are so heavy. I've never known a country so corrupt. I wanted to see the place for a change of view and because it seemed good for kids who don't get much Western rock. The whole place reminds me of *The Third Man*.'

The irony of the Polish débâcle was that it blackened the début of the tightest band Clapton had thus far produced. When tempers had cooled and they were safely in the West, Forrester mused that his sensitive artist did not need to live through such a trauma. Eric, he said, preferred the simple life: 'Marks and Spencer fleecy-lined slippers, a Labrador, and a pipe by the fireside.' He was not joking.

En route to Israel, Clapton had to smile. He phoned Pattie to ask her to join him in Tel Aviv. 'Here I am in Poland, missing the green and pleasant of England, and asking my wife to come over and she tells me she's just been to tap-dancing lessons in Guildford and that it will be awkward to come to Tel Aviv because she has to judge a fancy dress competition on Saturday. Oh my God, I just want to go home.'

Within a month of that traumatic experience in Poland, Clapton and his new band were in Japan for concerts at the Budokan, Tokyo. Although he dislikes the principle of live recordings, believing the moment cannot and should not be recaptured, the album *Just One Night* proved him wrong, artistically and commercially. Featuring some of the British line-up's best work, including particularly accessible versions of 'Blues Power' and 'Double Trouble', the double album tore into the top five both in the USA and in Britain.

Back in Britain for Christmas, a contributory factor to Eric's prolonged alcoholism was his innate acting ability. 'Only the people who were very close to me had any inkling of how bad it was,' he admits. 'Unless you came close up and smelled my breath, I could appear to be sober and rational when in actual fact I was ten sheets to the wind. I could go all day like this ... even at lunchtime, I'd be stoned out of my brain but would appear to outsiders to be fairly *compos mentis*.' In the pub, Eric always chose to drink in the public bar, rather than the saloon bar, so that he could mix with 'real people'. They were always less monied than him. The complexity of his character showed in his enjoyment of driving away from the pub, and waving goodbye to the workers from the comfort of his Ferrari. He considered this classless behaviour.

'I had the ability to let my drunkenness out of the bag only when it was in an appropriate setting. In the pub, where it was OK to be drunk, I'd behave twice as drunk as I was! But most days, I was generally much drunker than I appeared to be. My manager and my close friends knew the problem, but they were frightened of telling me they knew because of the rage that would ensue.' He became very defensive and aggressive whenever anyone touched on the subject of his drinking habits: 'Don't tell me how to live my life.'

In private meetings, Pattie, Roger, Eric's mother Pat, Guy Pullen and Nigel, rather like a committee, pondered what to do about Eric's drinking. They agreed that he was so stubborn he would have to decide for himself. No one could persuade him that it was becoming dangerous. Getting Eric to eat, to offset the alcohol, was difficult. Inevitably, the years of hard drinking, erratic sleeping, poor eating, travelling and pressurized work when it came were going to hit him. The thunderbolt happened when Eric and his band were eight dates into a projected forty-five-concert tour of America in 1980.

For months before the tour, and particularly when it began, Eric had had a pain in his back. 'I didn't know what it was and I didn't tell anyone,' he says. When the tour began, it worsened. He stepped up his dose of painkillers, and together with the consumption of at least a bottle of brandy a day, his appetite for food had virtually gone. Nigel Carroll kept the painkillers and became increasingly alarmed at the knocks on his hotel door at four in the morning from Clapton wanting more tablets.

Eric said he thought the pain in his back had come from a very hefty Irishman's slap on the back during Eric's visit a few months earlier to Barberstown Castle, County Kildare, Ireland (the beautiful eleventh-century hotel which Clapton had bought as an investment and visited for hard-drinking weekends). But Forrester and Carroll decided that, as Eric's knocking on the door for tablets increased to two or three times a night, and a mighty long concert tour lay ahead, they could not risk carrying on without medical help. Before his next show, he needed a pain-killing injection from a doctor.

Eric played the concert at Madison, Wisconsin, and came off stage doubled up in agony. Watching the show from the side of the stage, Forrester sensed that the situation was now very serious, but knew he would have trouble persuading Clapton to go to hospital. On the band's midnight charter Viscount plane to Minneapolis St Paul, Eric was ashen, quiet, not drinking and clearly in trouble. 'I was desperately worried,' says Alphi O'Leary. 'He was just slumped in his seat, out of it.'

Eric had to be helped from the plane into the limousine. Forrester told the driver to go straight to the hospital. Eric sleepily grumbled that he didn't understand why he was suddenly travelling separately from the band. Forrester said: 'This time, you need help. You're having a check-up.' At the United Hospital, St Paul, they checked him over and asked him to return later that morning. After some X-rays at the second session, the doctor asked Roger and Nigel to phone them later. By the time they had returned to the Radisson Plaza Hotel, the doctor was on the phone: 'Get him back here immediately. He's got an ulcer that's about to explode into his pancreas. We want him back in.'

Forrester's reaction was: 'Well, if it's that serious, we'll fly back to England straight away.' The doctor chillingly rammed home the urgency: 'I don't think you've got time even to get to the airport. I'll have to lay it on the line to you. We think he could die at any moment.'

Eric had returned to his room. Forrester called Carroll, who had a pass key. A knock went unanswered. They opened the door and saw Eric's jeans lying on the floor – still inside his cowboy boots. 'We could only see the trousers and the boots. It looked like his body was inside them round the corner. We assumed he was lying on the floor, and we went *white*,' says Forrester. They were relieved to find him asleep on the sofa. Forrester woke him and didn't speak a word. 'I'm going in, aren't I?'

said Eric. 'Yes,' said his manager. 'Let's go,' said Eric, 'I'm in so much pain.'

Within forty-five minutes Eric was on an intravenous drip, with a camera confirming the worst suspicions. He had five ulcers, and one was so big, the size of a mandarin orange, that it was like a time-bomb that could have exploded at any moment. It was so big that at first the doctors thought it was a shadow.

Eric's dramatic illness, and his four-week stay in the United Hospital, was big news throughout America. Gradually, with drugs, his ulcers were diminished and he returned from the precipice. Pattie flew in from London. Pete Townshend and country singer Don Williams were among the visitors, and more than 5,000 cards, flowers and gifts flooded the hospital. Eventually there were so many that the florists were asked by Eric to divert anything sent to him to other local hospitals, and the dozens of teddy bears sent to him went to the children's wards. Eric's nurse, Delia Flynn, had the tough job of coping with Eric's moodiness. As he responded to treatment, Eric went out for two hours each day. By then, obsessed with fishing, he found a local shop where he built up a collection of about twenty-five rods. He used to pretend to cast, with weights on the end, in the hospital corridors, a sight that amused the nursing staff. He became such a local news item that one radio station established a point in the city for people to congregate and sign a get-well card to him each day. 'Eric Clapton's get-well card today will be displayed at the corner of . . .' And thousands went to sign it.

Eric was allowed out of the hospital quite often during his month there. On one occasion he decided to visit a fishing friend in Seattle, one of his favourite cities. It was part of his therapy. Over dinner, he ordered a glass of milk and then asked the waiter to put brandy in it. Infuriated, Nigel Carroll ordered the waiter not to. He told Eric that because of the drugs he was taking for his ulcers, alcohol was wrong. But Clapton was annoyed at his personal assistant's schoolmaster-like attitude. He asked a girl sitting in the restaurant party to drive him back to his car. Terrified at having a superstar as her passenger, she shot a red light and crashed into a taxi. Eric suffered bruised ribs, and a Seattle doctor diagnosed that he had now also developed pleurisy.

He was immediately flown back to Minneapolis. The doctors said that he now had a lung condition: the bottom half of one of his lungs had partially closed. They put a steamer in his room, which finally convinced Eric that he should go home. 'If I've got to sit in a room breathing damp air from steam,' he said, 'I might as well go home to England where the air's *naturally* damp. I can get it by sitting in my garden!' He flew back to London next day.

The doctors did not tell him until he was leaving how close he had been to disaster. One estimate said he would have had forty-five minutes to live if the giant ulcer had not been brought under control in time. 'I had been in agony, but I'd anaesthetized myself so much by booze and pills that I never knew how truly painful it was,' says Eric. 'I never saw the tunnel, never actually visualized myself dying. I just recall feeling very bad on the plane and then recovering in hospital. It's still hard to believe how close I ran to mortality.' Medical advice on leaving hospital was tough on Eric. He was told to avoid spicy foods, a particular blow because he had a taste for Indian curries, loved Rose's pickled onions and ate a jarful at a time and enjoyed eating lots of raw peppers. But on the question of alcohol, Clapton had skilfully negotiated himself a compromise. Basically, he was told not to drink. But Eric said that a total ban might be too much for him. 'They made deals with me. I said: "Well, if I moderate and cut it down to two or three Scotches a day . . . would that be all right?" And they all said yes. They didn't know they were dealing with a completely obsessive alcoholic to whom two or three Scotches were just for breakfast.'

The pull of the bottle triumphed over any medical intelligence. 'Within a couple of months of being out of that hospital I was back on a bottle or two bottles a day. And I didn't give a damn about my health.'

For Roger Forrester, the long years of constant worry about whether his friend would survive began to take their toll. By 1981, with Eric back to heavy drinking, a decisive conversation between them took place in Tokyo during Eric's tour of Japan, where the fans adore the depth of his music. 'The day of the Toyko show, for the very first time ever, Eric said to me he didn't want to appear on stage. I couldn't believe it.' Despite all the traumas of his life, Eric had remained steadfastly professional. He knew when he played badly, but the audience rarely guessed how far he sometimes pushed himself.

'Then that night in Toyko he showed me what was wrong with him,' says Forrester. 'His whole body was covered in an enormous rash from head to foot, right down to his fingers. Someone said it was food poisoning, but I knew it was alcohol. It was his liver reacting to the booze. Now, I'd been sweating for eight years through literally every number on stage, wondering if he'd get through the show. That night, I had to say something, even though I don't believe in ultimatums. I said we had to do something about this. I said: "I'll cancel all your work, Eric, until we get you together. I don't *think* you drink to excess, Eric. I don't think *anything*. I *know* that you're an *alcoholic*."' It was the first time Eric had the word applied to him. "You've got a problem," I said.' Eric says he did not believe Roger at first.

'We got back from Japan in December 1981,' says Forrester. 'I insisted that something had to be done.' 'Let me have Christmas at home,' a rational Eric finally replied, 'and if I agree to go into a clinic for treatment, I'll call you. Give me no more than twenty-four hours' notice, and take me away.'

The death in November 1981 of fifty-eight-year-old Sid Perrin, who had lived with Eric's mother for five years, had a deep effect on Eric. Sid was a thoroughbred Ripleyite, who worked in the aircraft industry and endeared himself to Eric by what Clapton calls a 'W.C. Fields-like panache'. He was a raconteur and the best footballer, cricketer and singer in Eric's village. Eric warmed to his sense of humour. They were frequent companions, particularly in the pub, where Sid fuelled Eric's male chauvinism.

'He was a beautiful man, a childhood sweetheart of my mother. But he was also a very hard-drinking man and when he fell ill and couldn't drink, I think he died from a broken heart because he couldn't have a good time any more,' Eric recalls. 'He had a love of life and was something of a hero to me. When he died, Ripley died with him to a certain extent. The good times stopped. It made me determined to stop the boozing. I saw it all as being a dreadful waste of time, and I could end up going the same way as Sid, after stomach disorders.'

Christmas 1981 was the worst. By eight o'clock on Christmas morning Eric was 'well on the way to being drunk,' says Pattie. She planned for a house full of both their families and friends, and set about cooking a turkey. By lunchtime she realized that Eric had been missing from the house for hours. He had said he was going off to see the gardener. 'I wandered round the garden looking for a slumped body in the snow. I was in floods of tears because I couldn't find him anywhere. I was furious with all the guests because they'd encouraged him to drink so much, too. I thought he'd passed out. And I found him asleep, absolutely drunk, among the pile of logs in the basement. It was a hideous Christmas.'

After Christmas, Forrester asked Clapton if he felt he could undertake treatment, though the clinic had already been booked. 'Yeah, I agree, go ahead,' said Eric. But as requested, he was not told until the day before departure that he was on his way. When Pattie told him the flight was only a day off, Eric was livid at the fact that final plans had been made behind his back. He poured himself a large brandy.

On 7 January 1982 Forrester collected a jittery Clapton and drove to Gatwick airport. Eric had no idea which country he was going to. A North West Orient flight took him to Minneapolis St Paul, scene of his ulcer drama only six months earlier. Immediately on landing, Eric, already full of aeroplane brandy and lemonade and feeling like a condemned man, asked to be taken to a bar near the airport for a final drink before treatment. Forrester refused his request.

Eric was checked into a clinic specializing in the treatment of alcoholics. Forrester stayed in a nearby hotel and was told not to visit Eric for the first two weeks, until he had overcome the worst. Becoming institutionalized, one of a crowd, Eric learned to recognize the problems inherent in everybody else's alcoholism as well as his own. It was an intensive four-week treatment which worked. Describing his visit to the Hazelden Foundation, the rehabilitation clinic for alcoholics, Eric says: 'It's quite a way out in the middle of nowhere. It looks like Fort Knox as you approach it, a very forbidding-looking place, low, concrete, government-type buildings, like a top-security prison. Most people arrive there either pissed or dying for a drink, or they've got so much alcohol in their system they need to be detoxified.

'So they put me on a drug called Librium for forty-eight hours. This helps you to come off the alcohol and balances you out. It eases you into the place. You feel very woozy for two or three days. You don't really know who you are, or who these other people are, or what you're doing there. I got pissed on the plane on the way there and I was sobering up when I arrived. I was panicking! I'd braved it through up to then and I wanted to go through with it until I saw the place. You sign some papers and start checking in and they put you into one of a number of units into which the place is divided, all named after famous people connected with Alcoholics Anonymous.

'Each unit contains twenty-eight people. All these people have been through the same thing, so their attitude is: here comes a new boy who's bouncing off the ceiling. You get looked after by all the other inmates, for the first three or four days. Then suddenly you're given a schedule of things you've got to do, and details of how you have to contribute to the welfare of your unit. And the unit runs itself, so immediately I had a ton of responsibility which I had not had for years. Mine was obviously to look after myself and make my own bed – which I'd never done before! – and then I was given the job of laying the table for my unit every mealtime and tea break. That was quite hard for someone who had never done *anything* domestic.

'Apart from that, I was given projects which involved lots of brain work, thinking and research. There were psychological tests: for example, what would the effect of a certain drug and alcohol be on three members of your unit, as compared with the effect on three other members of the unit. By this method you were supposed to get to know everybody and what their dependence was, and how it compared with what you had been through. So in a very short time you got to know everyone very quickly.

'I thoroughly got my teeth into it all. The one thing that was very hard was not being able to drink and having dreams about drink; waking up feeling drunk when I wasn't, which is an established syndrome among the inmates. I was actually sleeping with four other alcoholics in a billet – it was army-style accommodation.

'On top of that, there's group therapy three or four times a day: prayers, lectures, a thousand things to keep you occupied. At one o'clock in the morning I was still struggling to keep up with the work they'd given me to do during that day. When I got to bed, I passed out from complete mental tiredness. That was great, because sleeping was something I had always found difficult to do naturally when I was a drunk – I had to drink to go to sleep. So this was great.

'I was there in January and the temperature was far below freezing, with a very cold wind, which was a bit of a shame because it was too cold to spend much time outdoors. But we did go out for walks a little. I came to realize that in many ways alcoholics are some of the best people in the world. Some of the people I met there, and had to muck in with, were fantastic characters who had had amazingly hard lives. And some of them had been into that place four or five times, real hard-liners. Before going into Hazelden, I thought I had had a really tough time and was hard done by. Suddenly I was faced by the rest of my unit of twenty-eight people, many of whom had much worse stories to tell than me.'

Working on integration with the other people in there was just as important as the treatment. 'Every man is expected to pull his weight, and anyone who doesn't is letting the whole team down,' says Eric, 'so it's all integrated. And on top of that I *wanted* to do well. When you see all these other tough guys breaking down and crying, but still making headway, you realize that you're not that badly off.' Many times Eric felt he could not go through with the full four-week period of treatment. Some patients did leave after coming to the conclusion that they could not cope. 'One bloke, a very wealthy man, had his wife fly a private aeroplane into the nearest field and he left in the middle of the night.'

Some people recognized Eric, but few took much notice of his role as a superstar guitarist. 'The credentials for being there were simply that you were an alcoholic, a drunk. Apart from that, you weren't meant to delve too much into people's lives. Anonymity was the only way you could get on in the place – you couldn't pull any kind of rank.'

Eric underwent many physical and psychological tests. 'There were all kinds of questionnaires which, if you read between the lines, were supposed to spell out whether you were a possible psychotic or whether there was a chance of being one in the outside world. I managed to get through most of those.'

After about three weeks, Eric felt he was coping well with the institutionalization of the place 'but at the same time there was still this rebellious thing coming out. That part of me said I was playing for time, playing the game, but when I got out I would go back to being how I was before.' But that rebellious streak was finally crushed through a foolproof method used by the clinic authorities: they wrote to the patients' loved ones and asked them to fill out questionnaires. 'They ask questions like: Did your husband ever rape you? What was he like when he was drunk?' says Eric. 'It surprised me then, though it doesn't now, because my wife was suddenly given the opportunity to say something destructive or honest because she knew it would help her husband. And when I read out to some of the other clinic inmates what Pattie had said in her questionnaire, how I had treated her without me realizing it – that broke my heart. I was made to understand that I'd behaved like an animal. And that's when I cracked. It was powerful stuff. They judge whether the inmate is fit enough to face it and then they call you into the head counsellor's office, where it's read out in front of the others. It definitely showed what a bastard I was. They said they'd got a letter from home for me. I went to pick it up and when I read it, it was this questionnaire. I read it out in front of a couple of other inmates. And I broke down. Then I went to see one of the counsellors about it. He said it was a mistake that I'd been given it. But it wasn't a ploy by the counsellors.'

'It *was* very personal,' Pattie confirms. 'The questions were particularly severe, asking what amounted to an intrusion into one's personal life with one's husband. But

I decided that the only reason they had asked those questions was to help Eric rather than be intrusive. I knew he was taking the course very seriously, but a part of me feared I could be letting him down by exposing him to my thoughts because he is a famous person.' She had told nobody of the problems she had had with her husband's behaviour and his drinking problems. It was a difficult decision but she rationalized in favour of telling the whole truth.

Having done so, the next agonizing decision was whether to agree to Eric being shown the questionnaire. 'Finally I decided that he *should* be shown how I felt, because for several years before he went into Hazelden I wasn't able to really talk to him at all. There wasn't one minute, on any day, when he was completely sober, so he had absolutely no idea how I felt. So this wasn't a vicious or vitriolic situation I was making use of; it was a method of getting through to him for me.' Conversely, while she knew what she wrote about him would 'hurt him dreadfully', she felt protective towards him. Yet it would be part of his therapy.

'Up until then,' Eric goes on, 'at the back of my head I was playing the role of Jack the Lad in there. But when I heard what she'd written, it cracked me. And the people in there wait for that – at some point a man has to give way in a situation. At first, when you go into the clinic, you battle through. You're tough. But that's not the way it's going to work. You're going to have to break. You have to understand what you've done and what you're facing up to. And once I'd been broken down I felt a lot better, although it did hurt me very deeply. From that point, though, I started to develop a little bit of dependency on the place. It suddenly felt like home. It was safe there. The Jack the Lad man was gone.

What was left was a very insecure human being, a little bit frightened of the outside world. That was the point where it started to get a little bit worrying. I needed building up again.'

But Eric knew, after that month, that he had at least completed the initial work. 'It isn't all done there. All they do is pick you up and point you in a different direction. I knew they had managed to do that with me, but after that it's up to the person. What to do with life from that point on is your own choice.' He had made several friends there, and has since corresponded with several Americans who went through the course with him. Without a doubt, he says, he could not have conquered his alcoholism without going to Hazelden.

Pattie says she leaned on the bottle, ironically, during her husband's absence because she was 'worried that this new person was going to arrive, a freshly scrubbed baby returning to the nest, and he might not love the person he had previously seen through a haze. I expected him to be back, crystal clear and sharp, and thought *I* might not go down too well with *him*.'

Her problem was partly solved by therapy for herself. She flew out to Minnesota and into Hazelden for an intensive five-day course designed to teach relatives, dependants or friends how to cope with people like Eric when they returned home from the 'drying-out' process. 'It was a great relief to mix with other people who had experienced the same problems as I'd had,' says Pattie. 'I had to learn how to live with somebody and not have an automatic reaction to how I thought they would behave, as an alcoholic. Which is how I used to live: I'd hear the door open and immediately react to the prospect of a drunk falling or sliding into the house. So I had to unlearn all of that ready for Eric's return home.' They saw a little of each other at Hazelden, and she was struck by how 'severely clean' he appeared. 'He was crisp and smart, not at all the person I knew. In fact, he was a bit too clean: he'd been through the dry cleaners a few too many times! He was full of praise for Hazelden and he'd been through an almost religious experience.'

On his return, a rejuvenated Eric committed himself to Alcoholics Anonymous and craved as much work as Forrester could get him. In his pocket he continually fingered the medallion given to him by the clinic as a sign that he had successfully completed the course. A major factor in his achievement had been their treatment of Eric's alcoholism as no different from anybody else's, despite his financial ability to buy as much drink as he desired. Now he wanted a quick return to life as a musician. He immediately astonished all around him with his eye-flashing alertness.

'For the first year, he was nervous of being around people who were drinking too much,' says Pattie. 'I took all the hard liquor out of the house and just kept the wine there, which he didn't mind being left in the wine cellar. He never drank wine anyway. He was very much quieter and he withdrew into himself terribly. He seemed very, very insecure. It showed in the way he became obsessive about buying beautiful and very expensive Italian clothes *every week*.'

During his first year of sobriety, Eric believed work would be one of the greatest therapies. 'It was a rash decision,' he says now. 'The experts always counsel you after you've stopped and say you can expect a good year of completely irrational behaviour, and you shouldn't make any plans or decisions. And they're quite right. I felt within three months that I'd changed completely for the better having stopped drinking, and I was ready for work. In fact I wasn't. After five months, I did a tour of America and really didn't understand what I was doing.' But it gave him a great chance to attend a lot of American meetings of Alcoholics Anonymous. One meeting, after a show in Minnesota, proved to be lacking in anonymity. 'It was after I'd done a concert in that town and half the people at the meeting were wearing T-shirts with pictures of me at the AA meeting.' Generally, he found himself recognized more often in the US than in Britain but 'they are all good people who live by what they say. They don't go away saying, "Hey, guess who I saw tonight?" because that would put *their* anonymity in jeopardy.'

Smoking cigarettes had been not merely a habit of Eric's, but a recognized quirk of his stage act: the burning cigarette which stuck in the neck of his guitar became virtually an emblem. He had smoked at least forty Rothman King Size cigarettes each day for about twenty years, and when under great stress that figure rose to about sixty a day. As he spoke of stopping smoking, too, his friends shuddered to contemplate a Clapton who did not drink, or smoke, or eat spicy foods and did not, above all, feel integrated as 'one of the gang' on social occasions, in dressing-rooms or on the road. 'Eric needs to join in things with the people around him he likes,' said one of his mates around that time. 'It's hard enough for him to be dry. I can't imagine Eric without a cigarette.'

'He was like a little orange on a tree that had started to shrivel,' says Alphi O'Leary, recalling the drunken years. 'And then somebody put a little bit of fertilizer on the tree and the orange became an orange again. If you prick that fresh orange, a lot of zest comes out of it.' Like all the people around Eric during the seven years of hard drinking, O'Leary had seen a totally changed man since 1982. The worst aspect of Eric's drinking was the frightening unpredictability of his moods. 'Tremendous highs, and then terrible depressions,' recalls Roger Forrester. 'But he alway did the shows, sometimes to my surprise. They'd be fifty per cent good, fifty per cent bad, but it was so worrying. He could never last all day awake. He'd never be able to get up in the morning and still be awake by the evening for the show. He'd have to sleep the afternoon away.' When Forrester knocked on his door in the early evening to say it was time to get up, he often had problems rousing him. Once, in Dublin, he had to break the door down when there was no reply from the sleeping Clapton. But Eric had amazing powers of recovery when a show was due; not once did his manager have to cancel a show because of his condition.

In Clapton's fertile mind, one of his biggest worries about giving up the bottle was: 'What am I going to do with all that extra *time*?' He realized how many hours of his days and nights had been devoted to actually drinking, then sobering up adequately to face the world before returning to the bottle. 'All the time I'd spent devoted to the bottle, I'd put off doing things that were waiting to be tackled when I returned to real life. Abstract things: emotional problems or family situations. Suddenly, when you're sober again, you have to learn to live with all the problems you've created in your life but which have been cloudy. It doesn't go away.' Eric's membership of Alcoholics Anonymous was crucial: it absorbed his interest as well as helping him practically.

Like everything that makes an impact on his life, Alcoholics Anonymous is something he is still, in his own way, committed to. He never does anything half-heartedly. He feels that stopping drinking, particularly the quantity he was consuming, would have been impossible without going to group meetings once a week. On tour, anywhere in the world, he attended them, sometimes immediately after a concert when his adrenaline ran high and he needed sympathetic reassurance.

'I'm still active,' Eric said in 1985. 'I'm not such a good member as I could be, mainly because of my travels since I gave up drinking three years ago. My first year off it was good, the second year not so good, because I began to get the urge to drink again. And my third year was disastrous because I stopped going to meetings and gave in to the desire to drink. I did drink earlier this year and carried on for a few months.' He stopped before it took a hold, however. On one plane journey that year with Roger Forrester, he asked his manager if he minded if he had a beer. No, said Forrester. No attempt would be made to prevent Eric from drinking. Eric has a big guilt complex at being seen to let down those around him who worried about him. So he drank a beer and then stopped totally. But that odd beer was a far, far cry from the days when Eric's personal assistant carried a case with Courvoisier aboard each flight because Eric could not wait for the plane to 'level out' before needing a drink.

Of his AA endorsement, Eric says: 'A lot of people in show business and the music world don't go to AA. They would like to stop drinking and a lot of them do. But some of them have done it on their own, without the help of AA, because they fear being recognized, they fear being treated as a special case. Now for me, because of the way my career has developed overseas, I'm more recognized in America, if I go to a meeting, than I am in Britain. A lot of people in my local group meetings still don't know who I am and it's only after I speak for a little while, they realize that I'm in entertainment. But they have no idea specifically what I do. So now, in England, I'm still pretty anonymous, but in America now, I'm not.

'In America, they've got a slightly better handle on it than in Britain. They're a lot more outspoken and a lot less nervous about it than the British. It still seems to be a bit of a stigma in Britain to be an alcoholic. And the best members of AA in England are always old army types, who have been sober for a long time, or who drank for a long time. They are much tougher, whereas in America it seems to be a younger clan of people, more around my age group and younger, from all walks of life. They don't have that shame and guilt, which a lot of people in Britain still have.'

While he has conquered drink, he is careful not to claim that he will never return to it. He tried a sip of white wine at home in 1984, but hated the taste. 'It's only too often that it happens that people start again. I mean, it's any day! You can be sober for fifteen or twenty years and then one day you'll just put yourself into an impossible situation, whereby the only thing you can do is to pick up a drink. It's always premeditated. And God knows what brings it on half the time. You could set yourself up over a period of a year, as I did. I worked myself up to a drink, over a period of six months, at least, just *thinking* about having a drink ... until I couldn't stand it any longer and I had to find out whether I could take it or not. So you could set yourself up for years and you become very miserable and morose. But it is always possible, no matter how long you've been sober, to drink again. And the thing about AA is that they're always ready for you to come back. If you do drink again, all you've got to do is go back and say, "I've drunk again", and they'll take you in. There are no reprimands, because they all know that it could happen to any one of them, at any time.'

Eric has worked for AA, helping those less experienced than he in withdrawal from alcohol. 'After a couple of years of sobriety, or even just a year, you're invited at some point to give what is called "chair". That's when you sit at the head of the table and tell your life story. You tell how you drank and how you stopped drinking and how you're getting on in your recovery.' He has done several of those sessions. He enjoyed the therapy of that, and would do it again. 'Because I've never got it under control. No alcoholic ever has control. He is actually suffering from a killing disease which gets worse. Even if you're not drinking, it's getting worse. So I'm trying, as best I can, and that's not very well, to stay sober and to live and learn to live again as a sober human being. And any time that I fall prey to drink, I know that I stand the risk of killing myself within a very short time. And I've no control over that whatsoever, if that happens.

'I see it as being a completely logical chain of events, where when you stop going to AA meetings, there is only one other course of action and that is, if you're an alcoholic, you drink. So it's absolutely necessary if you are doing it properly to go maybe once a week, if not twice a week. Because if you're not there, you'll be in a pub, or you'll be at the bottle. So I think anyone who tries to drop alcohol needs this kind of help. If you try to beat it with your own willpower, that always falls down. Because you're just not strong enough on your own.'

His doctrine from AA is based on 'one-day-at-a-time'. 'They say, "Do not drink again *today*. Don't worry about tomorrow. You can have a drink tomorrow, if you like. But don't have a drink *today*.' Well, it's just based on the fact that you're never actually going to be here tomorrow. So if you don't drink today, you'll be all right. It's a struggle at Christmas time! It's always a struggle whenever you're around people who are having fun, or whenever you're having fun. For me the temptation to drink comes along when I'm most relaxed, or when I'm actually happiest, when things are really going well and I've got no problems. That's when I want to drink. When I'm struggling against adversity, when I'm in a bind, the temptation to drink doesn't cause me any problem, because I know that I have to get through that without any help from the bottle. And then I know for a fact that drink will only make it worse. It's always the times when you're most relaxed and there's nothing to bother you . . . that's when you feel like you could sit back and take it double easy.'

By mid 1985, Eric was 'enjoying a glass of wine or beer at the right time of day, drinking in moderation. But I do feel that the AA was very instructive and a great deal of help to me when I needed to stop drinking heavily. Now, there's no guarantee that I won't drink heavily again, just as there's no guarantee of anything. So I may have to return to AA at some time in my life. But at the moment, I feel I can drink in moderation. So for the time being, things are a little different. What I'm striving for in my life now is establishing a balance – being involved in a little of each of my interests instead of doing one thing to the exclusion of everything else. So when Gary Brooker says I will be a fisherman until the day I die, he's probably right. It's just that I don't need to do it every day of every week. I'm constantly striving to be a more consistent human being. I don't want to be predictable but I don't like the idea of people having to wait while I make up my mind about what I'm going to do next.'

Interestingly, Eric sees no connection between the way he ditched drugs and his ending the heavy drinking habit. 'They're totally unrelated,' he says. 'I conquered drugs through my own wish and will to survive, with the help of Meg Patterson and the help of her husband and family, who gave me love. That was the medicine I needed as much as, if not more than, the actual acupuncture which she was practising. It was a totally self-centred way of getting better, for my own benefit really, which is the same in AA. Except that in AA you're thrown in among a lot of other people who are having the same problem, so you have to *give*, whereas with me, coming off the drugs, I was just *taking*. When I stopped drinking and came into AA, I'd learned bit by bit and still am learning how to fill the vacuum with a belief in something greater than myself.'

Eric was self-analytical about his sobriety and the change it caused in all his relationships. For Forrester, his embattled friend and manager who had pulled Eric through the war zone, it was difficult to adjust. 'It was a lot easier for Roger when I was drunk,' Eric told me. 'Because I couldn't make decisions on my own and because of the chemistry between us, the father–son relationship that exists there, it was actually quite preferable in many respects. He could make decisions which I would just follow on with, without questioning at all. When I stopped drinking, and I did wake up, there were a lot of things that I wanted to change by myself, including my lifestyle and my attitude towards music.

'And it all came into focus. Roger had to deal with that, had to rescind a great deal of his authority over me, and a great deal of his responsibilities. They had to come back to me so that I could learn to live again on my own two feet. I think once he made that transition, which took him a long time, probably about a year and a half, for him to fully accept that I could make rational, non-compulsive or non-impulsive decisions, he was happy. He's happy again now because he's dealing with another human being and not a vegetable. But it took him a long time to get over it.'

Pondering the drinking years, Eric remembered 'every day I was setting up or proposing or getting involved in projects that were totally insane. And it was Roger's job either to dissuade me from doing something or to smooth it out after I'd already decided. I'd get involved in all kinds of crazy schemes and ventures that he would have to deal with. So I would think now, it's a lot easier. It's a lot quieter life. Although he and I both have a pretty eccentric sense of humour. A lot of that was great fun.'

The new, dry, alert Eric was the talk of his friends and relatives. It was almost frightening to observe his changed persona. 'I prefer it. I'm vividly awake all the time. I really only get six hours' sleep. I'm wide awake. That's wearing off, but for the first couple of years after drinking I was so hyper-sensitive it was untrue. Now it's getting a little better.

'My character as a drunk was a lot more forthright. But when you're drunk, a lot of the time, the frontal part of your brain says "Pack in". Your instincts take over a lot. Because I'm awake now, I'm allowing my intellect to make judgements on what my instincts tell me. And that often leads me astray, sometimes, still. Whereas my instincts I just trust. They're very good. And my intuition is quite strong. But because I'm still learning how to intellectualize everything, I find that I muddle it up a bit sometimes. Don't allow my instincts and my intuition to really come through to the fore. And that applies to my sense of humour, to the idea of having fun, or being relaxed. These are still things that I find quite a lot of difficulty with. Because my intellect says that that may lead to drinking, or that may lead to something else, or is it valid. I tend, at the moment, to take myself quite a lot too seriously.' He believed he could 'change that to make myself a better person to be with . . . which is quite important because I don't really want to end up alone, you know, or be regarded as an intimidating person'.

That was precisely how people described him at that time. He agreed, adding: 'It's all to do with insecurity and protection. Because of the sensitivity and because of my inability to give or open myself up completely to people, they find it intimidating that I don't always say what I'm thinking and feeling, I think. And I'm consciously working on that. But it takes a lot of practice.'

EIGHT

THE MARITAL
STORM

'H E'S MUCH more emotional than anyone ever
sees on the surface. There are tears just behind
that poker face. He's actually very, very soft
inside, no matter how much we all see him as a strong
man,' says pianist Chris Stainton.

The keyboards player in Eric Clapton's band since
1979, Stainton has made a study of astrology. He knows
Eric purely from being in his band; apart from the
expected talk between musicians, they don't have a
particularly close relationship. Yet Clapton inspires great
personal loyalty and concern among those who go, like
Stainton, on the road with him or record with him. It's
not just his music that commands their admiration.
There's something especially unpretentious about him.
And yet, he is in no doubt. Everyone around him believes
Clapton is totally aware of his status and his talent. He
tends to push it away, and never allows it to be seen that
he knows about it or accepts it. That's his form of
protection against conceit. It is also his reason for
pushing himself onwards to try to improve his work.

Born under the sign of Aries, Eric is, according to
Stainton: 'direct, forceful, energetic, outgoing, impulsive

and loses his temper quickly. He's full of life and energy, a pioneer. But then he has Scorpio rising, which makes him very secretive and poker-faced. You don't know what's going on behind the mask. He might be perfectly sweet on the surface, but somewhere else he might be loading his gun ready to shoot you. He has powerful emotions but they're bottled up . . . and they can only get a release through his music. Hence the intensity of his playing.

'His moon is also in Scorpio, which doubles the effect. This means he has a great need to eliminate things from his life. Drug addiction and alcoholism serve no purpose and he knows that. So he has now eliminated them from his life and they're gone for ever. That's the strange thing about anyone with a strong Scorpio element: he has to undergo a period of trial, a deep and intense test period like Eric underwent. Without that, as just an Aries with a spirit of pioneering and leadership on its own, he wouldn't have the Scorpio spirit of tenacity, the ability to persevere doggedly on. Scorpio in Eric provides him with incredible resistance to setbacks. Nothing will ever put him off. He'll carry on, grinding onwards.

'There's another side to him, really sweet and graceful. He has Venus and Taurus in him, which brings a softness. He is heavily ruled by Mars in Pisces, which means that he's far more liable to break down and is much more emotional than we see on the surface. Pisces figures in Eric because it's the sign of music. That's his outlet for all his emotions. Without that sign figuring in him, I don't know what he'd do. Without music coming out of him, Eric would go berserk. Beneath the gruff exterior, there's gold in that man . . .'

Chris Stainton's reading of Eric comes from one who has returned from the slippery road of drugs himself. As

a pianist accompanying such big stars as Joe Cocker and
Elkie Brooks, Stainton had by 1979 acquired a reputation
as an intuitive, highly melodic rock 'n' rolling pianist.
Clapton hired him when he sought a particularly all-
British band. And yet Stainton was a slightly dangerous
hiring. Unemployed when Clapton phoned out of the
blue to offer him an audition, Stainton was, as a known
former drug-user, a potential hazard for a 'clean'
Clapton.

The two men have developed a bond, with the
perceptive Stainton observing his boss from the vantage
point of amateur psychologist and sideman on stage and
in the studio. 'He's a natural bandleader,' says Stainton,
contradicting Clapton's own theory of himself as an
unnatural leader. 'He always knows what he wants, but
maybe he doesn't realize the kind of power, or authority,
he has over people. If anyone tries to usurp him, it's all
over for that person. He has to be in control of all
situations, and as long as he is, fantastic things can
happen on stage, where Eric is at his best.' But to judge
the man takes years of study. 'If a show has gone badly,
a certain poker-face comes over him, and you don't go
near him. Best to let him alone to suffer in silence.'

When Clapton is sailing away with the right backing
from his musicians in a live concert, 'God knows where
it comes from, the stuff he plays,' says Stainton, shaking
his head. 'He'll hit notes that make me float away. And
even Eric says he feels himself lifted two feet off the
ground. It's as if the music is coming through him, from
somewhere else . . .'

Yet the sensibilities of the man should never be
mistaken for any lack of a sense of destiny. Self-preser-
vation is inherent in his make-up. Grasping his career
since ceasing to drink may have been an essential therapy,

but it came to him quite easily. He had hitherto spoken of his difficulties in grappling with the job of bandleader. But now with a dry Clapton came a changed demeanour; he became dedicated to his own survival.

He had always relied on his ability, his example, as his passport to leadership. But he had always stopped short of exerting the authority that came with it. Grappling with the task of handling people had never come easily to him. But in the recording studios in the Bahamas in July, 1980, Clapton became restless with the British quartet of musicians he had been praising so much in the past year. The album that resulted, *Another Ticket*, disappointed. It was partly salvaged from the aborted album being produced by Glyn Johns. By now, Eric's voice had matured into a rich, bluesy and natural instrument; his rendition of Sleepy John Estes's 'Floating Bridge' was exceptional. He also excelled on a Muddy Waters track, 'Blow Wind Blow'. Overall, though, the album lacked personality. The title, 'Another Ticket', was Eric's tongue-in-cheek jibe at a friend who was continually asking for 'another ticket' for Clapton concerts. As a pointer to Eric's immediate future, the two words were ominous.

He agreed with many friends that it lacked a blues feeling. Without that, Clapton was directionless. There was a feeling throughout the Clapton camp that new energy was essential . . . and it took a sober Eric and a wise producer like Tom Dowd to realize it – and act. Dowd's history was impeccable, and Eric respected him; his production experience dated back to the days of the famed Stax label, which produced legendary names like Otis Redding, Sam and Dave, Booker T and the MGs and Aretha Franklin. He had produced the Allman Brothers and knew all about blues feeling.

Eric decided for the first time in his life to break with virtually the entire band on the spot. Chris Stainton, Gary Brooker, Henry Spinetti and Dave Markee were on their bikes. Only the star guitarist Albert Lee remained, partly because his style complemented Clapton's work – and also because having such a lauded player in the band was quite a coup for Eric. 'I'd always used the old maxim of giving people enough rope and letting them cook themselves,' says Eric, 'rather than calling a halt to it at an early stage. But down at Nassau, we'd tried every method there was to record a couple of songs. It wasn't happening.' After two weeks they had hardly got one track complete. 'I said nothing to the musicians. In the old days, I used to let people make mistakes because I hadn't got the guts to say: "This is wrong."'

'The idea of being with English gentlemen was a break,' Eric told Robert Palmer in a *Rolling Stone* interview in June, 1985. 'They just wanted to play good music and that was really easy for a while. Unfortunately there were some things they just couldn't do. And one was to play the blues. I guess I was under-achieving a little bit.' Justifying to himself the diversion he had taken, he added that as a blues player, which he was 'by birthright', 'you can't face it all the time . . . sometimes you need to hear some harmonic softeners . . . to quench the fire and calm yourself'. He was fond of Don Williams's music as an antidote, and for a period enjoyed good country music, infusing it into his work on songs like the ever-popular 'Promises'.

Advice given by counsellors at the American clinic where Eric had dried out played a key part in his decision to change the band. 'They had kept telling me that if something bugged me, I should be assertive about it. If I wasn't happy with situations, I should say so rather than bottle it deep inside, or moan about it, or resent it. So losing the band was partly me exercising that advice purely for the sake of it, being decisive for the first time in my life.'

He amazed himself with the firmness of his action. 'I gathered them all together in one of the little chalets near the studio. I told them there was nothing personal, they were a great band for touring with and going on stage with, and nice people to be around. But because I'd been out of the studio for so long, and this album we were preparing was so important as a result, I said I didn't think they were up to the standard required. I said I'd have to bring in some professional studio people, so there was no point in them being there any more. They'd have to go home. I added that I'd give it some time before thinking whether or not I would bring them back into the working situation on tour.'

For Clapton, who treasures friendships, it was the most momentous decision allied to his career since he had kicked heroin. 'It was a terrible thing to have to do, and it was probably over the top,' he reflects. But it was the right move for him at the time. 'They were my mates. They'd been working for me through my years of drunkenness, and they'd seen a very sloppy individual who was almost incapable of making any rational decision whatsoever. And here I was, making a decision which concerned their working lives. They must have thought that I was actually flipping out.' Dave Markee and Gary Brooker took it particularly badly, but Clapton's friendship with his old fishing companion Brooker continued.

Chris Stainton went back to London and sent Eric a postcard to Nassau. 'I think you've done the right thing,' Stainton wrote wryly, 'and it was a bloody long audition.' As a result of that postcard Stainton was immediately rehired and continues to be in Eric's 1990s line-up. Eric says: 'He forgave me immediately and saw the whole thing for what it was. There was no doubt about that band being lethargic. It would have been very difficult to get the album done in the time required. I'm a blues guitarist, and that just wasn't a good blues band.'

The departure of the British musicians was at least as important psychologically to Eric as musically. 'With those guys, I'd been trying to get a *band* together with that unique British feeling. I'd be able to hide and continue losing myself within it – just a band of mates, doing pub gigs and village halls as well as the bigger concerts. I was after a *feeling*. But when I remembered what they'd told me in the clinic, about being assertive, I realized I was fooling myself to carry on. Firing the whole band, it left me back on my own. I'd employ musicians who suited me. It was the restart of my solo career, really.' Significantly, when Roger Forrester flew into Nassau to be told of the plan, he had asked Clapton if he wanted him to deal with the practical problem of telling the band. The manager had become accustomed to pulling Eric out of awkward situations: the gullible guitarist was always committing himself to ideas and projects that needed Forrester's veto and action at the eleventh hour. 'No, I'll deal with it,' Eric said. There was a stunned silence when he broke the news to them. 'They were all very, very shocked.' For Clapton, that moment emphasized a dominating part of his character: come drugs or drink or shyness, he could usually apply a streak of ruthlessness when it meant survival.

Who would replace them? Tom Dowd mentioned some possibilities to Eric: what about Duck Dunn, the rock-solid house bassist at the Stax label during the mid-sixties? Dowd knew that Eric held him in high esteem for his work with Otis Redding, Booker T and many other giants of soul music. How about drummer Roger Hawkins, the man Eric had once played alongside on an Aretha Franklin album, and who was known for his robust work as one of the regulars at the Muscle Shoals studios? Maybe Ry Cooder could be persuaded to guest, Dowd added.

Clapton laughed off such ideas with genuine modesty. 'You'll never get people of *that* level here. Why should they come and be on my album?' Dowd assured him that his reputation was bigger than he thought; a few phone calls later, and despite other work, two of those three top musicians virtually left their homes at once for Compass Point. The electricity between the new band worked well. Duck Dunn and Eric struck up such a firm rapport, and the bassist's work proved so intuitively right for Eric's music, that he went on to tour the world with Eric's band from 1983 onwards.

When Dowd said the maestro of slide guitar Ry Cooder might also drop in, Eric laughed again. 'Don't tempt me with these names! If it's not possible to get them I don't want to be frustrated by good-sounding impossibilities!' But Cooder was elated when he heard that a new Clapton album was under way and jumped at the invitation to drop in on the record. Suddenly, there was a new dialogue when Ry arrived, different again from the excellent relationship that had been struck up between Eric, Duck and Roger. Cooder's roots, like Eric's, skirted jazz, and the communication between the two men, musically as well as out of the studio, was firm. As a master stroke, the talent of Albert Lee was deployed to the concert piano, while Roger Hawkins spent a complete day buying a new set of skins for his drums to achieve a very special sound which Eric required.

The resulting collection, *Money and Cigarettes*, had its moments of triumph, with Eric's voice ruggedly mature. There was massive radio play around the world for the lilting '(I've Got a) Rock 'n' Roll Heart', while purists loved the old Albert King favourite, 'Crosscut Saw', and the Sleepy John Estes classic, 'Everybody Oughta Make a Change'. For the Johnny Otis song, 'Crazy Country Hop', Otis was excitedly on the phone to Clapton to remind him of the lyrics during Eric's recording session. The maudlin songwriter inside Eric shone through with 'Man in Love' and 'Pretty Girl', another unashamedly tearful song to his wife. The album contained his cutting message to her about alcohol, 'The Shape You're In', which presaged their matrimonial strife. Eric told me this was a 'tongue-in-cheek' song about Pattie's drinking. But in reality, for any man to record a song of such negativity about his wife showed a terrible lapse of taste – particularly after the majestic 'Layla' and 'Wonderful Tonight'. Conversely, Eric made his own vital statement on his renunciation of dope and drink with a song which received little attention. 'Ain't Going Down', with breakneck guitar runs and splendidly bluesy vocals, laid bare the dangers he had survived in his thirty-seven years, and set forth his determination to carry on living.

It was not a great album, but a solid, important one. It marked a turn in his confidence. Tom Dowd, who helped to mastermind the changed stance on *Money and Cigarettes*, says: 'I have never found him easy to handle. He's not the kind of person of whom you can predict that if he gets up one morning and takes two steps one way, that's the direction he's going for the whole day – or even for the next couple of hours! He can tire of any route very quickly. He changes on a whim. So people who play with him, or work with him as I do, have to go with his beat or give up. I think Eric thinks spherically rather than in straight lines. And so it's difficult to achieve a balance of judging when he is re-entering the planetary system. But then, he's an artist, and it's essential never to curb his energy. I try to direct it carefully, the way he instinctively thinks it's going.'

Eric has lurched from one craze to another. 'I don't think I'll ever level out, until I get very old,' he says. 'I go from one obsession to the next. It's something I'd really like to beat but I don't know if I can. I try in every way I can to do things in moderation – but the impossibility is precisely what made me an alcoholic. We're all obsessive. You know, you can always spot an alcoholic. If you leave a bowl of peanuts on the table, he'll finish the lot. He can't manage with just two or three. I'm like that. And if I decided to paint a room, I have to do it in one day, or until I'm completely knackered.'

So when he stopped drinking and tried to fill all his time, Eric plunged into another hobby, fishing, with an all-consuming zeal.

It began through his friend Gary Brooker. The pianist, who lived a few miles from Eric, often went to the local pub with him, and one day said to Eric: 'I'm going fishing tomorrow.' Clapton replied: 'Ah, I used to go fishing over in Ripley when I was a kid. Caught a perch once.' He was persuaded by Gary that fly fishing was different: it called for a psychological victory over a delicious trout or salmon, rather than coarse fishing which produced carp or perch to be thrown back. Intrigued, Eric saw it as a potentially healthy obsession, one that might contrast with his heavy drinking. Fishing and drinking did not mix well. Brooker, a skilled fisherman, taught Eric to cast, and within weeks it was totally dominating Clapton's life. He bought a place on the River Test in Wiltshire and went trout fishing for days on end – and those absences added to the strain on his marriage as a now bemused Pattie stayed at home. When he returned with trout, she gutted them and prepared them for the deep freeze, but inwardly pondered the new 'fence' that fishing had built between them. Yet it was not without Clapton's dry humour. Once, after a day without a catch, he wanted to impress Pattie with his prowess, so he went, like many another fisherman before him, to Mac Fisheries and bought some trout in a crazy attempt to fool her.

Eric agrees his days of fishing were 'very selfish' but argues that as an alcoholic coming off the booze, he needed to be selfish. 'It was my *life* and if I hadn't started taking steps to get straight again, I was going to die. Because even if I wasn't drinking, I could have died of misery. You can end up committing suicide while sober. So for me fishing was great contemplation, meditation, and a way of getting physically fit again. For that first year, it was absolutely necessary to have some kind of exercise – with fishing you tend to have to walk a lot. It could have been tennis, squash or golf, but I chose fishing for the first year off booze. The second year, I should have eased off and maybe started setting up a new lifestyle. But I carried on fishing. And that's when it became anti-social. It definitely contributed to a division between Pattie and me.'

The American tours for up to six weeks, the concerts all round the globe, and the recording sessions, all without Pattie, added to the strain on the marriage.

Eric's obsessiveness made it difficult for him to contemplate changing his ways. While Pattie nursed her grievances, he in turn felt very aggrieved when, returning home from the airport after a long tour, he found her absent. Hardly surprisingly, since his phone calls to her from 'the road' were rare, she often forgot when he was due home.

Roger Forrester, with the world-weary look of one who had observed Eric's fetishes a thousand times, said fishing would not last. Meanwhile, when Eric's concert tours were planned, Forrester was asked to book only hotels near fishing facilities. Eric spent many hours of each day out on lakes, alone, and a new worry loomed: that he would be so tired from such a long day in the fresh air that he wouldn't have enough energy for the show.

'We went fishing everywhere,' says Gary Brooker. 'In Japan we had a boat and drifted downriver in the rapids and didn't catch anything at all. But Eric said it was much better than being stuck in the hotel room. And he got so immersed in it that the last thing he wanted to do was stop off at a bar for two hours' rest. Booze is not part of the sport, except in America where they load the cooler full of beer as soon as you take the boat.'

Back home after a tour, Pattie's role as a 'trout widow' increased. Eric left at 7.30 in the morning and did not return until late at night from his solitary fishing outings, usually with three or four trout for Pattie to clean and freeze. He collected rods and reels and all the paraphernalia with predictable feverishness. On tour, as soon as the party arrived in a town and he had checked into his hotel suite, Eric was scouring the local phone directory for the name and location of the fishing tackle specialist.

The phone would ring in Nigel Carroll's room: 'Right. I've found the shop. Let's go.' He bought dozens of rods and reels, but gave many to his friends.

The intensity of the fishing days and nights surprised even Gary Brooker. Eric went to a lake not far from his home in Surrey, or to his position on the River Test for five-hour sessions at night, or to Scotland, or to one of the four trout lakes run commercially by ex-Who singer Roger Daltrey in Sussex. 'His casting's good and he's sometimes caught fish when I haven't,' says Brooker. 'Once, down at Roger Daltrey's, I caught one and he caught five.' Eric took great delight in boasting of his expertise. 'Did you see what they were feeding on, Hornby?' he said, using his mocking nickname to Brooker. 'It was a pheasant tail nymph,' he said, describing the fly he had chosen.

Clapton enthusiastically told Brooker several times that fishing had replaced alcohol in his life. Gary recalls one outing which emphasized how seriously Eric had immersed himself in the sport. 'There were some fish in the river, and a trout rising underneath a branch. It turned to his fly three or four times. It was difficult to cast the fly to it, too. And Eric chirped up like a little boy: "I've got a real challenge on here, Hornby. I'm not gonna give *this* one up!" Eric loves the confrontation of fishing, as well as encouraging Pattie to cook the trout. Gary Brooker believes he will never completely give it up. But by 1985, Eric's keenness on fishing had gone on to 'hold'.

In 1983, celebrating his twentieth year on the road, Eric played a short series of splendid concerts along with some other British veterans. His old friend Ronnie Lane, former singer alongside Rod Stewart in the Faces, who was suffering from multiple sclerosis, helped to organize a series of gala concerts to aid ARMS (Action Research into Multiple Sclerosis). At the Royal Albert Hall, London, on 20 September, Eric joined a line-up including Jimmy Page, Jeff Beck, Joe Cocker, Andy Fairweather-Low, Steve Winwood, Charlie Watts, Chris Stainton, Ray Cooper and Bill Wyman. Taped for a video to raise cash for the cause, the night had 'a special atmosphere,' Eric recalls. 'Although all of us had been around for all those years we were playing together for the first time. I don't think we'd ever have done it for the money. There would have been too much aggravation. But because it was for multiple sclerosis and Ronnie Lane, it seemed right. We all put down our egos and got on with it. It was a circus, and great entertainment.'

The producer was Glyn Johns and an unrepeatable moment came when Clapton, Page and Beck joined together on the Led Zeppelin classic 'Stairway to Heaven'. A second night's concert was to aid the Prince of Wales' Prince's Trust. So successful was this enterprise that the show moved on to New York, Los Angeles and San Francisco, filling the 20,000-seater stadiums.

The international admiration society for Clapton's work, which had been building for two decades, reached its zenith around that time. Sometimes, it seemed, Clapton would submerge his blues identity in favour of his need to please a friend by 'sitting in' in a recording session, irrespective of the alien genre of the artist. With such a curious logic of making himself far too easily available for sessions, he found himself, in August 1983, recording in London for Roger Waters. The ex-Pink Floyd composer/guitarist/singer was creating his solo outing with his project called 'The Pros and Cons of

Hitch-hiking' and along with the gifted American saxophonist David Sanborn, Clapton's input gave the project
a musical validity.

To fill the vacuum caused by distancing himself from
drink, Clapton was hungry for as much work as he could
get. But the bankrupt music meant even Clapton could
not stamp his proper authority on the project. Worse
followed, for Clapton was then persuaded by Waters to
go on stage at London's Earls Court on 21 and 22 June
1984. This diversion, perhaps the weakest career move
he ever made, was against the advice of a fuming Roger
Forrester. Clapton was far too established to play what
amounted to second fiddle around the world on a project
with which neither he nor his music had anything in
common. But he loyally followed through, and did
European and American dates, having told Waters he
would.

Clapton originally liked the idea because it gave him
the chance to submerge himself within a band led by
someone else; he fancied a world ticket with no responsibilities; the musical company, including Michael Kamen
(keyboards), Andy Newmark (drums) and Mel Collins
(saxophones), sounded interesting. But once on the
road, he quickly tired of what he regarded as a preten-
tious atmosphere. It was more like a travelling five-star
hotel, with a mental distance between the players, a sharp
contrast with the camaraderie he enjoyed in his own
band. Tensions developed. Eric felt lonely, exposed.
Once, in Stockholm, at an after-the-show dinner hosted
by Waters's record company at a luxury restaurant, a
hungry Clapton grew tired of waiting ages for food from
obsequious waiters. He said to Nigel Carroll: 'I could do
with a Big Mac and French Fries.' Carroll left and
returned with the fast food fifteen minutes later. Eric

enjoyed watching the expressions on the faces of the dinner guests as he tucked into his burger at the table while they still waited for their culinary delights.

Musically, as well as socially, Clapton was utterly unsuited to the Waters show. By far the finest musician on the stage, he had no natural place in such theatricality and posturing. The show came to life only when Eric played. But he looked uncomfortable, bored, and smoked endlessly to relieve what he saw as the dreariness of the stage show. Fed up from the start, he could hardly wait for the tour to end. The iciness of the music and the bad vibes of the touring entourage depressed him. It was, however, another example of the breadth of respect held for Eric by artists of many hues. And when the tour went to Europe, Eric went to see the film *Purple Rain*. He was deeply impressed by Prince.

Back in London from the Waters tour, a relieved Eric knew he had once more to change his approach to his next album. Songs, he reflected, had to carry simplicity and emotion to get the best response from his strongest weapon, the guitar. 'I can sing other people's songs,' he said, if the material touched him. 'Or I can write them, if I'm feeling secure enough. Or insecure enough!'

The relevance of those last three words could not have been more appropriate to the period. As he spoke, his marriage was creaking.

Eric's ardour for Pattie continued, and he would articulate his adoration of her to anyone who asked. He would never love another woman so intensely. Pattie was, however, always a personality in her own right. For twenty years, her resonant observations and individuality had been submerged by two high-achieving rock heavyweights. And she felt the need to shape her life beyond the confines of the Surrey countryside while Eric plunged into his work. It was a classic case of a husband's professional duties taking priority over his marriage.

A new studio setting had been booked for Eric to make his new album. This time, it would be George Martin's Air Studios in Montserrat. Eric needed to write some songs. But, he told me, 'the home situation was getting sticky'. Normally, Eric wrote comfortably in Surrey, but suddenly he felt 'exposed'. The tension between him and Pattie was unbearable and not conducive to creativity.

'So I took myself off to Wales and wrote in a little cottage there for two weeks . . . and all this stuff came out, which made no sense to me at the time. It was almost like writing nursery rhymes. It was abstract.' Only later, as events unfolded, could he see that he had been writing autobiographically about his threatened relationship with Pattie, and the apparent inevitability of their separation. 'I only hope it isn't too late,' he said to me at the time. 'There are a couple of songs that are actually quite positive. It seems to me that one of the heartbreaking things about being an artist is not knowing what the hell you're creating until you've finished it. And then it may be too late. Other people can see what you're saying, but you can't. I was just opening my mouth and letting it come out.'

But he felt nervous about the degree of angst in the songs he had prepared. Songs had to have simplicity, 'something that twangs me emotionally. I can sing other people's songs if they do that to me . . . At the moment, I'm in a very difficult [matrimonial] position in the case of writing. Because if I say the wrong f.....g thing, I could actually turn the applecart right over. If everything

resolves, or gets better, or even if it gets worse, then I'll
be able to write in a safer position. Because it'll either be
so far gone, irretrievable, or it'll be back and I'll be able
to write about that. You need a firm base to be able to
write about that.' Faced with an emotional trauma at the
centre of his life, the songwriting prospects were good,
whichever way the problem went.

As he flew into the West Indies to record under the
production baton of Phil Collins, the prophetic nature of
the songs would become even more apparent. One song
was called 'She's Waiting', which, as Eric explained later,
was all about how Pattie was waiting for another man to
love, 'And I had no idea about who this was . . . it didn't
seem to me that I knew anyone that was doing this.' It
was 'about predicament and how I blew it . . . except
that I hadn't blown it when I wrote the bloody song!
That's awful, isn't it – to predict what you're going to do
unconsciously, and then go ahead and do it.' 'Just like a
Prisoner' ('probably about me inside our relationship')
and 'It All Depends' carried a similar, if oblique, commentary on the problem, while even compositions by
others ('Forever Man' and 'Tangled In Love') continued
the theme of self-questioning.

Eric tore into one song with a feverishness which none
of the musicians had seen in him before. Playing and
singing his own personal favourite on the record, 'Same
Old Blues', he was full of fire in his guitar power and in
his raging, but still mellow, vocal work. So impulsively
fierce was his playing and singing that the 'guide vocal'
was impossible to improve upon; it went on to the final
album unvarnished. His studio performances often
gained bite from tensions, real or imagined, that surrounded him. One of the reasons for Clapton's fury on
that particular performance was a reflection of his pride

and character. Around the studio, he had heard that his band and crew were enjoying themselves, indulging in excesses of drink. But nobody had told him in advance of these sessions; he only heard about them later, accidentally. He disliked the fact that he wasn't told about the 'action' and given at least the option to join in.

'He got this feeling that everyone was holding out on him, unnecessarily protecting him from getting close to anything like drink or drugs, because he wasn't considered sensible or moderate enough to know better,' recalls Phil Collins. 'He was very, very annoyed. Everyone was denying it. I was oblivious to it all, and didn't even know he was angry when we went in to record 'Same Old Blues'. It was great! He played and sang really aggressively and we stayed with that first take.' (Eric told me the song was about 'Pattie and me and my relationship with the road'.)

Next day, Clapton called Collins aside. 'Come here,' he said, reprovingly. 'Why are you holding out on me?'

'What are you talking about?' said a bemused Collins.

Clapton was furious with him, and with the whole company, for not allowing him to know what revelry was going on when he was out of the way. He strongly resented people treating him with kid gloves and excluding him from everything that was happening around him. He felt he was being mollycoddled. Having taken full control of his drugs and drink problems during the previous ten years, he disliked any whispering campaign that spreads rumours implying he might be 'fragile' when addictions and indulgences were being discussed.

'Somebody's been holding out on me,' Eric finally told the assembled musicians. 'Now you guys, listen, I'm not a kid. I want to know everything that's going on.' This was no posture. It was an angry man who convinced everyone that in the future everything should be 'out in the open'.

For Collins, who has been friendly with Clapton since 1978, it was an eye-opener. Familiar with the complexities of the man, he was treading with difficulty while combining comradeship with his first production role on an album by one of his heroes. While Eric knew little of Genesis and Collins's musical history, Phil had been weaned on the music of Cream and was in awe of the guitar work. In the sunshine of the West Indies, Collins was charged with the tough job of refreshing Clapton's music: Phil felt Eric had sounded jaded on the album *Money and Cigarettes*. Although he had not touted for the work, Collins had been suggested as the kind of contemporary 'ear' to give a new production edge to what would be a vital record.*

Renowned for his devotion to the sound of the guitar, Eric was warily coming to terms with the modern effects of technology in music-making. He bought a Roland guitar synthesizer and featured it a little on his *Behind the Sun* album. 'The coming of the synthesizer took a long time for me to pick up on,' he says. 'It crept up on me through the use of keyboards, which came about through my working with Phil Collins. When he came

---

* Living a few miles from each other in the Surrey countryside, Clapton and Collins had become great mates, visiting each other's homes; on one visit, Eric played guitar quietly in the background in Phil's home studio during the recording of 'If Leaving Me is Easy', which appeared on Collin's *Face Value* album. But their friendship went far deeper than musical compatibility. It had its base in Clapton's deepest values, the strongest of which are honesty and unpretentiousness. Like Clapton, Phil Collins loathes phoney show-business preening, and the two men are very close, despite Eric's ignorance of Genesis's music.

on as producer, my recording sound changed, and what happens on stage follows suit to a certain extent. When I do the older stuff, it stays pretty much the same, and my actual songwriting is motivated by the same things. It's hard for me to see, from where I am, what's going on musically because I feel I'm basically doing the same thing all the time. I was lucky in working with Phil, not just because he's a good friend, but because he wanted to produce an album that would show lots of different sides that hadn't been seen or heard before. It really didn't matter to him whether it was commercial or not, as long as it was true. Working with Phil was like falling off a log.' Clapton likes fast action. 'We finished recording in a month and mixed it in a month, and by today's standards that's quick.'

Although the two men are firm friends, Collins surprised Eric by admonishing him in the studio. 'After a month, when it was almost finished, I started getting a bit loose, mucking about, and Phil gave me a bollocking that I'll never forget, in front of everybody. Almost nobody had ever talked to me like that. It was unbelievable. But it straightened me out and I was very grateful for it. The only other person who's ever done that to me was Pete Townshend. Both he and Phil are professionals of the old school. Admirable stuff!'

His moment of heartache in song came with 'Never Make You Cry'. Similar in flavour to 'Wonderful Tonight', this simple ode to Pattie reflected the inner torment of a man about to lose his love. Coming in at an extraordinarily long six minutes and five seconds, the song was, in Eric's description, 'a very positive, loving song . . . actually *the* love song of the album and my favourite'. In his mind, it replaced 'Wonderful Tonight' as his ultimate love song. But he didn't think anyone would want to put it out as a single; it was 'far too sentimental'.

When he returned from Montserrat, Eric had played 'Never Make You Cry' to Pattie, saying: 'This is from me to you.' But the other songs, 'I just let them ride because I thought that she would be able to pick the words up as she went along or that she would be able to form her own interpretation of it. But I think she knows what it's all about.'

The album's title song, 'Behind the Sun', clinched the theme. 'It's from one of Muddy Waters's songs called "Louisiana Blues",' Eric recalled. 'The first line of that song is: "I'm going down to New Orleans, baby, behind the sun." I always loved the phrase, "going down behind the sun". It's been used in other tunes, too, in a blues context.' He wrote the song shortly after Pattie told him she was leaving their home alone. 'I was talking about how my love had gone behind the sun.' At the time he considered it maudlin, but that was how he felt. In fact, it stands as one of his most poignant, and neglected works.

Phil Collins believed this was a new, dynamic Eric, off the booze and with a new muse. But to add to Eric's personal dilemma when it was completed, he flew back to London and a confrontation with his record label. Warner did not care for the record. 'They decided it needed more oomph, needed some hit material on it,' Clapton said. He and Forrester were initially aghast and furious at the attitude by Warner towards such a major artist, but when he calmed down, Clapton took a more phlegmatic, long-term view. The Warner Records promotion department told Forrester there was not a 'radio play' track on the record, and every album needed that thrust.

At that time, many established artists were being dropped by record companies. Clapton was not at risk, but he read the signals of the music business and acted, as ever, in a self-protective manner. 'I decided that, in order to stay sweet with the record company, I ought to find out what hit material was. And they sent me some songs which I did like. Swallowing my pride and ego, I went to Los Angeles and recorded the songs. I liked what I'd done quite a lot, so I thought: well, if they can mix it in with what's already there, then that's playing the game with the record company and also maybe helping the album become more successful.'

Three songs written by Jerry Williams, whom Eric admired, were recorded, and produced in California by Ted Templeman and Lenny Waronker. Eric felt 'a certain loss at what we had to sacrifice because the album as it originally was, had been more of a concept. Even if it hadn't been successful it would have been more of an artistic production. But I still don't feel we lost that much. I mean, I wouldn't have actually compromised all the way. I made the first step by going to L.A. But after that it wasn't much of a compromise.'

Eric's finely attuned eye and ear for criticism of his work surfaced during the making of the *Behind the Sun* album. Back in London, Phil Collins was mixing the tracks at the Town House studios in Chiswick, west London. A few weeks earlier, in a magazine interview, Clapton's old engineer from the John Mayall days, Gus Dudgeon, had echoed the view of many of Clapton followers that Eric's playing had lost something of its power. The guitar sound was 'too clean and I preferred Eric when he was at full tilt'. Collins challenged Dudgeon in the corridor at the studio. 'Are you Gus Dudgeon? Are you the guy who was complaining that Eric doesn't play with any bollocks any more?' 'Yeah,' Dudgeon answered. Later, in the studio restaurant, Eric caught sight of Dudgeon, who expected to get a 'severe roasting' from his old friend, whom he had not seen for nearly twenty years. Eric walked across to him. 'Gus,' Clapton said to him as if he was continuing a conversation, 'you'll be pleased to know that I have just gone back to using valve amplifiers,' a move that would beef up his sound.

No Clapton album was ever so starkly heartrending. As the jaunty 'Forever Man' hit the airwaves around the world, the melancholia of the song hit home. The man who had faced the darkness of drugs and drink now confronted his marital storm with commendable honesty. But it was too late. Before the album was released in 1985, Eric went off on a tour of Australia and Hong Kong. When he returned home in September, Pattie had left the Surrey homestead and rented a flat off Harley Street, London, only a few hundred yards from Eric's management offices. She seemed to enjoy the solitude, telling me of her plan to consolidate her talent as a photographer. (During that difficult period of her relationship with Eric, Pattie took the striking photograph of him that was used on the first edition of this biography, published that year in Britain.)

Eric was distraught. He begged, pleaded and cajoled Pattie to return, even though he, like she, had found a temporary partner. But just as their love affair had blossomed in the least orthodox fashion, this separation was bizarre. They spoke by telephone several times a week, went for lunch together, and Pattie confirmed to Eric that she was still in love with him. Yet, she said, she felt she had to assert her own individuality, away from him, and pursue interests beyond staying at home as a rock star's wife. Eric conceded that perhaps he had been rather chauvinistic and he talked openly to all his friends about his desperation to win back Pattie's total commitment to him. 'I will never love another woman as much as I love Pattie,' Eric told me during the separation.

His self-confessed chauvinism was, he felt, 'curable'. As a result of his childhood, he had 'always had a dreadful respect for woman, and I've been over-awed by their power. And when I began to drink and began to spend time courting women, that's when the male chauvinism took over as a form of protection . . . as a way of getting some power over them!'

The Women's Liberation movement was 'often very misguided,' he continued. 'I think it's gone out of proportion in a lot of ways; it's actually become a masculine thing more than a feminine thing. It's almost like Men's Lib now. But I see a lot of it as being very valid indeed. And I think they've achieved a great deal. But they've put even the most normal man in a very precarious position as to his own identity. Because I think if you take either of the sexes and try and liberate it on its own, too far, the other one is obviously going to be left standing. And I think it's much better to think of any of these things as being a human problem rather than a female problem. So both the sexes can travel upwards together and grow together rather than one leave the other behind.'

Had he had such a discussion with Pattie? I asked. 'No,' Eric answered. There had 'always been a kind of feeling that Pattie wanted to have something of her own to express herself with. But in my male chauvinism, I didn't really take that very seriously. I thought that it was just a kind of boredom or trap, that she was always around me too much in my work and that made her frustrated.'

He believed that kind of wish could be illusory. Wives of some of his friends were saying similar things, that turning forty they had not created something of their own: 'Even having kids, you can see that a woman apparently can still feel she's missing out in achieving something in her life. And I think that can be got over; it may be a phase that can be got through without doing too much damage, or you can go and search and find out for yourself. But I think it is dangerous, if it's based on an illusion, or on Women's Lib. Because ideals are great, they are really good things to have. But they're not real. And it can cause a lot of unhappiness.'

He had always taken the role of the women, in the house and by his side, for granted. 'I've never had a great deal of friction to worry about in my personal life. Relationships before my marriage were always very light and disposable, for me at least. Up until now, when my marriage is in a very shaky state, I always really thought that everything was all right.' If his wife's urge to achieve something was based on being around someone who is creative, then he 'would take it one step further and think: "Well, she should be f.....g lucky she isn't." Because for me being creative is often a very painful business. You have no idea when you're actually going to put pen to paper. You just know you've got to. And you can run around and have miserable days waiting for something to come out. And that's something I wouldn't wish on anybody. I am what I am but there's no doubt that life could be a lot easier if I wasn't a creative person.'

So he felt that a partner's creative urge 'may not be best for their marriage, or love life, or relationship. Especially if they don't talk about it, or if it's something they allow to fester inside. Then all kinds of resentments build up.'

At home, alone in his mansion, he seemed a sad, lost man. He thought Pattie was making a bad mistake because they were destined to live together, 'But whatever she does during this period away from me, she is still my wife and I have to support her.' Some people close to him advised him to 'play it cool'. It was advice which Clapton utterly rejected. 'No, I'm not that kind of person. She's got to know I *care* and I want her back. I don't feel in the least bit cool about it! Besides, George Harrison played it cool and look what happened . . .'

Despite Eric's regular phone calls and his complete belief in their marriage, Pattie proved hard to pin down. They spent Christmas 1984 separately. He remained at home and played host to his mother and grandmother and friends; she went to her family home in the West Country. In January, Pattie flew with some friends to Sri Lanka, telling Eric that she would decide on her return whether to go back to live with him.

She wavered in her decision, but by February Eric had persuaded her to go away with him for ten days in the sun so that they could have some proper conversations. They flew to Eilat, Israel, mingled with holidaymakers, and returned sun-tanned and in a positive frame of mind. A week later, Pattie had moved back in with Eric after a six-month absence. They went out together – to the making of a video for Eric's new single, and to the première in London of the film *Brazil*. And they held hands and cuddled like two young lovers.

Eric ascribed their split to his absence when touring or recording out of Britain. 'When I came home I was tired and I just wanted to lie down and that in turn led to neglect for Pattie,' he told Anne Nightingale in the London *Daily Express*. 'At one time Pattie used to come on tour with me and I think now that it was a good thing. When I stopped taking her on the road we started to lead different lives. I would now like to say to any musician, or anyone who can learn by my mistakes, that if one values one's marriage, it's got to be the first priority.' Splitting up had been 'hell' for him but he kept the door open, sensing there was a possibility of a reconciliation. In a flash of rhetorical candour, he asked: 'Why *should* my personal life be plain sailing after all those years of being drunk or stoned, neglecting my home life? It's something I should have worked on. Pattie coped with all that but it was gnawing away at her and it was very destructive.'

Here was a fragile, almost fairy-tale reunion which both delighted and unnerved all Eric and Pattie's friends and well-wishers. Though he was consistent, how could she cause him so much anguish and then return to him with such apparent passion? Pattie explained to me that she was looking for 'space' during the separation; both said they found if difficult to live without the other. 'I did not realize how much I loved this woman,' Eric said. He was certain that the period of separation would mark his life. Physically and mentally, he was at sea during Pattie's absence, and his determination to win her back was another example of his grit in the face of adversity.

The obsessiveness in Eric surfaced: he bombarded Pattie with red roses during her absence and never eased up in his determination to persuade her to return home. When she eventually did, he relaxed his ban on her joining him on tour. She joined Eric for part of his marathon US tour in 1985, but before she flew out to him, Pattie had to get used to a new tactic by her husband to convince her of his affection. As soon as he reached America, for the start of the tour, Eric telephoned Pattie twice daily. She found the transformation in Eric's attitude overwhelming, but an improvement.

NINE

THE ELDER
STATESMAN

CLAPTON HAS always combined the twin aspects of his make-up, spirituality and materialism, to produce a creative conclusion. His art is the extension of the inner man, and the crises in his life have been the dangerous sources he needed. Conversely, he has never had any difficulty in enjoying the fruits of fame. The 'Ripley lad' mentality, comfortably hanging out at a pub or walking down King's Road, Chelsea, in the unrealistic guise of an anti-star, contrasts with the free spender whose wealth has at times put him into psychological conflict. In the early years of his success, he was disinclined to enjoy money lest he be considered flash, particularly by old friends whom he wished to keep. Today, he spends gigantically and visibly, especially on clothes, travel and restaurants, and his collection of art.

For several years, until the late 1980s, an old-fashioned perforated brown wages envelope was regularly delivered to Eric at his home. It contained £150 in cash. He did not particularly need the money, but he insisted on the 'feeling' of getting a wage packet in his pocket, just like millions of other workers, every week. And he liked the discipline of living within a cash budget. He was gleeful when he under-spent and had a few pounds' profit to carry forward seven days.

Typically of people who earn a lot, Clapton spends very freely but is careful with the small change. One of his friends testifies to his largesse, but several people used to confirm his meanness at the bar: 'He's over-generous. If a friend admires something in his house, however big, he'll say: "Take it." But in a pub, he often has to be reminded that it's his round.' There was even a joke when he got his wallet out. '"Look out," said his mates, "that Red Admiral will fly out in a minute!"'

For a period, he compared his salary with those of the people who worked for him, men like Nigel Carroll and Alphi O'Leary. 'How much are you earning, then? Oh, I'm getting twenty quid more than you. Suppose that's right, really. I'm the guitarist!' He was, however, serious about making his salary work on a daily and weekly basis; by Wednesday, during his heavy drinking period, he would say to his friends: 'I can't go out till Friday. I've spent out!' And he meant it.

Clapton has made a very strong, conscious effort to stay in touch with the basic values of the working man. Determined to be 'one of the lads', he used to go drinking daily with the villagers. Some people close to him feared he was distancing himself too far from his natural stardom.

He is a stickler for 'playing the game' with money. In cards, he puts his money on the table and refuses to start playing until everyone has done the same; he hates debts or promises that betting money, however small, will be paid later. At a London recording session for an American friend, singer-songwriter Stephen Bishop, Eric was going through a period of feeling exploited. 'No work until you've paid me the £200 in pound notes,' he said to Bishop. The singer peeled off the cash there and then, and the music began. Eric was not joking.

Enjoying his wealth, he thinks nothing of flying, on a whim, to Rome, Milan or Florence for a day. He goes there specifically to add to his huge collection of designer suits, shirts and shoes. Conversely, his wish to retain contact with reality, and remain unpretentious about his roots and aspirations, has never left him. Once, when his limousine broke down on the way to a gig, Eric enjoyed switching to a hijacked fish van.

His attitude to money shows a blissful naïveté that probably comes from having amassed plenty early in his life and never having needed to worry about it, except during his lowest ebb when he had to pawn his guitars to support his habit. But his manager and those around him are still floored by his innocence. A cheque for several thousand pounds once arrived at his house and he put it in a drawer and forgot about it. He had never paid a cheque into a bank in his life. Weeks later, Roger Forrester asked if he had received the cheque which was due to him. Yes, said Eric, but he didn't realize anything had to *happen* to it. He had no idea at that time in the 1980s about banking systems, credit cards or cheques – and he was amazed when a store refused his cheque for over £50 without a supporting bank card. 'What's a bank card?' asked Eric. Since then, he has been given credit cards, though for a long time he gave the impression that he did not fully realize they are substitutes for money. In a dressing-room once, a band member said: 'Wow, great jacket, Eric. How much did it cost you?' Eric replied, in all seriousness: 'I didn't buy it. It was nothing. I got it on a credit card.' His pride and joy, a 1957 Tour de France Ferrari, cost him £40,000 but he quickly forgot the price. Twenty grand, he said, when a friend asked him how much it had cost only a few days after he had bought it.

Forrester is able to detect and define Eric Clapton's gullibility and impulsiveness from wide experience. On a trip to the South of France, Eric caught sight of a speedboat on the water and was immediately enraptured. He asked Roger to buy him one immediately. Forrester agreed. It cost £47,000, but the holiday it was planned for didn't happen; Eric never set foot on the boat and it did not even leave its original packing crate. Forrester sold it about a year later.

After several years of staying there during working trips to Ireland, Eric bought the magnificent Barberstown Castle Hotel in County Kildare. Visiting Dublin over the years, playing some of his greatest concerts at the Stadium, Eric found it a marvellous base from which to enjoy fishing. He 'fell in love' with the eleventh-century hotel and bought it as an investment, as well as for his pleasure. But while many local people went to Barberstown hoping to see Clapton as mine host, the staff believe one of the reasons Eric cut Barberstown out of his life was that it reminded him too much of his heavy drinking and he could not face abstaining in his own hotel. By 1985 Eric had returned there, determined to enjoy regular visits, but he sold the property a few years later.

Eric says he enjoys his money, mostly because he rarely thinks about it. 'Oddly enough, I think that having money has made me insecure. It's distanced me from certain people who don't have so much as me, or from people who know how to handle money and respect it, which are qualities I don't have. My relationships with those sorts of people have become insecure. And I find it impossible to have a relationship with people who have a complete monetary understanding, because to me money is simply something to be used. The value of it is not as important as what it's used for!

'I've been a collector of guitars, then weapons for a short time, then cars, then fishing rods, and no hobby lasts for long. I'm obsessive while it lasts and then it's on to the next. Materially, I've always got more than I ever need, which is quite annoying to me. I'd really like to live in a more spartan fashion but it's hard to keep a rein on my spending. I still buy too many clothes. My wardrobe is always too packed. That enthusiasm for clothes which came early in my life has never left me. I still enjoy seeing what other people wear. I enjoy judging a town, or a country, by the clothes its people have. The spirit of people manifests itself through what they wear. There's perhaps a dormant designer, or art historian, or fashion historian inside my fascination somewhere!' He likes what he calls 'street clothes' and particularly likes British fashion-consciousness.

The intricacies of Eric's personality are strongly connected with feeling free – with people, with money, with material goods. He has an utter horror of locked doors.

Italy, home of the Armani suits which he had always admired, had attracted Eric for years. On one trip in the late autumn of 1985, he went to a party and met Lori Del Santo. She became pregnant by him. Midway through Lori's pregnancy, Eric went to Los Angeles and at the Sunset Sound studios, under Phil Collins's production, recorded the songs that would comprise his new album, *August*, named in honour of his son's birth. With two songs, he showed his convoluted attitude to fidelity. 'Miss You', a new Clapton classic which he would rarely perform in the future, sounded like a lachrymose farewell to Pattie. But 'Lady of Verona', an upbeat celebration of Lori, which could well have been a big single hit, was excluded from the resulting album. With words like 'I fell in love with the Lady of Verona', it was deemed politically unsuitable for the world's ears.

In May 1986, while Eric was recording in California, Lori told her story in the Rome-based magazine *Novella*, alongside a picture of herself cuddling Eric. Saying they had met over a plate of spaghetti at a midnight dinner party in Milan, Lori was reported to have said: 'Eric called me the very next day and invited me for a drink.' His childless marriage to Pattie, who had once suffered a miscarriage, would not survive this news. Once, with the cathartic honesty he derived from filling in his daily diary, Eric had written a message to Pattie saying that he would 'always be a naughty boy'. Their partnership had weathered several difficulties, but this marked the end.

Even Eric seemed reconciled to the split. Pattie eventually went to live in Fulham, west London, in a flat with clean, modern lines and the daylight she craved both metaphorically and physically. Importantly to her, it overlooked the River Thames and she enjoyed the serenity of the view, with its wildlife and fine skyline. She launched herself into more photography and into running a new model agency called Deja Vu. And her inquiring spirit began a fresh chapter of her life.

Conor Clapton was born on 15 August 1986. Eric and Pattie were divorced in 1987. They remain friends.

'Layla' and 'Wonderful Tonight' continued to be Eric's primary manifestos. Many Clapton enthusiasts found this odd, and still do. As crucial signposts of his life, he might have been expected to drop them from his repertoire, or perhaps restrict his performance of them to mark the end of an era. But for ever, it is now certain, those two compositions will have an almost biblical importance for him. For example, during the time his marriage was rocky, he gave concerts in the US, and seemed to be playing with more manic intensity than ever as he hopped from a studio session at Gary Brooker's studio in Farnham, Surrey, to a concert at Hartford, Connecticut, on 1 May 1985. This venue has always generated an especially infectious atmosphere among genuine Clapton fans, and his playing always responds. 'Layla' and 'Wonderful Tonight' were, even during this difficult time, mandatory in his armoury.

He then moved on to appear at the world's biggest-ever rock extravaganza, to help the starving people of Ethiopia. 'Live Aid' took place simultaneously at JFK Stadium, Philadelphia, and Wembley Stadium, London, on a sweltering day, 13 July 1985. It was rock's finest hour, as the superstars of the sixties and the younger idols of the seventies submerged their vanities as well as their bank balances and ignored any conflicts over top billing. The aim to raise cash to help the afflicted struck a chord with hundreds of artists and with the millions of people who comprised the world's television audience.

The London audience of 80,000 at Wembley saw a cast including Elton John, Queen, Dire Straits, Status Quo, The Who, Phil Collins, Elvis Costello and Bryan Ferry. In Philadelphia, an estimated 101,000 people saw Bob Dylan, Billy Joel, Paul Simon, Stevie Wonder, Jimmy Page and Robert Plant, Waylon Jennings, Mick Jagger, Bryan Adams and Neil Young.

Clapton needed no persuasion to become involved. A phone call from Pete Townshend alerted him to the planning of the spectacular charity concert, and Eric agreed immediately to appear. There was a problem: he would be in the middle of an American tour on the day of the Live Aid concert. 'We were playing Denver just before the Live Aid show, and going to Philadelphia meant cancelling a show in Las Vegas and flying to Philadelphia to spend the night there before the concert,' says Clapton. 'Then we had to fly back to Denver for another show immediately afterwards, so there were some fairly big leaps. Thank God we were in good shape! The band was really playing well at that time. Everyone was up for it, and that made the travelling part of it a lot easier. I'd have been terrified if we'd just started the tour. I heard that some artists were pulling out because they weren't up to it, and I understand why.'

There was eager anticipation for Eric's performance at the JFK Stadium, as the hot afternoon became twilight. Although Eric has a large and faithful following in America, his status among many of those watching on television around the world was that of a famous name with whom they had lost contact. It was important exposure for Clapton, therefore, and the enormity of the event as well as the size of the audience played on his nerves.

'The atmosphere in Philadelphia was just buzzing,' Eric remembers. 'The moment we landed, you could feel music everywhere.' He checked into the Four Seasons Hotel to find players in every room. 'This was Music City. I was awake most of the night before the concert. Couldn't sleep with nerves.' Next day, he watched Live Aid on television before his scheduled appearance in the evening – probably a psychological mistake.

'That was very hard, watching people all day on TV knowing I was going on at night. Very few people got rehearsals. Mick [Jagger] did because he was doing something special with Tina Turner. But anyway, we were touring, so we didn't need it. But I still got really nervous. I'd guess I was about a hundred times more psyched up than for a regular gig. Being in the presence of all these great artists caused that. By the time we got there, I and a couple in my band were feeling very faint. I was so psyched up, I couldn't talk to anybody, and I became completely tongue-tied. We were put into a trailer to change, and we stayed there. Duck Dunn and I confessed to each other that we'd been close to passing out. The temperature seemed about a hundred and twenty degrees, and combined with nerves and trying to keep ourselves together, Duck and I and others in the band came very close to toppling over.'

The show began inauspiciously for Eric, who is very sensitive to the atmosphere around him just before he is going to play. 'As I was going through the tunnel from backstage to the stage, I had to wade through what seemed like thousands of security people. They were probably necessary, but they definitely felt in the way and that threw me slightly. Getting near the stage, the first thing I saw was my guitar roadie throwing the amplifiers on the floor, screaming in blue Glaswegian. They'd provided the wrong amps, according to what he had specified, and he was just freaking out. This got through to the whole band. It was pretty chaotic and didn't help my nervous condition.'

Worse was to follow. Clapton's choice of first song stunned and delighted the vast crowd. He hadn't performed the Cream classic 'White Room' for eighteen years, and had had to be taught the chords by Paul Shaffer, the resident keyboards and musical director on the David Letterman TV programme, in New York, when he had performed on the show on 8 May 1985. People climbed up on the sound tower to get a better view of Clapton as he launched into this unexpected song. But few of the audience could have sensed what he was going through as he began. Only the presence of an old friend, Atlantic Records chief Ahmet Ertegun, to his left on stage, giving him the thumbs-up and a big smile, carried Clapton through another crisis.

'As I kicked off that song, I went up to the mike and was going to sing the first line when I got a great big shock off the microphone. This hadn't happened to me since God knows when. I didn't think it was possible in these days of technology. This made everything worse, because I had to concentrate on singing with my mouth not quite touching the microphone but close enough to hear myself, because the monitors weren't very good. So that added another dimension of nerves.'

The crowd went wild as the unexpected chords of 'White Room' filled the stadium. Then came more cheers as Phil Collins's face suddenly appeared on the giant projection screens on either side of the stage. He was playing drums alongside Jamie Oldaker; Phil later admitted that he had never played the song before.

The end of the Cream epic was mixed with thunderous applause, and Eric went straight into 'She's Waiting', the two drummers pounding out the basis of the raunchy song from *Behind the Sun*. Although many in the audience didn't know the song, they had been won over by 'White Room'. Next, the familiar bluesy guitar introduction segued into 'Layla'. The stadium crowd erupted as Eric drove into one of rock 'n' roll's perfect anthems. What Eric could not have guessed was Pattie's reaction. Watching the show live on television at her London home, she was numbed. How could Eric stand there and sing a song so personal, during such a delicate period in their lives? It was not as if he did not have a colossal repertoire to choose from. She was clearly affected by the realization that he was not going to adjust his sensibilities . . . or recognize hers.

When he finished the set, the entire audience was on its feet. As he often does, Clapton shouted 'God Bless You'. He recalls: 'When we finished, it was like we'd not been on! It seemed like when various incidents happen in your life, or you get involved in a car crash and think back about it later. You just can't remember any of it. Your mind probably protects you from the shock.'

Eric says one of his greatest memories of Live Aid was the performance of the Four Tops. 'To my mind, they were the best act there, with that fantastic big Motown orchestra combined with all their energy. They're playing better than ever.' He regularly watches the video of their act.

Proof that a new young record-buying audience was warming to Clapton came in the weeks following the Live Aid concert. According to *Billboard* magazine, the top albums sold were *Led Zeppelin IV*, *Layla* and *Cream*.

Clapton is his own sharpest critic, able to recognize the fact that he has weaknesses and is not very good at sustaining relationships. Yet, even given the rich tapestry of life and work, he has been unwilling or unable to learn certain sensibilities from his rigorous self-examination.

On 11 June 1988, he made a guest appearance with Dire Straits, who joined several other major names for a 'Free Nelson Mandela' concert before 80,000 people at Wembley Stadium. The arrival ten years earlier of Mark

Knopfler's lyrical guitar in Dire Straits had slightly worried Eric; the first time he heard this new British musician, he felt threatened. But gradually the reality dawned that their styles were different, Knopfler much more a precision worker than Clapton, more determined to repeat every show note for note. Eventually, the two men developed a friendship.

Their performance proceeded predictably, Dire Straits leading with their established hits 'Romeo and Juliet' and 'Money for Nothing'. Before his appearance, Eric had met Pattie, who told him that she would be watching. She was therefore astonished that for the one song of his own he performed that day, Eric chose to sing 'Wonderful Tonight'. Of all the hundreds of Clapton tunes possible, she pondered, why did he yet again have to choose one that evoked such a personal time for them? She was embarrassed by what she considered his insensitivity. But Eric sees it differently. He could never contemplate deleting that song, or 'Layla', from his shows. To him, they remain part of his musical spine. Just as he confronts his own peccadilloes head-on, he expects the world to accept what happened, without sentiment affecting the reality of history. Ultimately the songs remain, to him, slices of his life. It would be difficult to imagine his audiences in the US, Britain and Japan (where the cry is 'Rayra! Rayra!' – a rare display of theatricality from the genteel audience) going home from a Clapton show satisfied, without 'Layla' being performed. And the show-business side of Eric, more finely attuned inside him than many might think, knows how to pace a show and play to the gallery with his greatest hits.

*

Throughout the 1980s, Eric's appetite for work of any kind was insatiable. He turned up to other people's recording sessions unexpectedly, to the delight of many musicians. It is endemic for musicians of Clapton's vintage to 'jam'. The 1960s were not merely more innocent years for rock 'n' roll, but also a period of discovery and exchange of ideas. There was a keen competitive edge among the players, which was healthy in a commercial sense, but at the core there was more to share, artistically, than the players of the 1980s and 1990s can enjoy. 'The nostalgia for the 1960s is for a period of discovery: British musicians were lucky to be discovering black Americans' rhythm-and-blues music, and Caribbean music, and welding this into the power of fashion which unified and identified them. All these things were completely new to people who came through the 1960s,' says Pete Townshend. 'And it was completely free, like finding a crock of gold. In those years, we post-war young British people were coming into adulthood and realizing that the black community, who were still regarded as second-class immigrants, did have a fantastic culture. Which we really couldn't borrow. We were allowed to observe it, but there was no way we could become part of it. So there was this obsession with American music ... and that crock of gold just isn't there any more.'

It was against this background that the pleasure of jam sessions stimulated players like Clapton in the 1960s and 1970s. Today, when rock music is generated more by big business and video than by instrumental inspiration, it's difficult to grasp the pleasure of jamming to musicians and audiences alike. Eric still enjoys the impromptu nature of it and indulges in a 'jam' when it feels right.

His most notable jams in 1985 were with Sting, Dire Straits, Buddy Guy, and in different situations with Lionel Richie and Stevie Ray Vaughan. 'When I went to see Sting in Milan, he more or less verbally forced me into it,' says Eric. 'He's a lovely man and I felt like it, and it was great. I enjoyed it and was glad I did it. But it's not always that easy, because depending on how I get into the theatre, I'm probably going to be on or near the stage anyway. And if they start beckoning you up, what are you gonna do? I love to play but it's getting quite worrying now. When I want to see a concert, the convenient, accepted way is to get a limo and have someone drop me at the back door, get a couple of passes, go and say hello and then sit down. But then I face the prospect of being asked to play. And sometimes I really don't feel like it. Yet if I say no, I might be denying myself a great pleasure and there's also the danger of insulting the person who's asked me.'

A visit to an Elton John concert in London posed no such problem. 'I don't think I'd have helped or fitted in on that stage. Everything was so well worked-out, properly planned. Davey Johnstone, Elton's guitarist, came on at exactly the crucial points and played just the right thing. There was no place there for a jam involving me or anybody else.' The Dire Straits shows at London's Hammersmith Odeon were different. Eric jammed on stage on both nights of the band's gigs. Impressed by the guitar fluency of Mark Knopfler, Eric continued to believe that Mark's playing could eclipse his own status. Such is the insecurity of Clapton. 'I play down my own ability so much,' he admits, 'that I tend to think of myself as small potatoes when a great new talent comes along. I'm still in awe of Mark Knopfler. I don't know where he gets it from! But this business of comparing myself unfavourably with people of his calibre happens all the time. All I'm doing is allowing myself to enjoy something. The unfortunate thing is that to do that, I have to put myself into the background.'

When the moment came and he went on stage with Knopfler, Eric says he 'really didn't feel any less of a musician than him. I felt quite adequate and on the same sort of level. We both have our own method of doing things and I felt I complemented him. I didn't go on stage and freeze and become paranoid, so we had a good time. We were ourselves. So you see, that *awareness* of the strengths of other people is only my way of allowing myself to enjoy the music.' As well as Dire Straits songs 'Two Young Lovers' and 'Solid Rock', Eric played 'Cocaine' and 'Further up the Road'. From the applause, he need never have worried.

Until *Behind the Sun*, Eric's album titles usually carried the nonchalant air of a man determined not to strike any poses. The music did the talking. *There's One in Every Crowd*, *E.C. Was Here*, *Slowhand*, *Backless*, *Just One Night*, were all unmemorable. *Money and Cigarettes* was a private aside, reminding himself that those were the two items he checked he had in his pocket when he left his house. Such a personal habit, converted to a title, was lost on the record buyers.

This uncomplicated theme was due to have been continued with his 1986 album, scheduled to bear the tour-related title of *One More Car, One More Rider*. But all that changed when Eric's son was born. Puzzling the public again with such obtuseness, he called it by the month of Conor's arrival: *August*. Fuelled by colossal public interest in Eric Clapton, the album was a massive international seller. Musically it was patchy, the ethereal 'Holy Mother' (the simple style of which set the tone for 'Tears in Heaven'), the ferocious 'Tearing Us Apart' duet with Tina Turner and 'Behind the Mask', perhaps a self-examining title, redeemed an only average collection of songs. Phil Collins was criticized by some Clapton followers for trying to point Eric in the lush, soul-inflected ballad direction of Lionel Richie. To Eric, this was not valid criticism, as he admired Richie and had recorded with him. The album design for *August* reinforced the new Clapton. Recruiting his friend Terry O'Neill to take his photograph, Eric looked alone, outwardly strong but, as often, inwardly troubled.

Eric was naturally touched by the enormous international grief at the death of Conor; the messages of sympathy that poured into his home and management offices were unquantifiable, and Eric asked that anyone wanting to make a donation in the boy's memory should do so to the American children's charity administered by Variety Club International.

Eric celebrated his fortieth birthday on 30 March 1985. For some ten years, he had been heralded as a virtuoso who could virtually write his own ticket to a concert hall or recording studio. But he preferred to live on the edge, stay contemporary in his tastes, such as clothes and music, and regard every session as a challenge. His ethos of not wanting to be judged on past glories was to come into play now, in the mid 1980s. Because with the collapse of his marriage and with the death of his son in such cataclysmic circumstances, Eric Clapton decided to re-invent himself.

As his public profile rose to a height he would have preferred not to receive through such sympathy, he needed high security gates at his country home. Not surprisingly with such a focus, his self-awareness, always substantial, went to a higher level. In came a stylishly floppy hairstyle, the Armani and Versace wardrobe accelerating his man-about-town image. He had been a Concorde traveller for some years, but now he looked and acted the epitome of the jet-setter ten years younger than his reality.

The world's greatest rock and blues guitarist seemed, also, to embrace a more eclectic attitude towards music. Years earlier, with George Harrison, he had delineated the difference between his own style and musical preference as blues-guitar style versus George's penchant for rockabilly. Now, on 21 December 1985, Eric and George again stood side by side, on stage at London's Limehouse Studios for a rockabilly session.

The event was a video recording with the legendary guitarist Carl Perkins, composer of 'Blue Suede Shoes'. Perkins was celebrating his thirtieth anniversary in music, and alongside noted guitarist Dave Edmunds and in a line-up that included Ringo Starr at the drums, Clapton slipped deftly into the rockabilly mode, on such songs as 'That's All Right Mama', 'Blue Moon of Kentucky' and 'Whole Lotta Shakin' Goin' On'. Clapton told me that though he was not well acquainted with rockabilly 'the atmosphere was infectious and we all enjoyed it so much because we respect Carl'. The inevitable finale, 'Blue Suede Shoes', was rousing testimony to the identity, in a crowd, of Eric's playing. There also, for observers of irony, was Eric yet again side by side on stage with George Harrison. While the tabloid press had for twenty-five years considered Clapton the 'man who stole a Beatle's wife', the actual parties had harmonized as friends, on and off stage. With his usual forthrightness, Eric has said that although an underlying tension still existed, they were far too mature and respectful of each other to let it mar their friendship. Eric described their relationship as 'jostling'.

Eric had arrived at that television studio for the Perkins show after a long Japanese tour which was hugely successful for him; and *en route* back to Britain he had visited Alaska and become the first major British rock star to play a concert in Anchorage. 'It was a freaky concert, just like another century up there. And the whole band had never felt jet-lag like we experienced: on the night of the gig we were all meeting in the hotel lobby at seven-thirty and someone phoned Tim Renwick's room to find him sound asleep. When we got back to England we were still in that condition. I never had such bad jet-lag and never slept so much in my life as I did during that period.'

There was an outlandish aspect to the Alaska experience for Eric involving Renwick, who was the newest recruit to the band (Clapton had first met him during the Roger Waters 'Pros and Cons of Hitch-hiking' tour). 'Tim and I flew north of Anchorage about seventy miles, to do some fishing, and nearly killed ourselves. We were fly fishing for trout – in Alaska! – and didn't catch a damned thing. Tim's wader leaked and we were totally stranded for two hours when we tried to fly back. I don't know what we were doing all this for . . . trying to be macho, I suppose.'

Not all jam sessions are as pleasant or as musically fruitful as those Eric enjoyed with Dire Straits, Carl Perkins and Sting. 'I met Stevie Ray Vaughan in Australia in 1985; he was just leaving and I was just arriving in the hotel lounge. Suddenly he said as we were about to split: "Let's jam!" – and it set up this feeling of postponement, that sooner or later we'd be in the same town at the same time and there'd be this mammoth jam.' A few months later Eric, on a day off in New York State, flew into Manhattan for a day to do some shopping. 'That night, the word got out that Stevie Ray Vaughan was going to be in a rehearsal studio until about twelve o'clock. So I went to the rehearsal studio and proceeded to get loaded waiting for him. He didn't show up until four in the morning, fresh as a daisy having slept all day and into the night! So he was ready to *go* and I was *gone*. It was almost the same situation as Australia, except that I was checking out and he was checking in. And I tried to play, and I made such a fool of myself. It was really horrendous. So yes, there are definitely times when I regret jamming.'

How competitive, then, is a jam? 'Between me and Stevie Ray and anyone else I'm jamming with, there's nothing. We're musicians and we must play. But there *is* competition between the people around us. You can feel that vibe. And that goes on, like ripples in a pond, out into the world, out towards our respective followers, supporters, fans.' Does that interaction get back to the individual musician? No, says Eric. 'Not when you have a good one-to-one relationship, which should have caused the jam in the first place. Because our understanding goes a lot deeper than what happens on the outside.'

Buddy Guy, an early hero of Eric's from the period when he was about to launch Cream, visited London in late 1985, and with his taste for jamming whetted, Eric tracked him to his hotel. 'I said "I'm coming down to see you at Dingwalls," and immediately he said "You gonna play?" I said dunno, see what happens. When Roger [Forrester] and I got to Dingwalls it was packed. I'd been there before but I'd forgotten how bizarre the place was. We went in the front door, got hassled by different kinds of people, couldn't see or hear the band because people were jammed in with their heads two inches from the ceiling!' Eric sought an easier way of seeing and hearing his friend, via the stage door, 'which actually opened on to the stage, or the floor next to it'.

'So there we were pressed up to the stage and Buddy was perfectly aware we were there. He carried through the show and they were getting pretty loose. It seemed like they were making it up as they went along, and it was a great show. Then he just called me up. And there was no way out. What was I gonna do? He gave me his guitar – and that's always the hardest thing, playing a strange instrument. Half one's "front" is getting up, the next is trying to look as if you know what you're doing, on an instrument you've never played before. This was a brand new custom-made guitar and I broke a string straight away. It was a blues jam, real jamming, and it was fantastic. I finished after about three numbers and came off stage absolutely soaking wet. Had to change my shirt out in the open air, it was so wet. And that was a true jam, a great night.'

Another happy link was with the fine singer Lionel Richie, who was on his way to the Live Aid concert in his car when he heard Clapton's slot on that show, on his car radio. 'He remembered meeting me years before, and liked what he heard, so he wanted me to play on his record,' says Clapton. 'From that point on, he was following my itinerary around the States and trying to get me into the studio, to play on his record. Finally he caught me in Seattle. He got on stage with me and sang on "Knock on Wood" and "You Don't Know Like I Know". Great fun. He'd flown in with tapes of his new album, a producer and an engineer. And he booked some studio time – so we went to the studio and I put guitar on one of his tracks. That was a great honour, because I like Lionel's work such a lot.'

Like moths to a flame, outstanding and empathetic musicians continued to be drawn to Eric's side. No artist in the history of contemporary music has commanded such sincere respect from his peers. And while he's aware of that position in the rock pantheon, Clapton has never taken this status for granted. He is admired because, particularly on stage where there is the risk factor, he works tenaciously, pushing himself hard to go beyond the level of competence that's always there.

An excellent result from the requirement of his record company to re-record songs for *Behind the Sun* led Eric to meet two fine musicians, bassist Nathan East and keyboards player Greg Phillinganes. They would help him shape his next few years, giving a new dimension, and added muscle to his sound. Most importantly, along with guitarist Tim Renwick who also joined his occasional line-ups, their innate ability kept him alert. Drummer Steve Ferrone and percussionist Ray Cooper have rounded out a band loyal to Clapton. For the players, the credibility of having been in Clapton's band will always be a calling card, but they know they cannot stay indefinitely. Part of Eric's method for survival entails the changing of the guard regularly, not because they become stale, but because he needs the feed of new stimulus by his side.

And he expects them to berate him if he performs below par. His old problem of leadership has been replaced by a healthy blend of benevolent dictatorship and traditional rock 'n' roll co-operative. At least now he accepts that he's the boss.

As a player, Eric has always operated on an economy-of-notes principle. Dazzling instrumental pyrotechnics have never impressed him, and the idiom of his choice ran counter to the preening of some players who played ten notes when one meaningful note would do. It was always how to articulate, bend, shape that note that commanded Clapton's study. For that reason, he always admired Miles Davis: 'he hit the notes perfectly'.

Despite the turbulence of his private life, he went through his forties with a relaxed ambition. His lucky escape with his life intact from his thirties' indulgences seemed to give him a new zeal. It was time to stretch. Concert appearances and albums would continue, but his reputation would not rise or fall on the basis of either one. With his position secure, he needed a diversion, and it came in the form of movie soundtracks.

Eric had always loved film, and when John Hurt was working on *The Hit*, he remembers that 'there was only one person to think of, when music for the project came to be discussed. Not just because he was a friend of mine and was therefore approachable. But because I knew his mind would be able to take it and he has a tremendous dramatic understanding.' Although Eric's contribution to the film was small, at the start, Hurt believes he 'managed to set the feeling very accurately and inventively'.

Next came Eric's song entitled 'Heaven Is One Step Away', chosen for the Steven Spielberg film *Back to the Future*, while in Britain, Eric's first major success and exposure as a writer of soundtrack material came with his work for the BBC 1985 television drama series, *Edge of Darkness.*

Clapton's enjoyment of the movie soundtrack medium grew slowly. 'Ever since I saw *Paris, Texas,*' he says, 'I have thought there was room for me in some capacity in the movie theme world.' He says he finds it both challenging and natural for him. 'It's easy to do in one respect because all it requires is music, not a lyric. The hardest part of what I do, to me, is singing and writing words. The music is my favourite part of my working life, and I can cope with that till the cows come home. Provide me with an image, from a movie, and I'm as happy as a sandboy provided the image is harmonious to the way I make music.

'For *Edge of Darkness,* they sent me a cassette of the first episode and I was so knocked over by the dramatic content that it was the easiest thing in the world for me to write the theme for that and make the music. Nothing could have been easier. And what I really liked was that it could lead to something. It was like a door opening for me. It did not require a mad effort and it was nothing to do with commercial success. For me, that aspect has gone, to a certain extent, from making records. Artistic content has always been first to me, but it doesn't seem to be so with records for everyone else. It's so commercially based.'

So Clapton agrees with John Hurt's opinion. 'It's easy to make mistakes in the film field and I'm hoping it won't happen in that way. I hope I'll be presented with ideas and themes that are good, and, most importantly, that I'll be able to get into the right place at the right time.'

'Most of the work for *Edge of Darkness* was done at Pete Townshend's Oceanic Studios at Twickenham.' Eric was given guidance by an experienced composer, Michael Kamen. 'I'd just written a theme which Michael dressed up with chords and we watched as many episodes as we could. Then it was just a question of making incidental music, and, for him, dubbing it on the film. It was totally new. I was faced with a whole technological frontier that I'd never been exposed to before.'

In the late 1980s, Eric became one of the favourite artists of the royal family, since he joined artists including Elton John, Paul Young, Ringo Starr, Phil Collins and Mark Knopfler at events in London to boost the Prince's Trust charity. The resulting photographs of Eric shaking hands with the Princess of Wales sealed Eric's arrival in the upper echelon of celebrities.

The role of elder statesman of rock suited him, but, dangerously, he began drinking again in 1987. He returned to Minnesota in December that year for treatment. This worked well, marred slightly by the embarrassment, during his stay there, of the showing on television around America of an advert for Michelob beer which featured Eric singing 'After Midnight'. In a room full of alcoholics at the clinic, he watched the commercial. 'Is that *you*?' they asked. 'Yep,' he replied. Since that period of recovery, Eric has applied himself steadfastly to staying dry. Conceding that he has a weak trait in his make-up, he is acutely aware of the danger to his life if he slipped down the alcoholic road again.

TEN

THE FRUITS OF STARDOM

Eric Clapton has effortlessly acquired the charisma of stardom. While his artistry has grown, his friends of more than thirty years have seen a man increasingly sanguine about his work, and, since his music must be the product of his soul, eager to stretch himself by finding fresh company in his work. He takes the mildest rebuke of his performances seriously.

Pete Townshend, a lifelong ally, reflects on his sparring relationship with Clapton, which has seen peaks and troughs: 'In 1982, when I'd come away from Meg Patterson's treatment myself, I did an interview with *Rolling Stone* in which I had a little crack at Eric. I said then what I know as a former heroin addict to be true: that you *do* change permanently. It could be a change for the better, but you *do* change. And I think that unfortunately it does reduce you slightly, because I think it denies you the true experience of the years that you spent as an addict. For me, mercifully, that was a short time. For Eric, it was two and a half years or something. I mentioned that he'd lost two and a half years and maybe they were precious years and no one will ever know what might have happened had Eric not done that.

It wasn't meant to be a criticism. But Eric was extremely hurt that I should talk in public about him in any way that was critical, or that I could abuse a friendship.'

Townshend says he wrote to Clapton to apologize – 'but also to defend what I felt was the case. It's strange. Show-business friendships are built on so much fatuousness . . . this is the real world and you know what makes it go round: gossip, success, scandal and controversy! That's what makes life worth living, and if you don't feed the machine occasionally, nothing happens. In a relationship like I have with Eric, or similarly with Paul McCartney, they should be strong enough to take it occasionally. Maybe it's a bit romantic, a bit stupid to think that we're all members of a great clan and we can knock one another in public. But we should know that behind the scenes we're still friends. With Eric, perhaps that isn't true now.'

Eric's response to Townshend is succinct: 'He thought I was very shallow because he believed I was upset that I didn't win a Best Guitar Player award. This wasn't actually true. He had heard that second-hand. I wrote to him to say that it wasn't true, but even if it was there was nothing wrong with wanting to be the best guitar player in the world. It was that very idea that had kept me going through all my hardship. So I ticked him off and said that if he felt that way about me, why didn't he tell me face to face, or on the phone instead of blabbing to the papers? I felt strongly that if people like Pete were going to comment on what they *heard* people were saying, it was dangerous because it was second-hand. It was Pete's supposition of what I felt that I objected to.'

But Townshend has enormous admiration, and even a little envy, for the way in which Eric has marshalled his art. 'What he's doing is what I've desperately wanted to do, which is to age with dignity in this business. It's partly because he still maintains he's a blues performer. But it's greater than that: people like Muddy Waters and B. B. King aged with fantastic dignity. Eric has a trace of that but his dignity has come from allowing his inner spirit *freedom* as he plays. That is the biggest step any musician can take. So few people have ever done it. Charlie Parker, John Coltrane and Jimi Hendrix did it, and now Eric has done it. And once free, it can never be contained. This flower has blossomed. Eric's life has been the most fantastic romance.'

Townshend continues: 'What is ironic is that in the years he was going through the *motions* of playing the blues, he had nothing to say. He was a purist, very much an apologist. Now he's risen above that. He might use the same keys on the typewriter, but he's speaking from a difference within. With something really important to communicate – a feeling of real human aspiration, of the real qualities of dignity and openness, "take me, warts and all", Eric had it at his fingertips, from his original sources, to communicate that. And now he's doing it.' In late 1984, after seeing Eric 'change the colour of the atmosphere' by his playing at the bleak Roger Waters concert, Townshend went up to Eric and said: 'Well, it's true, after all these years, Clapton is God.' Pete felt stunned at the fact that he's said it, but he stands by it. 'This was Eric making communication from heart to heart. It was divine.'

Townshend believes that one of the reasons for the poetry of Clapton's guitar playing and vocals is that: 'He doesn't do *anything* else. He just plays. He doesn't make speeches, have a band to struggle against – music is all to Eric. So in a way, Eric's like royalty. He's always very polite, considerate, upright, dignified, moral overall, but he survives on being, above all, not strong but a gentleman.'

Although Eric has great respect for Townshend's intelligence, he has sometimes had reason to resent Pete's tactlessness in dealing with his sensibilities. 'Pete's an important influence on the life of anyone who's ever met him or heard him,' says Eric. 'Once you've got him as a friend, he's there. That's *it*. He's probably the kind of friend that you sometimes really don't want to have, because he's the most honest man you'll ever meet, and he'll tell you stuff you don't want to hear. But in the long run, it's good for you. So you have to value it.'

The man who is able to set his spirit free on stage is capable of iron self-discipline when his off-stage survival is threatened. Nothing and nobody will stop him from attending an AA meeting anywhere in the world when he feels the need. In Antigua in 1992, a visiting Ronnie Wood was having a great time with Eric at his home when Eric said he was going to a meeting. 'Come along,' he told his guest, 'and give me some strength. But don't dare open your mouth.'

'Afterwards,' the Rolling Stone says, 'we walked out of the meeting and Eric said to me: "I suppose you want a drink now?" I said: "You're dead right." He came up to the bar with me and said: "Go ahead, enjoy yourself." He was very strong, and very sweet about it. I really respect that in him.'

Adopting the twelve-step cure for alcoholic addiction was essential for him. But a non-smoking Clapton was always too difficult to comprehend. A forty-a-day man (sixty-a-day during crises), Clapton volunteered for hypnotherapy in London in late 1993 to help him stop and the treatment succeeded. Friends feared that a non-smoking, non-drinking Clapton would be boring, but it was all part of his clean-up campaign for the 1990s, which would see him hit age fifty on 30 March 1995. This accent on health was in sharp contrast with the years when the hungry, hamburger-eating Eric's choice phrase to his driver on tour was 'Pie stop'; when he would enjoy fry-ups with the band and crew; and when his friend Robbie Robertson of the Band warned him: 'The road has taken a lot of the great ones; it's a goddamn impossible way of life.' That comment, plus the loss of so many dear friends, forced Eric to examine his working lifestyle as well as what he was doing to his body.

As with many celebrities, the rollercoaster of his life and his status sometimes obscures to his new public his masterly work as a guitarist. Because Eric's songwriting, and his voice, have elevated his profile in parallel with the tragedies that have beset him, the man's first love, his dedication to the guitar, is in danger of being down-played. His love affair with the instrument that captured his heart as a boy has never diminished. The guitars he owns, well over 100, vary in style, shape and vintage and he says they are needed to fulfil various roles. 'A Spanish guitar for a classical melody or a Spanish sound, an acoustic for a country or folky or even a very old rural blues, and an electric guitar, depending on the size or quality of the amplifier, if it's country, rock or blues. And my songwriting can be affected by the guitar that comes into my hand at the moment I'm composing.'

Of his mighty collection, a highly personal guitar which he assembled himself occupies a special place as his favourite. Nicknamed 'Blackie', it is a 1956 black Fender Stratocaster. In 1970 Eric was in Nashville filming a TV show with Johnny Cash when he walked into a store and bought six guitars, including some old Fender Stratocasters. Though, as Clapton recalls, Les Paul models had been 'ruling the roost', he had a strong affinity with the 'Strat', a model which had begun life in 1954. It had been adopted by country and western players, particularly in California; they loved its trebly, twangy tone.

The 'Strat' was created by Leo Fender, whose first big invention was the Telecaster (initially called the Broadcaster) in 1950. The Telecaster was the first massproduced electric guitar with a solid body (as opposed to those hollowed-out like acoustic instruments). It was virtually a plank that could be plugged in. The Stratocaster, thus named to reflect the embryonic 'space age' of the 1950s, featured three electronic pick-ups for more tonal variety, a patented vibrato (often called a whammy bar) and a contoured shape. It was to capture the imagination, and the musical hearts, of the new generation of rock players. In the rock era, Buddy Holly played one (a fact which impressed Eric), as well as the Beach Boys, and later Bonnie Raitt, Mark Knopfler, Robert Cray and thousands of others. Crucially, Jimi Hendrix played the 'Strat', and famously set fire to one on stage at the Monterey Pop Festival in 1967. Many consider that Hendrix's use of the instrument was responsible for its surge in popularity.

When Eric returned with those six guitars from Nashville, he gave a model each to Steve Winwood, Pete Townshend and George Harrison. 'Out of the three I had left, I made one from the best ingredients of each guitar, right down to the machine heads or the volume control. That guitar has been with me through all kinds of scrapes. I remember in Jamaica, rehearsing the band I had for *461 Ocean Boulevard*, drunk out of my mind, in the middle of the night in this cinema which we'd rented. We could only get to play in it during the night from twelve o'clock to six o'clock in the morning. I remember ending a Chuck Berry number by falling flat on my face. That was the cue for the drum beat to end the song, and I crushed some parts of my Blackie guitar underneath me. And within half an hour it was playing as good as new, just with a few little running repairs. The body and the neck and everything else were totally gone and I thought: This guitar is my *life*. It can take as much damage as me! And I've never felt quite that secure with any other guitar. I can pick it up, drop it or bounce it off the wall and it will still be in tune and still play with heart and soul. It's irreplaceable'.*

On stage, Eric changes guitars to suit a song's style. 'I switch sometimes because of tuning . . . because I use a few different tunings to play slide. But Blackie is the core guitar. Somehow, with that guitar, I can make sounds that are truly me. I can do my total thing, whereas if I use a Gibson, it will sound like a Gibson.'

Since he regards Blackie almost as one of his limbs, few people are allowed to touch it. At the Montserrat recording studios where he was recording his 1985 album *Behind the Sun*, one of the occasional visitors was American musician Stephen Bishop, an old friend of Clapton. (Eric had guested on Bishop's albums.) 'After we'd recorded one song, Stephen, as an afterthought, went in to add some electric guitar. He went back into the studio, picked up my special guitar, and began

---

* In 1994, as Clapton celebrated his thirtieth year as a professional musician with a special tribute issue from Billboard magazine, the Fender Stratocaster was marking its fortieth anniversary. At London's Royal Albert Hall, to mark both anniversaries, Eric was presented with a solid silver and gold nine-inch Strat replica.

playing it – very brutally. This felt to me as if someone had taken a dagger and plunged it into my arm and was twisting it. I screamed, ran into the studio and grabbed it off him. Really, it was that bad, a physical feeling, painful. I believe that guitar has got some of me in it. So to see someone else pick it up and abuse it was unbearable.'

After Eric had stopped drinking, he went through a phase of wanting to change all his surroundings – and he planned to spray Blackie a lurid green. His guitar roadie, Lee Dickson, flatly refused to allow him to do it. Though Eric is the owner of the guitar, Lee is its custodian. He ensures that it is treated with enormous care. But on one fact Eric is adamant: it is rarely far from his side, and unlike most of his guitars, is kept at his home. 'What's special about that guitar,' says Eric, summing it up, 'is that it came from a period in my life when I was so conscientious, and it's actually got that feeling in it. My attitude now is much more lax. I could pick up a guitar and if it worked, great and if it didn't I'd put it down again. But the idea of taking three or four guitars and working on them meticulously, as I did, to get one perfect just isn't in me any more. I value Blackie for that, too.'

His audience used to be mostly male. But with his new status and public display of sensitivity that has changed. His followers are now evenly split between male and female. While both admire his musicianly qualities, women also find him sexy. This double-edged power is remarkable, because Eric has never needed to employ sexual gyrations in his concert appearances like hundreds of other rock stars. His charisma stems from his 'less is more' principle, his understatement, his vulnerability, his gentleness which contrasts with the rugged eloquence of his guitar-playing. Many of the men want to be like Clapton, the man and guitarist; many of the women want to date him. The sexuality of his soaring instrumental power turns on millions of women around the globe.

Whether Eric heads for romantic stability or re-marries has no bearing on his illustrious career, but his exploits with women continue to fascinate a world aware of his lifelong amours. Appearing on the David Frost television show on 16 June 1994, Eric reiterated his known 'open' view of his future: he said he would like to get married and establish a normal family relationship, but whether it would happen was another matter. He was not ruling it out. His beard now grey, his crew-cut growing the same colour, he looked his age, but then, Clapton has never been one for evading reality. As he spoke, he was back in Olympic Studios, Barnes, turning full circle, recording for a new album some of the blues songs that had ignited his love of music and sparked his career, three and a half decades earlier.

Contrasting with the animation of his playing, Eric is fundamentally shy, a characteristic he shares with his friend Bob Dylan. This has been an endearing hallmark of the man all his life. 'He was shy when I first met him in 1966 when he was with John Mayall,' Harvey Goldsmith says, 'and he's remained just the same. He's always very friendly, but it's important for people around him to maintain their position, to do their jobs and keep a healthy distance.'

While he often gives an illusion of being casual, Clapton expects unswerving professionalism from those who work around him. 'You don't know what I *do*,' his tour assistant Alphi O'Leary said to him once, implying that there were a million things to attend to backstage to ensure that there were no blips in the machinery around Eric. Even though he was in his drunken phase at the time O'Leary said that, Eric fixed him with a stare and said: 'You don't *think* I know, but I *do*.' Roger Forrester confirms that Eric will never tolerate inefficiency around him.

Protecting and projecting Eric skilfully and strategically has been Forrester's job for some twenty-five years. Many of the most successful artist-manager relationships in popular music have gone beyond the boundary of business and have become brotherly, symbiotic, possessive: Brian Epstein with the Beatles, Colonel Tom Parker with Elvis Presley, John Reid with Elton John, Gordon Mills with Tom Jones, Andrew Oldham with the Rolling Stones. The perfect chemistry of the low-profiled Forrester and Clapton has been an important ingredient in his survival and success. Unswervingly dedicated to Clapton (the only artist he manages), Forrester has positioned Eric so that he is never over-exposed with too much visibility, but has enough work in his diary to keep him energized. It sounds logical, but achieving that balance for an often mercurial personality has sometimes been difficult. 'Roger has really made Eric's talent work,' observes Harvey Goldsmith, 'because unlike the greedy managers, he has always kept to the philosophy as a manager that I've adopted as a promoter: if you can sell 12,000 seats, book a 10,000-seater hall. That way, the demand is always kept.'

Forrester has been at his artist's side in his darkest days and nurtured him into the world star he is today. 'Before Roger took control,' Goldsmith recalls, 'there were so many people hanging around backstage, so many hangers on and people of ill repute, that it was stopping the job being done.' This was partly because Eric encouraged a party atmosphere, the drink flowing freely. 'Roger decided the only way he was going to control Eric and the people around him was to literally close the doors, erect a Berlin wall.' Forrester decided that once Eric had arrived at the theatre, 'nobody went backstage,' Goldsmith says. Gradually, the backstage atmosphere has been pared down to simplicity and familiar faces. Dozens of rock bands ask for champagne, fancy food and more backstage. 'Eric asks for nothing,' notes Goldsmith.

Now it is obvious that he will never hang up his guitar, Eric seems the epitome of the almost swashbuckling image of the blues players of yore whom he so revered. 'As I get older, I get stiffer,' he says. 'My fingers take a little bit of time to get loose. I'm still doing exactly the same thing, except that it's a little bit more refined and polished.' Knowing that he can always rely on himself to turn in a professional performance of a good standard, he is constantly hoping for that inspirational flourish that lifts any concert or recording session to a special altitude.

'I've gone through periods of thinking I'm retiring, and others wondering if I'll continue making records and touring until the day I die. I'm constantly changing my mind about it. I think I'll carry on until I can't do it any more – because something will stop me, like arthritis or fatigue. Aside from that, I can't see myself doing anything else. What else is there? Grand Prix driving, maybe? I don't know. It would have to be that exciting because I'm used to such a buzz, a thrill, playing on stage in front of an audience. You can't get that from writing film scores. So I think this is my destiny.' He says he now *needs* audience applause as part of his life. 'I've worked towards making that integral to my whole being,' he says. 'It's not just being successful by making hit records, but being true to myself as a musician. Knowing I get applause for that is very satisfying.'

After three full decades, he is confident most shows will achieve a satisfactory level of entertainment. And blues artist that he is, he is aware of the wider show business requirement – the need to send audiences away satisfied. If the function of art is to provoke and stimulate while the role of entertainment is to reassure, Eric Clapton sits comfortably astride both with a natural expression and manufactured show business. The challenge, now, is to elevate the concert, or the album, or the writing of the movie score, to the second tier, of transforming his muse into art. 'My career is nothing more than a collection of sounds in my head. That's it. It's just a question of if I hear some notes in my head, how do I get them to sound the best that I can get them to sound, through my fingers on the guitar. That's an ambition. That's my career.'

'I was singled out to pick up the guitar,' Eric declares. 'I think it was probably destiny. And I feel also that I am meant to carry on because I have been in many life-threatening situations and have got through by the skin of my teeth. And I think that is all for a reason. Without getting almost religious about it, I feel I have a purpose.' He added, during a British television interview with Sue Lawley, that he worked very hard because there is 'a definite vacuum in my personal life'.

Immediately after the death of Conor, Eric moved homes. After two decades in the Surrey countryside, he reverted to his 1960s London milieu, choosing a house in Chelsea. With his home on Antigua assuming a new importance to him as a sanctuary, a new Clapton appeared. It was ever thus: every decade had wrought new slants to his outlook, his lifestyle, his daily habits.

The 1990s Clapton, emerging from turmoil at the onset of the new decade, quickly became more focused than ever before. The enigma remained. He stayed introspective but gregarious, loyal yet sometimes pragmatic and ruthless, professing insecurity but displaying unflinching application to his career. Clear of alcohol, his concert work became more consistent, if less improvisational. Although a tour features the same set of songs in the same order night after night (which hard-core Clapton fans comment on), the unpredictable player of the 1980s has been succeeded by a more certain performer.

Back in 1974, when she was a fifteen-year-old schoolgirl, Virginia Lohle saw Clapton literally having to be carried off the stage after eight songs at the Roosevelt Stadium, South Jersey. Since then, as one of his most devout followers, she has seen him on every tour, totalling more than 100 shows, and like many others from other countries she travels from her New York home every January to see every concert in his season at London's Royal Albert Hall.

Like all his ardent fans, she is not blinkered to his faults. 'Our greatest criticism is that he *will* keep the same set for more than two years with very slight variations. I understand that he is obligated by the demands of his audience, especially first-time people, to play 'Layla' and 'Wonderful Tonight'. And it's good that he changes his band every two years or so. But in spite of his greatness as an artist, as a live performer he doesn't grow as much as he could. He might do so as an individual, as a player, as a songwriter. But apart from a new confidence and maturity, he does not stretch himself on stage. I think he would derive a lot more pleasure for himself if he mixed up the set with a little flexibility. It's music, not a computer programme.'

If Clapton's professional life has prospered by virtue of organic talent, his personal life has been a tabloid gossip columnist's dream in the 1990s. Here was the audacious romantic who stole a Beatle's wife by writing gorgeous songs to her. The heroin addict who went into oblivion on a seven-year alcohol bender. The heroic rock star whose talent stayed ablaze and whose career kept rising, with hit after hit album and sell-out concert tours around the world. The illegitimately born star who sired a son by a pretty Italian. And here was the fairy-tale marriage to Pattie that, after years of being on and off, finally ended in divorce, while their friends predicted a reconciliation. And here were former lovers speaking in tabloids around the world about their affairs with Eric. Long before 'Tears in Heaven', his story bore all the ingredients of an exaggerated novel about a rock star who self-destructs. The twist in Clapton's real-life story is that not only did he survive it all, but his artistry became embellished with each turn of his page.

And then came womanizing and hedonism. Although he controlled himself over drink, drugs and cigarettes, his addiction to women has been constant, and played out in public. Here was Eric stepping out with beautiful actresses and models: Marie Helvin, Julia Smith, Carla Bruni, Naomi Campbell, Kathy Lloyd, Patsy Kensit, Tatum O'Neal, Valerie Golino, Davina McCall, Yelitza Negrete. Always looking contemporary, ahead of fashion or in tune with it from his hair down to his shoes, Eric took his seat as a gentleman rocker opposite such women at San Lorenzo, the London restaurant which has become a citadel for celebrities. (Frequented by such glitterati as the Princess of Wales, Joan Collins, Rod Stewart and Gina Lollobrigida, San Lorenzo is London's equivalent for star-spotting to New York's Four Seasons or Los Angeles's Le Dome.) The paparazzi follows him there but that's not why he goes; unlike many celebrities, Eric is equally comfortable in simple eateries. For years, he and Roger Forrester wandered from their office near Regent's Park, London, to the Sea Shell in Lisson Grove for fish and chips, and today he often visits the Stockpot in Chelsea for traditional English food in a distinctly non-showbiz setting.

In 1994, Eric made his début in the list of Britain's richest 500 people published by the *Sunday Times*. Stating his wealth to be £30 million, the paper said that his company paid him £3.8 million in 1991. In 1992 and 1993, *Forbes* magazine placed him among the world's highest paid entertainers for the first time with total earnings in those years of $14 million and $19 million respectively.

Some say he has become tougher, more 'career hard', in the past year or so. 'I don't think he's a hard man, even now, with all the changes,' says Alphi O'Leary after twenty years by Eric's side. 'Deep down he's soft. When you see a man cry, as he does, you know he's a man but you also know he is real and definitely not that tough.' Always demonstrative and affectionate towards his boss, O'Leary says: 'I've seen him go through a lot of different phases and when I see him I hug him because that's how I am. Whether he likes it or not is irrelevant; that's the way I feel towards him and others, and he cither has to hug me back or say: "Oh, leave it out!" It's interesting that Eric never gets embarrassed with that type of show of feeling. He *needs* that level of attention. Eric actually *needs people*.'

Like those who have seen the old and new Clapton, O'Leary sees a difference. 'He's changed, obviously for the better. He's not as much fun as he was. He still has his amusing moments but in the late 1980s it was all wind-ups. He's more serious now, and is very dominant. At work, he expects everything to be done properly. Do your job properly or get on your bike. If people are not delivering, he will tolerate it for a while and then suddenly he will blow. And when he does that, it's the end of the story. That person is history.'

Although Eric is now among the show-business hierarchy, and a focus by the media on his private life is inevitable, his schedule since the mid 1980s should have been enough to have kept him out of the newspapers for anything other than work. There was the show in St Louis on 16 October 1986 for the album and film *Hail Hail! Rock 'n' Roll* to celebrate Chuck Berry's sixtieth birthday (Eric was joined by Keith Richards and Robert Cray as well as Berry). The following month he moved ahead in his movie career, appearing on the soundtrack of *Lethal Weapon* alongside David Sanborn and Michael Kamen in sharply evocative, and highly praised, music. And in 1987 came sessions (alongside Elton John) for George Harrison's album *Cloud Nine* at George's Friar Park studios, located at his house at Henley-on-Thames. Eric was featured playing 'The Robbery' on the soundtrack of the film *Buster*, which starred Phil Collins; and the movie career continued with his performance on eight songs in *Lethal Weapon 2*.

His championing too, of fresh talents has been one of his most endearing contributions to the music scene: he has introduced to British audiences Buckwheat Zydeco and Robert Cray, the US blues guitarist who seems destined to follow Eric's authentic tradition.

His compulsion towards his work, and his confrontation with his drugs problems of yesteryear, surfaced in October 1993 when he gave three concerts (with Joe Cocker) in Birmingham in aid of the Chemical Dependency Centre projects. This raised £250,000 for SHARP (Self-Help Addiction Recovery Programme), a day-care programme that is one of the CDC's main projects.

He has also assumed the dignified aura of one of rock's statesmen. On 9 January 1994, it fell to Eric to induct the Band into the Rock 'n' Roll Hall of Fame. In the ceremony at the Waldorf-Astoria Hotel in New York, Clapton's heartfelt speech pinpointed the impact on him of one of the most influential sounds to have reached his ears: he described the Band as 'one of the few white bands who ever got it right'. He referred to the Band's guitarist and songwriter Robbie Robertson as his brother and went on stage with the group to perform the Band classic 'The Weight'.

In September 1989, as the guest 'castaway' on the BBC's *Desert Island Discs*, Eric profiled the central ingredients of his turbulent first forty-four years. His guilelessness and candour evoked a man full of self-criticism, not entirely at ease with himself, and conceding that most of his personal problems had been self-induced. He was unsure whether he would ever fully be clear of turmoil. Asked by Sue Lawley whether he was simply one of those people who attracted trouble, Eric laughed and said that was probably right. 'Even now my private life is in complete chaos and it probably always will be. I'm stricken with this disease of being ill-content . . . the minute I start to see a satisfying situation, I will do something myself to upset the apple-cart. Maybe it's a subconscious thing. I don't seem to have any control over it.'

Tracing his childhood years, Clapton said how he now understood the agony his mother must have felt at having seen him being raised, 'watching from a distance'. The confusion of realizing, at the age of nine, that Rose and Jack, his grandparents, were not actually his parents contributed to his 'massive inferiority complex'. It was 'traumatic', and he had not yet fully recovered: 'It takes all your life.' He stated that he had a fine relationship with his mother, Pat, now: 'We are actually great pals . . . it's more like brother and sister.'

Citing his love of Pattie and 'the hopelessness of that situation' together with the death of his grandfather 'whom I adored' as two possible causes for his descent into drugs, Eric spoke of his use of marijuana and black bombers in his youth through to cocaine and on to heroin. He considered it was 'foolish' to go down that road 'because you end up with too much regret and that can be overbearing'. This remark seemed a cautious reverse of his view in earlier years that he should not issue warnings about drug use.

Asked by Sue Lawley if perhaps he needed to play out the role of the 'suffering genius' to pursue his muse, Eric said no, he could not really accept that. Rather, he had to face the reality that he had never properly grown up, or was growing up late in life. 'Life is calming down . . . the fact that I don't take any substances any more is a lot better for me . . . I wake up every day feeling fresh . . . I don't think it will ever really resolve . . . I'm a bit of a wanderer.' Conor's birth three years earlier had stabilized his life. Fatherhood had brought a 'massive change' for him: 'I love him dearly.'

Choosing his records for the desert island to which he

was imaginarily consigned, Eric listed opera from Puccini which 'gives me tranquillity'; Robert Johnson's 'Crossroads Blues'; Muddy Waters's 'Feel Like Going Home'; Stevie Wonder's 'I Was Made to Love Her'; Ray Charles's 'Hard Times'; Freddie King's 'I Love the Woman'; and 'Purple Rain' by Prince.

Eric said he had considered rock 'n' roll might be dead until he heard the genius of Prince, whom he described as a combination of Little Richard, Jimi Hendrix and James Brown. If he were forced to take just one record to the island that would be the one. 'As a fisherman, I could catch enough to eat and I would get great sustenance from music.'

His reading matter on the island would be Charles Dickens. Of his fame, Eric said he would prefer to be recognized as a good musician but also have anonymity. 'But that is a Utopian dream.' He realized that stardom brought with it interest in his private life.

Desert island castaways are allowed one luxury item. Here, Eric's pleasure in possessions shone through. He felt perhaps he could take a Versace suit, so that he might dress up once a month; or a car so that he might have fun driving around the island. But when Sue Lawley pointed out that a guitar would not automatically go with him, even as his working material, he had to rescind the suit and the car in favour of an instrument, presumably his cherished Blackie Fender Stratocaster. 'There is no choice,' he said.

There are, then, at least two Eric Claptons. The serious, conscientious blues musician whose fragility and life experiences have meshed with his natural talent to produce a player of stature; and the unashamed show-business icon enjoying his wealth, spending a fortune on clothes and cars. Even in that role, he is substantially more thoughtful and analytical than most transparently show-business figures.

To his credit, his enjoyment of the good life has not lifted him from the reality which his music requires. He says: 'I do buy things for newness every now and then, or to turn me on, but it doesn't last very long and I don't walk around polishing everything or looking at it and saying "This is what I've got."' Material goods did not in themselves bring him lasting pleasure. 'I found that for me happiness is a completely interior thing, nothing to do with the outside and the material world at all.' There is no certainty that he will find relaxed happiness: somehow, the word 'contentment' does not sit accurately on Clapton. And if he ever truly found it, would he then be able to play the blues?

To my suggestion that his desire for possessions might have diminished when he realized his freedom to buy anything, he replied: 'I don't think I've ever really been materialistic. I've been a collector of things I've got bored with but I don't put any real lasting value on them. It immediately becomes transparent.'

Royal Albert Hall, London, 24 February 1994. Expensive perfume wafts around the audience. Champagne corks pop. Eric's audience for this year's twelve-night season at his special venue is supremely self-aware; they might have paid up to £150 for a ticket from those wretched touts, but Eric would be worth anything to them. The leader of the rock 'n' roll nobility, he has now captured a partly 'corporate' affluent audience that seems to know he represents quality but is not quite sure why. His tragic-hero reputation has sealed his stardom.

Heading for his forty-ninth birthday, Eric tonight looks something like a twenty-year-old Yardbird. His hair is shorn, his apparel simple but consciously pared down: white shirt, black trousers, Doc Marten boots. Thirty years on from his Ivy League suits, he's still in the vanguard of fashion as he enjoys re-inventing himself. His spoken words to the crowd are as tentative and as banal as ever: 'Hello and welcome to the Albert Hall for the annual stint. This year I'm doing some blues . . . by the end you'll probably find it a complete mish mash . . . we'll start with some songs by Robert Johnson.'

Sitting on a stool, Eric is comfortably solitary as he slides into 'Terraplane Blues', and the difference between him and all his contemporaries is immediately delineated. His sad voice, now more at home than ever on the blues, and his incandescent guitar work, combine to finally present a natural, searingly personal performer. As he moves on into the Leroy Carr song 'How Long', he could be back in the Ken Colyer jazz cellar on the edge of Soho in the late 1950s: Eric achieves a lazy swing. Refreshingly, for what will emerge as a watershed evening when he reclaims his earliest role as a bluesman, he prefaces each song with the name of the composer: 'We'd like to do a couple of Big Maceo numbers', before the band helps thicken the sound for a Howlin' Wolf composition. He switches guitar for most songs to suit their texture, moving through Muddy Waters ('Standing Round Cryin'') to two songs by Jimmy Rogers, the country-ish 'Going Away' followed by 'The Blues All Day Long'. And so it continues: more Muddy, a brilliant reading of his classic 'Hoochie Coochie Man', Eric's voice raging like sandpaper, on to Elmore James's 'It Hurts Me Too', and a couple of Freddie Kings, Eric surprising with the emotion in his voice on 'Someday After a While'. There were homages, also, to Leroy Carr and Jimmy Rogers. To augment his recognizable voice, he demonstrates a formidable grasp of myriad blues guitar techniques.

This declaration of his blues roots to his most glitzy audience seems at once an affirmation and a challenge. In returning to the cradle of his inspiration; it was as if Eric wanted to confront his age with the dignity which his blues roots afford him. And his memory of all the intricacies of those songs, with their differing styles, techniques and words, with an especially rich reading of the Bessie Smith classic, 'Nobody Knows You When You're Down and Out', made for a momentous set, the bluesy repertoire of which stamped his autumn 1994 album *From The Cradle*.

The audience applauded politely, knowing it was special, but many had come for the hits. Thereafter, it was a home run: the crowd was virtually blinded as the house lights were up, shining into their faces as 'White Room' began. And the rest of the show assumed predictability: 'Badge', with his fingers well up the fretboard singing and ringing; seguing in an immaculate execution of the changed mood of 'Wonderful Tonight' and the Jimi Hendrix song 'Stone Free'. The two songs relating to the death of his son, 'Circus Has Left Town' and 'Tears in Heaven', sung solo with tender power, melted the crowd before Eric plunged into 'Tearing Us Apart', 'Crossroads' and the rolling blues of 'T'aint Nobody's Business If I Do' as an encore, featuring Chris Stainton's florid piano. As ever, Clapton ignited 'Layla'; the crowd went wild; a fan rushed up to the stage with red roses. He has no peer.

'The extraordinary thing about Eric Clapton, the reason he is as wonderful as he is, is that he's not a technical musician in any way,' says Glyn Johns. 'I have this theory: his music goes straight from his heart to his fingers. It doesn't go via his brain at all. And there's nobody in the world like that . . .'

Shortly after he had stopped drinking, Eric went to Wales to visit his old friend Ben Palmer. Clapton gave Palmer a book about the peregrine falcon, and Ben became fascinated by the characteristics of the bird. It has astonishing eyesight, can see for some twenty miles, and hunts by dive-bomb action. When Eric had left and Ben had absorbed the book, the analogy of birds of prey and his friend's life struck Ben forcefully. 'There's a tension that a hawk at 1,000 feet will feel from the wind. The bird's mathematical certainty, drive, strength: it's something very similar to Eric's movements which have followed his life.'

Palmer reflects, too, on a conversation he recalls from 1963 with the ambitious Eric. The two friends were debating the importance of money. 'But what would you do if you were down to your last sixpence, Clappers?' Eric replied: 'I'd buy a Mars bar.' Says Ben: 'That's how he saw it then and that's how he sees life still.'

ERIC CLAPTON
ON RECORD

This discography of Clapton's prodigious work lists all of his singles, albums and compact discs from the début with the Yardbirds in 1964 until 1994. It is compiled by Marc Roberty and represents a chronological look at Eric Clapton's recording career.

THE YARDBIRDS

Singles

'I Wish You Would'/'A Certain Girl'
Columbia DB7283 released 6/64.

'Good Morning Little School Girl'/'I Ain't Got You'
Columbia DB7391 released 10/64.

'For Your Love'/'Got to Hurry'
Columbia DB7499 released 2/65.

Albums

Five Live Yardbirds
Columbia 33SX 1677 released 2/65.
CD version Charly 182.

Sonny Boy Williamson and the Yardbirds
Fontana TL 5277 released 1/66.

Remember . . . The Yardbirds
Regal Starline SRS 5069 released 6/71.

Shapes of Things
Charly BOX 104 released 11/84.
CD version Decal LIK BOX 1.
Re-released in 1993 by Charly as 'Train Kept a Rollin'' in a
remastered form. The long form box also included a T-shirt
and badge.

JOHN MAYALL'S BLUESBREAKERS

Singles

'I'm Your Witchdoctor'/'Telephone Blues'
Immediate IM012 released 10/65.

'Lonely Years'/'Bernard Jenkins'
Purdah 3502 released 8/66.

'Parchment Farm'/'Key to Love'
Decca F12490 released 9/66.

Albums

Bluesbreakers with Eric Clapton
Decca SKL4804 released 7/66.
Available on CD.

Looking Back
Decca SKL5010 released 9/69.
Available on CD.

Back to the Roots
Polydor 2425 020 released 6/71.

Primal Solos
Decca TAB66 released 83.
Available on CD.

Archives to Eighties (revised versions of songs originally
recorded for the *Back to the Roots* album of 1971 which
now include new vocal and drum tracks).
Polydor 837127 released 88.
Available on CD.

CREAM

Singles

'Wrapping Paper'/'Cat's Squirrel'
Reaction 591007 released 10/66.

'I Feel Free'/'N.S.U.'
Reaction 591011 released 12/66.

'Strange Brew'/'Tales of Brave Ulysses'
Reaction 591015 released 6/67.

'Anyone for Tennis'/'Pressed Rat and Warthog'
Polydor 56258 released 5/68.

'Sunshine of Your Love'/'Swlabr'
Polydor 56286 released 9/68.

'White Room'/'Those Were the Days'
Polydor 56286 released 1/69.

'Badge'/'What a Bringdown'
Polydor 56315 released 4/69.

Albums

Fresh Cream
Reaction 593001 Mono 594001 Stereo released 12/66.
Available on CD.

Disraeli Gears
Reaction 593003 Mono 594003 Stereo released 11/67.
Available on CD.

Wheels of Fire
Polydor 583031 released 8/68.
Available on CD.

Goodbye
Polydor 583053 released 3/69.
Available on CD.

Best of Cream
Polydor 583060 released 11/69.
Available on CD (Japan only).

Live Cream
Polydor 2383016 released 6/70.
Available on CD.

Live Cream Vol. 2
Polydor 2383119 released 7/72.
Available on CD.

BLIND FAITH

Single

Instrumental jam (Island change of address)
Island promo released 6/69.

Album

Blind Faith
Polydor 583059 released 8/69.
Available on CD (UK version has two bonus tracks from
the abortive Rick Grech solo album sessions and are not
Blind Faith outtakes).

DELANEY AND BONNIE

Single

'Comin' Home'/'Groupie (Superstar)'
Atlantic 584308 released 12/69.

Album

On Tour
Atlantic 2400013 released 6/70.
Available on CD.

PLASTIC ONO BAND

Single

'Cold Turkey'/'Don't Worry Kyoko'
Apple 1001 released 10/69.

Albums

Live Peace in Toronto
Apple 1003 released 12/69.

Sometime in New York City
Apple PCSP716 released 9/72.
Available on CD.

ERIC CLAPTON

Single

'After Midnight'/'Easy Now'
Polydor 2383021 released 10/70.

Albums

Eric Clapton
Polydor 3383021 released 8/70.
Available on CD.

History of Eric Clapton
Polydor 2659012 released 7/72.
Available on CD (Japan only).

Rainbow Concert
RSO 2394116 released 9/73.
Available on CD.

DEREK AND THE DOMINOS

Singles

'Tell the Truth'/'Roll It Over'
Polydor 2058057 released 9/70 withdrawn 9/70.

'Layla'/'Bell Bottom Blues'
Polydor 2058130 released 7/72.

'Why Does Love Got to Be So Sad' (live)/'Presence of the Lord' (live)
RSO 2090104 released 4/73.

Albums

Layla and other Assorted Love Songs
Polydor 2625005 released 12/70.
Available on CD as original as well as a special 20th anniversary box set containing 3 CDs with various jams and unreleased outtakes.

In Concert
RSO released 3/73.
Available on CD.
Re-released in 2/94 as *Live at the Fillmore* in expanded form containing many previously unavailable tracks.

ERIC CLAPTON AND HIS BAND

Singles

'I Shot the Sheriff'/'Give Me Strength'
RSO 2090132 released 7/74.

'Willie and the Hand Jive'/'Mainline Florida'
RSO 2090139 released 10/74 in limited edition picture
sleeve.

'Swing Low Sweet Chariot'/'Pretty Blue Eyes'
RSO 2090158 released 5/75.

'Knocking on Heaven's Door'/'Someone Like You'
RSO 2090166 released 8/75.

'Hello Old Friend'/'All Our Pastimes'
RSO 2090208 released 10/76.

'Carnival'/'Hungry'
RSO 2090222 released 2/77.

'Lay Down Sally'/'Cocaine'
RSO 2090264 released 11/77.

'Wonderful Tonight'/'Peaches and Diesel'
RSO 2090275 released 3/78.

'Promises'/'Watch Out for Lucy'
RSO 21 released 10/78.

'If I Don't Be There by Morning'/'Tulsa Time'
RSO 24 released 3/79 in picture sleeve.

'I Can't Stand It'/'Black Rose'
RSO 74 released 2/81.

'Another Ticket'/'Rita Mae'
RSO 75 released 4/81 in picture sleeve.

'Layla'/'Wonderful Tonight' (live)
RSO 87 released 2/82 in picture sleeve.
RSOX 87 12in released 2/82.

'I Shot the Sheriff'/'Cocaine'
RSO 88 released 5/82 in picture sleeve.
RSOX 88 released 5/82 with bonus live version of
'Knocking on Heaven's Door' from the December 79
Budokan shows in Japan.

'I've Got a Rock and Roll Heart'/'Man in Love'
Duck W9780 released 1/83 in picture sleeve.
Duck W9780T 12in with bonus 'Everybody Oughta Make
a Change'.

'The Shape You're In'/'Crosscut Saw'
Duck W9701 released 4/83 in picture sleeve.
Duck W9701T 12in with bonus 'Pretty Girl'.
Duck W9701P picture disc.

'Slow Down Linda'/'Crazy Country Hop'
Duck W9651 released 5/83 in picture sleeve.
Duck W9651T 12in with bonus live version of 'The Shape
You're In' was planned but withdrawn before release.

'Wonderful Tonight'/'Cocaine'
RSO 98 released 4/84 in picture sleeve.

'You Don't Know Like I Know'/'Knock on Wood'
Duck 7-29113 released 11/84 in Australia only.

'Edge of Darkness'/'Shoot Out'
BBC RESL178 released 1/85.

'Forever Man'/'Too Bad'
Duck W9069 released 3/85.
Duck W9069T 12in with bonus 'Something's Happening'.

'She's Waiting'/'Jailbait'
Duck W8954 released 6/85.

'Behind the Mask'/'Grand Illusion'
Duck W8461 released 1/87.
Duck W8461T 12in with bonus 'Wanna Make Love to You'.
Duck W8461F 7in double pack with bonus live versions of 'Crossroads' and 'White Room' from 15 July 86 NEC show.

'It's in the Way That You Use It'/'Bad Influence'
Duck W8397 released 3/87.
Duck W8397T 12in with bonus 'Same Old Blues' and 'Pretty Girl'.

'Tearing Us Apart'/'Hold On'
Duck W8299 released 6/87.
Duck W8299T 12in with bonus live version of 'Run' from 15 July 86 NEC show.

'Wonderful Tonight'/'Layla'
Polydor POSP881 released 8/87.
Polydor POSPX881 12in with bonus 'I Shot the Sheriff' and a live version of 'Wonderful Tonight' from the Budokan 79 show.
Polydor POCD881 CD single with bonus 'I Shot the Sheriff' and 'Swing Low Sweet Chariot'.

'Holy Mother'/'Tangled in Love'
Duck W8141 released 11/87.
Duck W8141T 12in with bonus 'Forever Man' and 'Behind the Mask'.

'After Midnight' (1988 rerecorded version)/'I Can't Stand It'
Polydor PO8 released 7/88.
Polydor PZ8 12in with bonus 'Watcha Gonna Do'.

Polydor PZCD8 CD single with bonus 'Watcha Gonna Do' and an unreleased live version of 'Sunshine Of Your Love' by Cream from 7 March 1968 at San Francisco's Winterland.

'Bad Love'/'Before You Accuse Me'
Duck W2644 released 11/89.
Duck W2644T 12in with bonus live versions of 'Badge' and 'Let It Rain' from 15 July 86 NEC show.
Duck W2644CD CD single with same bonus tracks as 12in.
Duck W2644B box set single with exclusive live version of 'I Shot the Sheriff' from 15 July 86 NEC show and a family tree.

'No Alibis'/'Running on Faith'
Duck W9981 released 3/90.
Duck W9981T 12in with bonus live version of 'Behind the Mask' from 15 July 86 NEC show.
Duck W9981CD CD single with same bonus tracks as 12in.
Duck W9981B box set single with guitar badge and photos.

'Pretending'/'Hard Times'
Duck W9970 released 5/90.
Duck W9970T 12 in with bonus 'Knock On Wood'.
Duck W9970CD CD single with bonus 'Behind the Sun'.

'Wonderful Tonight' (live)/'Edge Of Darkness' (live)
Duck W0069 released 10/91.
Duck W0069CD CD single with bonus live versions of 'Layla Intro' and 'Cocaine' from the big band Royal Albert Hall 1991 shows.
Duck W0069CDX special limited collectors CD single

containing 2 exclusive live versions of 'I Shot the Sheriff' and 'No Alibis' from the big band Royal Albert Hall 1991 shows.

'Tears in Heaven'/'White Room' (live)
Duck W0081 released 1/92.
Duck W0081T 12in with bonus 'Tracks and Lines' and live version of 'Bad Love'.
Duck W0081CD CD single with same bonus tracks as 12in.

'Layla' (Live unplugged)/'Tears In Heaven'
Reprise/Duck W0134 CD 9362–40614–2

Albums

461 Ocean Boulevard
RSO 2479118 released 8/74.
Available on CD.

There's One in Every Crowd
RSO 247132 released 4/75.
Available on CD.

EC Was Here
RSO 2394160 released 8/75.
Available on CD with bonus full version of 'Driftin' Blues'.

No Reason to Cry
RSO 2394160 released 8/76.
Available on CD with bonus track 'One Night'.

Slowhand
RSO 2479201 released 11/77.
Available on CD.

Backless
RSO 2479221 released 11/78.
Available on CD with bonus full version of 'Early in the
Morning'.

Just One Night
RSO 2479240 released 5/80.
Available on CD.

Another Ticket
RSO 2479285 released 2/81.
Available on CD.

Time Pieces – Best of Eric Clapton
RSO RSD5010 released 3/82.
Available on CD.

Money and Cigarettes
Duck W3773 released 2/83.
Available on CD.

Time Pieces Volume 2 – Live in the Seventies
RSO RSD5022 released 5/83.
Available on CD.

Behind the Sun
Duck W925166–1 released 3/85.
Available on CD.

Edge of Darkness
BBC 12RSL178 released 11/85.
Available on CD.

August
Duck WX71 released 10/86.
Available on CD with bonus 'Grand Illusion'.

Lethal Weapon Soundtrack
Warner released 4/87.

The Cream of Eric Clapton
Polydor ECTV1 released 9/87.
Available on CD.

Crossroads
Polydor ROAD1 released 4/88.
Available on CD.

Homeboy Soundtrack
Virgin released 11/88.
Available on CD.

Lethal Weapon 2 Soundtrack
Warner released 9/89.
Available on CD.

Journeyman
Duck WX322 released 11/89.
Available on CD.

24 Nights
Duck WX373 released 12/91.
Available on CD.
Also available in a limited edition box featuring the double
CD set with bonus tracks 'No Alibis', 'I Shot the Sheriff'
and 'Layla Intro'. Also contained in this set is a scrapbook
including drawings by Peter Blake as well as rare back-stage
photographs with items of memorabilia pasted in by hand,
a commentary written by Derek Taylor, a printed envelope
containing copies of Eric's guitar picks, a button badge, a
laminate back-stage pass and a guitar string. All this is
available in a hand-made buckram solander box with gilt
tooling and the book is autographed by Eric and Peter
Blake.

Rush Soundtrack
Duck released 1/92.
Available on CD.

Lethal Weapon 3 Soundtrack
Warner released 6/92.
Available on CD.

Unplugged
Duck released 7/92.
Available on CD.

GUEST SESSIONS

Considering his stature as a solo artist, Eric Clapton could be forgiven if, in his thirty years at the helm, he had concentrated only on his own recording career. But this list of his guest appearances on records by artists of diverse styles, often removed from his own, prove at least two facts: his compulsion for making music, and his hard-to-challenge title as rock's most industrious 'session' guitarist.

OTIS SPANN

Single

'Stirs Me Up' (Decca)

Album

The Blues of Otis Spann (Decca)
Released 11/64.
Available on CD as *Cracked Spanner Head* (Decca).
Also available on CD as *The Blues of Otis Spann . . . Plus* (See For Miles)
Eric plays on 'Pretty Girls Everywhere'.

CHAMPION JACK DUPREE

Album

From New Orleans to Chicago (Decca)
Released 4/66.
Available on CD.
Eric plays on 'Third Degree', 'Shim-Sham-Shimmy'.

ERIC CLAPTON WITH JIMMY PAGE

Album

Blues Anytime Vol. 1, 2, 3, 4 (Immediate)
Released 1967.
Available on CD.
Later re-released as two double albums titled *Anthology of British Blues Volume 1 and Volume 2.*
Eric plays on 'Miles Road', 'Tribute to Elmore', 'Freight Loader', 'Snake Drive', 'West Coast Idea', 'Draggin' My Tail', 'Chocker'.

ARETHA FRANKLIN

Album

Lady Soul (Atlantic)
Released 3/68.
Available on CD.
Eric plays on 'Good to Me As I Am to You'.

GEORGE HARRISON

Album

Wonderwall Music (Apple)
Released 11/68.
Available on CD.
Eric plays on 'Ski-ing'.

THE BEATLES

Album

The Beatles White Album (Apple)
Released 11/68.
Available on CD.
Eric plays on 'While My Guitar Gently Weeps'.

JACKIE LOMAX

Singles

'Sour Milk Sea'/'The Eagle Laughs at You' (Apple)
Released 2/69.
Available on *Is This What You Want?* CD.

A side 'New Day' (Apple) (Eric does not play on B side)
Released 5/69.
Available on *Is This What You Want?* CD.

Album

Is This What You Want? (Apple)
Released 3/69.
Available on CD.
Eric plays on 'Sour Milk Sea', 'The Eagle Laughs at You',
'You've Got Me Thinking', 'New Day'.

MARTHA VELEZ

Album

Fiends and Angels (London)
Released 6/69.
Available on CD.
Eric plays on 'It Takes a Lot to Laugh, It Takes a Train to
Cry', 'I'm Gonna Leave You', 'Feel So Bad', 'In My Girlish
Days'.

BILLY PRESTON

Single

'That's The Way God Planned It' Parts 1 and 2 (Apple)
Released 8/69.

Albums

That's the Way God Planned It (Apple)
Released 6/69.
Available on CD.
Eric plays on 'That's the Way God Planned It', 'Do What
You Want To'.

Encouraging Words (Apple)
Released 9/70.
Available on CD.
Eric plays on 'Right Now', 'Encouraging Words'.

SHAWN PHILLIPS

Album

Contribution (A&M)
Released 1/70.
Eric plays on 'Man Hole Covered Wagon'.

VIVIAN STANSHALL

Single

A side 'Labio Dental Fricative', B side 'Paper Round'
(Liberty)
Released 2/70.

DORIS TROY

Singles

A side 'Ain't That Cute' (Apple) (Eric does not play on B
side)
Released 2/70.

B side 'Get Back' (Apple) (Eric does not play on A side)
Released 8/70.

Album

Doris Troy (Apple)
Released 9/70.
Available on CD.
Eric plays on 'Ain't That Cute', 'Give Me Back My Dynamite', 'I've Got to Be Strong', 'You Give Me Joy Joy', 'Don't Call Me No More', and 'Get Back' as a bonus track on CD edition.

LEON RUSSELL

Albums

Leon Russell (A&M)
Released 5/70.
Available on CD.
Also available on a gold CD edition with unreleased numbers from the original session.
Eric plays on 'Delta Lady', 'Roll Away the Stone', 'Prince of Peace', 'Indian Girl', 'Jammin' with Eric', 'The New Sweet Home Chicago'.

Leon Russell and the Shelter People (Shelter)
Released 6/71.
Available on CD.
Eric plays on 'Alcatraz', 'Beware of Darkness'.

JONATHAN KELLY

Single

'Don't You Believe It' (Parlaphone)
Released 6/70.

KING CURTIS

Single

'Teasin'' (Atlantic)
Released 7/70.
Available on *History of Eric Clapton* CD (Japan only).

STEPHEN STILLS

Albums

Stephen Stills (Atlantic)
Released 11/70.
Available on CD.
Eric plays on 'Go Back Home'.

Stephen Stills 2 (Atlantic)
Released 7/71.
Available on CD.
Eric plays on 'Fishes and Scorpions'.

GEORGE HARRISON

Albums

All Things Must Pass (Apple)
Released 11/70.
Available on CD.
Eric plays on 'Wah Wah', 'Isn't It a Pity', 'What Is Life',
'Run of the Mill', 'Beware of Darkness', 'Awaiting on You
All', 'My Sweet Lord', 'Out of the Blue', 'Plug Me In', 'I
Remember Jeep', 'Thanks for the Pepperoni'.

The Concert for Bangladesh (Apple)
Released 1/72.
Available on CD.
Eric plays on 'Wah Wah', 'My Sweet Lord', 'Awaiting on
You All', 'That's the Way God Planned It', 'It Don't Come
Easy', 'Beware of Darkness', 'While My Guitar Gently
Weeps', 'Jumpin' Jack Flash', 'Youngblood', 'Something',
'Bangladesh'.

ASHTON GARDNER AND DYKE

Album

The Worst Of (EMI)
Released 2/71.
Available on CD.
Eric plays on 'I'm Your Spiritual Breadman'.

THE CRICKETS

Album

Rockin' 50's Rock 'n' Roll (CBS)
Released 2/71.
Eric plays on 'Rockin' 50's Rock 'n' Roll', 'That'll Be the Day'.

JESSE DAVIS

Album

Jesse Davis (Atlantic)
Released 4/71.
Available on CD (Japan and Germany only).
Eric plays throughout the whole album.

BUDDY GUY AND JUNIOR WELLS

Album

Play the Blues (Atlantic)
Released 7/71.
Available on CD.
Eric plays on 'A Man of Many Words', 'My Baby She Left Me', 'Come on in This House', 'Have Mercy Baby', 'T-Bone Shuffle', 'A Poor Man's Plea', 'Messin' with the Kid', 'I Don't Know', 'Bad Bad Whiskey'.

HOWLIN' WOLF

Albums

The London Sessions (Rolling Stones Records)
Released 8/71.
Available on CD.
Eric plays on 'I Ain't Superstitious', 'Poor Boy', 'The Red Rooster (rehearsal)', 'The Red Rooster', 'Worried About My Baby', 'Do the Do', 'Built for Comfort', 'Sitting on Top of the World', 'Highway 49', 'What a Woman', 'Who's Been Talking', 'Rockin' Daddy', 'Wang Dang Doodle'.

London Revisited (Chess)
Released 10/74 US only release.
Eric plays on 'Going Down Slow', 'Killing Floor', 'I Want to Have a Word With You'.

BOBBY WHITLOCK

Albums

Bobby Whitlock (CBS)
Released 7/71.
Eric plays on 'Where There's a Will There's a Way', 'A Day Without Jesus', 'Back in My Life Again', 'The Scenery Has Slowly Changed'.

Raw Velvet (CBS)
Released 12/72.
Eric plays on 'The Dreams of a Hobo', 'Hello LA Bye Bye Birmingham'.

DOCTOR JOHN

Album

Sun Moon and Herbs (Atlantic)
Released 11/71.
Available on CD.
Eric plays on 'Black John the Conqueror', 'Where Ya At Mule', 'Craney Crow', 'Pots on Fiyo/Who I Got to Fall On', 'Zu Zu Mama', 'Familiar Reality-reprise'.

JAMES LUTHER DICKINSON

Album

Dixie Fried (Atlantic)
Released 2/72.
Eric plays on 'The Judgement'.

BOBBY KEYS

Album

Bobby Keys (Warner)
Released 7/72.
Eric plays on most of the tracks on this album.

VARIOUS ARTISTS

Album

Music from Free Creek (Charisma)
Released 5/73.
Eric plays on 'Road Song', 'Getting Back to Molly', 'No One Knows'.

FREDDIE KING

Albums

Burglar (RSO)
Released 11/74.
Available on CD.
Eric plays on 'Sugar Sweet'.

1934–1976 (RSO)
Released 10/77.
Available on CD.
Eric plays on 'Sugar Sweet', 'TV Mama', 'Gambling Woman Blues'.

THE WHO

Album

Tommy the Movie (RSO)
Released 7/75.
Available on CD.
Eric plays on 'Sally Simpson', 'Eyesight to the Blind'.

ARTHUR LOUIS

Singles

'Knockin' On Heaven's Door'/'Plum' (Plum)
Released 8/75.

'Knockin' on Heaven's Door'/'The Dealer' (Island)
Released 6/78.

'Still It Feels Good'/'Come On and Love Me'
(Mainstreet)
Released 7/81.

Albums

First Album (Polydor)
Released 8/75 in Japan only.

Knockin' on Heaven's Door (PRT)
Released 7/88 in a remixed form with Eric's guitar to the
forefront.
Available on CD.
Eric plays on 'Knockin' on Heaven's Door', 'Plum', 'The
Dealer', 'Still It Feels Good', 'Come On and Love Me',
'Train 444', 'Go Out and Make It Happen'.

BOB DYLAN

Album

Desire (CBS)
Released 12/75.
Available on CD.
Eric plays on 'Romance in Durango'.

DR JOHN

Album

Hollywood Be Thy Name (United Artists)
Released 12/75.
Available on CD.
Eric played congas at the session, but it is difficult to place which track(s) he actually participates on.

JOE COCKER

Album

Stingray (A&M)
Released 6/76.
Available on CD.
Eric plays on 'Worrier'.

RINGO STARR

Album

Rotogravure (Polydor)
Released 10/76.
Available on CD.
Eric plays on 'This Be Called a Song'.

KINKY FRIEDMAN

Album

Lasso from El Paso (Epic)
Released 11/76.
Available on CD.
Eric plays on 'Kinky', 'Ol' Ben Lucas'.

STEPHEN BISHOP

Album

Careless (ABC)
Released 12/76.
Available on CD.
Eric plays on 'Save It for a Rainy Day', 'Sinking in an Ocean of Tears'.

CORKY LAING

Album

Makin' It on the Street (Elektra)
Released 5/77.
Eric plays on 'On My Way'.

ROGER DALTREY

Album

One of the Boys (Polydor)
Released 5/77.
Eric definitely attended the sessions and even contributed some guitar. However, both he and Roger consumed much beer and the resulting work was either mixed very low or not used at all!

RONNIE LANE AND PETE TOWNSHEND

Album

Rough Mix (Polydor)
Released 9/77.
Available on CD.
Eric plays on 'Rough Mix', 'Annie', 'April Fool', 'Till the Rivers Run Dry'.

RICK DANKO

Album

Rick Danko (Arista)
Released 1/78.
Available on CD.
Eric plays on 'New Mexico'.

THE BAND

Album

The Last Waltz (Warner)
Released 4/78.
Available on CD.
Eric plays on 'Further On Up the Road', 'I Shall Be
Released'.

VARIOUS ARTISTS

Album

White Mansions (A&M)
Released 5/78.
Available on CD.
Eric plays on 'White Trash', 'Kentucky Racehorse'.

GEORGE HARRISON

Album

George Harrison (Dark Horse)
Released 2/79.
Available on CD.
Eric plays on 'Love Comes to Everyone'.

MARC BENNO

Album

Lost in Austin (A&M)
Released 6/79.
Available on CD (Japan only).
Eric plays on 'Hotfoot Blues', 'Chasin' Rainbows', 'Me and a Friend of Mine', 'New Romance', 'Last Train', 'Lost in Austin', 'Splish Splash', 'Monterey Pen', 'The Drifter', 'Hey There Señorita'.

DANNY DOUMA

Album

Night Eyes (Warner)
Released 8/79.
Eric plays on 'I Hate You'.

ALEXIS KORNER

Album

The Party Album (Interchord)
Released in Germany only 3/80.
Available on CD in the UK on Castle Communications.
Eric plays on 'Hey Pretty Mama', 'Hi-Heel Sneakers', 'Stormy Monday Blues'.

STEPHEN BISHOP

Album

Red Cab to Manhattan (Warner)
Released 10/80.
Available on CD.
Eric plays on 'Little Moon', 'Sex Kittens Go to College'.

PHIL COLLINS

Album

Face Value (Virgin)
Released 2/81.
Available on CD.
Eric plays on 'If Leaving Me Is Easy'.

JOHN MARTYN

Album

Glorious Fool (WEA)
Released 10/81.
Eric plays on 'Couldn't Love You More'.

RONNIE LANE

Album

See Me (RCA)
Released 7/80.
Eric plays on 'When Lad Has Money', 'Barcelona', 'Way Up Yonder'.

GARY BROOKER

Singles

'Leave the Candle'/'Chasing the Chop' (Chrysalis)
Released 4/81.

A side 'Home Lovin'' (Mercury) (Eric does not play on B side)
Released 3/81.

Album

Lead Me to the Water (Mercury)
Released 3/82.
Available on CD.
Eric plays on 'Leave the Candle', 'Lead Me to the Water', 'Home Lovin''.

SECRET POLICEMAN'S OTHER BALL

Album

The Music (Springtime)
Released 3/82.
Available on CD in the UK on Castle Communications.
Eric plays on 'Crossroads', ''Cause We Ended as Lovers',
'Further On up the Road', 'I Shall Be Released'.

RINGO STARR

Album

Old Wave (Bellaphon)
Released 6/83 in Germany, Canada and Brazil only.
Available on CD.
Eric plays on 'Everybody's in a Hurry But Me'.

CHRISTINE MCVIE

Album

Christine McVie (Warner)
Released 1/84.
Available on CD.
Eric plays on 'The Challenge'.

ROGER WATERS

Album

The Pros and Cons of Hitch-hiking (Harvest)
Released 5/84.
Available on CD.
Eric plays throughout the album.

COREY HART

Album

Corey Hart (EMI)
Released 6/84.
Available on CD.
Eric plays on 'Jenney Fey'.

GARY BROOKER

Album

Echoes in the Night (Mercury)
Released 9/85.
Available on CD.
Eric plays on 'Echoes in the Night'.

PAUL BRADY

Album

Back to the Centre (Mercury)
Released 3/86.
Available on CD.
Eric plays on 'Deep in Your Heart'.

LIONEL RICHIE

Album

Dancing on the Ceiling (Motown)
Released 8/86.
Available on CD.
Eric plays on 'Tonight Will be All Right'.

LEONA BOYD

Album

Persona (CBS)
Released 8/86.
Available on CD.
Eric plays on 'Labyrinth'.

PRINCE'S TRUST 10TH BIRTHDAY PARTY

Album

Prince's Trust 10th Birthday Party (A&M)
Released 10/86.
Available on CD.
Eric plays on 'Better Be Good to Me', 'Tearing Us Apart',
'Call of the Wild', 'Money for Nothing', 'Everytime You
Go Away', 'Reach Out', 'No One Is to Blame', 'Sailing',
'I'm Still Standing', 'Long Tall Sally', 'Get Back'.

PRINCE'S TRUST CONCERT 1987

Album

Prince's Trust Concert 1987 (A&M)
Released 8/87.
Available on CD.
Eric plays on 'Running in the Family', 'If I Was',
'Wonderful Tonight', 'Behind the Mask', 'Stand By Me',
'You've Lost That Loving Feeling', 'Through the
Barricades', 'Saturday Night's All Right', 'While My Guitar
Gently Weeps', 'It's the Same Old Song', 'I Can't Help
Myself', 'Reach Out I'll Be There', 'With a Little Help
from My Friends'.

BOB GELDOF

Single

A side 'Love Like a Rocket' (Mercury) (Eric does not play on B side).

Album

Deep in the Heart of Nowhere (Mercury)
Released 11/86.
Available on CD.
Eric plays on 'Love Like a Rocket', 'August Was a Heavy Month', 'The Beat of the Night', 'Good Boys in the Wrong'.

TINA TURNER

Single

'What You See Is What You Get' (Capitol) (12in version only)
Released 3/87.

Album

Live in Europe (Capitol)
Released 3/88.
Available on CD.
Eric plays on 'Tearing Us Apart'.

JOHN ASTLEY

Album

Everybody Loves the Pilot (Atlantic)
Released 6/87.
Available on CD.
Eric plays on 'Jane's Getting Serious'.

CHUCK BERRY

Album

Hail Hail Rock 'n' Roll
Released 10/87.
Available on CD.
Eric plays on 'Wee Wee Hours', 'Rock 'n' Roll Music'.

STING

Album

Nothing Like the Sun (A&M)
Released 10/87.
Available on CD.
Eric plays on 'They Dance Alone'.

BOB DYLAN

Album

Hearts of Fire (CBS)
Released 10/87.
Available on CD.
Eric plays on 'The Usual', 'Night After Night', 'Had a
Dream About You Baby'.

GEORGE HARRISON

Album

Cloud 9 (Dark Horse)
Released 11/87.
Available on CD.
Eric plays on 'Cloud Nine', 'That's What It Takes', 'Devil's
Radio', 'Wreck of the Hesperus'.

JACK BRUCE

Album

Willpower (Polygram)
Released 88.
Available on CD.
Eric plays on 'Willpower', 'Ships in the Night'.

BUSTER SOUNDTRACK

Album

Buster (Virgin)
Released 88.
Available on CD.
Eric plays on 'The Robbery'.

BUCKWHEAT ZYDECO

Album

Taking It Home (Island)
Released 8/88.
Available on CD.
Eric plays on 'Why Does Love Got to Be So Sad'.

GAIL ANNE DORSEY

Album

The Corporate World (WEA)
Released 10/88.
Available on CD.
Eric plays on 'Wasted Country'.

JIM CAPALDI

Album

Some Come Running (Island)
Released 12/88.
Available on CD.
Eric plays on 'You Are the One', 'Oh Lord Why Lord'.

BRENDAN CROKER

Album

And the Five O'Clock Shadow (Silvertone)
Released 1989.
Available on CD.
Eric sings on 'That Kind of Life'.

THE BUNBURYS

Single

'Fight' (Arista)
Released 1/89.

Album

One Moment in Time (various artists)
Released 11/88.
Available on CD.
Eric plays on 'Fight'.

CAROLE KING

Album

City Streets (Capitol)
Released 4/89.
Available on CD.
Eric plays on 'City Streets', 'Ain't That the Way'.

STEPHEN BISHOP

Album

Bowling in Paris (Atlantic)
Released 9/89.
Available on CD.
Eric plays on 'Hall Light'.

PHIL COLLINS

Album

But Seriously (Virgin)
Released 11/89.
Available on CD.
Eric plays on 'I Wish It Would Rain'.

CYNDI LAUPER

Album

A Night to Remember (CBS)
Released 11/89.
Available on CD.
Eric plays on 'Insecurious'.

ZUCCHERO

Album

Zucchero (London)
Released 11/89.
Available on CD.
Eric plays on 'Wonderful World'.

VARIOUS ARTISTS

Album

Nobodys Child (Warner)
Released 1990.
Available on CD.
Eric performs 'That Kind Of Woman'.

VARIOUS ARTISTS

Album

Knebworth (Polydor)
Released 8/90.
Available on CD.
Eric and his band perform 'Think I Love You Too Much',
'Money for Nothing', 'Sad Songs', 'Saturday Night's All
Right', 'Sunshine of Your Love'.

MICHAEL KAMEN

Album

Concerto for Saxophone and Orchestra (Warner)
Released 9/90.
Available on CD.
Eric plays on 'Sandra'.

YOKO ONO

Album

Fly (Apple)
Released 12/71.
Eric plays on 'Don't Worry Kyoko'.

THE ROLLING STONES

Album

Flashpoint (Rolling Stones Records)
Released 10/90.
Available on CD.
Eric plays on 'Little Red Rooster'.

BUDDY GUY

Album

Damn Right I've Got the Blues (Silvertone)
Released 7/91.
Available on CD.
Eric plays on 'Early in the Morning'.

RICHIE SAMBORA

Album

Stranger in This Town (Phonogram)
Released 8/91.
Available on CD.
Eric plays on 'Mr Bluesman'.

LAMONT DOZIER

Album

Inside Seduction (Atlantic)
Released 8/91.
Available on CD.
Eric plays on 'That Ain't Me'.

JOHNNIE JOHNSON

Album

Johnnie B Bad (Elektra)
Released 9/91.
Available on CD.
Eric plays on 'Creek Mud', 'Blues #572'.

VARIOUS ARTISTS

Album

Two Rooms (Mercury)
Released 10/91.
Available on CD.
Eric performs 'The Border Song'.

DAVID SANBORN

Album

Upfront (Warner)
Released 3/92.
Available on CD.
Eric plays on 'Full House'.

ELTON JOHN

Album

The One (Rocket)
Released 6/92.
Available on CD.
Eric plays and sings on 'Runaway Train'.

THE BUNBURYS

Album

Bunbury Tails (Polydor)
Released 10/92.
Available on CD.
Eric plays on 'Fight'.

RAY CHARLES

Album

My World (Warner)
Released 1993.
Available on CD.
Eric plays on 'None of Us Are Free'.

VARIOUS ARTISTS

Album

Bob Dylan's 30th Anniversary Concert (Columbia)
Released 1993.
Eric plays on 'Love Minus Zero', 'Don't Think Twice',
'My Back Pages', 'Knockin' on Heaven's Door'.

JACK BRUCE

Album

Somethinels (CMP)
Released 2/93.
Available on CD.
Eric plays on 'Willpower', 'Ships in the Night', 'Waiting on
a Word'. 'Willpower' and 'Ships in the Night' had
previously appeared on a Jack Bruce retrospective titled
Willpower which was released in 1/89 on Polygram.

THOMAS JEFFERSON KAYE

Album

Not Alone (Hudson Canyon)
Released 7/93.
Available on CD.
Eric plays on 'Tough Enough'.

VARIOUS ARTISTS

Album

Stone Free: A Tribute to Jimi Hendrix (Reprise)
Released 10/93.
Available on CD.
Eric performs 'Stone Free'.

KATE BUSH

Album

The Red Shoes (EMI)
Released 11/93.
Available on CD.
Eric plays on 'And So Is Love'.

VARIOUS ARTISTS

Album

A Tribute to Curtis Mayfield (Warner)
Released 2/94.
Available on CD.
Eric performs 'You Must Believe Me'.

VARIOUS ARTISTS

Album

Grammy's Greatest Moments Volume 2 (Atlantic)
Released 3/94.
Available on CD.
Eric performs a live version of 'Tears in Heaven' from the
Grammy Awards.

VIDEOS

Farewell Cream (Royal Albert Hall 1968)
Channel 5.

Sweet Toronto (Plastic Ono Band Live in Toronto 1969)
Parkfield.

Supershow (Staines 1969)
Virgin.

Superstars in Concert (Live Blind Faith footage from
Hyde Park 1969)
Telstar video.

Concert for Bangladesh (George Harrison charity concert 1971)
Warner.

The Last Waltz (The Band's farewell concert 1976)
Warner.

Old Grey Whistle Test (Live 1977)
BBC video.

Alexis Korner's Eat a Little Rhythm and Blues (Pinewood Studios 1978)
BBC Video.

Arms – The Complete Concert (Royal Albert Hall 1983)
Channel 5.

Live 1985 (Hartford, Connecticut 1985)
Channel 5.

Rockabilly Session, Carl Perkins and Friends (Limehouse Studios 1985)
Virgin.

Hail Hail Rock 'n' Roll (Chuck Berry's 60th Birthday concert 1986)
CIC.

The Eric Clapton Concert (Birmingham 1986)
Radio Vision.

Prince's Trust Birthday (Wembley Arena 1986)
Video Gems.

Prince's Trust Rock Gala 1987 (Wembley Arena 1987)
PMV.

All Right Now – Island Records 25th Anniversary (Pinewood 1987)

Island Video.

BB King and Friends (LA 1987)
Video Collection.

Prince's Trust Rock Gala 1988 (Royal Albert Hall 1988)
Video collection.

Knebworth (June 1990)
Castle Music.

Eric Clapton (Knebworth June 1990 – unreleased version of 'Sunshine of Your Love')
Castle Music.

24 Nights (Royal Albert Hall 1990–91)
Warner

Unplugged (Bray Studios 1991)
Warner.

Yardbirds (Retrospective)
Warner.

Fresh Live Cream (Cream rare live clips)
Polygram.

Tommy (Ken Russell's film of Who epic)
RSO.

The Cream of Eric Clapton (Compilation)
Polygram.

Eric Clapton – The Man and His Music (History)
Video Collection.

Cream – Strange Brew (Retrospective)
Warner.

24 APRIL

~~tuesday~~ williamsburg gig

this morning, my throat is even worse and its moved from one side to another not only that, but the gland is swelling pretty rapidly, so ning is trying to score some tetracycline, which is a drag 'cause i know how antibiotics can slow me down, and also i wont be able to drink ! arrrrgggh ! i think i will fly wifey in pretty quick, i am going down fast and who else but her can look after me. i tried to ring her but the line was busy. i finally got through and it was so good to hear her voice, what a setgsh bastard i am, what i mean is, if wifey called me and said she needed me right now, would i be able to drop everything and run to her ? answer, yes ! there must never be any doubt in my mind about that, or #i am lost — put your skates on darling, i cant hold out too long ! to top it all, roger says that i was moved to another room because, people were complaining about the smell coming from my room. i dont smell ! do i ? up just because i dont smother myself in poofdah perfume doesnt mean ive got b.o., bleeding nerve, i am almost tempted to get some stink bombs, and have a bath in them, then they would be a little more appreciative of my natural aroma, didnt say anything about me smelling so there ~ wild gig, i made about a million mistakes, broke about eight strings, but we made the best of it, especially our albert, who had a wale of a time, and he was still steaming on when i went to bed ~ mrs. clapton arrives tomorrow hurray ~ goodnight ~ EC

The following extracts are taken from Eric Clapton's personal diary all in love is fair ! ? ! ? ~

21 JUNE

thursday salt lake city gig

nigel has apologized for not being on duty last night, although im not sure he wasnt got his fingers crossed behind his back, anyway he has said that he will write out hundred lines, saying "i promise not to let barry forget to take the rottennes off the plant" later ~ we watched the buddy holly story on the tele, excuse me for a minute, but roger has just come for a chat, now, we all know what that means ~ "have you had anything to eat today" so my reply is: well i was just going to have a shower, so he says "are you sure you can fit both things into the same day" what a lovely man! anyway as i was saying, we watched the buddy holly story on the box, and i got very unhappy about it, i suppose i knew it would be wrong, but i was curious to see how far they would go to earn a buck. later ~ the gig was okay although after two days of kicking our heels we played a bit stiff, i couldnt get that film out of my mind either, i felt like an anachronism on display.... i mean by that, that i am something left over by the past, a sort of museum piece ~ you see, for all of the really young rock fans, who didnt grow up with rock and roll, gary busey is buddy holly! i know i am a purist at heart, but any damn fool over the age of thirty, knows the words to "thatll be the day", to top it all they changed jerry allison's name to jesse, and then went on to introduce a mediocre sax man as king curtis, who had already been dead for at least two years when that film was made. fuck'em, they made that bed and now they got to sleep in it ~ and i dont wish 'em luck. the high point of the night was getting olivia de havilands autograph, me and albert went and knocked on her door, and although she was probably already in bed, she passed her signature under her door, and her voice was just the same as i remembered it, so sweet ~ sssh ~ ec ~

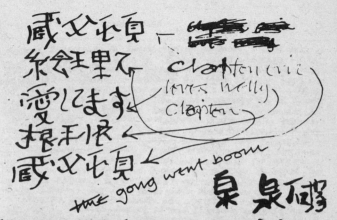

感父正頁
糸会王里乙
愛してます
根王仮
感父正頁

Clapton eric
loves nelly
clapton

the gong went boom

泉 泉礎

if i speak in the tongues of men and of angels
but have not love, i am a noisy gong or a
clanging cymbal. and if i have prophetic powers,
and understand all mysteries and all knowledge,
and if i have all faith, so as to remove mountains,
but have not love, i am nothing. if i give away all
i have, and if i deliver my body to be burned, but
have not love, i gain nothing.

love is patient and kind; love is not jealous
or boastful; it is not arrogant or rude.

love does not insist on its own way; it is not
irritable or resentful; it does not rejoice at wrong,
but rejoices in the right. love bears all things,
believes all things, hopes all things, endures all
things. love never ends; as for prophecies, they
will pass away; as for tongues, they will cease; as
for knowledge, it will pass away. for our knowledge is imperfect and our prophecy is
imperfect; but when the perfect comes, the
imperfect will pass away. when i was a
child, i spoke like a child, i thought like a child,
i reasoned like a child; when i became a man
i gave up childish ways. for now we see in a
mirror dimly, but then face to face. now i
know in part; then i shall understand fully,
even as i have been fully understood. so faith,
hope, love abide, these three, but the greatest
of these is love ～　　 amen ～

16

OCTOBER tuesday   warsaw .

i think i must have had a quarrel with
a steamroller last night ~ later ~
we held a press conference today, all
went well until this waistcoats piped
up with "is it true that david mills has
got a wooden leg? "then it got silly (as
it should be)... i was asked to name the
most famous person that i had been
on the road with, and came up with mondo
around the world with mondo pearvain
is the title of the next album, and so on...
seriously though, all things considered,
it was a good laugh ~ then we went
for a walk down the old town again
and i collected the seal that i had ord
ered yesterday... it turned out really
well, now that i look back on it, i wish
i had asked to see how it was done ~
while i was there i bought all the amulets they had left, which amount to
about thirty four and covers me for
everything but wba losing away at
southampton on saturday ~ roger
ordered a seal as well ~ nigel continues to act strangeley, if i take a step
backwards im standing on his toe ~
ah well ~ theres always one ~
im missing nelly so bad, and i cant get
her on the phone, ill try again now ~
later ~ the gig was great thanks to the
support we got from the marines (i kid
you not) when we got back to the hotel
i got a call from nelly which was like
a shot in the arm, she had just come
back from the tap dance school in
guildford and sounded wonderful, i could
actually smell her over the phone!...
watch out boys the real thing is arriving
on sunday ~ those amulets are no joke.
i had a good laugh and a chat with nigel
what more proof do you need? (only
joking nig')... good night all ~
                    sean ~

20

JANUARY saturday

(wba v. derby)
(home) cancelled

---

well woke me up at nine with
her alarm clock, to go to the game,
when i made it downstairs, the
postman was here, in the kitchen,
trying to figure out how to get
his van out of the ditch~ well,
i called roger, who called gordon,
who said the game would almost
certainly be off, kuszkars ~~
so i watched swap shop waiting
for a glimpse of kate bush, and
went to sleep and missed the whole
bloody thing, i woke to the theme
tune of grandstand and saw a
resume of albions most recent
goals, (even for a fanatic that wasn't
enough to make up for missing
a butchers at k.b.) not a good day
so far~

NOTES FOR JANUARY

make somebody happy
water on the ground
one and only son
something special
over the hurdles
holding back the tears (idea)
rose ~ bobby charles

so sacred is my love
i know that i've been blessed
my heart has finally come
to rest

and around the moon,
following the day, comes the night.
having no warning to the memory
of where one will begin,
or the other will end
but you can be sure as silver
that they whisper to one another
great words of love,
(that all can hear, if they so choose)
ensuring that they never drift too
far apart or come too close
together ~

⟨EC⟩

so someone said "look each way"
and i, being, as always, keen to
reply, muttered " how can you
possibly do two things at the same
time?" and the voice that i was
expecting (as always) said nothing
whatsoever ~ as always ~

⟨EC⟩

INDEX

Action Research into
    Multiple Sclerosis, 319
Adams, Bryan, 341
'After Midnight' (song),
    280, 358
'Ain't Going Down' (song),
    314
Alaska, 352
'Alberta, Alberta' (song),
    25, 247
Alcoholics Anonymous,
    290, 296–302, 362
alcoholism, *see* Clapton,
    Eric; Hazelden
    Foundation
All Things Must Pass
    (album), 142, 150,
    218
Allman, Duane, 219
Animals (band), 59
*Another Beatles Christmas
    Show* (TV show), 65
Another Ticket (album),
    309

Apple (record label), 121
Astley, John, 422
Atkins, Chet, 65
Atlantic Records, 169, 344
audiences: sex of, 366–7;
    treatment of, 238,
    253–4, 279–80
August (album), 339–40,
    349–50

Back to the Future (film),
    356
Backless (album), 268, 349
'Badge' (song), 125, 140,
    380
Bailey, John, 78
Baker, Pete 'Ginger', 90,
    93–8, 105, 115,
    124–5, 127–8, 278
Balding, Tony, 256–8
Ball, Kenny, 47
Band, The, 114, 119, 209,
    219, 237, 265, 375,
    413

Bangladesh Relief concert, 155, 157, 210, 221

Barberstown Castle, County Kildare, 283, 338

Barrett, Syd, 162

Beach Boys (group), 364

Beatles (group). 47, 52, 56, 62, 65, 86, 93, 121, 137, 205, 211, 368, 399

Beck, Jeff, 71, 76, 105, 232, 319

Bee Gees (band), 201, 269

'Before You Accuse Me' (song), 24

'Behind the Mask' (song), 350

Behind the Sun (album), 325–7, 344, 349, 355, 365

'Bell Bottom Blues' (song), 219

Benno, Marc, 414

Berry, Chuck, 53, 55, 248, 374, 422

Bilk, Acker, 115

Billboard charts, 200, 219n, 345

Bishop, Stephen, 237, 336, 365, 411, 415, 426

Blackbushe Festival, 265

Blind Faith (band), 127–34, 278, 386

Blonde on Blonde (album), 74, 265

Bloomfield, Mike, 111

'Blow Wind Blow' (song), 309

Blue Flames (band), 88

Blue Horizon Records, 263

'Blue Moon of Kentucky' (song), 351

'Blue Suede Shoes' (song), 137, 351

'Blues All Day Long, The' (song), 379

Blues Incorporated (band), 52, 88, 115

'Blues Power' (song), 218, 280, 282

Blues Project (band), 109

Bluesbreakers (album), 84

Bluesbreakers (band), 73, 79, 81–2, 89, 383–4; *see also* Mayall, John

Bond, Graham, 79

Booker T and the MGs (band), 309, 313

'Bottle of Red Wine' (song), 218

Boyd, Jenny, 141n, 208

Boyd, Leona, 419

Boyd, Pattie
    and Clapton: banned from touring, 213; courtship, 142–4, 149–50, 155, 184–5, 196–7; declaration of love, 206–7; life with, 210–15, 251, 285; London flat, 329; marital strains and break up, 5, 314–17,

321–34, 346, 372;
separations and
reunions, 222–7,
333–4; touring,
208–9, 229–32;
wedding, 227–9
alcoholism, 295, 314
career, 141
drugs conviction, 210
marriage to Harrison, 66,
140, 141, 206; divorce
20, 196–7, 208
model agency, 340
Boyd, Paula, 142, 149, 252
Brady, Paul, 419
Bragg, Melvyn, 42
Bramlett, Delaney *and*
Bonnie, *see* Delaney
and Bonnie
*Bridge Over Troubled
Waters* (album), 221
Brooker, Gary, 241–2, 248,
309, 311, 317, 341,
416, 418
Brooks, Bobby, 15
Brooks, Elkie, 65, 308
Broonzy, Big Bill, 24, 52,
53, 72
Brown, Pete, 116
Browne, Nigel, 15
Bruce, Jack, 74, 90, 93–9,
101, 103, 105, 112,
114–17, 125, 283,
423, 432
Bruni, Carla, 372
Buffalo Springfield (band),
121

Bunburys, The (band), 425,
431
Bush, Kate, 433
Bushbranch (racehorse), 256
Buster (film), 374
Butterfield, Paul, 111
'Bye Bye Blackbird' (song),
269

Cale, J. J., 250, 251
Campbell, Naomi, 372
Capaldi, Jim, 169, 425
Carr, Leroy, 379
Carroll, Nigel, 227, 283,
286, 336
Casey Jones and the
Engineers (band), 55,
56
Cash, Johnny, 363
Cass and the Cassanovas
(band), 55
Cassar, Brian, 55–6
'Cat's Squirrel' (song), 105
Cavern Club, Liverpool, 59
'Certain Girl, A' (song), 64
Charles, Ray, 432
Charlesworth, Chris, 208
Chas and Dave (duo),
243–4
Chemical Dependency
Centre, 375
Chicago, Illinois, 76, 104
China Garden restaurant,
Soho, 197–8
cigarette smoking, 278,
297, 362–3

'Circus Has Left Town' (song), 17, 380

Clapp, Adrian, 36, 161

Clapp, Jack, 2, 31, 37, 44, 45, 136, 154, 376

Clapp, Rose, 2, 31, 37, 39, 44, 45, 136, 154, 161, 165, 197, 233, 234, 376

Clapton, Adrian 33–4, 96

Clapton, Conor
  death and funeral, 4–10, 350;
  father's love for, 268 1–2, 4, 376;
  public sympathy, 350

Clapton, Eric
  acting ability, 268–70, 282
  alcoholism: affecting playing, 237–43, 267–8, 276, 287; Alcoholics Anonymous, 290, 296–302, 362; dependence on following drug treatment, 200; drinking with Pattie, 212; first taste of drink, 46; friends' concern at, 283, 286; hiding effects of, 282; manager's problems from, 261–2; medical warnings, 286–7; mixed with drugs, 189; moodiness, 298; pubs, 209, 215–16, 244, 248, 282, 336; recovery from, 300–5; return to, 358; treatment for, 11, 180, 289–97, *see also* Hazelden Foundation; wild behaviour when drunk, 255–6

  appearance: on stage, 61–2, 82, 86–7, 104, 113–14, 379; as a youth, 23, 47

  art training, 32–3, 37, 41, 42, 44–5, 48–9

  awards, 14, 26–8, 79, 112, 122, 217, 245

  birth and early years: birth 2; with grandparents at Ripley, 2, 30–6, 44–51; illegitimacy, effect of, 2, 186, 376; schooldays, 29, 33–6, 41–5, 48–51; sport, 36, 39

  character: addictive nature, 210; assertiveness, 311; chauvinism, 213, 222, 228, 330; coping with death, 12, 16; easy-going accessibility, 246–8; generosity, 38; gregariousness, 373–4; impatience, 321; love

of danger, 215;
meanness at the bar,
336; obsessiveness,
315; practical joker,
240; prickliness on
stage, 238;
professionalism, 235,
367–8; sense of
humour, 58, 245–6;
sexuality, 366–7,
shyness, 367;
solitariness, 38, 84,
154, 252–3; star signs,
306–7; superstition,
236; two sides of,
377–8

concerts: audiences,
treatment of, 133, 238,
253–4, 279–81;
Blackbushe Festival,
265; charity, 168–72,
319, 341–2, 345;
'comeback', 11,
169–72, 235; Earl's
Court, 265, 320;
Ethiopia Live Aid,
341–5; Guildford City
Hall, 249; Royal Albert
Hall, 3, 121–2, 319,
371, 378–81

diary, 241, 271, 340,
437–42

drugs: addiction, 15–7;
Alice Ormsby-Gore
and, 157–66, 171,
175; charity concert
under influence of,

168–71; comeback
album, 197;
consumption of, 173;
development of
problem, 191–3,
204–6; effect on
music, 183–7, 192,
220; farm work as
rehabilitation, 189;
medical cure, 173–82;
message to users,
195–6; reclusive life
with, 155–61;
recognition of
problem, 166–7, 376;
spending on, 158;
support from friends,
166–8; teenage
involvement, 45; will
to conquer, 191

films: appearances, 374;
soundtracks, 18–20,
356–8

friendships, 54–5,
144–5, 243, 265, 311,
325n, *see also* Forrester,
Roger; Harrison,
George; Townshend,
Pete

girl friends: actresses and
models, 372; Alice
Ormsby-Gore, *see*
Ormsby-Gore, Alice;
boyhood, 38–9, 45–7,
186; Cathy James,
206; Jenny McLean,
223; Lori Del Santo, 1,

4, 8, 12, 339–40;
Pattie Boyd, *see* Boyd,
Pattie
health, 283–8, 362–3
homes: Antigua, 17,
370; Barberstown
Castle Hotel, 283,
338; Chelsea, 370;
Paradise Island,
Bahamas, 209–10;
Pheasantry, 114;
Ripley, 135, 166
interests: calligraphy,
270–1, 437–42;
fishing, 234, 285, 302,
315–18, 338; football,
268; horse-racing,
256–8; model-making,
37
marriage, *see* Boyd,
Pattie
money: in Britain's
richest, 373; drug-
spending causing
shortage, 158, 162,
173; early carefulness,
335–6; lack of interest
in, 70–1; naïveté with,
337; opulent life-style,
135–6; ostentatious
spending, 335–9
musical career:
adulation, 75, 80; all-
British band, 276–8,
309–12; Blind Faith,
126–34; comeback
album, 197–8; Cream,

see Cream;
discography, 382–96;
disillusionment with
English music, 76–7,
80; future of, 370;
Glands, the, 78–9;
guest sessions,
397–436; loss of
power, 328–9; Mayall's
Bluesbreakers, 73–6;
overwork, 320; passion
for guitar, 38–41; 51,
262–4, 363–6; pub
and club circuit, 51;
recordings with other
artists, 217–18, 237;
sideman, 150–1; skill
recognised, 54, 61;
solo performer, 122;
videos, 434–6;
Yardbirds, 64–72
musicianship: black
musicians, 101; blues,
passion for, 40–3, 46,
53, 67, 73, 77–84,
244, 379–80;
contempt for
commercial music, 62,
70–1, 115, 117–18;
drug influenced, 183;
economy of notes,
356; guitar skills,
83–4, 267, 361, 363;
guitars, *see* guitars;
jazz, 47; musical
knowledge, 87–8;
'musician's musician',

91; producer's role, 274; recording techniques, 250–1, 272–3; respect from peers, 355; rhythm-and-blues, 52; song-writing skills, 12, 314, 321, 356–7; voice, 24, 95, 105, 198, 309, 314, 379–80; West Coast music, 111, 121
personal relationships, 5
racist remarks, 258–61
reclusive period, 155–61, 179, 194–5
record sales, 14, 26
religion, 34, 176–7, 183, 235–6
restaurants, 373
smoking cigarettes, 278, 297, 362–3
son's death, see Clapton, Conor
tabloid press, 372, 373
touring: Africa, 17; Alaska, 352; America, 17, 108–12, 125, 133, 154, 198–203, 208, 229–34, 283; Australia, 210, 329; Europe, 17, 262–3, 266–7, 275–81; Far East, 17, 329; idiosyncracies on tour, 153–5; incognito, 150; Ireland, 224; Israel, 236, 281; Japan, 20,

239, 281–2, 352; in middle age, 275; Poland, 17, 275–81; South America, 20; women banned, 213, 232, 274;
wardrobe: early days, 57–8, 61, 63–4; obsession with clothes, 86, 213, 296, 339; spending on, 337
Clapton, Patricia Molly (Pat) (mother)
Eric's birth, 2, 30
marriage to McDonald, 31, 58
relationship with, 186
visiting son, 160–1, 170, 233
Clapton, Pattie, see Boyd, Pattie
Clapton, Reginald, 2
Clapton, Sylvia, 34
Cloud Nine (album), 374
Club 66, 85
Coasters (band), 248
'Cocaine' (song), 250, 251, 254, 349
Cochran, Eddie, 40
Cocker, Joe, 169, 237, 239, 308, 319, 375, 410
Collins, Mel, 248, 320
Collins, Phil, 8, 323–6, 327, 328, 339, 341, 344, 350, 358, 374, 415, 426
Coltrane, John, 361

Columbia (record label), 64
Colyer, Ken, 47
'Come On' (song), 52
Cooder, Ry, 313
Cooper, Ray, 319
'Core, The' (song), 252
Costello, Elvis, 341
'Country Boy' (song), 279
'County Jail Blues' (song), 237
Cranleigh, Surrey, 246-8
Crawdaddy Club, 56-7, 62
Crawford, Randy, 19
Cray, Robert, 15, 364, 374
'Crazy Country Hop' (song), 314
Cream (band)
  albums, 104-7, 119, 344, 385
  American tour, 108-12, 241
  Clapton as leader, 94
  earnings, 120
  equipment, 100-1
  farewell concert, 121-2
  formation and launch of, 76, 90-6
  influence of, 122
  live shows, 100, 104, 107-9
  musicianship, 102-5
  popularity of, 103, 344-5
  relationships within, 90-9, 114-15
  sound, 106
  split up, 114, 118-25

Crickets (band), 217
Croker, Brendan, 425
'Crosscut Saw' (song), 106, 314
'Crossroads' (song), 122, 170
Curtis, King, 403

Daily Express (newspaper), 333
Daily Mail (newspaper), 225, 226
Daily Mirror (newspaper), 128
Dallas, Ian, 145-6
Daltrey, Roger, 412
Danko, Rick, 412
Dankworth, Johnny, 56
Davies, Cyril, 79
Davies, Ray, 45, 56
Davis, Miles, 356
Davis, Spencer, 87
de Burgh, Chris, 71
Decca Records, 67, 68, 82
Deja Vu model agency, 340
Del Santo, Lori, 2, 4, 8, 12, 340
Delaney and Bonnie (duo), 126, 151, 267, 278, 386
Dempster, Nigel, 225
Derek and the Dominos (band), 126, 146, 149, 152, 157, 158, 162, 165, 218, 221, 277, 388

Desert Island Discs (BBC programme), 375–7
Desire (album), 266
Detroit Wheels (band), 109
Dickinson, James Luther, 407
Dickson, Lee, 366
Diddley, Bo, 53
Dire Straits (band), 341, 345–6, 346–9
Disc and Music Echo (magazine), 122, 125
Disraeli Gears (album), 106–7, 113, 116–17
'Dizzy Miss Lizzy' (song), 137
Doctor John, 407, 410
Domino, Fats, 40
Donegan, Lonnie, 232
Dorsey, Gail Anne, 424
'Double Trouble' (song), 239, 282
Douma, Danny, 414
Dowd, Tom, 198, 203, 309, 312–15
Downbeat (magazine), 63
Dozier, Lamont, 430
Dreja, Chris, 57, 70
Dreja, Paul, 70
drugs
  deaths from, 153, 163
  medical treatment for addicts, 174–82
  work for addicts, 375
  see also Clapton, Eric
Dudgeon, Gus, 82–4, 93, 97–8, 329

Dunn, Duck, 312–13, 343
Dupree, Jack, 398
Dylan, Bob, 60, 73–4, 86, 155, 209, 221, 237, 265–8, 341, 367, 409, 423

E.C. Was Here (album), 235, 349
Earl's Court, London, 265, 320
East, Nathan, 18, 355
Edge of Darkness (TV drama), 357–8
Edmunds, Dave, 351
Elliman, Yvonne, 199, 203
EMI Records, 64
Epstein, Brian, 65, 90, 137, 142, 163, 368
Eric Clapton (album), 218, 219
Eric Clapton's Rolling Hotel (film), 269–72
Ertegun, Ahmet, 169, 344
Esquire (record label), 55
Estes, Sleepy John, 309, 314
'Everybody Oughta Make a Change' (song), 314

Face Value (album), 325n
Faces (band), 319
Fairweather-Low, Andy, 21, 319
Faithfull, Marianne, 128
Fame, Georgie, 88
Family (band), 128

Farlowe, Chris, 80
Fender, Leo, 364
Ferrone, Steve, 8, 18, 355
Ferry, Bryan, 341
Fifth Dimensional Show (US TV show), 108–10
film soundtracks, 18–20, 356–8
fishing, 234, 285, 302, 315–18, 338
Five Little Yardbirds (album), 64
Fleetwood, Mike, 208
Flint, Hughie, 74
'Floating Bridge' (song), 309
Flynn, Delia, 285
'For Your Love' (song), 68, 72n
Forbes (magazine), 373
'Forever Man' (song), 329
Forrester, Roger
  arranging work schedule, 17, 23, 201–2
  friendship with, 270, 287, 303–4
  influence of, 368–9
  manager, 202, 209, 213, 224–5, 240, 253–6, 261–2, 275, 280, 312, 337, 338
  protective role, 262, 264–5, 287–8, 298, 299
461 Ocean Boulevard (album), 198–200, 208

Four Tops (band), 345
Fraboni, Myel, 224, 227
Fraboni, Rob, 224, 226
Franklin, Aretha, 313, 398
Fraser, Robert, 145
Freddie and the Dreamers (band), 65
'Free Nelson Mandela' concert, 345–6
Fresh Cream (album), 104–5, 211
Friedman, Kinky, 237, 411
'From Me to You' (song), 52
Frost, David, 367
Fryer, Edward (Ted), 30
Fuller, Jesse, 25
'Further up the Road' (song), 349

Gaff, Billy, 101
Gallagher, Rory, 169
Galton, Ray, 91
Galuten, Alby, 199
Gardner, Ashton, 404
Geldof, Bob, 421
Germany, 266–7
'Give Me Strength' (song), 172, 199
Glands (band), 78
'Going Away' (song), 379
'Golden Ring' (song), 268
Goldsmith, Harvey, 85–6, 169, 265
Golino, Valerie, 372
Gomelsky, Giorgio, 56–7, 59, 64, 64, 68–70

'Good Morning Little
  Schoolgirl' (song), 64
Goodbye (album), 119
'G odnight Irene' (song),
  244, 247
Goon Show, 39–40
Gordon, Jim, 148, 150,
  151, 221
'Got to Hurry' (song), 69n
Graham, Bill, 110
Graham Bond Organization
  (band), 88, 90, 92, 93,
  94, 115
Grammy Awards, 26–8
Grateful Dead (band), 121
Grease (stage show), 201
Grech, Rick, 128, 169
Greenwood, Bernie, 78
Greer, Germaine, 114
Guildford City Hall, 249
Guitar Player (magazine),
  245
guitars
  acoustic, 17, 23, 25,
    182–3
  'Blackie', 363–6
  Clapton on, 77
  Clapton's sound, 83
  collection of, 136, 339,
    363–6
  Dobro, 199
  Fender Stratocaster, 152,
    218, 363–6
  Fender Telecasters, 218,
    364
  Gibson, 106

presentation of repoica,
    365n
  sale of to fund drug
    purchases, 158, 162,
    177, 337
  'shake' mastered, 56
  slide technique, 199,
    220, 313
  solos, 218
  suited to music, 363, 365
  synthesizers, 325
  'woman's tone', 104, 106
Guy, Buddy, 15, 150, 217,
  262, 348, 405, 429

Hail Hail! Rock 'n' Roll
  (album), 374
Hard Day's Night, A
  (album), 66, 141
Hare Krishna sect, 205
Harlech, David Ormsby-
  Gore, Baron, 145,
  167–8, 171, 172, 173,
  176
Harrison, George
  Clapton, friendship with,
    8, 21, 22, 65–6, 155,
    156, 169, 196,
    210–11, 221, 351–2,
    364; musical
    partnership with, 20–3,
    121, 351–2, 399, 404,
    413, 423
  Hare Krishna sect, 205
  marriage to Pattie, 140;
    divorce, 206–7;

problems, 196–7; *see also* Boyd, Pattie
musical career, 142, 150, 155, 218, 374
Hart, Corey, 418
Hartford, Connecticut, 341
Haslam, Michael, 65
'Have You Ever Loved a Woman?' (song), 221
Hawkins, Roger, 313
Hazelden Foundation
arrangements to enter clinic, 288, 289
drugs, 290
group therapy, 290–2
intensive treatment, 290
questionnaire, 293–4
see also Clapton, Eric, drugs
Head, Murray, 71
'Heaven is One Step Away' (song), 356
Helm, Levon, 237
'Help Me Angel' (song), 19
'Help Me Up' (song), 19
Helvin, Marie, 372
Hendrix, Jimi, 87, 106, 115, 121, 122, 150, 163, 170, 184, 266, 269, 361, 364, 380
Henke, James, 65
'Hey Hey' (song), 24, 53
Hit, The (film), 356
Holly, Buddy, 40, 217, 364
'Holy Mother' (song), 350
'Honey Bee' (song), 56, 262

Honolulu, 255–6
'Hoochie Coochie Man' (song), 379
Horler, Chris, 275
horse-racing, 256–8
'How Long' (song), 379
Howerd, Frankie, 91
Howlin' Wolf, 104, 217, 250, 379, 406
Hudson, Garth, 237
Hunt, Dave, 56
Hurt, John, 55, 215, 267, 356, 357
Hyde Park concert 1969, 128

'I Can't Hold Out Much Longer' (song), 199
'I Feel Free' (song), 105, 113, 116, 121
'I Shot the Sheriff' (song), 200
'I Wish You Would ' (song), 64
Idlewild South (album), 219
'I'm So Glad' (song), 105, 122
'I'm Your Witchdoctor' (song), 79
'Innocent Times' (song), 237
'It All Depends' (song), 323
'It Hurts Me Too' (song), 380
Italy, 339
Ivor Novello Award, 28

Jagger, Mick, 128, 145, 232, 341
James, Elmore, 199, 248, 380
Jan and Dean, 109
Japan, 20, 239, 281–2, 352
jazz
   jam-sessions, 95, 150, 248, 347, 352–3
   jazz clubs, 47, 56, 88
Jennings, Waylon, 341
Jennings, Will, 19–20
Jerusalem, 236
Joel, Billy, 341
John, Elton, 169, 341, 348, 358, 368
Johns, Glyn, 250–3, 267, 272–3, 309, 319, 381
Johnson, Blind Willie, 53
Johnson, Johnnie, 430
Johnson, Robert, 25, 53, 203, 379
Johnstone, Davey, 348
Jones, Brian, 52, 99, 163
Jones, Elvin, 90
Jones, Paul, 52
Jones, Quincy, 28
Jones, Tom, 368
Jones, Wizz, 48
Joplin, Janis, 163, 184
Jupp, Mickey, 248
'Just Like a Prisoner' (song), 323
Just One Night (album), 282, 349

Kamen, Michael, 320, 358, 374, 428

Katowice, Poland, 279, 280
Kaye, Thomas Jefferson, 433
Kelly, Jonathan, 403
Kensit, Patsy, 372
'Key to the Highway' (song), 170, 220
Keys, Bobby, 151, 407
King, Albert, 106, 314
King, B. B., 61, 262, 361
King, Carole, 426
King, Freddie, 106, 262, 380, 408
King of the Delta Blues Singers (album), 53
Kingston Art College, 42, 44, 45, 48–50
Kinks (band), 45, 56
Kirk, Roland, 150
Kissoon, Katie, 21
'Knock on Wood' (song), 354
'Knockin' on Heaven's Door' (song), 280
Knopfler, Mark, 348–9, 358, 364
Kooper, Al, 110
Korner, Alexis, 52, 79, 88, 115, 414
Kramer, Carlo, 55

'Lady of Verona' (song), 340
Laing, Corky, 237, 411
Lane, Ronnie, 247, 250, 318–19, 412, 416
'Last Waltz' (song), 265

Lauper, Cyndi, 427
Lawley, Sue, 370, 375–7
'Lay Down Sally' (song),
    250, 251, 279
'Layla' (song), 12, 20, 24,
    170, 196, 219n, 220,
    248, 249, 254, 314,
    340, 344–5
    inspiration for, 146–8
    words, 148
*Layla and Other Assorted
    Love Songs* (album),
    149, 152, 218–19,
    345
Leadbelly, 46
Leavell, Chuck, 18, 25
Led Zeppelin (band), 53,
    71, 319
Ledbetter, Hudde, 244
Lee, Albert, 229, 242, 244,
    276, 277, 279, 310,
    313
Lennon, John, 45, 137,
    138–9
Lester, Richard, 141
Let It Be (album), 221
'Let It Grow' (song), 199
'Let It Rain' (song), 170,
    218
Lethal Weapon 2 (film), 374
Letterman, David, 343
Levy, Marcy, 237
Lewis, Furry, 53
Lewis, George, 47
Leyton, John, 91
'Life is Like a Slow Train
    Going up a Hill'
    (song), 74
Lightfoot, Terry, 115
Lippmann, Horst, 266–7
'Little Wing' (song), 152,
    170, 221
Little Walter, 52
Live Aid concerts, 341–5,
    354
Live Peace in Toronto
    concert, 138–9
Lloyd, Kathy, 372
Lohle, Virginia, 14–15,
    371–2
Lomax, Jackie, 121,
    399–400
'Lonely Stranger' (song),
    17, 24
Louis, Arthur, 409
'Louisiana Blues' (song),
    327
Lovin' Spoonful (band),
    121
Lynch, Kenny, 52

McCall, Davina, 372
McCartney, Paul, 86, 172,
    232
McCarty, Jim, 58, 70
McDonald, Brian, 148, 34,
    209
McDonald, Frank, 31
McGhee, Brownie, 70
McGuinness, Tom, 52, 73n
McGuinness Flint (duo),
    52n
McLean, Jenny, 223–6

McLean, Susie, 223
McNeny, Larry, 227
McVie, Christine, 417
McVie, John, 74
Madison, Wisconsin, 283
Maharishi Mahesh Yogi, 162, 205
Malibu, California, 237
'Malted Milk' (song), 25
'Man in Love' (song), 314
Manfred Mann (band), 52, 88, 91, 95
Manuel, Richard, 237
Markee, Dave, 242, 310, 311
Marley, Bob, 199–200
Marquee Club, 85
Martin, Charlotte, 114
Martin, George, 322
Martyn, John, 415
Marvin, Hank, 122
May, Brian, 279
Mayall, John, 62, 73, 76, 77–89, 92, 95, 96, 278, 383–4, *see also* Bluesbreakers
Mayall Plays Mayall (album), 81
'Mean Old Frisco' (song), 251
'Mean Old World' (song), 220
Meher Baba, 162
Melody Maker (magazine), 77, 79, 91, 112, 117, 208, 217, 245, 260

Metropolis Blues Quartet (band), 57, 59
Miles, Buddy, 150
Miller, Roger, 28
Mills, Gordon, 368
Milton, Jake, 78
Milton, Ted, 78
Minneapolis St Paul, Minnesota, 286, 289, 358
'Miss You' (song), 339
Mlinaric, David, 145
Money, Zoot, 88
Money and Cigarettes (album), 314, 325, 349
'Money for Nothing' (song), 346
Montserrat, West Indies, 322–7, 365
Moon, Keith, 65
Morrison, Van, 265
Mothers of Invention (band), 121
'Move It' (song), 40
Murray the K, 108–9, 116, 162
Muscle Shoals studios, 313
Music from Big Pink (album), 114, 209, 224

National Film Theatre, 271
Negrete, Yelitza, 372
Nello (racehorse), 257
'Never Make You Cry' (song), 326

Newcastle upon Tyne, 59, 87

Newmark, Andy, 320

Nightingale, Anne, 333

Niles, Tessa, 21

No Reason To Cry (album), 266

'Nobody Knows You When You're Down and Out' (song), 24, 53, 170, 219, 380

Nordoff Robbins Music Therapy charity, 28

Novella (magazine), 340

'NSU' (song), 105

Nuremberg, Germany, 266–7

O'Dell, Chris, 227

'Old Love' (song), 22, 25

Oldaker, Jamie, 199, 229, 255, 268, 344

Oldham, Andrew Loog, 90, 368

O'Leary, Alphi, 236–7, 240–1, 280, 284, 297–8, 336, 367–8, 373–4

'One Day I'll Fly Away' (song), 19

One More Car, One More Rider (album), 349

O'Neal, Tatum, 372

O'Neill, Terry, 350

Ono, Yoko, 308, 137–40

Ormsby-Gore, Alice, 145–6, 155, 157–8, 163–4, 171, 178, 189–96, 205

Ormsby-Gore, Frank, 189

Ory, Kid, 47

Oswestry, Shropshire, 189

Otis, Johnny, 314

Oz (magazine), 114, 117

Page, Jimmy, 53, 71, 79, 114, 169, 319, 341, 398

Palmer, Ben, 51–5, 71, 73, 78, 101, 158–9, 229, 233, 381

Palmer, Robert, 310

Paradise Island, Bahamas, 209

Parker, Charlie, 184, 361

Parker, Colonel Tom, 368

Parrot Band, 248

Patterson, George, 176, 182–9

Perkins, Carl, 65, 350

Perrin, Sid, 288–9

Peter, Paul and Mary, 60

Pheasantry, 114

Philadelphia, Pennsylvania, 342–5

Phillinganes, Greg, 18, 355

Phillips, Shawn, 401

Pickett, Wilson, 109

Pink Floyd (band), 162

Plant, Robert, 53, 341

Plastic Ono Band, 137, 387

Playboy (magazine), 245

'Please Be with Me' (song), 199

Ploughman, Sandra, 38
Poland, 17, 275–81
Police (band), 279
Polydor Records, 91
Pop Weekly (magazine), 91
Powell, Enoch, 259, 260
Presley, Elvis, 40, 368
Preston, Billy, 400–1
'Pretty Flamingo' (song), 91
'Pretty Girl' (song), 314
Price, Jim, 151
Pridden, Bob, 162
Prince, 279, 321, 377
Prince's Trust, 319, 358, 420
Procol Harum (band), 241
'Promises' (song), 268
'Pros and Cons of Hitchhiking' (tour), 319–20, 352
Pullen, Guy, 34, 37–9, 215–16, 234
Puplett, Diana, 256
Purple Rain (film), 321
Pye International, 104
Pyke, Rex, 268–72

Q (magazine), 153
Queen (band), 279, 341

racism, 258–61
Radle, Carl, 151, 197, 199, 221, 229, 268
Rainbow Theatre, London, 168–72, 235
Raitt, Bonnie, 364

Rau, Fritz, 266–7
Ray, Bob, 78
Reaction (record label), 91
Redding, Otis, 309, 313
Reed, Jimmy, 46
Reid, John, 368
Relf, Keith, 47, 70, 76
Renwick, Tim, 352, 355
rhythm-and-blues, 52, 91
Rich, Buddy, 90
Richard, Cliff, 40
Richards, Keith, 8, 62, 145, 374
Richie, Lionel, 348, 350, 354, 419
Ripley, Surrey, 8, 30, 45, 135, 154, 215, 233, 335
Ripleyite (racehorse), 257
'Robbery, The' (film music), 374
Robertson, Robbie, 209, 219, 237, 265, 363
Rock Against Racism, 259, 260
Rock Legends (band), 21
rock 'n' roll, 40, 90, 112
Rock 'n' Roll Circus (film), 150
Rock 'n' Roll Hall of Fame, New York, 375
'Rock 'n' Roll Heart' (song), 314
Rogers, Jimmy, 379
Rolling Stone (magazine), 65, 310
Rolling Stones (band), 8,

10, 52, 57, 62, 64, 90, 93, 217, 368
'Romeo and Juliet' (song), 346
Ronettes (group), 67
Roosters (band), 52–4, 99
Rough Mix (album), 250
Royal Albert Hall concerts, 3–4, 121–2, 319, 371, 378–81
RSO (management company), 91
'Running on Faith' (song), 25
Rush (film), 18
Rush, Otis, 237
Russell, Leon, 156, 239, 402
Ryder, Mitch, 109

Sam and Dave (duo), 301
Sambora, Richie, 429
'Same Old Blues' (song), 324
Samwell-Smith, Paul, 57, 59–60, 64, 68–70, 265
San Francisco, 110–111, 120
'San Francisco Bay Blues' (song), 25, 48
San Lorenzo restaurant, 373
Sanborn, David, 320, 374, 431
Sanchez, Rev. Daniel, 227
Sarne, Mike, 91

'Save the Best Till Last' (song), 26
Saville, Jimmy, 65
Seaman, Phil, 90
Secret Policeman's Other Ball, 417
Self-Help Addiction Recovery Programme (SHARP), 375
Shaffer, Paul, 343
Shamley Green, Surrey, 161
'Shape You're In, The' (song), 314
Shapiro, Helen, 52
Sharp, Martin, 114, 116–17, 265
'She's Waiting' (song), 323, 344
'Sign Language' (song), 209, 237
Simon, Carly, 71
Simon, Paul, 340
Simon and Garfunkel, 71, 109, 221
Simpson, Alan, 91
Sims, Dick, 199, 229, 268
Sims, Judy, 125
Sinatra, Frank, 93
'Sitting on Top of the World' (song), 122
Slowhand (album), 251–2, 267–8, 275, 349
Smith, Bessie, 24, 53, 380
Smith, Julia, 372
'Smokestack Lightnin'', (song), 267
Smythe, Colin, 15

'Solid Rock' (song), 349
'Someday After a While'
    (song), 380
'Something' (song), 22,
    144
Sounds Incorporated, 65
South Bank Show (TV
    programme), 42
Spann, Otis, 67, 263, 397
Specials (band), 279
Spector, Phil, 67
Spector, Ronnie, 67
Spencer Davis Group
    (band), 63, 127
Spielberg, Steven, 356
Spinetti, Henry, 242, 276,
    310
'Spoonful' (song), 104, 111
Stainton, Chris, 238, 242,
    276, 306–8, 310, 319,
    380
'Stairway to Heaven'
    (song), 319
'Standing Round Cryin''
    (song), 379
Stanshall, Vivian, 401
Starr, Ringo, 221, 233,
    237, 350, 358, 410,
    417
Station Hotel, Richmond,
    59
Status Quo (band), 341
Stax record label, 309
Steele, Tommy, 80
Stevens, Cat, 71
Stewart, Rod, 319
Stigwood, Robert, 91–2,

104, 107, 121, 124,
    129, 131, 149, 167,
    176, 197, 201–2, 206,
    268–9
'Still in the Game' (song),
    19
Stills, Stephen, 108, 217,
    403
Sting, 348, 422
Stockholm, Sweden, 320
'Stone Free' (song), 380
Story of Layla and Majnun,
    The (Nizami), 146,
    270
Storyville Jazzmen (band),
    115
'Strange Brew' (song), 106,
    113, 117, 241
Sunday Times (newspaper),
    373
'Sunshine of Your Love'
    (song), 102, 106, 117,
    122, 125
Swallow, Roger, 246–7
Swaziland, 17

'T'aint Nobody's Business
    If I Do' (song), 380
'Tales of the Brave Ulysses'
    (song), 117
Talking Back to the Night
    (album), 19
'Tearing Us Apart' (song),
    350
'Tears in Heaven' (song),
    12, 19, 24, 25, 28,
    350, 380

'Telephone Blues', 79

'Tell Me That You Love Me' (song), 268

Templeman, Ted, 328

'Terraplane Blues' (song), 379

Terry, George, 199, 268

Terry, Sonny, 72

Test, River, 316, 318

'That's All Right Mama' (song), 351

There's One in Every Crowd (album), 209, 349

'Tipitina' (song), 280

Titelman, Russ, 18

'Toad' (song), 105, 122

Tommy (film), 207

Topham, Anthony, 57

Toronto, Canada, 138–9

Tosh, Peter, 200

Townshend, Pete
　art training, 45
　first meeting with Clapton, 62
　friendship with Clapton, 161–4, 165–7, 168–9, 171, 285, 341–2, 359–60
　musical work, 103, 237, 250, 347, 364, 412
　on Clapton's playing, 361–2; Cream, 109; drug dependence, 204–5, 359–60; Pattie Boyd and Clapton, 207–8
　studios, 357

Traffic (band), 126–7, 129–30

Transcendental Meditation, 162, 205

Troy, Doris, 401–2

'Tulsa Time' (song), 268, 279

Tulsa Tops (backing musicians), 268, 276

Turner, Tina, 343, 350, 421

'Two Young Lovers' (song), 349

'Under My Thumb' (song), 128

United Hospital, St Paul, Minnesota, 284

Unplugged (album), 26, 28, 53n

Unplugged (US TV programme), 23–5

Variety Club International, 350

Vaughan, Jimmy, 15

Vaughan, Stevie Ray, 16, 348, 352–3

Velez, Martha, 400

Vernon, Mike, 82–4, 93, 263

Via Delta (racehorse), 256–7

Village Recorders, Santa Monica, 18

Vincent, Gene, 40

Voorman, Klaus, 137
Warner Brothers, 327–8
Waronker, Lenny, 328
Waters, Muddy, 46, 52, 56, 67, 229, 262–4, 264n, 271, 309, 327, 361, 379
Waters, Roger, 319–20, 352, 361, 418
Watts, Charlie, 319
Way, Darryl, 248
'Weight, The' (song), 375
Welch, Chris, 91
Wells, Junior, 405
West Indies, 17, 209, 321–7, 370–1
Wheels of Fire (album), 113
'Where's Robin?' (song), 19
'White Room' (song), 122, 125, 344, 380
'Whiter Shade of Pale, A' (song), 241
Whitlock, Bobby, 151, 221, 406
Who, The (band), 62–3, 65, 109, 162, 166, 341, 408
'Whole Lotta Shakin' Goin' On' (song), 351
'Why Does Love Got to Be So Sad?' (song), 221
Williams, Danny, 52
Williams, Don, 268, 285, 310
Williams, Jerry, 328

Williams, Vanessa, 26
Williamson, Sonny Boy, 57, 67, 267
'Willie and the Hand Jive' (song), 203
Windsor National Jazz and Blues Festival, 104, 107
Winwood, Steve, 19, 29, 62–3, 87–8, 126–34, 168, 169, 278, 319, 364
Wonder, Stevie, 341
'Wonderful Tonight' (song), 22, 229–31, 249–51, 279, 314, 326–7, 341–8, 346
Wood, Ronnie, 10–11, 168, 237, 362
'Wrapping Paper' (song), 104, 116
West Bromwich Albion FC, 268
Wyman, Bill, 319

Yardbirds (band), 57, 59, 64–5, 67–72, 105, 115, 126, 278, 382–3
'You Don't Know Like I Know' (song), 354
Young, Neil, 341
Young, Paul, 358

Zanuck, Lili, 18
Zucchero (band), 427
Zydeco, Buckwheat, 374, 424